Hollywood Art

Hollywood Art

Art Direction in the Days of the Great Studios

by
Beverly Heisner

McFarland & Company, Publishers, Inc.
Jefferson, North Carolina and London

British Library Cataloguing-in-Publication data are available

Library of Congress Cataloguing-in-Publication Data

Heisner, Beverly.
    Hollywood art : art direction in the days of the great studios /
Beverly Heisner.
        p.   cm.
    [Includes index.]
    Includes bibliographical references.
    ISBN 0-89950-428-0 (lib. bdg. : 50# alk. paper) ∞
    1. Motion pictures—United States—Art direction—History.
    2. Motion picture studios—California—Los Angeles—History.
    3. Hollywood (Los Angeles, Calif.)—History.   I. Title.
PN1995.9.A74H45   1990
791.43′0233′0979494—dc20   89-42721
                                                                        CIP

Manufactured in the United States of America

McFarland & Company, Inc., Publishers
  Box 611, Jefferson, North Carolina 29640

To the memory of
Pauline Braun Heisner

Acknowledgments

I am indebted to the art directors and other art department personnel who took the time to share their experiences with me, particularly Arthur Lonergan, Rudi Feld, and John Mansbridge, who were very encouraging to me as I began my project, and also to Henry Bumstead, Gene Allen, Lyle Wheeler, Randall Duell, Tambi Larsen, Harold Michelson, Carl Anderson, Alexander Golitzen, Maurice Zuberano and others who shared their memories with me.

My research was funded in part by grants from the Academy of Motion Picture Arts and Sciences, the National Endowment for the Humanities, and the University of South Carolina Research and Productive Scholarship Committee and Venture Fund.

Institutional help is gratefully acknowledged from the American Film Institute, the Academy of Motion Picture Arts and Sciences Library, the University of Southern California, the University of California, Los Angeles, the Museum of Modern Art Film Archives, the University of Texas, Columbia University and the University of South Carolina. My appreciation goes to David Fischer who compiled the index.

A special thanks to my daughter Jennifer, who good-naturedly put up with my absorption in the motion pictures.

Table of Contents

Preface

The important subject of art direction has usually been touched on only briefly and peripherally in books on film. This volume has been written to focus on the history of art direction in American films, concentrating on the heyday of the great Hollywood studios and the classical American film, chronologically the period from the mid-twenties through the fifties. After this time, the old form of monolithic motion picture factory, one that housed all of the technological and artistic functions of the film under one roof, began to disappear, and the art director's conditions of work (although not the work itself) changed radically; this later period differs sufficiently from the first fifty years of film design to warrant a separate study.

The goals of this work and its organization have been geared to exploring several issues in the period of the classical American film, among them:

What was the role of an art director on a film?

Why have art directors been essential to films from their very beginnings?

How did the art director do his work as the studio system developed and flourished?

What was the nature and organization of the big studio art departments? What were the differences, along these lines, from studio to studio?

Who were the personalities involved in art direction? How were they trained?

To these ends, this book deals with both individuals and with the system itself. It explores the workings of just one of the several major technical departments that were the backbone of the studio system, examining the enormous power the art departments had in determining the visual appearance of motion pictures.

Beyond a discussion of these concerns, I wanted to address questions of style and content in American films and how these were affected by their art direction. This area of discussion is bound up with the question of each studio's "look." And although writers have repeatedly suggested that the Hollywood

studios had identifiable visual approaches, little effort has been put into defining these "looks" or to establishing who was responsible within the studio
system for them. The question I have asked here is: What part did the art
departments, with their many practioners of the visual arts (architects,
painters, illustrators), play in establishing the visual styles of the studios? To
this end, I have individually characterized *each* of the major Hollywood art
departments (United Artists, MGM, Warner Bros., Paramount, 20th Century-
Fox, RKO, Columbia, Universal).

The materials of the text have been organized in the following way: first,
a brief introduction examines some of the unique characteristics of film art
direction (a topic explored throughout the book). Chapter 1 then gives an account of the origins of art direction in early motion pictures (late 19th century
through the teens), a period that is difficult to document but one that was fundamental to establishing the possibilities of art direction. Chapter 2 presents
an overview of the organization of art departments and character of art direction in the period from the twenties through the fifties. The role played by the
art director in the creation of motion pictures at all of the big studios is
established. Remaining chapters (3–7) deal with each studio individually,
discussing the art departments from the time of their inception, and then
chronologically surveying their output until the fifties. Such an approach is
helpful in terms of establishing the evolution of each studio's screen "look."
It also aids in dealing with the major personalities and their careers, because
most of them stayed at the same studio throughout the greater part of their
working lives.

Filmographies of American art directors and a bibliography on the subject
conclude the text, which is followed by an index.

Introduction: Film Design

Aside from the WPA projects sponsored by the federal government during the Depression, there has been no more significant gathering together of American visual artists than in the movie industry when it flourished in Hollywood in the first half of this century. Painters, illustrators and architects were assembled under one roof, working for a single patron, on communal tasks. It was not a bad place to work, but like the other historic communal artistic efforts (the medieval and Japanese examples come to mind), the individual tended to get swallowed in the group. The collaborative nature of filmmaking together with a tendency, thus far, on the part of writers on film to focus on certain other important members of the filmmaking "team" (directors, actors, writers, cinematographers and even management) has meant that the role of the art director in the visualization of the screenplay has been largely ignored.

Because the contributions of art directors to the art of film have been so neglected, even such popularizing writers as Ephraim Katz in *The Film Encyclopedia* has been prompted to comment: "Probably the most underrated of cinema artists, the art director may dominate the visual quality of a film, and the caliber of his work often determines its mood and atmosphere." Citing the complexity of the art director's job, he continues,

> It requires knowledge of architecture and design, a good grasp of decorative and costume styles of all periods, graphic ability, business acumen, and a working knowledge of everything concerning film production, including photography, lighting, special effects, and editing.

Art direction is a branch of architecture in which environments are built, but seldom in their entirety and seldom to last. What the art director creates are spaces (internal and external), facades, and even entire towns. These are often seen by more people than will ever see any single building in the world. Beyond that, the art director, using only fragments of nature or architecture or manmade objects, can evoke mood, establish themes, and etch characters in films.

1

Stage direction has received far more attention than has film art direction, but recently interest has been shown in modern designs in American motion pictures in two volumes (*Screen Deco,* by Howard Mandelbaum and Eric Myers, and *Designing Dreams,* by Donald Albrecht). The literature still remains scant, with Léon Barsacq's *Le Décor de Film* giving the most sweeping appraisal of art direction and the Thames Television catalogue of an exhibition and broadcast programs on Hollywood art direction providing the most enlightening consideration of American art directors.

This book focuses on the history of art direction in American films during the days of the large integrated Hollywood studios—particularly the period from the advent of sound into the 1950s; the character and personnel of the studio art departments; and the role the art director played in formulating the visual "look" of individual studios.

Beyond the above, the text will try to uncover those characteristics unique to film art direction. Both art direction for film and stage design call for an infinitely high degree of invention, imagination, sensitivity to script and to actors. They sometimes call on the same conventions, but frequently do not. Early on, screen decor borrowed heavily from the example of stage decor, especially that associated with 19th century realism, but as the film medium matured, the tendency of art directors was toward independence from stage precedents.

One important respect in which art direction differs from stage design is that the film director can choose in each frame those elements in the decor that are seen by the audience. A stage set is at all times available to the audience, whose eyes may roam over it at any given moment. As Orson Welles put it, "In the theatre there are 1,500 cameras rolling at the same time—in the cinema there is only one."[1] But stage settings are usually appreciated by the audience as the curtain rises, after which attention shifts to the actors. On the screen, although an establishing shot frequently introduces the visual ambiance, the screen director may, and frequently does, direct the audience through the setting, or even to details in it—a bottle on a table, a knife on the floor—during the course of the action. In screen decor, details are often more important than they are on the stage.

In a film there are frequent changes of setting, rather than the significant one or two sets seen in most stage plays. A film art director must be extremely selective in deciding what to build, depending on how long and how much of it will be seen on the screen and upon the action: extremely small fragments of sets are often built, suggesting vast spaces beyond them. Conversely, what might be the entire setting for a play, may be seen for only 30 seconds in a film.

Because of the camera's flexibility, film art directors must visualize how their sets will appear from many points of view, rather than from the more or less fixed single viewpoint of the prevalent proscenium theatre. Screen decor is also highly manipulable, and the machinery of that manipulation need not be seen, no curtain needs to fall or wall to move, a cut or wipe or fade gets the viewer instantaneously to the next location.

Screen art direction calls for an intimate, minute-by-minute analysis of the action because of the intense focus of the camera eye. Cedric Gibbons, supervising art director at MGM, discussed this aspect of film design,

> A script . . . may state (as in *Captains Courageous*) that a sailboat race is taking place, and that, in the leading boat, the mast breaks. . . . [The art director] must determine a) what a sailboat looks like, b) what it looks like in a race in heavy seas, c) how a mast breaks, d) what a mast looks like when it is breaking, when it is falling and after it has collapsed.[2]

Screen decor can also include real locales — landscape, street scenes, ocean waves — so that scouting and preparing locations is a speciality of film art directors. This adds to the visual repertoire of the art director many devices for evocation of mood and character, but likewise creates difficulties in handling.

On the stage, although the actors make use of the set, their contact with it tends to be more limited than on the screen. The setting may help the actor in as many ways on the stage as on the screen, but the screen player more frequently finds himself in arduous contact with it. Actors often comment on the combat they have had to do with the settings or locations of their pictures. Alec Guinness recalled the making of *The Man in the White Suit:* "As I walked, horizontal to the ground, down the side of the house, suspended by the piano wire from a belt around my waist, the wire snapped when I was about four feet from the ground and I landed flat on my back."[3] While Guinness' experience is hardly comparable to such well-known stories as Lillian Gish's harrowing tale of filming a scene on an ice floe for D.W. Griffith's *Way Down East* (1920), it is illustrative of the kind of interaction with settings that are better done when the director can yell "cut."

While screen acting may be done in intimate conjunction with the set, Cedric Gibbons also noted a peculiarity of screen design,

> The stage setting surrounds the actors. In the movies, *once the scene is filmed,* you might almost say that the actors surround the set. Except in distant shots, the people are always in the foreground, the sets are but backgrounds against which they play. . . .[4]

As with stage design, art direction begins with the script. Films, however tend to divide their attention more equally between the written word and the action than do stage plays (with film action expanding to include everything from car chases to interplanetary travel). Screen art directors, by carefully designing their spaces and choosing their locations to facilitate the action, have the opportunity to greatly effect the pacing of the filmed story.

This book probes the role and imagination of the screen art director. It is the story of the large and skilled art departments then working to make great

in-house and, later, location pictures. There were certain constraints on art
directors then, that are no longer prevalent when most art directors work independently. But there were wonderful advantages, too, to working with the
backing of the other large technical departments that Hollywood studios
provided—the construction, property, and costume departments. The art
director then was privileged to have at his finger tips, under one roof, all the
tools of his trade.

Whatever their backgrounds, art directors of this period always claimed
that what they were aiming for was "realism."[5] This term was simply a catchall
for whatever they were doing. Each studio developed a visual "look" dependent upon many factors to be explored in the coming chapters, among them
the studio's film genres, the personnel of that studio (including cameramen,
directors, costume designers, and importantly their art directors), the preferred
way of lighting films, and the amount of hard cash that management was willing to put into settings.

Whatever types of films were made in Hollywood, the narrative was always
most important; screenplays leaning heavily upon symbol and metaphor were
not permitted. Perhaps for this reason no really expressionistic style of art direction developed in America as it did in Germany and elsewhere. Stylized decor
was never the preferred language in American films, but was permitted to a
degree in certain genres—musicals, futuristic and horror stories—where it
alternated with thoroughly unstylized settings. American film directors (and
their art director partners) of this period were not given enough artistic control
over their films to allow the exploration of idiosyncratic visual concepts; the
final cut, with few exceptions, always lay with the front office.

American art directors never developed elaborate theories of film decor as
did some of their European colleagues, especially the Russians and Germans,
perhaps because of the overall emphasis by the Hollywood studios on
"realism." Realism meant, in one form or another, a world that the audience
recognized. This did not have to be the contemporary world around the audience, it could be one known from paintings, photographs, or even the frequently quoted Biblical world of Sunday School cards and fans.

The illusionistic world seen in films, whatever it recreated, had to look like
its authentic counterpart. This was one of the primary goals of art directors in
the twenties: How do we make film sets look real? By the late twenties that
problem had been solved and art directors could convince an audience that
what they were seeing was the real thing, whether Ancient Rome or the pioneer
West. In the thirties art directors frequently commented with pride about this
aspect of their craft, the knowledgeable Cedric Gibbons wrote,

> One of the chief problems of the art department is to make something look real
> which is not. Because of the lack of time, it is impossible, for instance, to
> reconstruct a "mediaeval" castle, using real stones and mortar! We must therefore
> use materials which will appear to be solid rock, and so construct the castle that,

when fighting men, for instance, lunge against the wall, it does not "give" but will maintain the illusion of solidity and antiquity. . . .[6]

Making things appear "real" in film decor involved a lot of cheating, often accomplished simply by exaggerating effects. The independent art director William Cameron Menzies suggested this:

. . . in many cases, authenticity is sacrificed, and architectural principles violated, all for the sake of the emotional response that is being sought. My own policy has been to be as accurate and authentic as possible. However, in order to forcefully emphasize the locale I frequently exaggerate—I made my English subject more English than it would naturally be, and I over–Russianize Russia.[7]

Accuracy simply didn't always work in pictures, as Menzies went on to explain. For a Mary Pickford picture,

We had to have a Spanish city near Toledo and I put the Campanile of Toledo in to make it authentic. As you know, Madison Square Garden in New York has copied this campanile, and so many people recognized it and asked what Madison Square Garden was doing in the picture, that I had to change it.[8]

Menzies, one of the few American art directors to do any theorizing in print about film design, observed that a film setting may serve in several ways. It can be negative, as in the early days of film when it was often an "irritating distraction." It can be neutral—give the location but contribute little further that is meaningful to the film—often the case in thirties' crime films. It can even, to use Menzies' expression, become the "hero" of the piece, dominating the action and the actors—frequently the case in horror films. Or, the visual ambiance of a film may enhance its emotional dimensions, nonverbally further the plot, draw character profiles, and in enumerable ways add to the content of the film.

Film critics have frequently tried to analyze the effect that the *mise-en-scène* has on the content of a film (seldom do they mention the art directors who created it), but very few American art directors of the big studio days have left us their views on the subject. Again Menzies is an exception. Writing in 1930 about his own work, he said,

. . . if the mood of the scene calls for violence and melodramatic action, the arrangement of the principal lines of the composition would be very extreme, with many straight lines and extreme angles. The point of view would be extreme, either very low or very high. . . . The values or masses could be simple and mostly in a low key, with violent highlights. . . . In the case of pageantry such things as scale and pattern, figures, rich trappings against a high wall, through a huge arch are demanded. In comedy scenes the composition may be almost in the mood of caricature. In tragedy or pathos, or any scene photographed in a low key, the setting is often designed with a low ceiling, giving a feeling of depression.[9]

More recently several art directors have contributed their views on the means by which the settings compliment the script, among them Harry

Horner, who has written of his contributions to the emotional ambiance of William Wyler's *The Heiress* (1949). Horner was hired even before the screenplay writers because Wyler felt that it was better "to first let the visualizer, the designer, think of how this story . . . could be translated into a more visual or more varied interpretation of the story."[10] Horner's idea was to have architectural elements of the Victorian house in which the action all takes place express the conflict within the family between the father and daughter. Actress Olivia de Haviland's feeling of happiness and later bitterness and rejection were focused by Horner on her traversal of the main hall stairway, which was photographed from different angles and differentially lit to express her moods.

The short-lived magazine *Mise-en-Scène* published some excellent articles on the interaction between screenplay, player, and settings; one was on the use of decor in the master's house in Joseph Losey's filmed version of the Harold Pinter story *The Servant* (1963). The house interiors evolve from an early barren state to a correctly appointed and then unkempt state at the film's end when the servant has gained the upper hand over his "master": "the house [is] a metaphor which conveys social and human contradictions, reflects and defines the characters and comments upon them and their lives."[11] Unfortunately the authors of that article did not bother to mention the name of the art director who created the house. It was Ted Clements.

In terms of film content, sets can be evocative or discordant, they can set an overall mood for a film, or give it a sort of tonal quality (this is very prevalent in films today, like *The Cotton Club*, designed by Richard Sylbert).

Early art directors concentrated their energies on getting a built environment on the screen and weaving it together in a sensible pattern. A second phase of art directors built whole worlds inside movie studios. Lately art directors (especially those calling themselves production designers) have concentrated upon finding an overall concept, a visual idea around which the entire film is designed. This has only been possible as American art directors have gained artistic freedom and control over their product. Today it is American directors and art directors, rather than American film studios, that have a certain "look."

1
Early Art Direction

The use of three-dimensional sets in American narrative films was slow in evolving. In the early days, flat painted backdrops done by theatre scenic painters were used with a simple prop or two added as the plot required; the camera stood directly facing the background. The early silent studios, for economic reasons, continually reused their stock backdrops which customarily bore the company's monogram. Simply built sets with walls (reusable flats) made out of more durable wood and covered with lightweight material, like a store counter with shelves behind it, emerged during the first decade of the century. Lateral walls were added to the back wall, first one to create an L and then two to create a "box set" similar to those that had been used increasingly on the stage since the mid–19th century. These developments added a greater sense of depth to settings and also allowed the camera to take several points of view of sets, including into corners. In D.W. Griffith's *The Lonely Villa* (1912) (see **Illustration 1**), the Biograph studio monogram may be seen on the reusable flat at the back, while a wall with doors is shown laterally as the camera peers into the corner; decorative details, like the draped door, give additional realistic textures to the room.

By the time of the late silent films, sets had become as elaborate as they were ever to be, and art directors had emerged as important individuals in studio hierarchies. They had also developed almost all of the trick devices that were to be used in subsequent decades — glass shots (part of the image painted on clear glass is placed before the camera and filmed with the actors to create an illusion of a real set), forced perspective (the diminution in scale of objects into the distance to make them look like they are at a greater distance then they actually are), miniatures (miniature sets that when filmed and shown briefly on the screen look full size), and other special effects.

The earliest settings used in films varied from the actual locale, preferred in the documentary style of the Lumière brothers, to the elaborate fabrications based on stage designs, built by the fanciful Georges Méliès. Méliès, a conjurer by profession, first made sketches and models of his sets and backdrops,

1. *The Lonely Villa,* **1909.** Mother (Marion Leonard) and children (the eldest is Mary Pickford) are seen in a corner of the realistic interior of the villa formed by reusable flats that carry the studio's monograph (AB for American Mutoscope & Biograph Co.). The draped doorway, carpet, and paneled door provide textural variety in the set.

and then built them of canvas, wood, cardboard, clay and plaster. Everything had to be painted in grisaille (grey tones) because of the orthochromatic film in use at that time.[1]

Above all, Méliès preferred a great number of imaginative sets for such narrative pictures as *A Voyage to the Moon* (1902) and *The Conquest of the North Pole* (1912). He was expert at constructing mechanical special effects for his films, a carry over from his work in the theatre, and he also used double exposures and other purely cinematic effects. Already in *A Voyage to the Moon* Méliès used dozens of separate scenes in a variety of locations, as well as animation, stop-action photography, and double exposures. Méliès extended a fine visual eye to everything seen in his films from perspectival backgrounds to costumes. It is small wonder that Hollywood films, building a solely narrative tradition, should follow on and perfect artistic directions forwarded by the inventive Méliès.

Méliès' films were seen in America, where Thomas Edison, with Edwin S.

Porter at the camera, was also venturing into narrative film production with pictures like *The Life of an American Fireman* (1903). It featured location photography with thrilling sequential cutting that frightened audiences by having the fire brigade horses run directly into the camera. Earlier, in 1895, the Lumière Brothers had forced audiences out of their seats with a locomotive that seemed to come right off the screen.

Both Edison and Porter went on to make other popular films, in which, as in Porter's *The Great Train Robbery* (1903), much of the picture takes place on location and the interiors (a telegraph office and cabin) were very obvious painted backdrops. In this film, as in others of this early period, the characters moving from painted to real environments created what Frank Beaver has called, "a jolting contrast of scenic styles."[2]

B.P. Schulberg has reminisced about his days with Porter when scenic design was still a casual affair:

> I'd think up a plot and write it on Monday. Porter would cast it, paint his sets, and pick out locations on Tuesday. We would shoot the picture on Wednesday, by which time I'd be ready with the next one, which he'd case, plan, and shoot by Friday. On Saturday our two one-reelers were shipped off to the distributors.[3]

To mitigate the sharp contrast between real locations and obviously artificial interiors, by around 1910 sets began to be built occasionally in the open landscape so that the views through the windows were real. Details of the decor—fireplaces, window frames, and doors—were gradually built and furnishings were pushed further away from the walls, again to add a feeling of depth to the space.

In the teens, more money went into individual productions as they became longer. Greater attention was given to building the three-dimensional sets and filling them with accurate properties that were by this time being stored in a systematic way for reuse. Art directors (also known as technical directors), newly added to studio payrolls, used drawings and models to help plan the action of the film and some miniatures were made to be filmed as real locales. New emphasis was placed on research and films were promoted on the basis of their "historical" accuracy.

The multiple room set was conceived to further enhance the realism of interior settings. The additional room could be seen, usually directly behind the principal one. Such added spaces expanded the possibilities of differentiated lighting and provided more than one space in which the intricacies of plot might be developed. By the mid-teens such multiple room sets were commonplace.

In the Norma Talmadge melodrama of the early twenties, *The Sign on the Door* (1921) **(Illustration 2)**, technical director Williard M. Reineck created this type of interior with rooms aligned directly behind one another. In the foreground, the action is taking place around furniture placed in the center of

2. (Top) *The Sign on the Door,* 1921. Williard M. Reineck, technical director. Typically of 1920s sets, a view was given from one room directly back into another room (light streams onto the scene from a doorway held by Norma Talmadge here). Furniture was centralized so that action could take place around it. 3. (Bottom) *Risky Business,* 1926. Max Parker, art director. Rich and stylish contemporary settings were the hallmark of Cecil B. DeMille's modern dramas. A stair and garden may be seen through the back arcade.

the room, which is given medium light from the lamp above the desk. The back room with its massive fireplace is more dimly lit, while a bright light streams through the door right to further suggest a space in that direction. The walls are no longer planar but, as here, are cut into by a niche (right behind the door).

The mid-twenties Cecil B. DeMille domestic drama, *Risky Business* (1926) **(Illustration 3)**, further illustrates the treatment of multiple room interiors. A spacious living room is clearly defined by fully articulated side walls (windows, a fireplace, a mirror) by art director Max Parker. The furniture is grouped into the space away from the walls, so that the acting may take place in an integral way around it (note the chair and table left giving an added sense of depth to the room). A stairway and landing are seen at the back through an arcade (rather than a flat wall surface) adding to the spacial complexity of the interior, and beyond this a view into a garden is provided through windows on two levels.

As with many other elements of film design in America, it was D.W. Griffith who pioneered the elaboration of sets and costumes in his longer films like *Judith of Bethulia* (four reels, 1913) and especially in *Intolerance* (14 reels, 1916) **(Illustration 4)**. A Griffith biographer gives an insight into the way early silent film art direction was accomplished, of *Intolerance* he says:

> The day would begin with a conference between Griffith and Huck Wortman. Griffith would give his master carpenter notes and instructions on scraps of paper. From these scraps Wortman would make, and pass along to his crews, the orders turning Griffith's dreams into three-dimensional reality.[4]

While this may have been the way Griffith had worked on earlier films, there was more to it on *Intolerance,* for Griffith had hired theatrical scenic designer, Walter L. Hall to design the sets. Karl Brown, a Griffith photographer, has described Hall's importance and working methods:

> He could draw with superlative skill and paint better, or at least more accurately, than anyone I had ever seen work with paint and brush. . . . Hall combined the gift of an imaginative creative artist with the needlepoint accuracy of a fine architect. His preliminary drawings were all done with pencil on specially surfaced heavy cardboard, like title cards. . . . There was no tentative fiddling around; a bold stroke here, and half an arch was on the board; another stroke, and the entire arch was there, hard and clear and firm.[5]

Hall attended to the minutest of details in the design of settings, while Huck Wortman served as the master builder.

According to Brown, Hall became known as "Spec" Hall because of his insistence that everything in pictures be ruled by the "laws of perspective," he continues:

> Short, dumpy, and with a face and turn of speech hauntingly like Winston Churchill's, Hall took a schoolmasterly satisfaction by proving that our lives are ruled by

4. *Intolerance,* 1916. Walter L. Hall, art director. Babylon: a full-scale, multilevel set, drawing upon Ancient Persian, Egyptian and Roman art had rampant elephants on two stories and held hundreds of extras (note those on back upper wall).

our point of view. "Things seen from one *angle* look entirely different when seen from *another,* but *things don't change.* It's all in how we *look at them! It's all a matter of* perspective, *dammit!*"[6]

Huck Wortman was featured in an article in *Photoplay* magazine on *Intolerance,* which was among the earliest American motion pictures to receive extensive publicity and recognition for its settings, but, oddly, Walter Hall's contributions were not even mentioned.[7] The *Intolerance* sets depicting Babylon, Judea, Paris, and modern times were touted as the most sensational ever seen in American films and even staid *Scientific American* magazine commented:

For more than six months the carpenters, masons, concrete workers, and painters were busied with the set, and the cost of the work is reported to have been in excess of $50,000.[8]

The huge Babylon set **(Illustration 4)** is the most famous one from the picture; its avenue of gigantic undulating columns topped by balconies and rampant elephants held hundreds of extras in the scenes of extravagant decadence depicted by Griffith. The avenue is a series of broad stairways, terraces, and passages covered with bas relief, painting, and punctuated by sculpture and sheets of draped cloth. Designer Hall drew upon disparate sources from the ancient world, principally Persian and Egyptian art, and the Roman forea.

Even earlier than *Intolerance,* at Biograph in New York, Griffith had been interested in the decor of his films. He grew tired of the backgrounds painted by one Eddie Shulter and hired the architecturally trained Harry McClelland, an Englishman, to design and paint his sets. Encouraged by Griffith, McClelland colored his settings light grey, rather than the earlier "Biograph brown" which Shulter had preferred (and for which the crew had found other descriptive terms). Lighting could be varied more effectively with the new color scheme.[9]

Other silent film directors, particularly Thomas Ince, were not to be outdone by Griffith. In the same year, 1915, Ince had huge sets, valued at $35,000, built for his ambitious film *Civilization* (1916). In a modern sequence (**Illustration 5**) sailors are seen in a boiler room that is complete to the minutest detail, the metallic gleam of the machinery is accentuated by a prominent pattern of welded bolts that runs over all the surfaces. The film's pressbook, inflating the figures, called *Civilization* "a million dollar production" for which real cities had been built and destroyed. Neither of these early big scenic films were box-office successes; their stories did not appeal to a public that was not coming to movies just to see sets.

The Italians in particular had more success and were even slightly earlier than the Americans with immense scenic films. Enrico Guazzoni, who had previously been a painter and decorator, directed and designed several films, including *Quo Vadis?* (1912), that were filled with stunning sets.

The Italian film, *Cabiria* (1914) (**Illustration 6**), with a story set at the time of the Punic Wars, also had dozens of awe-inspiring sets, props, and elaborate special effects that included the volcanic eruption of Mt. Etna. Director Giovanni Pastrone (the art director is not credited) did not confuse periods and stories, as did Griffith in *Intolerance* and Ince in *Civilization,* and his fast paced film sped along more logically than theirs had in spaces that reconstructed the magnificence of ancient Carthage: its marketplace, houses, and temples. Multiple space interiors (**Illustration 6**) were fully developed with three-dimensional columns, planar walls, stairways, differentiated floor levels (note the figures on the upper balcony in the center of the image), plants, illusionistic surfaces of all kinds (marble, fresco, brick, stone) and, in addition, electric light was used to backlight and cast enormous shadows (the man's shadow right).

Cabiria's sets were based upon earlier book illustrations and paintings, as were Griffith's sets, and with similar elements of pure fantasy entering in at times. In this respect *Cabiria*'s Temple of Moloch, with its huge maw into

6. *Cabiria,* Italian, 1914. Art director uncredited. Roman splendor was evidenced in the columns, pilasters and wall frescoes. Illusionistic surfaces represented marble, brick, and stone and created sets unsurpassed in the period for richness and imagination.

which children must be sacrificed, is analogous to the fabulous Babylonian imagery in *Intolerance,* with its enormous avenue of sculpted elephants. Films like these were an open invitation to art directors, allowing them to prove that they could create almost any imaginable scenic device and on any scale for films.

The building of such expensive and lavish sets, many of exterior facades on lengthy streets, eventually led, by about 1915, to the phenomenon of standing back-lots. Streets, domestic and foreign, and ancient sets were left standing on property adjacent to studios and were redressed for reuse. Interiors were still built within studios, but especially on the West Coast were also built outdoors (those at Universal were open to the public for a small charge). In the late teens, studios east and west were artificially lighting their interiors and this was one of the primary reasons for the introduction into film art direction of

5. *Civilization,* 1916. Art director uncredited. The modern ship's interior was all metallic surfaces, with the repetitive welding carried to a "realistic" extreme.

prominent scenic designers from the Broadway stage who had had practical experience with inventive lighting.

Photoplay magazine, as early as August 1916, ran a complete article on
the novel subject of "The Art Director." Mentioned in it were Wilfred
Buckland and Robert Brunton as Thomas Ince's art directors, Charles Chapman at Vitagraph, and Hugh Ford, "artistic executive" at Famous Players. According to *Photoplay,* in early pictures the property men did the sets,

> But that was before the days of the art director, known also as the technical direc-
> tor. And it wasn't so long ago either, as the art director is so new that in a number
> of well known studios there is no suspicion of such a personage about the "lot."[10]

The qualifications for the job, according to *Photoplay,* sounded glamorous:
". . . the technical director is a well read and much traveled gentleman, who
has broken bread in the poor man's hovel, and wine glasses in the rich man's
palace."[11] *Photoplay* especially credited Thomas Ince for his adoption of "real
sets in place of painted canvas" and prophesized "the art director has come to
stay and he will survive every revolution, because he is the actual exponent of
realism."[12] *Photoplay*'s crystal ball was quite right about the staying power of
the art director, and "realism" in one form or another was always cited as the
primary aim of art direction as it developed in the teens. Early art directors
defined their role in broad terms, and expected to take part in the decision
making process for set design, lighting, and camera positioning.

A more accurate definition of the art director's job and talents than
Photoplay's was published in the informative volume *The Blue Book of the
Screen* (1923), a few years after the big scenic films of Griffith and Ince were
circulated, and it could be used with little revision today. The art director must
have

> new ideas and rapid visualization . . . a knowledge of how to fake so as to cheat
> the camera. . . ; how colors photograph; where to light the set. All of this is gained
> only by experience. A careful study of the story and discussion with the director
> enables him to make his plan to fit the action, and design the set to fit the mental-
> ity of the character for whom it is built. The art director generally gives the
> cameraman the "set-up" for his long shot, after which the director shoots as he
> pleases.[13]

It was Wilfred Buckland's **(Illustration 7)** entry into the Hollywood milieu
in 1914 that was a milestone in the recognition of art direction as an integral
part of movie making. Buckland, a prominent theatrical designer, had worked

7. (Top) Wilfred Buckland, pioneering art director. A stage designer, Buckland was
called to Hollywood by Cecil B. DeMille. His innovative lighting techniques were
copied throughout the industry. 8. (Bottom) *Joan the Woman,* 1916. Wilfred Buckland, art director. Joan (Geraldine Ferrar) struggles before Buckland's recreation of a
French medieval village square. The thatched lean-tos in the middle ground add
authentic details to the provincial stone building.

for David Belasco creating sets, lighting, and as his stage manager. Joining
Famous Players Lasky in 1914, Buckland created rich and authentic settings for
pictures like *Joan the Woman* (1916) **(Illustration 8)** through the use of klieg
lighting for both interiors and exteriors. This innovation, nicknamed "Lasky
lighting," added great dramatic potential to settings which had previously
been daylit overall, producing a flat effect. Buckland's spotlit interiors for *Joan
the Woman* and *Robin Hood* (1922) **(Illustrations 80–82. See pages 162–164)**
revolutionized the industry. His large built exteriors **(Illustration 8)**, like the
medieval village in *Joan the Woman* were rich in authentic detail and textures,
like the thatched lean-tos on the side of the building (middle ground) behind
the struggling heroine played by Geraldine Ferrar.

On Broadway Buckland had successfully produced, as well as designed,
plays, and in Hollywood he insisted on being involved with all aspects of the
shooting on his films. Directors, in particular Cecil B. DeMille, objected to his
"interference" and Buckland's career began to founder already by the late
twenties. His personal life too was tragically marred and despite a testimonial
dinner given for him in 1941 by the Society of Motion Picture Art Directors,
by the time he died in 1946, having spent his last years doing odd jobs in the
MGM Art Department, he was an all but forgotten figure.[14]

Other famous theatrical designers soon followed Wilfred Buckland into
films. Among the best known was Joseph Urban who joined William Randolph
Hearst's Cosmopolitan Productions which had been formed in 1919. Urban was
both an architect and scenic designer, and his success with the Ziegfeld Follies
was probably what prompted Hearst's invitation to design elegant sets for pictures starring Marion Davies. Reflecting his education at the Academy in
Vienna, his work remained informed by that of the Wiener Werkstätte. He
emigrated to the United States in 1911, ran a swank New York interiors shop,
and received design commissions from the Boston and Metropolitan Opera
companies. In 1920 he told *Photoplay* in glowing terms that the new medium
of film "is the art of the twentieth century, and perhaps the greatest art of
modern times."[15]

Urban's decor for the Hearst film, *Enchantment* (1921), starring Davies,
is credited with introducing modern concepts to the American film. A dining
alcove reflected the geometric bias of the Werkstätte group; with a heavily patterned wallpaper, reminiscent of William Morris' work, as background. Urban
used high clerestory windows, modern light fixtures, and painted squares to
further a crispness in the design that the use of airy Thonet chairs further
enhanced.

Joseph Urban went on to put his ideas into the built milieu in the
marvellous Central Park Casino, New York (1929, not extant), with designs
that hark back to his work on *Enchantment*.[16] His most significant extant
building is the New School for Social Research, New York City, built in 1929–
1930, where he turned for inspiration to International Style modernism.[17]

While still doing screen work, Urban was among only six architects invited by the Soviets to submit a design for the Palace of the Soviets (1932).

It has been suggested that the upswing in the numbers of art directors in silent films, and their professionalism, may not have been without its problems. Friction occurred between them and the carpenters who built the sets, and had earlier been responsible for much of their design, and, also, with some of the directors. Silent film director Henry King commented,

> Many times, art directors will build lavish sets. I've had them standing around chewing their fingernails thinking, are we *never* going to see this big set? Well, the set is nothing but a set. To me, it is completely wrong to photograph it just because it's lavish.[18]

Despite King's reservations, film sets did improve significantly in the late teens and the public approved, as Kevin Brownlow has commented:

> The art directors were responsible for much of the improvement in the appearance of pictures around 1920; before that, the interiors of many of the straightforward, routine productions had a thin and empty look, like a rehearsal runthrough.[19]

While not much is known about the methods and opinions of early art directors, one or two, among them Hugo Ballin, were interviewed by the popular press. Ballin had come to Goldwyn Studios in 1917 leaving behind him a successful New York career as a painter and designer and an affiliation with the Thomas Edison Studio in Bedford, New York as an art director. A typical piece of studio hype of the teens was the article on him in *Motion Picture Classic* of March 1919 called "The New Studio Art." Ballin, who had painted the murals in the Wisconsin State Capitol, is described as one of America's leading painters and a member of the National Institute of Arts and Letters. Goldwyn had apparently brought him west to do the sets for *Thaïs* and *The Silver Star*. His first film in Hollywood was actually Allan Dwan's *Fighting Odds* which, although panned, was touted as having the "Goldwyn quality" due to Ballin's refined sets. Hugo Ballin explained his philosophy of set design in lofty terms:

> Every emotion can be expressed in terms of form and color. Thru physical marshaling of objects, thru contours and balance (not balance of weight, of course, but art balance), thru light and shade and their gradation, the world's grief and the world's laughter may be deftly and exactly expressed. Despair and hope, doubt and decision, hypocrisy and sincerity, these and other traits may be convincingly suggested by the physical surroundings of the people who are supposed to feel them.[20]

Among his goals was the simplification of settings. Ballin planned to revolutionize film decor, but his more idiosyncratic ideas, sounding very expressionistic, did not catch on.

> Some day (Ballin) will save his studio thousands of dollars by building most of his scenery out of draperies and shadows. He has the hardihood to believe that it

doesn't pay to build solid compo-board walls with carved moldings that are almost entirely hidden in the deep shadows of the best modern lighting. Doors, fireplaces, furniture — and light and shadow — these are all a photoplay needs.[21]

Beside Ballin, the Goldwyn Studio, in their quest to establish the "Goldwyn quality," employed other well known artists like Everett Shinn and W.H. Cotton in the teens. Shinn made only one picture for Goldwyn, *Polly of the Circus* (1917). In 1920 he worked on *The Bright Shawl* for Inspiration Pictures, and then took a final stab at art direction working on William Randolph Hearst's production of *Janice Meredith* (1923). On that film Shinn proved decisively that he was not cut out for film art direction, when he balked at using the million dollar budget Hearst wanted to put into the picture. This was a period in which studios were self-consciously promoting better visual effects in their pictures and were willing to spend more on them; art departments began to grow.

In *The Love of Sunya* (1927), Gloria Swanson starred in a series of romantic vignettes in Ballin's lavish sets. This spectacular production was chosen to open the fittingly enormous and opulent New York Roxy Theatre in that year. In one scene, Swanson manages to remain charming looking in cloche hat while atop a ladder (**Illustration 9**) fending off a barking dog. Ballin's opulent paneled library is filled with paintings, china figurines on brackets, and marble columns flanking the fireplace.

Hugo Ballin seems to have the distinction of being the first well known American art director to turn to the directing of motion pictures. In the twenties he made several films, *Jane Eyre* (1921) and *Vanity Fair* (1923), most of them starring his wife, silent film star Mabel Ballin. Later, other art directors like William Cameron Menzies and Mitchell Leisen, would make the crossover to direction from art direction, with England's Alfred Hitchcock having the greatest success. Ballin was to make another significant contribution to American motion picture art direction as the teacher and mentor of Cedric Gibbons.

By the teens, individuals had clearly set themselves up as specialists within the field of art direction. One such individual was Ferdinand Pinney Earle, whom *Photoplay* interviewed in November of 1918. Earle, who is described as a "well-known New York artist," had established a scenic painting studio for Metro, where in the words of the magazine, "he is devoting the finest of artistic educations and years of old-world experience to the improvement of motion-picture scenery and subtitles."[22] Mr. Earle, who called his work "motion painting," sagaciously predicted, "that the painter will go hand-in-hand with director and cameraman in achieving future symphonies for the eye."[23]

The *Motion Picture Studio Director and Trade Annual,* an early industry publication (1921), listed "Assistant, Art and Technical Directors" together under one heading.[24] Of those listed 33 used the title art director, many times coupled with the term technical director. Several names that were to become

9. *The Love of Sunya*, 1927. Hugo Ballin, art director. Gloria Swanson holds off a dog in Ballin's fine wood paneled library, in which oil paintings, oriental carpets, and expensive bric-a-brac are elegantly harmonized.

important for art direction, such as Ben Carré, Mitchell Leisen, Warren Newcomb, Harry Oliver, and Max Parker, provided short resumes of their educations and experience in the *Annual*. Others, whose names are unfamiliar, also detail their careers, some of which go back over a decade in films. This makes clear that there were many more trained specialists doing art direction and at earlier dates than has previously been assumed. It is practically impossible to trace the careers of these individuals because of the habit in the teens, and well into the twenties, of omitting screen credits for art direction. Certain studios, like Paramount, were particularly lax in this regard.

By the mid-twenties, Hollywood art departments were becoming better established and were attracting first rate talent from a greater variety of sources, not just from the Broadway stage or from illustration and painting. Architecture departments of universities became particular targets for recruitment of art directors by the late twenties — in the 1921 *Annual* there had been only three art directors who listed their education as in architecture (Alfred Wright Alley, Robert A. Odell, and Max Parker). Some trained architects joined art departments because of the scarcity of architectural jobs as the Depression began, but others were attracted by the variety of work and the lively atmosphere of the studios. Arthur Lonergan, who graduated with an architecture degree from Columbia University in the thirties, and worked for MGM and then for 20th Century-Fox, put it this way:

> You had all the advantages of working in an architectural firm and none of the headaches of construction. The milieu was fun, much less deadly than your ordinary architect's office. I liked the element of fantasy you could employ and the variety of tasks you were asked to do.[25]

Art directors of the studio departments have been somewhat self-effacing about their role in the making of motion pictures, partly because of studio politics. Unlike directors, none, except the emigre art directors Eugene Lourie and Ben Carré, have left memoirs of their creative lives. Lourie's account focuses primarily on his relationship with Jean Renoir and is more revealing about European than American practices, while Carré's account is best on the silent era in which his career thrived.[26]

Ben Carré, who began his career in 1906 in France as a painter of scenic backdrops, relates that

> At Gaumont, we'd be given an assignment to build a set. The set would be built, and the director would come in to direct without knowing anything beforehand about the set. I came to America in 1912, and I wanted my director, like Maurice Tourneur, to know in advance the sort of set he would get. I would show him sketches....[27]

He succeeded in giving Tourneur what he wanted; they worked together on the highly regarded production of *Blue Bird* (1918), and on 33 other films.

Carré had moved to California in 1918:

> I worked with everyone; I watched the studios grow. I came back from a trip to Europe in 1925, and was amazed to see how MGM's Art Department had developed. They had draftsmen, set dressers, prop men — people doing things that I was used to doing all by myself.[28]

A founding member of the Academy of Motion Picture Arts and Sciences, Carré had among his formidable accomplishments the intricate catacomb and backstage of the Paris Opera designs for the first *Phantom of the Opera* (1925) (see **Illustration 10**) and the sets for *Riders of the Purple Sage* (1931), the first western in sound to be shot on location.[29] During the last twenty years of his career, by his own choice, Carré reverted to painting scenic backdrops at MGM. Among his memorable credits in this field are the backdrops for *Dante's Inferno* (1935), *Meet Me in St. Louis* (1944), *The Wizard of Oz* (1939), and *North by Northwest* (1959). Carré died in 1978.

Art direction as a film profession grew out of the desire by studios for a refinement and elaboration in their product. After the original novelty of films wore off, audiences came to expect more in the area of verisimilitude and

10. *The Phantom of the Opera,* 1925. Drawing by Ben Carré. Charles D. "Danny" Hall, art director with Carré, E.E. Sheeley, Sidney Ullman. Carré's drawing is reminiscent of the gloomy interiors of Giovanni Battista Piranesi's etched *Prisons* (1745).

in spectacle from the motion picture. What was first the province of scenic painters, prop men, and carpenters slowly, in the first and second decades of the century, was turned over to art directors, trained in art, architecture, and theatre design, who were more involved in the total look of the film — the decor, lighting, and camera angle — than their predecessors had ever been. By 1920 film decor had already evolved through several stages, from a simple backdrop into a realistic three-dimensional box set, then into multiple room sets that could be seen clearly in all fields through the use of deep focus cinematography (all areas from the foreground to the background of the field are kept in sharp focus) by cameramen. The era of the big studio art departments was about to begin.

2
Art Departments
Under the Studio System

"We perceive that the once insignificant movie backgrounds of the Twenties, Thirties, and Forties, observed but taken for granted at their first showings, prove increasingly precious to us as the century rushes to an end; they are transformed into documents of historical importance, to be read and studied like any other document." — Brendan Gill. [1]

The heyday of Hollywood studio art departments was in the 1930s and 1940s, when dozens of architects, illustrators, model makers, and set decorators were employed in the movie industry. [2] Most of these art departments were formed in the twenties, Cedric Gibbons was the head of MGM's Art Department from the formulation of the company in 1924 and other studios also selected strong individuals to shape their departments in that decade.

The departments, numbering between 50 and 80 people, were structured hierarchically, with the supervising art director (the department head) overseeing all of the functions of the department, and coordinating the unit art directors and assistant art directors. The production of the departments was so great, involving as it did every one of the 50–60 features made each year that, according to Arthur Lonergan who was at MGM for nearly a decade (1936–1945), each art director worked simultaneously on a feature in pre-production, one in production, and one in post-production. [3]

The assignment to a film as unit art director meant that the individual assumed charge of the art department's contribution to that production. On "big" films, especially musicals, it was common to assign an assistant art director, but most pictures had only one. The unit art director was then assigned a sketch artist to carry his ideas out in detailed renderings. Some art directors and sketch artists were regularly teamed on certain types of films — like westerns or crime films or "character" films (lower class melodramas) — and became resident experts in these genres. As continuity sketches came into use, production illustrators also worked with the art director and director to develop the storyboards that traced the action in each frame.

Routinely subsumed under the aegis of the art department were the matte

25

shop, scenery painting (**Illustration 11**), the model and miniature shop (**Illustration 12**), property shop, special effects, the research and the location divisions.[4] The art director had close contacts with every other service division of the studio, especially the construction department.

The primary responsibility of the art director was to visualize the script and his role varied a good deal depending on each picture's director, specifically, how much help he required or would take in the process of visualization. Some directors, like Vincente Minnelli, were very certain about their requirements for the visual settings, but others, like George Cukor, were open to suggestion for both visual ambiance and camera set-ups. However, as Gene Allen, Cukor's art director for 18 years, recalls, detailed research had to be done prior to any suggestions being made.

> Before sets were even thought of, Cukor would have books of research done on every aspect of life in the time in question. What people ate, drank, their other habits, political and economic life, everything had to be researched. Then when Cukor was satisfied that we all knew something about the period, we could proceed with the sets. At that point he would leave the visualization with me ... only checking it and offering occasional suggestions. Cukor was the kind of director who would fight for the sets he wanted with a deliberate campaign.[5]

The art director was among the first in the studio to see a new script. Powerful supervising art directors like Lyle Wheeler, head of 20th Century–Fox's Art Department (1947–1962), were often given a book or screenplay before it was purchased and asked for an opinion as to whether it could be visualized.[6]

At early production meetings between the director, producer, art director and other members of the production crew, the number and types of sets were discussed and specific ideas for a movie's decor considered: cost estimates and preliminary sketches followed. The art director established the physical setting of the picture, including selecting locations. The economic level of the characters and their personal habits dictated their physical environment.

Prior to committing himself on set requirements, the art director analyzed the picture's action, as art director Harry Horner put it, "Directors want to know how do you get into a scene and how do you get out of it."[7]

In establishing the sets the art director was assisted by the studio research staff. Art directors relied heavily on the research department, which prepared detailed reports on locales (including photos) and every other aspect of each picture's setting. At 20th Century–Fox, the research department prepared bound volumes of materials for each film that was going into production.

Research departments collected contemporary art and architecture magazines, together with books so that a library was established in each studio. The art departments felt a proprietary interest in these libraries, so much so that Lyle Wheeler talked Daryl Zanuck into allocating $500 in each picture's

11. (Top) Scenic painted cityscape. Note storage numbers along top and man at right (for scale). 12. (Bottom) Camera-ready miniature of a small town with cyclorama behind it.

budget at Fox to be given to the research department for new acquisitions. Already in the silent era researchers were important — especially to period films. For the 1922 Douglas Fairbanks' production of *Robin Hood*, a research group led by Dr. Arthur Woods assembled a library of materials on the period and subject of Robin Hood.[8]

Most of the valuable studio research collections were sold off piecemeal or discarded when the studio system broke up in the fifties and sixties. As exceptions, the Goldwyn Library survived through purchase and the Warner Bros. Library is in the Burbank Public Library. John Mansbridge, long-time supervising art director of Disney Studios, managed to rescue a collection of photographs of architecture from the old research files of the RKO Art Department.[9] The rest of that department's contents have disappeared since they were transferred to Desilu as part of the sale of the studio in 1957.

The accuracy of historical settings based upon research was not always a matter left entirely to the art director. Some directors, like Otto Preminger, insisted on accuracy, while others were happier with a more fantastic jumble of historical styles.[10]

The type of director who was totally undemanding was apparently the biggest headache to art directors, as Arthur Lonergan remembers: "If a director told you to just go ahead and do anything you wanted with the sets, you knew you were in trouble." The art director and director had to present a united front to the producer in order to get a variety of sets. And, according to Gene Allen, directors who started out without precise ideas often got them in the middle of production, after the art director and his crew had put in weeks of work developing the sets.

Immediately following the research and preliminary sketch stages, finished sketches in a variety of formats, sizes, and materials — ink, charcoal, watercolor and pencil — were made. Some sketches of all kinds survive in public and private collections, but not in anything like the vast quantity in which they were produced. Contractually all sketches, plans and "ideas" of art directors belonged to the studios that employed them.[11] The studio saved a few sketches, mostly within the files of the art departments, some found their way over the mantles of producers, directors and movie stars, but most were discarded. The majority of art directors possess little of their own original art work from their days in the big studios.[12]

The finished sketch was followed by blueprints and a model. The models were executed by craftsmen under the art director's supervision. The scale and detail of the models differed from studio to studio, but models were always made on major pictures in the thirties and forties (**Illustration 13**). They provided directors and photographers with a three-dimensional representation of the setting so that action could be decided and camera angles established before sets were built and shooting began. After the completion and acceptance of the model, further alterations to the sets were not usually permitted.

13. MGM Art Departments, 1940s; a model may be seen on the desk in the foreground.

Under Lyle Wheeler at Fox complete models with colors and decorative details were preferred, while at MGM, according to Arthur Lonergan and Cedric Gibbons, the models were more simplified with only essential architectural elements indicated and were done in white. Models were too bulky to keep and were thrown away immediately after their use.[13]

The importance of production models was discussed in a 1951 article by art director Herman Blumenthal, who claimed they had become

> one of the major mediums of motion picture illustration . . . [because] a model will pave the way for better understanding between the Producer, Director, Cameraman, and Art Director, since it will give at a glance and in a few minutes all the important information as to design, action, and production, and technical problems.[14]

Blumenthal suggests that economics prompted the development of the use of models:

> Budget-wise, models help to achieve the elimination of those portions of the set which would not be seen on the screen but which are suggested by the script. A Producer and a Director can, by means of the model, restrict his shots to his basic action by pre-planning on the model itself, make his corrections for proposed action, and relay those changes to the Art Director before the final working drawings are released for construction. . . . This same method is of great help in the proposed lighting of a set for the Cameraman, the use of matt shots for ceilings and additional structures above, and the value of backings, cutouts, and miniatures.[15]

Important mechanical devices were developed in model shops to aid the
director and art director in assessing the set. Eldo Chrysler at 20th Century–Fox
designed a miniature periscope, "which gives the viewer a typical camera set-up
and the equivalent of a 35 mm lens in order to see the exact amount of the
set that will be on screen at any given time."[16] A miniature camera, the work
of Fox set designer, Walter Myall, could photograph from within a model the
camera set-up as it would actually be made.

> This method of photographing a model is of tremendous saving of time when it
> is necessary to prepare a series of continuity sketches to aid the Director in his
> shooting of a scene since it can be photographed before the set is constructed.[17]

Like models, extant blueprints are hard to locate, but art director Richard
Day left a few blueprints from his films to the Academy of Motion Picture Arts
and Sciences. For the sets of *Beloved Enemy* (1936) and *Marco Polo* (1938) these
are ordinary architects' blueprints: plans, elevations, and sections of sets, with
indications of their dimensions and decorative detailing; the camera positions
are pin-pointed. "Wild walls," walls that could be removed to enable camera
movement, were indicated on the plans—often by an oval around the specific
wall that was to be wild.

Continuity sketches, drawings made by the art director or at his instiga-
tion for individual shots in a film, were sometimes used in the thirties and forties.[18] Anton Grot was a pioneer in the twenties, along with William Cameron
Menzies, in the use on continuity sketches. For *Mildred Pierce* (1945) **(Illustration 14)** he did a complete set, and they are illustrative of how this technique
was practiced at the time. The camera's angle is shown in each of the sketches,
together with the position of the actors and the background setting. Above
each sketch Grot included explicit written directions for camera shots and—
based on the screenplay—what moods were to be evoked by the special effects
(wind and water) and by the actress, Joan Crawford. Still in use today, continuity sketches assisted the director in visualizing the script and charted the
picture's actions so that production problems could be worked out in advance
and expenses curtailed.[19]

The most famous continuity sketches in film history are William Cameron
Menzies' for *Gone with the Wind* (1939) **(Illustration 15)**. Their unprecedented
completeness is widely credited with having shaped the picture's cohesiveness
despite its numerous directors: "In *Gone with the Wind* the design element
was paramount so that camera angles, the positioning of actors, and inevitably
even the editing were deployed to suit the designer's aim."[20] As Anton Grot's
sketches demonstrate, the same thing might have been said for many other
films of the period. The term production designer was agreed upon by producer
David Selznick, art director Lyle Wheeler and Menzies to define the latter's role
in the making of *Gone with the Wind,* and is widely used today when the art
director is given sweeping responsibilities for the visual appearance of a film.

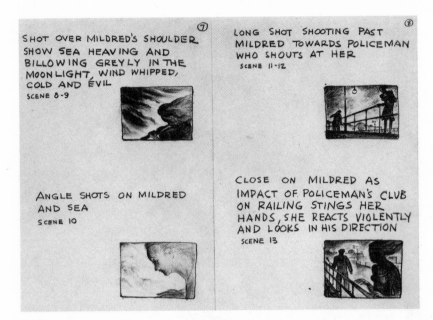

14. *Mildred Pierce*, 1945. Sketches by Anton Grot, art director. Grot manages to capture the action and mood of each frame with his free, undetailed drawing technique that silhouettes the figures.

Storyboards may have originated with the animated film, particularly those of Walt Disney, in which case they were absolutely essential.[21] Who first introduced them to the nonanimated film is difficult to determine, but continuity sketches and storyboards were a part of the parlance of art direction beginning in the mid-twenties (*The Thief of Bagdad*, 1925) and were an established technique in the forties.

The actual building of sets was done by three construction crews working around the clock, with the night shift doing most of the actual construction. As Arthur Lonergan recalls, "Many times this meant you had to get up and check the progress on the sets in the middle of the night, so you knew what would be ready for the next day's shooting."

With the completion of the sets, the set decorator took over their dressing—the placement of the props, furniture, and draperies. The set decorator, who had been consulted during the sketch and model period, was charged with the leg work of finding the things that the art director wanted in the set. The properties for the sets came first from the studio's own property department, then from other studio's property departments, and finally through rental companies or by purchase. It was the art director's job to monitor the accuracy with which his ideas were executed in dressing the sets, but set decorators gave essential advice and added touches that built on the

overall conception. Gene Allen found that property men and set decorators could sometimes be overly zealous in initiating details: "Throughout the shooting, you had to be on the sound stage almost constantly checking the accuracy of the sets." Despite such caveats, set decorators were experts in articulating sets and worked closely with art directors. They coordinated the work of many of the other craftsmen preparing the sets, including: upholsterers, drapers, greens men, and prop men.

Sets were, to some extent, coordinated with costumes. With the introduction of Technicolor in the twenties, backgrounds and costumes had to be analyzed in conjunction with the Technicolor consultants. Art directors agree that this was one of the most traumatic periods for art departments. The adjustments were profound in moving from sets that had been designed primarily in green and greys to ones in full and bright color. Technicolor consultants kept tight control of the colors used in sets, but in the early experiments with color full-length films, art directors also played an important part.

For the first live-action, three-color Technicolor film *La Cucaracha* (1934), the Broadway stage designer Robert Edmond-Jones was hired as art director because of his inventive use of colored lighting on the stage. Along with art director Wiard Ihnen, he also worked on the production of Rouben Mamoulian's pioneering *Becky Sharp* in the next year. This film demonstrated that both bright and soft coloring could exist within the same film. Robert Edmond-Jones expressed his feelings and probably those of many other art directors about color at the time: "the possibilities are unlimited. . . . Now that we have color — and very good color — to work with, we must learn to think in terms of color."[22]

Despite his enthusiasm, Edmond-Jones did not have an easy time on *Becky Sharp,* Wiard Ihnen relates:

> As it turned out Jones had been promised he could direct and produce the picture, but Lowell Sherman was made director and Kenneth MacGowan producer. . . .
> Jones turned the sets over to me. I made the sketches and built the sets in conference with Sherman. Jones was used to the theatre where the whole Modus Operandi was different. . . . He thought of himself as the artistic director and color coordinator. . . . Lowell Sherman died suddenly and everything stopped for a few weeks when Rouben Mamoulian was engaged. The sets had all, or mostly all, been built.
> He approved the sets and filming was resumed. In the meantime Jones had been designing the clothes and having them built.
> It ended rather sadly because Mamoulian would not let him on the sets! He had flats built around them and Jones had to content himself with a little portable office on the stage and busy himself with costumes.[23]

15. Art director Lyle Wheeler holds up production designer William Cameron Menzies's continuity sketches for the burning of Atlanta sequence in *Gone with the Wind* (1936). They are in contrast with the more finished production sketches propped up beneath them.

The talented Jones returned to New York, taking Ihnen's set sketches with him.

Early color lighting was unusually intense, flooding the actors and sets with light from all angles. This lighting increased the amount of detail that could be clearly seen by the audience and consequently art directors had to think more in terms of such detail and its accuracy.

The Technicolor Company hired a Parisian, Andre Durenceau, to head their own art department, a part of the "Color Advisiory Service" to clients. This service included color charts to be followed for each set. When faster and better film was introduced by Technicolor in 1939 some of the intense lighting could be toned down, but detail remained an important element in the creation of sets. Cedric Gibbons seems to have understood this instinctively and MGM sets, like those he did with William A. Horning covering 25 acres for *The Wizard of Oz* (1939), set high standards for finely crafted Technicolor settings.

Other than Technicolor, Cinemascope, introduced in 1952, had the most disruptive impact on art direction. Cinemascope and other wide-screen processes meant designing on the horizontal. Art directors found problems in filling the much vaster screens with settings that didn't disappear into the background or, conversely, dwarf the actors.

In the post-production period the art director supervised the sets during retakes. Retake sets were based upon the set and property stills which were routinely taken for each scene just before shooting. There are set and property still-books extant for many films; some of these have several hundred shots of sets alone (**Illustrations 16 and 61.** See page 129.). These still-books were preserved and kept for reference, while original materials like sketches were destroyed, because many of the sets would be stored, redressed and used over.[24]

The studios kept inventory books of their standing sets, exteriors and interiors. These provided quick references for their own directors and art directors, and were shown to rental clients.

Two still-books representing the available standing sets at Warner Bros. Studio and Ranch circa 1938–1939 indicate what the art department at that time had to work with.[25] On the Warner lot, as might be expected, there were an abundance of urban settings including streets entitled: New York, Western, French, Brownstone, Frisco, Russian, New England, Viennese, and Canadian. Other Warner sets included: a theatre interior, a lake, a court house, Robin Hood Tower, tourist cabins with gas station, a house, airplane hangers, and trenches. At the Warner Bros. ranch there was a Swiss cabin that rented for $200 a day, and an entire Mexican village, the set for *Juarez* (1939), that went for $1,500 per day. With so many standing sets available one of the challenges to the art directors and set decorators was inventing different disguises for them.[26]

Differences existed between the major studios on the frequency of their

16. *A Streetcar Named Desire,* 1951. Richard Day, art director. The atmospheric New Orleans tenement, exterior and interiors, fashioned by Day are the film's principal set.

reuse of sets. At all studios, the designation of a film as either A or B was an important determining factor. The B pictures merited few, if any, original sets or props. Warner Bros., with tight-fisted Jack Warner pulling the economic strings, was strong on the reuse of settings; some of them, for the mystery and crime films, became almost as familiar to viewers as the old silent scenic film drops had once been. Conversely, at Selznick International or 20th Century–Fox, Lyle Wheeler seldom felt pressured to use existing sets, and not at all on the quality films he designed for David Selznick like *Gone with the Wind* (Illustration 49), which had 90 original sets, and *Rebecca* (Illustration 50), for which he built Manderley, when a suitable mansion and permission to burn it down were not forthcoming (see **Illustrations 49 and 50,** pages 110 and 112).

The budget for sets was drawn up by the art director, reviewed by the supervising art director, and then sent to the construction department for confirmation. The art director made a scene by scene breakdown, listing sets, properties, locations, and their individual costs.[27] The big studios had separate budget departments to assist art directors but, with experience, there apparently was little difficulty in this part of the job.

Checking production records on budgets for routine B films, the crime melodrama *The Cop* (Universal, 1937) turns out to be rather typical. On such B films art departments had to look close to home for their settings. The picture was given a favorable review in *Variety* (July 28, 1937) under its release title *Man in Blue;* directed by Milton Carruth it featured Robert Wilcox and Nan Gray. The total budget for the film was $117,260 and it came in under at $105,152. Of that sum, R.J. Riedel, the art director (Jack Otterson was supervising art director), was given $15,260 for the settings — this sum included their design, construction, dressing and striking. Martin Murphy, long-time construction manager at Universal, okayed each daily sheet on this film. Murphy's records show with what care he scrutinized every item of Riedel's budget of less than 15 percent of the picture's cost. Bigger budgets, of 20 percent or more of the film's cost, were allotted to A pictures. (Designers in the 1980s frequently find themselves working with much less than either of these figures because of the salaries given to star actors.)

The art director was himself in a central position for keeping costs on films down by calculating how much of the action would be seen in each shot. As a rule, nothing was built *"above what the camera saw."* This rule created difficulties for some actors who found it disconcerting to perform in fragmented environments; if they could get away with it in their budgets, art directors frequently built ceilings and other details to assist actors.

There were directors who tried to ignore the rule of "nothing built above camera," and as Lyle Wheeler relates, wanted whole cities constructed with little sense of costs or purpose. He tells the story of a director who insisted that the entire interior of Grand Central Station be built in the studio (it was wartime and travel to distant locations was prohibited). After analyzing the script, Wheeler suggested that,

> In terms of the action, the director could photograph the characters as they emerged from a studio built train gate, then use stock footage of the Grand Central Station interior, and return in the next shot to the characters being greeted in a studio built corner of the Station when the narrative picked up again.

Suggestions like this from art directors routinely saved studios thousands of dollars.

Another tale about the excesses of directors, which recurs with variations in the anecdotal repertoire of art directors, has to do with location shooting. As told by Gene Allen:

> The art director shows the director a required camera set-up framed by trees and leading off into a distant landscape. The director looks it over, is unimpressed and tells the art director to have a tree brought over to a nearby spot with a superior view. The director leaves; the art director has the crew dig a hole at a distance and fill it back in. The next day the director checks out the camera set-up — in its original place — notes the "tree" hole, and satisfied, says "See, didn't I tell you it would be better over here?"

Fundamental to the art director's job was faking things. The materials represented in films were seldom real; either because they were too expensive or too heavy. Art directors and their crews, all developed special techniques for attaining illusions. Proud and unsecretive about these techniques, they were often praised by others in the industry for the part they played in making movie "magic." The cinematographer Harry Stradling in an article on his work with art director Richard Day on *A Streetcar Named Desire* (1951), recalled a comment overheard in the audience at a screening of the film: "This show isn't phony. That was shot right down in New Orleans. I know the town."[28] Actually, 80 percent of the film was shot on one studio set designed by Day. Stradling continues:

> In my book, Art Director Day is one of the real masters at the business of making studio sets come to life. He has tremendous talent for realism, the knack of eliminating the freshly painted look. His sets always have a lived-in and worn-by-time appearance that gives them quality.[29]

Stories on art directors or art department activities were routinely prepared as part of the publicity materials for films in the thirties and forties, but their release was usually squelched by directors or studio executives who didn't want confusion in the public's mind over who was in charge on a film. Arthur Lonergan suggests that studio bosses didn't particularly want the public to know precisely how movies were made, thinking that if they did, the "magic" of movie magic might be gone.

Since the time of pioneer art director Wilfred Buckland's move into the Hollywood studio system in the teens, art directors have had to tread lightly in their relationships with directors. In the 1950s sensitivities surfaced when the Screen Director's Guild suggested that the term "director" be stricken from the art director's screen credit. But since the term art director went back as far as the origin of the job, the issue wasn't pushed beyond preliminary meetings between representatives of the two guilds. In today's terminology, art directors are frequently called production designers, and what used to be known as the assistant art director is now often listed as the art director.[30]

The big studio art departments experienced yearly changes in personnel, but most people remained for relatively long periods of time—a decade or more—in one studio. The longevity of the heads of departments had already been mentioned. A feeling of competitiveness within art departments is seldom admitted by art directors and apparently was not deliberately fostered. Hal Pereira, while head of Paramount's Art Department (1950–1967), reportedly created in-house competitions for certain films, but this was not the common practice. Art directors heard of specific properties coming up for production and asked to be assigned to them, but the final decision always came from the supervising art director.

Excepting the writers, the educational level of the members of the art departments in the thirties and forties was above that of most other studio departments. Whatever their backgrounds, the art directors of this period admit that most of their training for film work was "on the job."

The architecture trained art directors who began to dominate in the studios around 1930 had been trained in the Beaux-Arts traditions prevalent in American architecture schools in the 1920s. Fundamental to such training was the absolute recall of historical styles, which came in very handy for their work in films.

Some of these architecturally trained art directors had the opportunity to build small private architectural practices. What they built shows no particular stylistic bias and is highly eclectic in character. Lyle Wheeler built the still handsome Beverly Hills Post Office in a simplified renaissance revival style. Art director Randall Duell, who was highly successful in reverting entirely to architectural practice after many years in films, designed amusement theme parks around the country. Cedric Gibbons designed his own house in 1930 as a paradigm of modernism, which even as late as 1980 prompted a *New York Times* architecture critic to comment:

> His house is Le Corbusier's Villa Stein gone Hollywood, and it is full of wonderful possibilities — how differently might we view the history of modern architecture in Los Angeles if Cedric Gibbons hadn't spent the rest of his career designing movie sets?[31]

But how differently we would have viewed the movies!

Although there was some of the usual studio versus studio jealousy, it does not seem to have run particularly deep in the studio art departments. This was due, in part, to the fraternizing done by the art directors in the Cinemagundi Club. Although they generated no real artists' colony in Hollywood, the art directors did form a confraternity as early as 1924 called the Cinemagundi Club (named after the famous New York artist's Gundi Club). Among the charter members were Robert Odell, Ben Carré, William Cameron Menzies, and William S. Darling. The Cinemagundi Club later evolved into the Society of Motion Picture Art Directors, which flourishes today, approximately 350 strong, as Local 876 of the International Alliance of Theatrical Stage Employees and Motion Picture Machine Operators of the United States and Canada.

The original purposes of the Cinemagundi Club were primarily social, but gradually, professional concerns took a more prominent part in the group's activities. The unionization that came along in the mid-forties was due partly to working conditions and partly to pressure from other unionized segments of the industry. Today, as a result of union rules, the art director is locked into certain duties and locked out of others which earlier he was free to do. For instance, he is not supposed to make any finished sketches, a task left to sketch artists.

An informative source for the varied activities of art directors in the studio system was a short-lived publication of the Society of Art Directors, *Production Design*. Begun in January 1951 (with then Guild president Arthur Lonergan a prime instigator) as a typewritten monthly bulletin with short articles and news of Society activities, by February of the same year an editorial board from the membership, composed of Daniel Cathcart, Randall Duell, Robert Peterson, Leo Kuter and Seymour Klate, had been appointed and the size and format of the publication expanded to produce a short magazine. Illustrated articles on the work of well known art directors now appeared, written by other art directors. Among those profiled were Edward Carrere, Anton Grot, Robert M. Haas, William A. Darling, Harry Horner, Richard Day, and Maurice Ransford. This ambitious publication, produced solely by busy art directors, faltered by August 1952, with only one edition appearing in the following year.

Production Design reported that the Society proposed several innovative projects — the formation of a permanent collection of members' sketches and the establishment of an art research library, for instance — which, like the magazine, were soon abandoned. The Society, realizing that the work of their members affected American taste, did for a while give out awards of merit to manufactured products (cameras, refrigerators, and the like).

Even in the silent era, art directors and set decorators had noted the immediate impact their ideas on interior decor had upon the American public. George James Hopkins, already a noted set decorator in silent films, noted in *Production Design* that the sets

> proved to be of interest to the American housewife, and we began to receive a great number of letters relative to home building and decorating problems. Studio heads were faced with the undisputable fact that a large number of people came into theatres to see settings, as well as actors. The Art Director and the Set Decorator ceased to be looked upon as an experiment.[32]

In the thirties art directors like Cedric Gibbons were credited, and correctly, with affecting public taste. *Theatre Arts Monthly* opined that Gibbons had introduced film audiences "to the modernistic settings now so much in vogue."[33] Yet Gibbons was not alone in using modern decor; movie sets of the thirties were frequently done in Art Moderne and Art Deco styles. Van Nest Polglase and Carroll Clark's sets for the Fred Astaire and Ginger Rogers pictures at RKO are superb examples of modern design ideals stemming from, among others, the German Bauhaus architects and designers and from the work of the Swiss Le Corbusier, and the French Robert Mallet-Stevens. Contemporary architects and interior designers in America must have found it easier to sell their clients modern concepts once they had been seen in the movies.[34] The impact of film design on built design deserves much more study.

Aside from trying to uplift American taste in design and present professional profiles, the greatest number of articles in *Production Design* were practical how-to pieces, like John Meehan's on how he prepared the shot looking upward at William Holden's body floating in the swimming pool in *Sunset Boulevard* (the camera at the water's surface looked through a piece of glass and photographed the body reflected in a mirror at the bottom of the pool).[35]

Several other articles, like the long one by Eugene Lourie about working in India on *The River* (1951), dealt with problems of art direction in a foreign country.[36] These articles in *Production Design* discussing location shooting problems seem indicative of the growing importance of foreign and domestic location work for art directors in the transitional 1950s. Fewer films were being made on the major studio lots and the large art departments were beginning to disintegrate. Television and the changing economics of motion picture production were intervening. For a variety of reasons, not the least of which were the inexperienced crews, it took twice as long to shoot pictures in foreign countries, but they still could be done less expensively than in Hollywood studios.

American taste in movies was changing too — altered by television and the postwar changes in society. The public was used to seeing foreign places from newsreels, and many Americans, former soldiers in particular, had actually seen foreign lands. Fifties movies shot in London, Paris and Rome prompted nostalgia in some, and a desire to travel in others. For art directors, used to studio life, they caused innumerable headaches.

Beginning in the sixties there was a gradual drifting of television trained directors into the motion picture industry, and they accelerated the demise of the studio art departments. These directors brought with them a skepticism about what could be done in a studio, premised on their television studio experience. Their attitude was that it had to "be real to look real." They did not know how to use the resources that the studios had to offer and perhaps, given their comparative youth, were intimidated by the older, more technically knowledgeable studio personnel, including the art directors. With the closing down of the old studio system, art directors had to look for work as independents or retire.

3
United Artists and the Independent Art Directors

While most of the Hollywood studios fell into the same basic pattern in the development of their technical departments, United Artists broke different ground. United Artists was not a major studio in the usual sense, but a company of independent artists who distributed their films under the same banner, hoping to keep the profits. Founded in 1919 by Mary Pickford, Douglas Fairbanks, Charlie Chaplin and D.W. Griffith, it added to its roster other artists, producers and directors over the subsequent decades, including, Samuel Goldwyn (1925), Gloria Swanson (1927), and Howard Hughes (1930). The individuals associated with United Artists made their pictures at a variety of studio locations in Los Angeles, so that the company did not develop any large technical departments. Despite this peculiar situation, certain well known art directors are associated with the studio, either because they started their careers or spent a major portion of them in association with one of the company's principals. Like them, these art directors, most importantly William Cameron Menzies *(The Thief of Bagdad, Gone with the Wind)* and Richard Day *(Greed, On the Waterfront)* who are discussed here, are independents.

Menzies and Day to a lesser extent, moved from studio to studio, often working under non-exclusive short term contracts. This was unusual for their time. Menzies' and Day's work represents the best that Hollywood art direction was ever to achieve—its intense variety, use of the history of architectural styles, and imaginative thrust are indicative of artists of the first rank. Their efforts effected and continue to effect others in their profession.

William Cameron Menzies was born (1896) and educated in New Haven, Connecticut; he attended Yale and then studied at the Art Students' League in New York City **(Illustration 17)**. His first jobs were in advertising, doing magazine layouts and illustrating children's books. After service in the Navy in World War I, he was befriended by art director Anton Grot, who managed to have him taken on as an assistant at the Fort Lee Studios in New Jersey.

41

17. William Cameron Menzies, independent art director.

Menzies first picture was Pathé's *The Naulahka* (1918), directed by George
Fitzmaurice. For it, Grot conceived a

> set representing the interior of a huge Hindu temple, with the foreground 30 feet
> deep where the action was to take place. The remaining depth of the set was built
> in "forced perspective." Although the actual depth of the entire set was no more
> than 50 or 60 feet, it appeared on the screen to extend for at least 200 feet.[1]

Grot taught the novice Menzies this technique and others, particularly the
function of the continuity sketch, which both were to use successfully
throughout their careers.

Invited to come to Hollywood by Raoul Walsh, Menzies worked for him
many times in the early twenties on *The Deep Purple* (1920), *The Oath* (1921)
and others, and finally on a film which was to be a landmark in his career and
establish him as one of the most influential art directors in silents, *The Thief
of Bagdad* (United Artists, 1924), starring Douglas Fairbanks. Always concerned about the sets for his pictures, which were frequently virtual "costars"
in the action sequences, Fairbanks was one of several movie stars (Mary
Pickford was another) to have an important impact on the expansion of art

direction as a craft. For *The Thief of Bagdad* Anton Grot now worked as Menzies' assistant, as did Irvin J. Martin, Park French and others.

Menzies' widow (he died in 1957) recalls that Fairbanks at first thought the art director too young for the job (he was 28!) and that to convince him of his abilities, Menzies

> worked and worked on these paintings day and night, then he asked for another appointment. He went over carrying all these drawings on his head because they were heavy, and he walked into Douglas Fairbanks' office with these boards balanced on his head and said he'd come to show him that he wasn't too young. He got the job.[2]

Menzies' masterful design of *The Thief of Bagdad*, is evident from these refined drawings, which even at this early stage in his career are in purpose like those he was to do throughout it. The setting is shown, as are the actors and actions of each scene, and the lighting and camera angle are indicated.[3] When his drawings were transformed into settings, as in the elaborate oriental city on a river **(Illustration 18)**, they come alive with exotic detail; a winding stair (center of the still) leads into the city—a place of countless different levels, where over a dozen separate roof lines may be counted.

The great cinematographer James Wong Howe was later to comment on the thoroughness of Menzies' technique, when they worked together on the Sam Wood picture *King's Row* (1942):

> Menzies designed the sets and sketches for the shots; he'd tell you how high the camera should be, he's even specify the kind of lens he wanted for a particular shot. The set was designed for one specific shot only, if you varied your angle by an inch you'd shoot over the top... Menzies created the whole look of the film. I simply followed his orders. Sam Wood just directed the actors; he knew nothing about visuals.[4]

In *The Thief of Bagdad* Menzies successfully wed semiabstraction to ornate detail in the exteriors and interiors of the palace and streets of the city **(Illustration 19)**. Previously, semiabstraction in film decor had been brilliantly achieved in silents by several designers, particularly Natasha Rambova in those films she conceived for film great Nazimova, *Camille* (1921) and *Salome* (1923). But the troublesome Rambova, second wife of Rudolph Valentino, was not to have a sustained career, due to her egomaniacal, disruptive behavior on film sets.[5] The stepdaughter of the cosmetic magnate, Richard Hudnut, Winifred Shaunessey Hudnut had reemerged with the name Natasha Rambova on the advice of a psychic who said she could only achieve fame using the new name. Schooled in England, Rambova's education in the visual arts was slight; undeterred she emerged a self-styled artist in several media. She had wanted to be a dancer, studying and touring with the Russian ballet's Theodore Kosloff, before meeting Nazimova and turning her talents to costume and scenic design.

The Thief of Bagdad, 1924: 18. (Top) William Cameron Menzies, art director. Exotic in detail, Menzies' Oriental city winds vertically upward from a river. Towers with conical, pyramidal and pagoda caps create a background for the stairways, terraces, balconies and facades of the city. 19. (Bottom) The barren wall (right) is in sharp contrast to the ornately detailed palace facade (rear).

Rambova's concept for *Salome* (**Illustration 20**) is dependent on the illustrations on the same theme by *fin-de-siècle* Englishman Aubrey Beardsley. His distinctive graphic vocabulary of sinuous curving vines and flowing peacock inspired ornamental patterning is evident in Rambova's settings. Photographed in the black and white of the period, her sets, like Beardsley's drawings, have a stark, expressionistic effect with a portent of evil lurking just beneath their surfaces. Rambova frequently emptied the screen, as may be seen in this still, of all but a few linear devices, thus heightening the effect of Nazimova's highly stylized acting.

For *Camille* a similar exotic, sensuous vocabulary of surfaces had been chosen by Rambova for the boudoir of the star (**Illustration 21**) — her circular bed is seen through the transparent arch at the rear. The planarity of the walls and spare simplicity of the set design, alternating with floral and abstract motifs, link it to the Art Deco style then gaining in popularity.

Menzies would certainly have known Rambova's innovative work. His own palace for *The Thief of Bagdad* is resplendent with floral and linear detail, reflected, as are the sumptuous costumes, in a brilliant shining floor. Although the "big white set" is usually thought to have been developed in the thirties, Menzies' sets look vast and white, especially the streets. This is due to the abstraction of expanses of blank wall in the city and in the palace that is only punctuated by some giant scenic device — a sweeping stair or giant window. These relatively unadorned backgrounds serve as perfect foils for Douglas Fairbanks' acrobatic and balletic leaps and stunts. In contrast to this, at other times, as in the princesses' chamber, the screen is filled with rich detail. There, diaphanous curtains rise to a silken canopy over the bed, and a floral patterned ramp sweeps across the background.

The Thief of Bagdad lobby book took unexpected note of the sets and did not exaggerate their magical effect:

> First of all, there was the basic fact that when a thing is photographed, it is given substance and reality. This was overcome by building acres of glazed floor, which reflected high lights along the base line and destroyed the reality of solid foundations. This imparted the illusion of floating so that the magnificent structures, with their shadows growing darker as they ascend, seem to have the fantastic quality of hanging from the clouds rather than of being set firmly upon the earth.

To heighten the feeling of fantasy, Menzies designed a decor in which the proportions of objects — vases, flowers, windows, stairs — were vastly out of proportion to the human actors (see **Illustration 19**). The huge palace exterior in this crowd scene is not diminished by the dozens of extras, and Menzies, like Walter Hall on *Intolerance,* skillfully places people throughout several vertical levels of the set. The film was tinted in tones of green, rose and gold so that the total effect was foreign and sensual. Menzies' creativity, throughout his career, flourished when he was asked to do highly imaginative or exotic decor.

His reputation firmly established, Menzies went on in the later twenties to design Valentino's last three films: *Cobra* (1925), *The Eagle* (1925), and *The Son of the Sheik* (1926). United Artists had refused to renew Valentino's contract if his quarrelsome art director wife, Rambova, were involved in any more of his pictures. Valentino's adventure / romances allowed Menzies to further his vision of far off and romantic places.

Menzies' work in the later twenties also involved a stylized Gothic Paris for *The Beloved Rogue* (1927) starring John Barrymore, and two films for D.W. Griffith, *Lady of the Pavements* (1929) and *Abraham Lincoln* (1930). In the thirties Menzies began to direct films, many of them in conjunction with others. He codirected films with Kenneth McKenna, Marcel Varnel, and Henry King. Altogether he directed or codirected over a dozen films.

The most memorable of his own films was based on the H.G. Wells science fiction novel *Things to Come* (1936), which Menzies directed for London Films and whose designer was Hungarian-born Vincent Korda, then one of England's top directors.[6] Korda and Menzies worked with American special effects expert Ned Mann (with whom Menzies had collaborated on effects for *The Thief of Bagdad*) to create a futuristic vertical city like those foreseen by Le Corbusier in his influential writings of the twenties. The city rises to unknown heights as seen from below, this through the use of three-dimensional sets for the actors, cleverly interfaced matte shots (this is like a glass shot: a matte is a painting which is used in a composite shot with other live or still elements) and hanging miniatures. In many sequences (**Illustration 22**), as here, the actors appear minuscule in the overpoweringly sleek, white and Streamline Modern environment through which they move over avenues in the skies, on transparent elevators, and in futuristic flying machines. This British science fiction film, which had been built on concepts developed in Fritz Lang's classic *Metropolis* (1927), was in turn to serve as a prototype for other such films of the next two decades.

In 1930 for the *Cinematographic Annual* Menzies had written a short history of art direction and his theories pertaining to it. He noted that in some cases, "The setting might even become the hero in the picture...," an apt description of what happened on *Things to Come*.[7] The American public was to see something approximating Menzies' and Korda's vision a few years later at the 1939 World's Fair at Flushing, Long Island, and billed as "The World of Tomorrow."

What was Menzies' virtue as an art director — creating the visuals — seems

20. (Top) *Salome,* 1923. Natasha Rambova, art director. A stylized background of flowers and vines fit the stylized acting of Nazimova (shown here). Rambova's sets were based on Aubrey Beardsley's illustrations. 21. (Bottom) *Camille,* 1933. Natasha Rambova, art director. Nazimova and Valentino luxuriate among plush satin cushions and fur rugs in a room defined by dark planar surfaces with gilt edging. Through a transparent arch (rear), a circular bed could be seen.

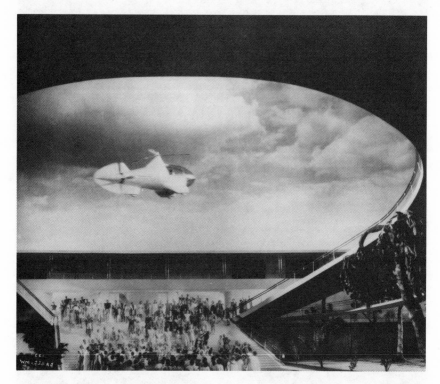

22. *Things to Come,* 1936. Vincent Korda, art director. A stair is filled with actors who appear minuscule in comparison with the sleek building (matte) and circular ramps that create a court (hanging miniature) surrounding them.

to have been his vice as a director. Lyle Wheeler, supervising art director at 20th Century–Fox, thought Menzies' films dwelt too much on the settings. He commented,

> Generally, art directors don't make good directors. There have been only two good directors who came from the field: Alfred Hitchcock and Mitchell Leisen. Leisen had designed sets and costumes and was very adroit at comedy. When Menzies worked as a director, I used to tell him, "Bill, you're no damn good as a director." The first thing he would ask for when he came on the set is, "Dig me a hole in here," and that's where he would put his camera. He wanted to photograph ceilings and didn't give a damn what the actors were saying. But when Menzies had Sam Wood working with him, he had Wood to control him. *Our Town* and *King's Row* are good examples of a collaboration in which the two men took turns at the camera.[8]

Wheeler is right in that Menzies' most successful long term collaboration was with director Sam Wood in the forties. Wood was an independent, like Menzies, and their films were made for almost every studio in town. Their work together includes: *Our Town* (1940) with Harry Horner, *King's Row* (1941) with Carl Jules Weyl, *The Devil and Miss Jones* (1941), and *For Whom the Bell Tolls* (1943) with Hans Dreier and Haldane Douglas.

The problems involving the design of *Our Town* stemmed from the producer Sol Lesser's desire to be as faithful as possible to the spirit of Thornton Wilder's popular 1938 Pulitzer Prize winning play, while making it cinematically interesting. The play had been staged with almost no scenery and only a few props — tables, ladders and chairs. It was decided that this approach would not work on the screen, and simple, turn of the century settings were devised by Menzies and Horner to visualize the town.

King's Row (Warner Bros., 1942) was adapted from a bestselling novel by Henry Ballamann about corruption in a small midwestern town at the end of the century. It starred Ann Sheridan, Robert Cummings and Ronald Reagan in a serious, realistic narrative. Menzies' sketches, which James Wong Howe has described above, showed the attention to detail that make these sets of ordinary households so intricately and inconspicuously a part of the tightly woven fabric of the story.

Menzies' was a singular visual talent in the movie industry, his development of the continuity sketch, his imaginative, exotic settings for *The Thief of Bagdad* and the Valentino pictures, his skill at handling every historical style earned him a reputation unparalleled among art directors. Working as an independent, Menzies did not tie himself down to one studio, which made the going rough at times, but it also seems to have provided him with the freedom to experiment and also to satisfy his ambition to direct.

How it felt to be an independent in the days of the big studios has been described by Russian-born art director Eugen Lourie, whose major work was done in Europe with director Jean Renoir, but who migrated to Hollywood during the Second World War, and has left a memoir of his career,

> I was amazed ... by the loyalty each film crew had to their respective studio, a Hollywood tradition that was new to me. I met some art directors who remained with the same studio for all their professional lives. They would have found it inconceivable to change studios.... In Europe we tried hard to work with some preferred directors or to choose films interesting in content or visual ambience. But in Hollywood I met designers working regardless of the film content, guided only by their loyalty to the studio. In my early Hollywood days studio art directors looked upon their independent colleagues with a condescending suspicion; they made me feel like one of the "irregular" intruders. This attitude changed in later years when the reign of the big studios ended.[9]

Menzies surely felt some of this insider/outsider conflict, but probably not as much as European Lourie did. One thing that freelance art directors had to face that their studio colleagues did not was the possibility of long spells without a paycheck. Menzies did not work for periods of several months duration, and even considered leaving art direction at those times.

Richard Day's career, like Menzies', did not adhere to the Hollywood norm. It was connected over long periods of time more with certain directors, like Von Stroheim, or producers, like Sam Goldwyn, than with a particular studio.

Sam Goldwyn had put together his own independent film production company, Samuel Goldwyn, Inc. Ltd., in 1924, after a falling out with several partners on earlier deals. Goldwyn decided that he wanted to be in complete control of what he called "The Goldwyn Quality." He had his own facilities at 1041 N. Formosa Avenue in Los Angeles, but frequently used rented space for the few movies he made each year—usually only three or four.

Goldwyn Productions had technical departments, but on a much smaller scale than did the major studios. Goldwyn was always choosey about his technical personnel and oversaw all areas of employment on his films. Gregg Toland was his photographer of choice, and his favorite early choice for art director was Ben Carré, who designed several films for him including 1924's *Cythera* and the very successful *Stella Dallas* (1925). By 1928 he turned to William Cameron Menzies for a series of films that included *The Awakening* (1928), a Vilma Banky vehicle, and *Bulldog Drummond* (1929), featuring Goldwyn's number one male star, Ronald Colman.

In 1930 Goldwyn hired Richard Day **(Illustration 23)**, who had formerly teamed with director Erich Von Stroheim on his major films, and then worked at MGM. Day was put to work on the screen version of the Eddie Cantor Broadway musical, *Whoopee!* This began Day's residence at Goldwyn Pictures, where he designed almost every major feature done by the Studio in the years 1930–1938. Day's work was nominated for an Academy Award frequently in this period; he won in 1936 for *Dodsworth*. In the late forties, Day returned to the Goldwyn lot for five pictures, bringing his total number of features designed for the Studio to 36, almost half of the 80 that were ever issued.[10]

At Goldwyn Pictures, Day had the chance to do every conceivable type of picture, from musicals with Cantor and the Goldwyn Girls cavorting around large sets, to historical pieces like *Barbary Coast* (1935). *Kid Millions* (1934, director Roy Del Ruth) was a typical Eddie Cantor vehicle, with Cantor doing his perennial juvenile routine (plus, at one point, his black face routine). The film starts out in rather ordinary settings—a fragment of a music store, a tugboat on the East River (the river back projected)—and then proceeds to a modern ocean liner (again seen in fragments). The boat arrives in Egypt and the settings change completely, moving into the realm of fantasy—an Oriental bazaar, and most importantly a sheik's palace. The palace follows the Menzies' tradition from *The Thief of Bagdad;* it is semiabstract with luxuriant details, like an ornate garden pond, which serve as backdrops for the Goldwyn girls who flit in and out of the film performing musical numbers that have little or nothing to do with the plot. The spectacular grand finale was filmed in Technicolor and directed by Willy Pogany. It takes place in art director Day's

23. Richard Day, art director.

futuristic ice cream factory set (don't ask why), which is filled with wonderful huge props and cute kids. Such thirties Goldwyn films lack the visual continuity Richard Day could have given them because of the plot preferences of the Cantor genre.

Sam Goldwyn is best remembered for films with contemporary themes and some of Day's best designs along modern lines, *Arrowsmith* (1931) and *Dodsworth* (1936), occur among them. *Arrowsmith* followed the career of a medical doctor (Ronald Colman) from a South Dakota town to world famous McGurk Research Institute in New York City to the islands of the West Indies. Dozens of ordinary sets were needed, with the most extraordinary being the Streamlined Moderne research facility which is used as a symbol for the sterile, antihumanistic values ascribed to in the "pure" science idealism of Dr. Arrowsmith.

Seen from the exterior and interior, the McGurk Research Institute is a stark, oppressive 30 story tower that dwarfs its inhabitants. The vast scale of the place and its pristine orderliness is felt in Day's interiors; an elevator corridor appears to run into infinity. Only five elevator doors were constructed and the dozens reaching into the distance are a painting in forced perspective. Day

cast about in the waters of architectural modernism for the look of the interiors of his research institute, which is at some distance from skyscraper construction in America in 1931, with only a few like George Howe and William Lescaze's Philadelphia Saving Fund Society Building of the same year looking as Streamlined in its interiors. Day built only fragments of most of the interiors, with mattes being used extensively. Director John Ford's camera angles, especially a carefully chosen overhead shot which shows Colman entering for the first time the Institute's marble lobby through doors 30 feet high, enhances Day's conception of monumental scale at the service of lofty, but heartless ideals.

Dodsworth is more relentlessly modern throughout than was *Arrowsmith*. Like the earlier film it deals with a clash of modern values with more traditional ones regarding marriage, fidelity, and work. Photographed on Hollywood sound stages, the film's convincing continental flavor comes from Day's sets and from the second unit's location photography of European sites that was skillfully back-projected in several scenes.

The film begins in Zenith, Ohio, where Sam Dodsworth (Walter Huston), a wealthy, unassuming automobile manufacturer, is about to retire. Day's offices of Dodsworth's Union Motor Company **(Illustration 24)** are anything but unassuming, they project power and wealth; their modern glass curtain walls overlook the mammoth plant (a built forced perspective, rather than a painted one, which looks more realistic in scenes in which the shot will be held for a longer period of time. The camera must be fixed in such shots to maintain the illusion.) The Dodsworths embark on a European grand tour and the rest of the story takes place in posh hotel rooms and on board that beloved icon of artistic modernism, a steamship.

Steamship motifs recur frequently in the modern architecture of the twenties, in the buildings of Le Corbusier (the Villa Savoy), Robert Mallet-Stevens (the Tourist Bureau, Paris, 1925) and others, but Day didn't have to settle for single motifs, he got to design an entire ship. His exterior upper deck is a spare, glistening, white-on-white set, complete with funnels, lifeboats, and stairs with metal railings. Steamships, on the model of the real *Normandie* and *Île-de-France*, were frequently the playground of the rich in films of the thirties; the Dodsworths are supposed to be going abroad on the Art Deco *Queen Mary*. Oddly, the real ships were seldom used in films, and so art directors got to build innumerable Art Deco or Streamlined staterooms, nightclubs, pools and even grand stairways on studio lots. But for once, movie decor was not exaggerating the elegance and beauty of the real thing.

Richard Day's later films of the fifties, whether the rather ordinary Dick

24. *Dodsworth*, 1936. Richard Day, art director. Walter Huston stands at a desk in the Bauhaus modern offices of the Union Motor Company. The factory seen through the glass curtain wall is a built forced perspective.

Powell *film noir* vehicle *Cry Danger* (1951) or Elia Kazan's brilliant *On the Waterfront* (1954) (see **Illustration 126** on page 272), are arresting in their use of street locations. He seems to have been the most adaptive of art directors and changes in film style only fired his creativity. Day's son recalled, "My father was always extremely interested in documentary films and studied, among others, the work of Pare Lorenz, a pioneer in the field. He was able to put some of these ideas to work in the film *On the Waterfront*."[11]

In *Cry Danger,* directed by Robert Parrish, much of the action takes place in a trailer park that Day has situated on a hill overlooking Los Angeles. The city becomes a teeming backdrop for the unfolding of a sleazy tale of criminal betrayal. The opening sequences are placed in the Los Angeles Union Railroad Station — a not very original idea but handled with great originality. Powell strides toward the camera down a cavernous ramp which silhouettes his dark solitary figure against a bright light. We sense that he is already trapped, held within the confines of something out of his control. This fatalistic tone pervades the settings of the picture as it moves from tawdry bars to decrepit trailers to soiled police stations. Powell, who has been wrongly imprisoned for five years, finds that he was framed by his best friend and his ex-flame. In the closing shot a reversal of the opening sequence occurs, with Day's locations again commenting on the narrative. Powell strides from the camera down the hill away from the trailer court. A diminishing figure, awash in bright sunlight, he is free from the confines of architecture which trapped him in the opening frame. His parting comment, thrown to a solicitous cop who asks him how he feels to be proven innocent after having spent five years in jail, is "How would you feel?"; ironically, it is the Los Angeles Hall of Justice, that we see in the far distance.

Day's early and unforgettable work as Erich von Stroheim's art director only proved preparatory to a long career that stretched over four decades. His inventive work, as much as any art director's, encompassed every sort of picture, from the gritty realism of 19th-century San Francisco in *Greed,* to the glitzy modernism of *Our Dancing Daughters,* to the sober street realism of *On the Waterfront.* There has been no more sensitive and competent artist of screen decor than Richard Day.

The succeeding chapters trace the story of the development of Hollywood art departments and make it abundantly clear that independent art directors, those who signed short term contracts (for a picture or a series of pictures) were relative rarities in the days of the big studios. The studios preferred having contract art directors, as they had contract players, directors and other technical personnel. The factory like nature of their production would have been inhibited by a constant search for talent. Menzies and Day were exceptions to the rule; and there is good evidence that they too, from time to time, sought the steady employment of long-term contracts. Day, in particular, seems to have wanted to be a supervising art director, and was for a while at 20th

Century–Fox. It is not surprising that it was frequently at United Artists, and with such independent minded producers and directors as Douglas Fairbanks, Jr., Sam Goldwyn, and Sam Wood, that Menzies' and Day's talents found employ.

4

MGM and Selznick International

During the golden age of the Hollywood studio system, each of the majors had a characteristic visual style, determined in large part by the designers at each studio. —Louis Giannetti.[1]

METRO-GOLDWYN-MAYER

The following chapters trace the development of individual studio art departments, introduce their major art directors, and examine the visual styles of each. Metro-Goldwyn-Mayer, largest and in many ways the most definable of the Hollywood studios, had, in its great days, the biggest of almost everything as far as technical facilities were concerned. But while the visual "look" of each studio in the thirties and forties was a direct result of decisions by contemporary management, directors, and art departments, indirectly it was also a result of the way the studio had developed: the philosophy of its earlier management. Metro-Goldwyn-Mayer, with its modest company slogan "More Stars Than There Are in Heaven," had been formed in 1924 through the merger of the distributing company Loew's Incorporated, headed by Marcus Loew, Goldwyn Pictures, where Samuel Goldwyn had been a prime mover until 1922 when he became an independent producer, and Metro Pictures, the proving ground for Louis B. Mayer.

Although Sam Goldwyn played no part in the newly formed company, he did bequeath a legacy of his filmmaking style to MGM through Goldwyn Pictures. Goldwyn, while a part of the Jesse Lasky Feature Play Company, had helped it gain a reputation for the production of high quality features, among them *The Squaw Man* (1913) and *The Virginian* (1914). Talents like director Cecil B. DeMille, cameraman Alvin Wyckoff, and actors Dustin Farnum, Blanche Sweet and Sessue Hayakawa were part of the Lasky organization.

At the Goldwyn Picture Corporation (1916–1922), which he formed with the Selwyn Brothers, Sam Goldwyn (*née* Sam Goldfish) self-consciously promoted his films through nationwide magazine ads touting the "Goldwyn Quality," an extension of those concerns with details of production which had begun at Lasky. He hired well-known theatrical designer Robert Edmund-Jones and artists like Hugo Ballin and Everett Shinn for the company and launched a publicity campaign focusing on their improvement of the scenic decor of Goldwyn films. He paid top salaries to lure these individuals, and others—actors and writers—into his company.

Goldwyn's trademarks, the roaring lion encircled by a banner carrying the inscription *Ars Gratia Artis* (Art Thanks to Skill), were taken over by the new MGM, but more importantly, his insistence on highly crafted production values and his belief in the "star" system found a ready reception in the new company. Goldwyn's greatest bequest to MGM in terms of art direction was the soon to be legendary supervising art director Cedric Gibbons.

When Sam Goldwyn went into independent production in 1922, he continued to insist on quality in details of costumes, settings, and actor's performances. In this vein the Samuel Goldwyn Studio was later to produce such motion picture classics as *Wuthering Heights* (1939), *The Little Foxes* (1941), and *The Best Years of Our Lives* (1946), notable for just those production values that he favored even in the teens. As has already been discussed, Goldwyn hired such excellent art directors as Richard Day on his independent pictures.[2]

At the newly formed MGM, Louis B. Mayer was named to head the management. While working at Metro Pictures, which he had helped found in 1915, Mayer had, like Goldwyn, grown aware of the power of the newly emerging "stars" to bring people into theatres. A hard-headed business man, he was not as self-conscious about technical quality in films as was Goldwyn, but he brought into his organization an associate who was, Irving Thalberg. Thalberg had begun working for Mayer in 1923 and went with him into the new company as its chief of production.

A part of what later became identified as MGM's visual style was the result of early business decisions made by these men. First and foremost, MGM films were to gather as wide an audience as possible, and out of this decision emerged "the studio policy of never allowing the lighting to be below a certain wattage so that all their films could be shown even in the poorest equipped cinemas."[3] Full high-key lighting, bright and relatively shadowless, came to be synonymous with MGM productions and in close-ups a kind of glamorous back-lighting called "Rembrandt" lighting was developed for their male and particularly for their female stars. This type of lighting was also used in the many glamour still photographs of the stars that came out of the studio, particularly in the thirties and forties.

Louis B. Mayer's reactions to films were direct and he knew what he liked and wanted. Gary Carey, Mayer's biographer, summed up his approach to the filmed image when describing Mayer's reaction to an early MGM film starring John Gilbert and Greta Garbo, *Flesh and the Devil* (1926) **(Illustration 25)**; it was directed by Clarence Brown and skillfully photographed by William Daniels. Carey says

Brown and Daniels had indulged in a lot of fancy photographic effects — shadows, chiaroscuro lighting and all the other distorted mannerisms that characterized the then-fashionable school of expressionistic filmmaking. Mayer despised this kind of arty stylization. He believed people went to the movies not for silhouettes or landscapes or pretty pictures, but to watch the actors, and that therefore the leading man and woman should be well lit and at the center of the frame whenever possible.[4]

Viewing Cedric Gibbons and Frederick Hope's exquisitely designed settings, full of period detail, it is not easy to understand Mayer's objections today. *Flesh and the Devil* was a colossal success but Mayer did not change his mind; *film noir*, which later used expressionistic techniques, did not become a speciality of the company.

A man of broader tastes than Mayer, Irving Thalberg's genius lay, in his ability to take a failed motion picture and recut and reshoot to salvage it and even make it into a hit. His reputation for savagely redoing films had been established in the early twenties when he was production manager for Carl Laemmle at Universal. Foremost among his reasons for reshaping a picture were problems of plot, but he also reworked pictures when their production values did not meet his standards. At MGM, Thalberg found that he had inherited several films with the merger — including the big budgeted *Ben Hur* — which were to put his talents to the test.

Another Thalberg asset, and one which was to greatly impact on MGM studio policy, was his taste for lavish productions. At Universal, Thalberg had launched that company's first super-production with the filming of Victor Hugo's *The Hunchback of Notre Dame* (1923), in which he had cast the relatively unknown character actor Lon Chaney.

Thalberg envisioned *The Hunchback* as a spectacle as well as a horror film. He ordered the construction of a huge set which slavishly duplicated the facade and courtyard of Notre Dame as it was in the mid-nineteenth century.[5]

Even this did not satisfy Thalberg, and he ordered the almost finished film back into production, adding new scenes and reshooting others "to enhance their pictorial values...."[6] Thalberg's eye for pictorial values and his perfectionism set the tone for the development of the great technical departments which were to flourish at MGM in the next two decades.

MGM came to have the most glamorous company of players in Hollywood. Among them were Greta Garbo, Clark Gable, Joan Crawford, the Barrymores, John Gilbert, Katherine Hepburn and Judy Garland. Their stable of directors included George Cukor, Victor Fleming, Mervyn Leroy, Vincente Minnelli and Busby Berkeley, whom they lured away from Warner Bros. in 1939 to stage musical numbers and direct films.

The studio began from the start, under Mayer's direction, to build their professional departments, so that eventually in the company's most successful

26. MGM Property Department, 1940s. MGM had the largest technical departments in the movie business. The prop department collected antiques and had others copied; seen here are rows of Louis XV furniture.

years, 1936–1945, theirs were the largest costume, property **(Illustration 26)**, and art departments in the industry. By the thirties MGM had 23 fully-equipped sound stages and 117 backlot sets **(Illustration 27)**.

Together Mayer and Thalberg decided at the time of the merger to retain Cedric Gibbons from the Goldwyn Company and make him the head of MGM's art department. Gibbons remained uncontested head of that department until his retirement in 1956. They could have made no better choice, for Gibbons, an urbane man of sophisticated tastes, had the ability to marshal the talents of other creative people to the mammoth job of designing the 52 pictures and 40 shorts per year, which became the production norm for the studio by the late thirties[7] **(Illustration 28)**. Gibbons was the chief architect of what became the most powerful production department at MGM.

From the start Cedric Gibbons' contract stipulated that his name should

25. *Flesh and the Devil*, 1926. Cedric Gibbons and Frederic Hope, art directors. Greta Garbo greets John Gilbert in an exquisite period boudoir with canopied bed at the rear.

27. **MGM backlot, 1940s.** A 19th century town square is seen right foreground; a water-front, steamboats, and a river are seen in the background.

appear in the credits of all films made in the United States by the company. MGM also listed the names of the unit art directors. This way of crediting became customary in the industry, and other supervising art directors — Van Nest Polglase, Hans Dreier, and Hal Pereira among them — regularly had their names appended to films on which they had only minor creative involvement. At other studios, but not at MGM, assistant art directors were usually named. Arthur Lonergan recalled, "If an art director [at MGM] was in trouble or had an overload those of us without assignment would assist without credit."

Several art directors have left their impressions of life in the Gibbons-run

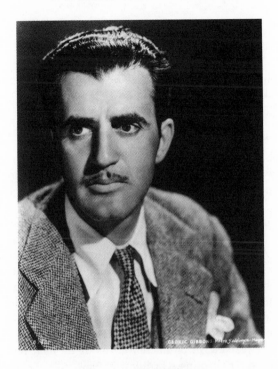

28. Cedric Gibbons, supervising art director, MGM. Contractually Gibbons' name was appended to every picture made in the United States by MGM in the period of his tenure there (1924–1956).

MGM art department. Gibbons was totally in charge; he demanded high quality work from his staff, but stood behind them when mistakes were made. Lonergan put it simply, "He always took the blame."[8]

Gibbons was formal in bearing, an egoist, always sartorially resplendent, an admirer of beautiful women—his first wife was the glamorous Mexican-born Hollywood star Delores del Rio. Art and special effects director A. Arnold "Buddy" Gillespie, who worked in MGM's art department from 1924 onward, has commented,

> He was quite a person: probably the finest executive on the lot at that time. He gathered around himself competent people and gave them almost complete autonomy, but he knew every minute what was going on. Even though there was a separate wardrobe department, he often was involved in costumes. There was another separate department, the set dressers under Ed Willis, but Gibbons was over all of them, too. ... Gibbons was so admired by the people on his staff, I don't think they ever felt any resentment that he would get the acclaim for a picture. I used to insist that certain of the men that worked for me had credit. He could never understand that, you know. He thought, "Hell, Buddy, you're the guy who's in charge."[9]

A bit of an actor himself, Gibbons carefully staged his daily entrances and exits from the Art Department, Herbert Rymann has described Gibbons' routine,

> He would arrive in his Deusenberg, in the grey homburg hat and the grey gloves, and he would walk up the stairs to the Art Department. By the time he was on the landing one glove was off and his grey homburg was swept off, and he would walk in and say good morning to his secretary, with all of us in the Art Department watching him appear and disappear with this elegant procedure.[10]

Everyone at the studio addressed him as "Mr. Gibbons"; a degree of distance from his staff was established in this way—yet they admired him and his sartorial style even to the extent of copying it—"but not too closely," according to Lonergan.

Clearly, Gibbons ran the Art Department on the model of an architectural office, a model that he knew from his own early experiences in New York. Among MGM Art Department memos is one explaining to a relief secretary what was to be expected on a regular basis, and it gives an insight into the tight organization of the department. Among *weekly* reports Gibbons received were: 1) Newcombe report (mattes), 2) Sets dressed, 3) Miniature department report, 4) Construction notes, 5) Weekly departmental cost report, 6) Weekly departmental personnel report, 7) Screen credits check, 8) Scripts (Active, Near-active, Inactive, New, In-production). Among the *daily* reports that Gibbons checked were: 1) Shooting schedules, 2) New stills, 3) Newcombe shot stills. Essential to the smooth flow of all this activity was the intervention of art director William A. Horning, who is listed in personnel records as Gibbons' assistant. Horning fielded questions prior to their being brought to Gibbons' attention, providing a screening process, that had much to do with Gibbons maintaining such a heavy work load.

Some of Gibbons' coworkers were not quite so benign in their appraisal of his authority as were Buddy Gillespie and other departmental workers. Director Vincente Minnelli has described his first meeting with Gibbons in caustic terms:

> My first exposure to the art department as a director was the first in a running series of battles. It was a medieval fiefdom, its overlord accustomed to doing things in a certain way . . . his own. Few directors took exception to this. I did.[11]

Part of the personality clash between Minnelli and Gibbons stemmed from the fact that the director had been himself an art director on Broadway. Minnelli worked as a designer of decor and costumes, first at the Radio City Music Hall and then for the Schuberts directing and designing their musicals. When he came to pictures, as opposed to many novice film directors, he knew exactly what he wanted in terms of sets and costumes. Gibbons surely saw Minnelli as intruding into his province. Later Minnelli concedes, "We eventually adjusted to each other's styles, and our differences were worked out."[12]

Jack Martin Smith, who worked in the MGM art department from 1939 to 1953, when he left for 20th Century–Fox, where he eventually became supervising art director in 1961, provides another vivid portrait of life under Gibbons:

> I worked as a sketch artist at Metro, under Cedric Gibbons. . . . There was never anything at Metro about "Would you like to do this picture?" You came back from lunch, the script was on your desk. You immediately made a list of sets, made a breakdown, got that list in. No funny business there.[13]

Smith became a specialist in musical pictures and made seven of them with Vincente Minnelli. Musicals, Smith noted, "usually had two art directors: one to design the book, the other the musical numbers."[14] Despite the hard work—the art department put out at least one film a week—the art directors who worked at MGM in the thirties and forties all seem to agree with Smith that "Metro was a marvelous place then."[15]

Gibbons himself described the MGM art department (which he favored calling the "Architectural and Engineering" department) in 1938 when he provided the chapter on the art director for the book *Behind the Screen: How Films Are Made*.[16] He described an art department in that day as having between 50 and 80 "trained specialists." "Blue prints are made by the dozen," he said, "one for each of the many departments and men who will be concerned: construction, painters, plasterers, electricians, property men, sound men."[17] Time and transportability were the principal nuisances in designing decor for films.

> We have to make reservations for stage space days ahead. Every foot of available room is utilised, with the result that sets for several pictures will be standing on one stage simultaneously. . . . In a year a big studio will produce from fifty to sixty feature-length pictures. Each one will require from thirty-five to fifty sets. Thus, with an average of, let us say, 2300 sets to be designed every year, the amount of creative work involved may be imagined.[18]

Art departments like Gibbons describes have vanished.

Aside from his duties as supervising art director Gibbons was called upon for assignments as varied as designing the interior of Irving Thalberg's bungalow (1933) (his own was designed by Buddy Gillespie) and "Cohn Park" on the studio lot. The latter was named after MGM's general manager Joe Cohn, whose negative attitude toward shooting on location, because of the expense, prompted the park's construction.

By 1935 the studio in Culver City was topographically divided into two general areas, Lot 1, where the front office was located, and Lot 2, where the sound stages, 22 by that time, were located. There was already a mixed assortment of permanent sets in place on the backlot: a village, several town squares, city streets, and a waterfront. Cohn suggested creating a park so that landscape locations could be shot on studio property,

When I suggested building a park on the lot, people told me I was crazy. But I
went ahead — Cedric Gibbons laid it out and it cost about $8,000.... No one used
it for a while except for some of the extras who did their "courting" there, but eventually a director decided to shoot at the "park" instead of spending three days in
Pasadena, and what he saved by working on the lot made a big impression.[19]

Cohn's park eventually grew until it covered approximately 180 acres. By the
mid-thirties MGM was employing 4,000 people and many of them were kept
busy by Cedric Gibbons and his department.

Austin Cedric Gibbons had been born into a family of architects probably
in 1893 in New York City and started his career as a junior draftsman in 1911
in his father's office. Attracted to illustration and painting, as well as to architecture, he had taken a study year in Europe and then enrolled at the Art Student's League (c. 1906 or 1909–1911) leaving there after several years to appren-
tice himself to muralist Hugo Ballin. His career as an art director in films began
as an assistant to Ballin at the Edison Studios in New Bedford, N.Y., in the
years c. 1912–1915.

Even on his first job, Gibbons became known as a champion of built sets
rather than scenic backdrops. Constructed sets were becoming increasing prevalent in the 1915–1920 period, and Gibbons tried to contribute a sense of realism to his sets; he became known as the designer who "put the glove on the
mantlepiece," both for his attention to detail but also because the mantlepiece
was now three-dimensional (and thus a real glove *could* be laid upon it).

In 1916 Ballin and Gibbons joined the Goldwyn Company at their studios
in Fort Lee, New Jersey. When Sam Goldwyn brought Ballin to Hollywood in
the same year, again Gibbons accompanied him. In the early twenties Ballin
decided to try his hand at directing and producing films and Gibbons fell heir
to his job as chief of art direction. Even at Goldwyn Studios, Gibbons was
called "supervising art director," a title which seems to have been invented
either by him or for him; either way, it fit him perfectly.

From his earliest days in films, Gibbons was a stickler for research. At
MGM he built an enormous research library, supervising the purchase of many
volumes himself. But sometimes research paid off and sometimes it didn't. In
1925 during the filming of *Paris* he brought Irving Thalberg a collection of
photographs of that city to prove that a love scene should not be enacted before
a moonlit ocean. Thalberg's reply was,

We can't cater to a handful of people who know Paris . . . audiences only see about
ten percent of what's on the screen anyway, and if they are watching your
backgrounds instead of my actors the scene will be useless. Whatever you put
there, they'll believe it.[20]

In the first years of its existence MGM released several large scenic films,
particularly the epic *Ben Hur* (1925), which had been carried over in the merger
from Goldwyn Pictures. The monumental sets for this film including the

Circus Maximus had been built in Rome according to the designs of Camillo Mastrocinque, the film's first art director. But as the costs and calamities of this notorious production proliferated, Thalberg and Mayer prevailed upon Marcus Loew to bring the company, including director Fred Niblo and stars Ramon Novarro and Francis X. Bushman, back to the studio in Culver City.[21] Art director Gibbons, by then in charge, and assisted by Buddy Gillespie and Horace Jackson, began designing a new version of the Circus Maximus for the crucial chariot race **(Illustration 29)**. A mammoth set, it cost $30,000 and was meant to be photographed together with a detailed miniature model by Gibbons and Gillespie. The new set, surprising for the technical wizardry of its special effects, included fake galleries with thousands of tiny moveable people in it who could wave and stand or sit. Silent film historian Kevin Brownlow has described the set thus:

> The camera photographed miniature and full-size stand together. Since the motion picture is not three-dimensional, the perspective is destroyed, and the model appears to be an integral part of the main set. But most extraordinary of all, Gibbons and Gillespie designed the miniatures so that the camera could pan over them, and not lose register. . . . This gave the cameraman complete freedom, and saved M-G-M hundreds of thousands of dollars.[22]

In the silent era, art directors contributed the special effects to films, as Gibbons and Gillespie did for *Ben Hur,* but even in the twenties some of them, like Gillespie, were beginning to specialize to some degree in this aspect of film design.[23]

James Basevi, hired as an art director at MGM in 1924 along with Gibbons, was another art director who became known very early for his skills in creating special effects. During the period of the introduction of sound, Basevi was named head of a Special Effects Department at MGM. The memorable earthquake sequence in *San Francisco* (1936) was the work of his department. Buddy Gillespie, who succeeded Basevi as head of special effects in 1936, recalls that, for obvious reasons, "They called it the disaster department. . ."[24]

The story of *Ben Hur* written by General Lew Wallace and first produced for the Broadway stage in 1899, has been an almost continuous challenge to motion picture art directors. First filmed in 1907 as a one-reeler by the Kalem Company, the staging was in the style of the fabulously successful Broadway play. The sets, depicting Roman sites, were huge painted backdrops which opened on several levels to allow action to take place. The actors stood on hidden platforms camouflaged by the drops; to heighten the realism, live horses encircled the set entering from one side and exiting on the other side of the screen during the chariot race. Groups of people milled about in front of the set, to create the illusion of the teeming Roman populace. A later version of *Ben Hur* released in 1959 by MGM was mounted at a cost of $15,000,000. Directed by William Wyler, it starred Stephen Boyd and Charleton Heston. Its thousands of sets **(Illustrations 30, 31)**, estimated by various sources as

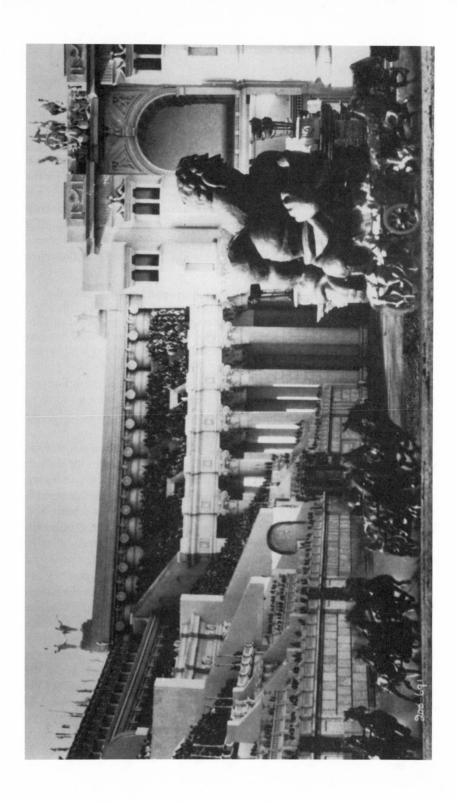

between 2,000 and 3,000, won Oscars for art directors William A. Horning and Edward Carfagno. Filmed in Panavision, color, and with the innovation of stereophonic sound, it like its predecessors was a box-office hit. The set of the Circus Maximus with central colossi and obelisk (Illustration 31) again stunned the eye, as it had in the 1925 production, through sheer scale which dwarfs the charioteers in the long shots. It too was flanked by stands, but this time built to accommodate the 50,000 extras recruited from the actual populace of Rome where it was filmed.

Aside from *Ben Hur,* another 1925 release notable for its scenic values was King Vidor's *The Big Parade* produced by Thalberg. A tale of a World War I soldier, played by John Gilbert, Thalberg made sure that its scenery did justice to the European locales represented in the action. Art director James Basevi's pictorial realism in the representation of French villages (Illustration 32), with their rutted streets and sparse vegetation, matched the grim realism of Vidor's battle scenes.

In the twenties, MGM produced a potpourri of excellent productions by such individualistic talents as Buster Keaton (*The Navigator,* 1924, and *Go West,* 1925) and Erich von Stroheim (*Greed,* 1924, and *The Merry Widow,* 1925). Differences between these talents and MGM, particularly in the person of Irving Thalberg, soon led to their leaving the studio. By the thirties, MGM was producing a steady flow of predictably plotted musical operettas featuring Jeannette MacDonald and Nelson Eddy, and a series of literary classics mostly starring the Barrymores or Garbo.

Von Stroheim had been working on *Greed* for several years before the production passed into the hands of MGM at the time of the merger in 1924. The film was designed by the director and his longtime associate, the talented Richard Day. Day's prolific career as a film designer began sometime around the year 1918 when he moved to Hollywood from his native Victoria, British Columbia. He began working for the volatile Erich von Stroheim on the film *Blind Husbands* (1919) and was also involved in the subsequent *The Devil's Pass Key* (1920) done at Universal, but received no film credit. It was von Stroheim's preference at that time to direct the film, design the sets, write the scenario, and sometimes act the leading part. Particularly when he added acting to his other roles, von Stroheim began turning to Day to take over the design aspects of his films, on which he still continued to collaborate. Day received credit as art director beginning in 1922 on *Foolish Wives* and continued in that capacity on von Stroheim's *Greed* (1925), *Merry-Go-Round* (1925), *The Merry Widow* (1925), *The Wedding March* (1928), and the uncompleted *Queen Kelly* (1929).[25]

29. *Ben Hur,* 1925. Cedric Gibbons, Arnold "Buddy" Gillespie, Horace Jackson, art directors. Chariots careen around the Circus Maximus whose screen scale was achieved with assistance from an intricate miniature.

For *Greed*, von Stroheim's demands for the settings were wholly different than for *Foolish Wives*, which had been studio built. Instead, the *entire* film was to be shot in locales—in San Francisco and the Mohave Desert—corresponding exactly to those found in Frank Norris' novel *McTeague* on which the script was based. Unprecedented problems faced the director and art director, first, because the San Francisco of *McTeague* had largely been destroyed by the earthquake and fire of 1906, and second, because no one was certain what to expect when filming in the scorching temperatures of Death Valley.

Day and von Stroheim spent weeks prowling around San Francisco and finally found, "A tenement section of the 1900 era . . . at the corner of Hayes and Laguna Streets."[26] The spaces within the tenement were left untouched, but all of the details and furnishings were added to respond to the period and story. Von Stroheim was interviewed by Idwal Jones of the *San Francisco News*, who accompanied him on a tour of the yet to be transformed tenement building, and explained how it would become the ambiance for greed, treachery, and murder **(Illustration 33)**:

> Right here in the bay window will be McTeague's dental chair. Just around the corner will be the car conductor's coffee joint. . . Just across the street is the saloon where he listened to Marcus Schouler's socialistic talk. And in the back there is an alley where you can almost smell murder. That's where Zerkow's junk shop will be.[27]

Von Stroheim's scenes of decadence and evil are seen through Day's gauzy lace curtains over the bay window, McTeague's dental chair sits beneath a bird cage, stark hanging lamp, and fly paper. Day found the memorable Sieppe family dwelling in Oakland at the foot of 34th Street next to the railway tracks. Idwal Jones reported Day's description of the house and its inhabitants: "Five people lived in that house—gloomy, filthy, musty. They could not understand why I came to offer them money for the use of their home. They stared vacantly and were relieved when I left. . . ."[28]

Greed was photographed throughout with brooding and highly interpretive lighting, ranging from the semidarkness of the opening shots of McTeague working in the Big Dipper Mine to the final glaring light of the desert sun when McTeague murders Schouler in Death Valley. Characteristically for him, director von Stroheim reverses the usual iconography of light and place in films and art, for McTeague in the dark mine is the enlightened and good man, while McTeague in the openness and glare of Death Valley is the damned.

Ben Hur, 1959: 30. (Top) Sketch, artist unknown. William A. Horning, Edward Carfagno, art directors. Atmospheric production sketches like this one of a domestic courtyard helped define the many sets in this epic. 31. (Bottom) The central colossi of the spina of the Circus Maximus borrow from the 1926 conception, while the stadium detail is less elaborate than in the earlier version (Illustration 29).

33. *Greed,* 1924. Richard Day, Erich von Stroheim, settings. McTeague's (Gibson Gowland) dental chair sits in the bay window of an actual tenement building in San Francisco that was converted by relevant detail (lace curtains, hanging lamps, birdcage and fly paper) into his office.

During the editing of *Greed* the merger of MGM took place and von Stroheim found himself working for Louis B. Mayer and Irving Thalberg rather than Sam Goldwyn. Richard Day went with the director to MGM. Thus began an association for the art director, not always happy, with that studio which lasted until the end of 1930. Day worked with von Stroheim on his later and

32. *The Big Parade,* 1925. James Basevi, art director. War torn French towns with dirt streets and sparse vegetation created authentic looking World War I locales.

final masterpieces, and through his association with MGM also encountered a wide variety of talented directors.[29] Von Stroheim's career as a director was to end tragically in the late twenties, a result of his own extravagant personality and the changing economic and managerial climate of Hollywood, but Day's as an art director was only beginning and he worked profitably in the industry for the next four decades.

At MGM, the fact that Cedric Gibbons' name was appended to works on which he was not the creative force rankled Day. His son reports that "he soon began to feel that he was being held back under the shadow of Cedric Gibbons."[30]

Day joined Samuel Goldwyn at the end of 1930 and worked almost exclusively for him through 1938. He then went to 20th Century–Fox, where he served briefly during the war years as supervising art director. When Lyle Wheeler was assigned that job permanently at the war's end, Day left Fox and freelanced during the rest of his career.

Although he may have chaffed under Cedric Gibbons' direction of the art department, it was at MGM that Day became the versatile art director of everything from comedies, *Beverley of Graustark* (1926), to musicals *Our Dancing Daughters* (1928), to melodramas like the Greta Garbo films, *The Divine Woman* (1928), *The Kiss* (1929), and *Anna Christie* (1930). He worked with many of the great directors whom MGM was attracting, including Sidney Franklin, King Vidor, Tod Browning, Fred Niblo, Ernst Lubitsch, Victor Sjostrom and Clarence Brown. It was in designing contemporary drama that Day was most at home throughout his career, and perhaps his only really unconvincing sets are for history pictures like the tiresome George Arliss vehicle *Cardinal Richelieu* (1935), where the cumbersome plot is equalled by the fussy costumes, and the actors are placed before phony-looking scenic backdrops of a Versailles which wasn't even a baroque palace during the crafty cardinal's lifetime.

Day's sensitivities to authentic locations, developing out of his association with von Stroheim, continued in later years, as his son explained:

> In the course of going about Southern California looking for these (locations) . . . my father became absolutely encyclopedic in his knowledge of the Southern California area, where you can find a reasonable facsimile of almost every kind of scenery in the world fairly close to the metropolitan area.[31]

While Day was not entirely happy at MGM under Cedric Gibbons, over the years many talented art directors were. They included: James Basevi, Buddy Gillespie, Preston Ames, Edward Carfagno, Daniel B. Cathcart, Randall Duell, Paul Groesse, Urie McCleary, Hans Peters, Stan Rogers, Ward Rubottom, Jack Martin Smith, Leonid Vasian, Arthur Lonergan, and many others.

When Gibbons commented on the aesthetics of art direction, which he

34. *Our Dancing Daughters,* 1928. Cedric Gibbons, Richard Day, art directors. Expanses of unarticulated wall are punctuated in this modern set by abstract reliefs, paintings, and semiabstract sculpture.

seldom did, his remarks seemed to center on clarity and style. As Gary Carey has put it, "All his designs were drawn in accordance with what he called his philosophy of the uncluttered—they were clean, functional and often highly stylized, a look that was to cause a major revolution in movie decor."[32] Carey seems to be referring to the films Gibbons designed in the late twenties that are much under the influence of Art Deco and Art Moderne in stylistic terms, like *Our Dancing Daughters* (1928 with Richard Day), *Our Modern Maidens* (1929), and *Our Blushing Brides* (1930 both with Merrill Pye).

Our Dancing Daughters set the tone for the series **(Illustration 34)** with its nude walls and geometric abstraction of stairs, arches, and fireplace. The floors are sleek and uncarpeted while modern sculpture, paintings and furnishings minimally punctuate the interiors. In *Our Modern Maidens,* a film having music and sound effects but no dialogue, directed by Harry Beaumont, Joan Crawford starred as the "epitome of carefree youth" in a tale of "wild life" among the wealthy. Newspaper criticism of the film all mentioned the decor, giving it glowing reviews. Said one,

The setting is ultra and neo. If the players depict the development of flapperism, their environment is not lagging. We believe it is the first time that the screen has shown such a faithful picture of the great revolution the French mode in home furnishings is about to effect. The moderniste motif is carried out even to architectural details, and it will afford no end of keen amusement to see square, solid, severe lines and the quixotism of strange lighting arrangements.[33]

In one scene Crawford and Johnny Mack Brown, the love interest, are seen posing first in a colonial setting and then in an Art Deco setting; this is a reflection of how their modern love affair differed from those of the past. According to the *Detroit Times,* this juxtaposition made "a big impact." They further opined that the house Crawford lived in "could only be conceived on the West Coast."

Cedric Gibbons was interviewed in the *New York Telegram* about his sets, and in a lengthy statement seems to admit to having gone too far in his decor for *Our Modern Maidens,*

The settings of major productions of the past years have undoubtedly reached their goal in regard to spectacle, detail and cost. It is practically impossible to go further. Now is the time to effect a more dramatic and simple background. This may be accomplished by a greater understanding of dramatic values on the part of the set designer. In the past the designer of settings has built a notable background for the action of a story. Now he must go one step further; he must design a dramatic background of corresponding value to the theme of the picture. By that I mean a background that augments the drama transpiring before it. The keynote of this is making the set act with the players.[34]

In 1930 the press was similarly impressed with the Gibbons and Pye sets for *Our Blushing Brides,* but this time gave them mixed reviews; said *The Spectator,* "Throughout the production an energetic contest seems to be waged between the art direction and the story to see which could attract the most attention."[35]

Hard-working model Joan Crawford works in Jardine's Department Store. Her apartment is realistic, but the store is Streamlined Modern. This time it really was — much of the principal action was shot in the May Company in Los Angeles — "Beaumont (the director) arranged to 'hire' the May Company . . . the occupancy to begin after closing time on Saturday night and ending before opening time Monday morning. . . ."[36] Gibbons and Pye had created dummy sets at the studio for rehearsals, and no time was lost at the location.

The most unusual studio set for this picture was built in the top of a tree. It was department store heir Robert Montgomery's "studio" in which he woos Miss Crawford. An iron stair swung down from the studio and one entered a huge interior. One critic commented:

Lo and behold the studio is approximately three times as big inside as it is out. The triumph over architectural restrictions is indeed a tribute to Hollywood genius, but personally we would find it dismaying to open a closet door and find that a ballroom had been there all the time.[37]

That Gibbons was drawn to the modern is attested in his own house designed in that mode in 1930; the elegant Art Deco and the uncluttered Bauhaus style in architecture were well suited to his impeccable tastes. The MGM sets Gibbons designed at this time were often in advance of much of what was actually being built in America; and he seems to deserve the credit given him as an innovative American architectural modernist through his film work.

The key production for defining the Gibbons' values in terms of modernism, and one with flawless settings, is the *Grand Hotel* (1932) directed by Edmund Goulding, with Cedric Gibbons and Alexander Toluboff credited as art directors. Toluboff, a Russian, had studied architecture in St. Petersburg at the turn of the century, and had come to MGM as a unit art director in 1926. In 1935, Toluboff became associated with Walter Wanger productions, which he supervised until his death in 1940.

Grand Hotel, costing $700,000 grossed $1,650,000 in 1932, and also garnered the Oscar for best picture of the year. The distinctive sets, all modern in conception, reflect a maturing and moderation over those done earlier for *Our Modern Maidens* and *Our Blushing Brides,* and are among those which established Gibbons as a master in this genre. As one writer put it, Gibbons "has set many fashions in interior decoration, notably certain modernistic trends which had their beginnings in his work."[38] While these trends may not have had their origins in Gibbons' work, it could certainly be argued that they had their popularization there.

The many stars who played in the screen adaptation of author Vicki Baum's *Grand Hotel* (Greta Garbo, John and Lionel Barrymore, Joan Crawford, and Wallace Beery), are frequently seen in the film traversing the magnificent lobby of the Grand Hotel—the picture's principal set **(Illustration 35)**. The vignettes of their lives, the substance of the film, are played out in the confines of the lobby and the other rooms of the hotel—corridors, restaurant, private rooms. The lobby is defined in sleek modernistic terms, with abstract forms and glossy surfaces predominating. Gibbons developed marked contrasts of black and white in the lobby's decor, especially so in its marble floor, done as a geometric diamond pattern. During the film's course the magnificent sweeping curves of the lobby were filmed by Goulding from every conceivable angle, including directly overhead. Art Deco decorative patterns, many abstracted from Egyptian art—geometric fan and pyramidal shapes—recur in the hotel interiors. In John Barrymore's and in Wallace Beery's bedrooms these Deco patterns are particularly sharply defined. Abstract paintings hang on their rooms' unpapered walls, while the wood furniture, beds, chairs, tables, are elegantly Art Deco in design. The lamps, wall sconces, and ceiling lighting all bear the stamp of the Deco's refined version of modernism.

35. *Grand Hotel,* 1932. Cedric Gibbons, Alexander Toluboff, art directors. The Art Deco lobby, with its polished surfaces, circular reception desk, and rich floor pattern, was central to the film's action.

In *Grand Hotel* Greta Garbo's hotel bedroom, from which she utters the desolate, "I just want to be left alone," is Deco but with feminine touches. A satin bedcover defines the ample bed she will share with Barrymore (not on screen, of course) as their stories unfold. Behind it, the luxuriant drapery of the same material covers the wall. Toluboff's and Gibbons' sets have a simple and uncluttered character, making them perfect foils for the convoluted and emotionally charged tales of author Baum.

Cedric Gibbons had attended the landmark Paris Exposition des Arts Décoratifs et Industriels Modernes held in 1925, whence the style, Art Deco (in French, Art Décoratif or Art Moderne), derives its name. At the exposition there were pavilions sponsored by prominent department stores, the Parisian Galeries Lafayette and others, and exhibitions of work by architects, textile and metal workers, and designers of furniture and decorative art.

Rooms were outfitted in the latest European fashion in a wide range, and included everything from the influential and elegant furniture of designer Émile-Jacques Ruhlmann to florid and decorative Lalique glass. Even the most decorative furnishings and objects were highly abstract by the standards of the recent past, and historic styles based on abstraction, like the Egyptian, were frequently emulated. The most radical departure from the past at the Exhibition was represented by the sleek and stripped-down cubic modernism of Robert Mallet-Stevens and Le Corbusier.

Le Corbusier's Pavillon de l'Esprit Nouveau was the single most revolutionary exhibit of the entire show. Both Mallet-Stevens and Le Corbusier espoused a crisp and clean modernism, using industrial materials like glass and concrete and based their aesthetics, in part, on an admiration for great contemporary machines, steamships, motor cars, and trains. Their nonhistorical style made no allusions to the art of the past as did Art Deco.

Cedric Gibbons understood both tendencies of the famous Parisian exposition; his own house follows Le Corbusier's ideas but in the *Grand Hotel* Art Deco reigns supreme. And in this film, there are no mixed metaphors, as in the earlier *Our Modern Maidens* and *Our Blushing Brides.* Deco is perceived as a modern style suitable for the telling of a modern tale. It was often to be invoked over the next decade when modern romances (Astaire and Rogers) or modern screwball comedy-dramas (The Thin Man series) were filmed, and nightclubs were invariably in this style. Art Deco was to serve as the formal language of many of the great skyscrapers and public buildings of the late twenties and thirties like the Chrysler Building and the Empire State Building, and American movie designers (Gibbons, Van Nest Polglase, Merrill Pye, Carroll Clark) were in the vanguard of its popularizers.

Although *Grand Hotel* was named best picture of the year, the trend-setting decor did not even receive a nomination. Nevertheless the film furthered MGM's reputation for finely crafted, meticulously detailed, and imaginative sets.

By 1936, the year of Irving Thalberg's death, MGM was settling into its preferred business-minded production of films with mass appeal. These pictures included several notable series: Andy Hardy, Tarzan, Dr. Kildare, The Thin Man, Maisie, and Boston Blackie. The sets for these films were reused with each sequel, keeping the costs of the series low and the profits high.

After Thalberg's death, several strong producers emerged at MGM, and they were to insist on imaginative and original sets. Among them was Albert Lewin who had worked as an associate of Irving Thalberg on MGM's prestige films, many of them adaptations of the literary classics, like *The Good Earth* (1937) and *Mutiny on the Bounty* (1935). The latter was the most expensive film of the year and won the Oscar as best picture. Its nearly $2 million budget was largely devoted to filming in the South Seas and the Art Department's design and building of an exact replica of the historic ship *Bounty.* Charles Laughton as Captain Bligh menacingly strides the ship's decks, while the crew, including Clark Gable as Fletcher Christian, try to avoid his cruelty in its passages. The ship set is seen in almost every frame. In this type of one-set film, the set is like another character in the story.

On *The Good Earth,* Harry Oliver, who had been an art director in the silent era, labored with Cedric Gibbons for two years on the settings. Oliver had worked in Europe on the making of *Ben Hur,* studied painting while in Rome, and in the twenties and thirties worked for both Fox and MGM.

The Good Earth was the culmination of Oliver's career and he retired when it was finished. The picture went through several directorial changes, but Oliver remained on it throughout the long production period, establishing its visual character. He even got to go on a research expedition to China (possibly with the original director, George Hill). It was certainly rare to go so far afield in those days to do research, but this trip was part of producer Irving Thalberg's quest for authenticity in all details.

Oliver brought back to the studio authentic props ranging from Chinese farm implements to livestock — two water buffalo. One of the doleful-eyed creatures achieved a star status as the main protagonist, Wang Lung's, only work animal, that had to be sacrificed in time of famine.

The locations, a small village and walls and part of a city, were built in the San Fernando Valley **(Illustration 36)**. Oliver's designs for these locations were based on photographs taken while in China. The film has a rich scenic density, seen here, with the town's market growing out of its walls, and the main street winding between it and a tangle of houses. Oliver grew particularly proud and proprietary about the Chinese gardens, rice, and wheat fields that he had had planted and which he tended himself sometimes.

The energetic production sketches **(Illustration 37)** fit the action to the sets built by Oliver. His imported Chinese farm machinery and gardens were lovingly photographed by director Sidney Franklin, who takes as much care with their handling as he does with the actor's parroting of the Chinese phraseology. Franklin alternates long takes of the valley with quick cuts in the action sequences. Especially affecting is the action during a plague of locusts, with special effects by associate art directors Arnold Gillespie and Ed Willis. The locusts swarm into the valley in a spectacular black cloud, settling on the farmer's fields; then Franklin cuts to close-ups of them eating everything in sight right down to the ground. A breeze comes into the valley unsettling the creatures who rise again in a cloud and fly out of sight; a harrowing image. *The Good Earth* attains a grandeur at certain moments, yet is uneven in writing and in acting; it never became the screen classic Thalberg had hoped it would be.

When the film opened at the Cathay Circle Theater, it was art director Harry Oliver's huge statues of the principals and his banners that adorned the facade. Oliver liked doing this kind of work, because "in early pictures I got used to mixing into everything."³⁹

Oliver was among the first group of art directors ever nominated for Academy Awards for his work on *Seventh Heaven* (1927/1928), and he received another nomination the next year for *Street Angel*. In a 1968 interview, his memories of these films were mainly of the technical wizardry that had been achieved:

I had moved the camera so many mysterious ways in *Seventh Heaven* that they encouraged me and in *Street Angel* I built a round set and had the whole floor

The Good Earth, 1937: 36. (Top) Cedric Gibbons, Harry Oliver, art directors. A road ran along the town's crenellated outer wall; peasant huts (left) and more affluent shops and houses (right) packed the set. 37. (Bottom) Production sketch, artist unknown (Tyrus Wong?). Production illustrations were consistently used by all major studios for economic reasons; they fit the action to the sets and helped the director plan sequences to be photographed.

moveable and a track up it and we got to everybody, moving close-ups and every-thing, but it wasn't easy.[40]

The Fox Studio considered his contributions to these films so great that his name appeared on their advertising billboards.

At MGM from 1933 to 1936, producer David O. Selznick's sense of style began to emerge in films like *Dinner at Eight* (1933) and *A Tale of Two Cities* (1935). Selznick injected his own preferences into even the minutest details of his productions, which he wanted to be of excellent quality.

In the thirties, the MGM film product became more and more recognizable, and as Frank Beaver has commented:

> The goal at MGM [was] producing entertaining star-studded films of high technical quality.... Production values (set design, costumes, artistic lighting) assumed great importance in products which displayed the studio "look" to its fullest advantage.[41]

M-G-M MUSICALS

Musicals became such a memorable part of MGM's output in the forties that the term itself has become almost synonymous with the studio. Yet it was Warner Bros. who brought sound to the motion picture and paved the way for the musical to develop as a genre. Warners did much to establish the early backstage musical format in pictures like *42nd Street* (1933), which along with the revue format, were the first types of musicals to be phenomenally successful with the public.

MGM produced a popular version of the backstage scenario with the ground-breaking *Broadway Melody,* the company's first all-sound picture which debuted at Grauman's Chinese Theatre on February 1, 1929, a year and a half after Al Jolson's *The Jazz Singer* had opened to rave reviews and turned the industry around about the acceptance of sound. *The Broadway Melody* was billed as:

THE NEW WONDER OF THE SCREEN!
ALL TALKING
ALL SINGING
ALL DANCING
DRAMATIC SENSATION

and became the first talkie to receive one of the newly (in 1927) created Academy Awards for best picture. With such an auspicious beginning, MGM seemed destined to take the musical genre seriously. They did new versions en-titled *Broadway Melody* in 1936, 1938 and 1940, and also created vehicles for Joan Crawford — *Our Dancing Daughters* (1928), *Dance, Fools, Dance* (1930), and *Dancing Lady* (1933) — that made her a star.[42]

The set requirements for backstage musicals involved theatres, both backstage and in front of a proscenium arch, and hotels or apartments. The plots predictably involved auditions and rehearsals, culminating in a great success — the grand finale of the picture, for which lavish sets were created. The art director's fantasy was allowed a range in the grand finale not permitted in the routine plotting of the rest of the film, and they seized the opportunity to create the only memorable sets from this early type of musical picture.

The filmed musical antedates sound, and MGM had produced its share of popular operettas and broadway musicals in the silent era, among them: *The Merry Widow, The Student Prince* and *Rose Marie.* These musicals could not excite the enthusiasm that the 1929 *Broadway Melody* did, and had not presented any special problems for the film's designers over other narrative pictures. The sound musicals, especially their finales, demanded larger, more spacious sets to hold the dozens of dancers and singers employed in these sequences. MGM responded as did the rest of the industry by immediately devising elaborate sound stage settings, each one vying to top the other in terms of opulence and gadgetry. Hollywood produced no fewer than 75 musicals in 1929, so many that the public soon tired of the type. What amounted to a moratorium on musicals occurred in the years 1930–1932, to be broken by the innovative *42nd Street* in 1933, beginning a new cycle that was to fade in popularity only in the late fifties.

The set for the title number of *The Broadway Melody* of 1929 (**Illustration 38**), performed by dancer Anita Page and singer Charles King, consisted of a system of painted flats depicting Manhattan in a distinctly Art Deco manner, with even the lettering of the billboard signs and the jagged patterning of the dancer's costumes suggestive of that style.

The Broadway Melody introduced what many have called MGM's musical anthem, "Singin' in the Rain," in a number featuring Cliff "Ukelele Ike" Edwards strumming beneath a silvery weeping willow tree while a chorus line dressed in slickers dance in a downpour.

Art director Merrill Pye worked as a unit art director on *The Broadway Melody* and later on *Our Modern Maidens* (1929), *Our Blushing Brides* (1930), and *The Great Ziegfeld* (1936), to become MGM's first resident expert in the field of sound musicals. Other directors, even Richard Day, were called upon to contribute to musical films, but Pye's handling of the idiom was so expert that he was constantly called back to it. Later he was to be joined by Jack Martin Smith, Preston Ames and others in this speciality.

In 1929 along with *The Broadway Melody* MGM produced an extravaganza using the second musical format, the revue. *The Hollywood Revue of 1929* featured Marie Dressler, Norma Shearer, Marion Davies, Joan Crawford, Conrad Nagel, Bessie Love, Buster Keaton and just about every other star or starlet on the lot. It was a tremendous box office hit. The film revue, modeled on live theatrical revues, let each actor do a turn, usually within a proscenium

38. *Broadway Melody,* 1929. Cedric Gibbons, Merrill Pye, art directors. Anita Page
and Charles King stand before painted flats depicting an Art Deco vision of Manhattan.
Not only the lettering but Page's costume have the geometric look of this style.

arch setting. The sets were tailored to each act, but uncoordinated with each
other. *Photoplay*'s description of the content of *The Hollywood Revue of 1929*
gives a good impression of the variety of sets that were called for in all such
revue pictures:

> Like Shakespeare? Well, you'll find Jack Gilbert and Norma Shearer as *Romeo and
> Juliet.* Like low-brow slapstick? Well, there are Laurel and Hardy in a comedy act
> as low as they come. Like big musical numbers with glorified gals singing and danc-
> ing? All right, there's the hit, "Singin in the Rain," and many breath-taking girl
> numbers.[43]

The following year saw MGM close down production on what was to have been their most lavish musical to date, *The March of Time;* it was never released. *Photoplay* reported extensively on *The March of Time* and, unusual for the period, published photographs of two of its sets. The caption to the set are still of a musical prison number featuring the Dodge Sisters and Austin Young advertised, "One of the largest and most exciting picture sets in the history of the films, devised and erected by Metro-Goldwyn-Mayer on the lot at Culver City. Officials say it is the highest so far built."[44] The Dodge Sisters are seen dancing in front of a full-scale, five-storied prison facade replete with iron stairs. There are five stories of banked lights surrounding the set on three sides indicating that it was lit in every detail. The other set still for *The March of Time* is for a production number called "Big Bull Fiddle" and illustrates one of the most common devices of musical sets, the giant prop—in this case a towering bull fiddle—before which a line of chorines dances on a gallery and at ground level another group sits playing their fiddles.

From the inception of musical films such enormous props were used in sets with great imagination. In the Warner's *Show of Shows* (1929) Winnie Lightner danced in a giant bathroom in a number called "Singin' in the Bathtub," which was a spoof on the "Singin' in the Rain" number from MGM's *The Broadway Melody.* Later Ruby Keeler and Lee Dixon in *Ready, Willing and Able* (Warner Bros., 1937) cavorted on a giant typewriter, parts of which were formed by chorus girls. Such out-sized props and rooms had been used by silent film comedians, like Buster Keaton and Laurel and Hardy, with great effect.

Sound musicals seem to have necessitated the use of large bland background areas so that the more numerous dancers could be clearly seen. In this context, oversized decorative elements as a means of defining a set became common. Giant decorative elements, looking surreal, punctuated and gave character to musical sets without creating any busy patterning. A wonderful example of the use of such decorative elements occurs in the "Begin the Beguine" number done by Eleanor Powell and Fred Astaire in *The Broadway Melody of 1940,* the last big MGM black and white musical **(Illustration 39).** Their dance takes place before a wall of mirrors with the dancers in "white" costumes reflected in them and again in the dark and shining bakelite floor. Occasionally they reflect an orchestra seated beneath huge semiabstract palm trees with stars twinkling behind to suggest the "night of tropical splendor" of the Cole Porter tune.

The most ubiquitous scenic device in musical finales, and in musicals in general, was the grand stairway—whether a single centralized stair, as in Universal's *King of Jazz* (1930), or multiple curving flights, as in *Paramount on Parade* (1930). The grand stairway had been used with great effect on the Broadway stage, especially in musical extravaganzas like the Ziegfeld Follies and Earl Carroll's Vanities. It migrated as a scenic tool to the motion picture

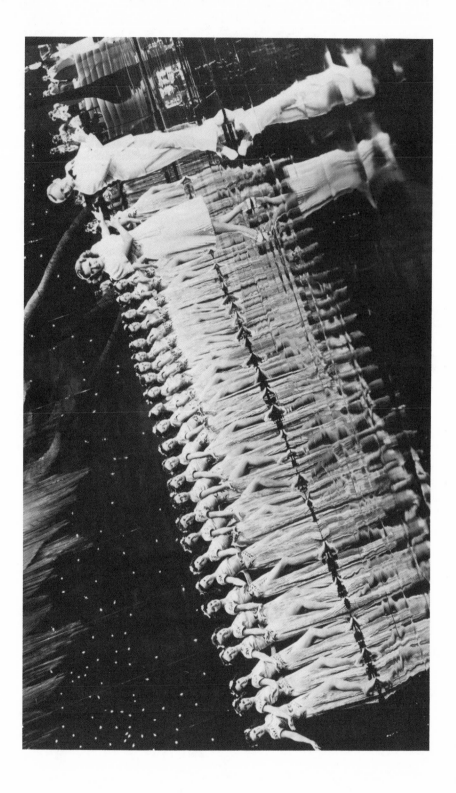

to be used for the same purposes as those of the stage. It even gained in purpose when Busby Berkeley devised his movie camera shots for musicals staged first at Warners and later at MGM. A stairway provided an architectonic device which was both open and passed vertically through the set. It could be used as a platform on which beautiful women posed or it could be danced and performed upon. Importantly, a grand stairway powerfully suggested elegant palatial surroundings unlike those the viewer was accustomed to in daily life.

In the course of the thirties the revue faded almost completely from the screen and even the backstage musical was superseded in popularity by the musical comedy. The forties were dominated by this type of musical where the story, a comedy with a light romance, was interwoven with song and dance numbers. There were still occasional spectacular settings for musical numbers, but they might occur anywhere within the film rather than being reserved for the end. The sets for musical comedies, again much affected by Broadway precedents, used mostly normative settings. The musical numbers tended to move the plotline along, and could not be set outside of the story. Several new forms began to appear in musical comedies and compensated for this relative normality of setting—like dream and fantasy sequences. Elaborate and fanciful settings could be continued in these sets. George Balanchine invented a dream sequence for the Rodgers and Hart Broadway musical *Babes in Arms* (1937) that gave impetus to this idea in films, and memorable dream sequences are a part of such musicals as *The Wizard of Oz* (1939), *Lady in the Dark* (Paramount, 1944), and *Yolanda and the Thief* (1945). Gene Kelly's fantasies of his love for Leslie Caron are the basis of the seventeen-minute ballet culminating *An American in Paris* (1951); fantasy had been used to great effect prior to this by Kelly in *Cover Girl* (Columbia, 1944).

Another device, the "show within the show," remained a popular conceit in musical films of the thirties and forties; show business crept into many of the plots even though the story was not a backstage "make good in show biz" musical. Fred Astaire, for instance, was connected with show business in the plots of several of his RKO and MGM musicals. The "show within the show" always provided the art director with the opportunity to create an extraordinary set.

The musical biography, a fourth musical format, flourished after the Second World War, but was tried earlier and with particular success by MGM in 1936 with *The Great Ziegfeld* starring William Powell, Myrna Loy and Luise Rainer. MGM called in John Harkrider, a former artistic director for Florenz Ziegfeld, to help do the sets for this film along with Cedric Gibbons, Eddie

39. *The Broadway Melody of 1940,* 1940. Cedric Gibbons, art director. In MGM's last black-and-white musical, Eleanor Powell and Fred Astaire dance on a bakelite floor before mirrors reflecting their images among giant palm fronds, and dozens of twinkling stars.

Imazu, and Edwin B. Willis. Harkrider brought the authentic Ziegfeld touch to the opulent sets which, with the costumes by Adrian, helped bring the film's cost up to $2 million and make it the most expensive MGM picture since *Ben Hur*.[45]

Harkrider was more than a bit of a showman himself. Born in Texas, he had played juveniles in silent pictures opposite Mary Pickford, Theda Bara, and Rudolph Valentino. He went on to design and stage the great spectacular numbers in such Ziegfeld Broadway productions as *Showboat, Whoopee,* and *Rosalie.* In Hollywood, off and on from 1929, he worked for Paramount, Goldwyn, MGM, and Universal designing numbers, sets, costumes, and titles.

The Great Ziegfeld had 23 musical production numbers, the most famous being "A Pretty Girl Is Like a Melody," whose spectacular set is a gigantic fluted column, designed by Harkrider, around which a spiraling stairway winds. As the camera moves upward it finds Dennis Morgan crooning (dubbed by Allan Jones) to dozens of chorus girls and boys dancing or posing on each tread. At its apex the column narrows to reveal Virginia Bruce posing in a rippling gown that echoes the flutes of the column. A huge white curtain whose top is never in sight has been rising slowly behind the revolving column. As the camera approaches the top, it pulls back and the full beauty of the set is revealed, but only momentarily. For as the viewer perceives the tiered lower level of the set with its confectionary scrolls and volutes, the curtain closes over the top portion of the column, and a proscenium curtain closes over the entire scene; a dream has been briefly realized and then as suddenly disappears. Harkrider had delineated this number in ebullient drawings that were built to his specifications on one of MGM's huge sound stages.

This set epitomizes the so-called "big white set" that Cedric Gibbons, Van Nest Polglase, Carroll Clark and other art directors brought into use in the thirties. Usually these big sets involved opening up two adjacent sound stages to create one vast space. The sets had large areas of detailed "true"-white architecture or props. Only when the use of incandescent lighting superseded that of arc lighting in the thirties did white come into usage by art directors. They had previously, to avoid glare, been using grey and other colors to designate contrastive "white" areas in their sets. The big white set allowed sharper value contrasts and fuller detail in decor.

The Great Ziegfeld won the Oscar as best picture for that year, and its many memorable sets had much to do with its success. Nominated for an art direction Academy Award, it lost to Richard Day's art direction for *Dodsworth*.

MGM did not always find grand sets a convincing vehicle for telling musical stories, and particularly in *Rosalie* (1937) Cedric Gibbons and the Art Department's sets often seemed to swallow up the star, Eleanor Powell. They in turn seemed to get lost in some sequences, like the wedding finale, which are "overstuffed" with hundreds of extras **(Illustration 40)**. *Rosalie* had been

40. *Rosalie,* 1937. Cedric Gibbons, art director. In this production still, dancers, cadets, and court officials mass on the set with its huge stairway. Bold, doughy decorative flourishes define the set so that its parts stand out among this cast of hundreds.

a Broadway hit for Ziegfeld in 1928 and the story about a princess who falls in love with a West Point cadet (Nelson Eddy) may have been beyond its prime. The grandiose sets cannot offset the trite story.

For the finale, a huge central stair placed before a semiabstract palace facade, is flanked by flowing scrolls and volutes (they look suspiciously like the lower portion of the big column set from *The Great Ziegfeld* of the previous year). Again an out-sized prop is important to the musical routine—this time enormous striped drums, graduated in size, are used for one of Powell's most acrobatic routines. She leaps from one to the other of them, and on reaching ground level twirls through cellophane flowers breaking them as she goes.[46] The camera, which has followed Powell's dance through all parts of the set, then pulls back for the long shot customary in finales, to reveal hundreds of extras crowded on the stairway. Star, set, costumes are all lost in a jumbled visual image that impresses mostly by virtue of its scale.

The Jeanette MacDonald musicals of the thirties, some with and some without Nelson Eddy, were regularly given lavish MGM productions, none more so than the sound remake of *The Merry Widow* (1934), which won Academy Awards for designers Cedric Gibbons and Frederic Hope. The challenge to create Parisian interiors of the late 19th century, including Maxim's, and the grand ballroom of the Ruritanian palace was splendidly met by the art directors who created an opulent yet light-hearted decor that perfectly suits Ernst Lubitsch's direction of the Franz Lehar operetta.

At the palace ball, the ensemble dance is performed against a background of carefully executed wall surfaces with carved entablatures, niches, and freestanding columns, all of which are reflected in mirrored wall panels reminiscent of those in Versailles' Hall of Mirrors. The team of Gibbons and Hope were again to recreate memorable *fin-de-siècle* Parisian settings for Greta Garbo in *Camille* (1936).

The Mickey Rooney and the Judy Garland "backyard musicals" popular in the late thirties and early forties usually took place in ordinary settings: on residential small town streets, in a school gym, or some other place large enough to house the climactic dance number. These films, although filled with strong performances, are mostly forgettable in terms of scenic values. However, Garland was to follow up her early films with two of the most memorable scenic musicals of all times: *The Wizard of Oz* (1939) and *Meet Me in St. Louis* (1944).

On the musical fantasy *The Wizard of Oz,* Cedric Gibons is credited as art director, with William A. Horning, who actually designed most of the sets, being cited as associate art director. Jack Martin Smith worked on the film as sketch artist and other members of the art department including Randall Duell were also drawn into the design process for the picture's more than 60 sets. The special effects, tornado, flying monkeys, and dissolving witch were all expertly done by Buddy Gillespie and his crew.

Using the cues given in the L. Frank Baum children's classic as inspiration Horning designed his sets and then had a model that was one-quarter life-size built. The film's producer, Mervyn Leroy, said, "They fabricated an entire model town, 122 buildings. It took months to finish that alone...."[47]

William A. Horning, a graduate of the University of California School of Architecture, was a perfectionist who worked from 9 a.m. until midnight and expected the same of his assistants. Randall Duell recalled, "Everything had to be done perfectly, and you had to stay all night until it was."[48]

The sets were built and then torn down in rapid succession as filming proceeded over a six month period. Multiple stages, six in all, were used off and on in the process, with the Construction Department's carpenters staying just about a week ahead of the shooting schedule.

Everything took extra time because of the filming in a Technicolor that really was to be "glorious." Randall Duell was assigned the task of finding the right color paint for the yellow brick road and it took him a week to do it because everything he tried looked green when filmed:

> Color film wasn't perfected then. We had to do a lot of testing and experimenting with the film to get the color to reproduce properly. We'd start filming a set a week or two before it was going to be used. We had to color-test each set not only for the paints on the set but for the background.[49]

Gibbons, another perfectionist, had Jack Martin Smith do a series of color sketches (three feet wide by two feet high) of all the sets so that he could check their colors. When Smith finished, Gibbons told him to start all over again, "He decided we should do an ethereal kind of thing, not full color but subdued color. So I had to turn around and do all the sketches over again, draw all the sets twice. It was an enormous thing to have to do them over again."[50]

The Wardrobe Department was closely following the illustrations by W.W. Denslow in the Baum book, but Denslow had done little with setting that Gibbons and Horning found useful. The designs for Munchkinland (**Illustration 41** were unproblematic according to Jack Martin Smith,

> You had something working for you. Doors are only this high because the houses are for midgets. Windows are only this high. Flower boxes have to be low enough for midgets to water them. Then we put grass roofs on the houses and shaped them like mushrooms, and that was Munchkinland.[51]

But the visualization of the Emerald City was giving Gibbons and Horning problems until the supervising art director found an inspiration in the Art Department's research department. Smith recalls,

> He found a tiny, a really minuscule photograph of a sketch that had been done in Germany pre–World War I. We looked at the sketch—it actually looked like test tubes upside down—and it crystallized our ideas.... We all thought the German sketch was right because it wasn't detailed. It didn't look like Rheims Cathedral. It didn't look like the Pyramids. It didn't look like King Tut's tomb. It looked like some strange thing we had never seen before.[52]

This description must be of the famous drawing of a "Crystal Mountain" by Bruno Taut from his 1919 volume *Alpine Architecture,* which was to inspire so many other modern artists, including Lyonel Feininger, who used the crystal motif for his delineation of the "Cathedral of Socialism" on the cover of the first Bauhaus proclamation (1919).

It was decided to do the exterior of the Emerald City as a matte shot with

the interior built sets; the same was true for the witch's castle. This film's sets illustrate what Gibbons had meant when he said,

> in the movies, tempo is directly related to design. For though the director is primarily responsible for the pace of a film, the best director in the world cannot inject a swift tempo into a film unless the designer ... has eliminated all "dead footage" from the sets.[53]

The Art Department's sets and props advance the action at all times, and Warren Newcombe and his associates in the matte department painted some of their most memorable creations, like the shimmering Emerald City for the picture, while the scenic painted backdrops were expertly done by the Scenic Art Department under George Gibson's supervision (see the background of Illustration 41).

George Gibson had come to MGM in 1934 from Fox where he had worked as a scenic artist, and he was to remain there until his retirement in 1969. In September of 1938 Gibson and a dozen of his colleagues began painting the enormous (400 feet long by 35 feet wide) white muslin backdrop that was to become in the course of three weeks a cornfield and hills. This was their first contribution, of many, to the film's decor, and was based, as were the rest of the scenic backdrops, on Smith's color sketches.

The mattes done at MGM were some of the best in the industry in the thirties and forties. Warren Newcombe headed the matte department at that time, and many of his mattes have survived in the archives of the Special Collection of the University of Southern California. Realistically drawn and painted in every detail, they were sometimes used for entire shots — theatre marquees, for example, were always done with matte shots which stayed on the screen for only a few seconds. More often mattes and live action, the combination of two separate shots onto one print achieved in the processing, were used. The matte was shot first with a hole in it, into which the live action was fitted. On the screen the image was seamless and the action seemed to be taking place in the setting created on the matte. Architectural backgrounds were perspectively drawn, like renaissance engravings. Directors found mattes especially useful for night scenes and foreign and fantasy locales like Oz or Xanadu.

Warren Newcombe must have come to his craft sometime in the late teens.[54] He and his then partner Neil E. McGuire placed an ad in the 1921 volume of the *Motion Picture Studio Directory* announcing that they did "Art Applied to Settings and Title Effects" in black and white and color from their studio on West 46th Street in New York City. They listed among their past productions such films as *Passion*, *The Inside of the Cup*, and *The Four*

41. *Wizard of Oz*, 1939. Cedric Gibbons, William A. Horning, art directors. Munchkinland consisted of thatched mushroom-shaped cottages on terraces around a pool that was surrounded by enormous flowers to make the tiny Munchkins appear even smaller.

Horsemen. Warren Alfred Newcombe was born in Waltham, Massachusetts, and educated at the Massachusetts Normal Art School and the Museum of Fine Arts, Boston. He then studied for two years with the painter Joseph DeCamp and the "colorist" A.H. Munsell. Newcombe is listed as an art director and in the early phases of his career is said to have been an "artist, portrait painter, illustrat[or] for books and magazines, designer of settings and costumes." In 1918 he began his association with motion pictures, and by 1921 he had already worked for "Selznick, Metro, Famous Players, etc." From 1921 to 1923 he had the partnership in the production of motion picture effects with McGuire. His interest in being a serious painter seems to have asserted itself at that time for he apparently produced two films, *The Enchanted City* and *The Sea of Dreams,* "both of which were made with paintings," according to his biographer. From 1924 until 1925 Newcombe worked for D.W. Griffith in Mamaroneck, N.Y. He came to Hollywood and joined MGM on a permanent basis in 1925, and headed the MGM matte department, nicknamed the "Newcombe Department," in the thirties and forties. He is mentioned from time to time in the chatty in-house "Studio Club News" at MGM, as when one of his oil paintings was exhibited in the annual Pennsylvania Academy Exhibit of 1937. Apparently his only Academy Award was for the sound effects for *Green Dolphin Street!*

Babes in Arms, another MGM musical hit of 1939, put Garland and Rooney into the hands of Busby Berkeley doing his first directorial stint at MGM; and also introduced songwriter Arthur Freed in the role of producer. Freed, a prolific songwriter, now began the formulation of his own production unit which was to be a prime mover in MGM's final phase of classic musicals of the forties and early fifties, some of them reprising his own songs, like "Singin' in the Rain" (1952).

Director Vincente Minnelli's impact also began to be felt at MGM in the early forties where he had come to work under Freed's auspices. Minnelli brought a refined expertise to the decor of his films. He knew exactly what he wanted in his sets, and had a particular genius for using them to enhance the story.

In the opening sequence of Minnelli's first big hit, *Meet Me in St. Louis* (1944), the Victorian residence of the Smith family is lovingly appraised from the exterior and then from the interior, in the first few minutes of the film. The main characters are introduced as the camera moves from room to room of the house and we hear the refrains of the title song in the background. This opening sequence, using only a few lines of dialogue, not only introduces the main characters in the story, but establishes their prosperous middle-class turn of the century lifestyle. The camera passes down Kensington Avenue **(Illustration 42),** into the Smith kitchen, down the entry hall, up the stairway, and even into the bathroom where the grandfather is found shaving and singing the strains of the title song.

42. *Meet Me in St. Louis,* 1944. Cedric Gibbons, Lemuel Ayers, Jack Martin Smith, art directors. Kensington Avenue with its elegant Victorian residences was based on period photographs of St. Louis. The graceful curve of the street, the yards, and the porches were repeatedly seen as the story unfolded.

Meet Me in St. Louis was designed by Cedric Gibbons, Lemuel Ayers, and Jack Martin Smith with assistance and sometimes fanatical supervision by Minnelli. The director insisted that Kensington Avenue be built in all details on the backlot. Because of Minnelli's moving camera technique, the Smith residence (based on old photographs of St. Louis) was built as a total unit, rather than as the customary independent sets.[55]

Minnelli was keenly aware of the potential of Technicolor, which he used to great effect in *Meet Me in St. Louis* and his subsequent films. The Smith residence is saturated with colors in a wide range of hues. Minnelli claims that he had a struggle over the color with the Art Department. Whatever these arguments may have centered on, MGM's Art Department had already had great success with color in infinite varieties and intensities in films like *The Wizard of Oz,* and they were subsequently to excel in its use in films with Minnelli and without him.

Minnelli's later films, where dancing is more central to the action, with

Gene Kelly in *The Pirate* (1948) and *An American in Paris* (1951) and with Fred
Astaire in *Yolanda and the Thief* (1945) and *The Band Wagon* (1953), are no
less dependant on memorable decor than was *Meet Me in St. Louis*.

Yolanda and the Thief, designed by the inventive Jack Martin Smith, has
imaginative settings that expertly serve the bizarre storyline. The picture is best
known for its production numbers; one finds dancers Fred Astaire and Lucille
Bremer amid stylized sculpted figures in 18th century costume on a dramatically wavy marble floor **(Illustration 43)**. The most famous sequence is the
dream ballet with a set modeled on the surrealist paintings of Salvador Dalí.
Astaire finds Bremer among rocks and tree fragments in what appears to be an
infinite, barren space like that found in Dalí's famous *The Persistence of
Memory* (1931, Museum of Modern Art). Dalí, who had collaborated with Luis
Buñuel on the making of *Un Chien Andalou* (1928) and *L'Age d'Or* (1930),
was himself involved in designing a memorable dream setting in the same year
for Alfred Hitchcock's thriller *Spellbound* (1945) (see **Illustration 51**). Dalí's
brand of surrealism was to be the common coin of dream and fantasy sequences
in forties films.

   Minnelli and Freed's 1951 Academy Award winning *An American in Paris*
is no less memorable for its lengthy concluding ballet than for the brilliant sets
that provide its ambiance. They were designed by Preston Ames and Cedric
Gibbons.

   Ames, who has left an account of his experiences in working with the principals of the film, indicates that Arthur Freed and Minnelli decided to combine
George Gershwin's musical suite "An American in Paris" with the style of
famous French painters in a ballet sequence.

> The intimate pooling of ideas by these men plus the enthusiasm of choreographer
> Gene Kelly started the formula of "No Formula" for this seventeen minute
> number. Supervising Art Director Cedric Gibbons, costume designer, Irene
> Sharaff, and I set to work to plot the various scenes.[56]

All of the French artists chosen for emulation were from the end of the
19th century and early 20th century, a well-known and romatized period of
early modernism. The artist Raoul Dufy was the inspiration for the rendering
of the Place de la Concorde and its huge central fountain **(Illustration 44)**.
Ames relates how Dufy's style inspired the designers: "his caligraphic style was
projected into a third dimension by the use of third dimensional forms such
as the obelisk and the fountain."[57] The painter Auguste Renoir proved the
source for the flower market on the Left Bank.

> The technique of the various painters had to be studied to the *n*th degree from
> the brush strokes on Renoir's "Pont Neuf"—to the palette knife technique of
> Utrillo. Color wise the artists themselves dictated the palette. Dufy, red, white and
> blue or Van Gogh with his yellow and white as used on his Sunflowers.[58]

43. *Yolanda and the Thief*, 1945. Cedric Gibbons, Jack Martin Smith, art directors. Amid statues wearing bizarre 18th century costumes Fred Astaire and Lucille Bremer dance on a wavey patterned floor.

For the streets of Montmartre, Utrillo was chosen because of "The damp, moldy walls, the dirty alley, rows of disreputable houses, his version of romantic Montmartre."[59] Four of the paintings of Henri de Toulouse-Lautrec "were faithfully reproduced," one of the dancer Chocolat at the Achilles Bar and the others of the Moulin Rouge. The post-impressionist Vincent Van Gogh, although not copied as exactly as Lautrec, was the source for the sets in the vignette at the Place de l'Opéra which, according to Ames, was "built in a series of planes" like those found in the painter's *Cypress* painted in the south of France. Even the primitive Henri Rousseau's type of stylized vegetation was called upon for the background of the scene of a carnival in a park.

Borrowing from paintings and engravings was done almost from the earliest days of the narrative motion picture, with a notable example being D.W. Griffith's use of the engraved *Battles and Leaders of the Civil War* as inspiration for some of the visualization in *Birth of a Nation*. Certain directors, Fritz Lang in particular, whose background was that of a painter, constantly made reference to well-known painted images in their pictures. But never before *An American in Paris* had the ideas of painters been so intricately wed to a cinematic expression.

44. *An American in Paris,* **1951. Cedric Gibbons, Preston Ames, art directors. Three-dimensional lanterns, fountain and obelisk were used to project French painter Raoul Dufy's calligraphic style onto the Place de la Concorde.**

Minnelli and Gibbons feuded, as was their custom, about the sets; this time about the monumental fountain in the Place de la Concorde on which Leslie Caron and Gene Kelly perform their sensuous dance to the Gershwins' haunting theme. Minnelli's version of the feud, certainly not intended to flatter Gibbons, indicates how closely the supervising art director oversaw the designs for the sets of major pictures and how he contributed ideas to them that were seldom ignored. Minnelli relates:

> Cedric Gibbons, the head of the art department, insisted it [the fountain] should be done differently. "That isn't in the style of Dufy," he said. "Dufy is all lines. Therefore, the fountain should be solid and the lines should be painted in."
>
> Gibbons didn't know my plans for light changes, but he remained steadfast in his opinion.
>
> "Cedric," I told him, "the solid fountain won't work. It will look just like a Henry Moore, you know, those doughlike figures. It'll be nothing."
>
> Gibbons still couldn't see my point. "But it doesn't look like Dufy," he insisted.
>
> A meeting of the entire production unit was called. When I explained why I wanted the original design, which would allow an interplay of light to suggest different emotions, Gibbons reluctantly gave in.[60]

Art director Preston Ames got on smoothly with Minnelli, who heaps praise upon him in several places in his autobiography. Ames, who had studied architecture in France and been hired by Gibbons in 1936, remained at MGM for most of his career. He became Minnelli's favorite art director and they worked together closely on many subsequent films.[61]

The fifties saw a waning of the original musical written for film, while a stream of adaptations from Broadway shows were done, like *The King and I* (Fox, 1956) and *South Pacific* (Fox, 1956). Fewer musicals overall were produced by MGM and other studios. Yet MGM's great *Singin' in the Rain* (1952) was still in the offing and even such a film as *Royal Wedding* directed by Stanley Donen and starring Fred Astaire and Jane Powell, although otherwise rather bland in terms of decor (done by Cedric Gibbons and Jack Martin Smith), was to have the most memorable prop room of musicals. A jubilant Astaire, in his London hotel room, to the tune of "You Are," suddenly dances on floor, walls, and ceiling. The room was constructed in a barrel and the furniture all nailed to the floor. The camera and barrel turned in unison; while Astaire seemed to be the one doing all the turning.

The sets for *Singin' in the Rain,* created by Randall Duell and Cedric Gibbons, range from the disarmingly simple street of Gene Kelly's dance in the rain to the elaborate sets seen in the fifteen minute "Broadway" dance number — at one point including dozens of huge flashing theatre marquees (**Illustration 45**). The set is a modernistic reprieve of Warner's *42nd Street* and MGM's own Deco set from the early sound musical *Broadway Melody.*

Randall Duell had joined MGM in 1936 and remained with the studio for over 25 years, designing over 60 films in the course of his career. Duell who received his B.S. in architecture from the University of Southern California in 1925, then worked as a designer in various architectural firms. He answered MGM's call to help design sets for Norma Shearer and Leslie Howard's *Romeo and Juliet* (1936) (**Illustration 46**), and ended up creating the Capulet House, but receiving no screen credit for it. In the banqueting hall, a perfectly polished, boldly patterned floor reflects the shimmering costumes of the ladies and gentlemen. A spacious arcaded interior, it is surrounded by tables laden with food and plate, with a stair leading to a loge. This is an MGM version of the renaissance; clean, shiny, flawless.

Historic films were much in vogue in the thirties when Duell joined MGM, and he also worked without credit on *Marie Antoinette* (1938), one of the studio's most extravagant scenic films of the decade. This Norma Shearer vehicle was much publicized for its 98 individual sets, as Bosley Crowther explained:

> Cedric Gibbons [was instructed] . . . to prepare the most exquisite and impressive settings that could be conceived. Versailles itself was slightly tarnished along side the palace Gibbons whipped up. He did some exquisite reproductions of the buildings of eighteenth century France. Ed Willis, the head of the prop depart-

45. *Singin' in the Rain,* 1952. Cedric Gibbons, Randall Duell, art directors. The "Broadway" production number found Gene Kelly amid dozens of oversized flashing theatre marquees; an updated version of earlier Broadway musical film sets (*42nd Street* and *The Broadway Melody of 1929*).

ment, was sent to Europe to buy furniture and rugs. He stocked his department for all time with the antiques for *Marie Antoinette. . . .* The studio's great technical departments were triumphantly tested on this film.[62]

The reviews were not overwhelmingly favorable, with the *Hollywood Spectator* summing up the general consensus, "*Marie Antoinette* too Long; Cedric Gibbons its Hero."[63]

By 1937 a full-fledged member of the art department, Duell had already risen from set designer (the person who prepares detailed set designs from the art director's ideas) to art director on B pictures, and was regularly being credited on MGM films. His first assignments to design A productions came in 1939 with *The Emperor's Stallion* and Garbo's *Ninotchka;* from that point on he did a wide variety of prestige films, preferring the historical ones (*The White Cliffs of Dover,* 1943) and musicals (*Anchors Aweigh,* 1944).

Duell's most memorable films include such realistic masterpieces as *The*

46. *Romeo and Juliet,* 1936. Cedric Gibbons, Frederic Hope, art directors. In the large, arcaded banqueting hall of the Capulet House, Norma Shearer (center) and company prepare to dance on a boldly geometric marble floor.

Postman Always Rings Twice (1946), *Intruder in the Dust* (1949) and *Blackboard Jungle* (1955). In *The Postman Always Rings Twice* the contrast between the openness of the exterior long shots of road, cafe, and countryside, done on location, and the claustrophobic interiors of the roadside cafe help to create the tension within the film. The authenticity of director Clarence Brown's adaptation of William Faulkner's novel *Intruder in the Dust* owed much to Duell's handling of the settings. All of them, exteriors and interiors, were shot on location in Mississippi. Care to detail, long typical of MGM set design, was now in the postwar period more frequently being applied to films with contemporary social content, like the Faulkner work or to stories of urban crime and violence like *The Asphalt Jungle* and *The Blackboard Jungle*. For the latter film, the first to examine violence in big city schools, Duell visited "a lot of problem schools in L.A." and then accurately duplicated their interiors. A careful practitioner of the art of art direction, Duell's sets are not marked by idiosyncrasies of personal style, but perfectly exist within his own definition of a well-designed picture as one that works "in the framework of the script to help the director interpret it in a concrete way."[64]

In 1958, with MGM studio production dwindling, Duell retired from the movies to return to architectural practise. In subsequent years his firm, Randall Duell and Associates, became the leading designers of amusement theme parks, including the Six Flag parks, Hersheypark, Opryland, Magic Mountain, and others. The imagination he had applied to set design in films, was applied equally well to the built world of fantasy in theme parks.[65]

By the fifties when Randall Duell left the studio, MGM was still doing its fair share of historical films, but much less frequently than when he started in the thirties. The Elvis Presley pictures, like *Jailhouse Rock* (1957), with art direction by Duell, called mostly for contemporary sets, and filmed plays, like *Cat on a Hot Tin Roof* (1958), now turned on current themes.

Urie McCleary, longtime unit art director at MGM, designed the sets for *Cat on a Hot Tin Roof* and they are representative of the MGM style continuing into the fifties. "Big Daddy's" mansion is tailor-made to the story, rich in color, careful in detail, but with a slightly artificial cast which tells you this is a movie and not reality.

McCleary's sets for the screen adaptation of Cole Porter's *Kiss Me Kate* (1953) provide a heavy dose of the fashionable fifties' modern and surreal mode in decor. Directed by George Sidney, the film has a range of sets, but the opening titles, surreal in motif, tip off the viewer about what to expect in the "big" sets. The principal musical sequences, part of a theatrical presentation of Shakespeare's *Taming of the Shrew* have Kathryn Grayson and Howard Keel squaring off as the shrewish Katharina and Petruchio, the gentleman from Verona. For a film, the set (see **Illustration 47**) is relatively shallow (simulating a Broadway stage). Its semiabstract composition, with palace to the right and behind it a townscape, is reminiscent of the painted images of Italian Giorgio de Chirico's work. The sky is painted an absolutely clear flat blue. The palace interiors, seen on Katharina and Petruchio's wedding night, exist as many flat fields of color on planar walls. These sets perfectly complement the action, especially a dance by Ann Miller, Bob Fosse, Tony Rall, and Bobby Van, but they make the rest of the film's very conventional decor seem unusually bland in comparison.

Occasionally at MGM, unusual concepts emerged in art direction through a sort of benign neglect on the studio's part because the film was not considered very important. Such was the case with the now cult science fiction film, *Forbidden Planet* (1956) on which Arthur Lonergan was the art director; Edwin B. Willis and Hugh Hunt were the set decorators. Science fiction was not an MGM genre, and this was a low-budget effort. It doesn't look it.

The film's director Fred McLeod Wilcox guided the actors through the innovative plot which involved Commander Adams (Leslie Nielsen) and his crew from earth's United Planets Cruiser visiting another planet, Altair IV, which is inhabited by Dr. Morbius (Walter Pidgeon) and his beautiful and innocent daughter Altaira (Anne Francis). Adams has been sent to discover what has happened to a colonization party of some twenty years earlier. He finds that Morbius and his daughter are its sole survivors and that the doctor has taken over the mysterious and malevolent mental powers of an ancient civilization,

47. *Kiss Me Kate,* 1953. Kathryn Grayson and Howard Keel, with Kurt Kasznar (left) pose in a city square whose forced perspectival building (right), tower, and flat painted sky could have come out of a Giorgio de Chirico surrealist painting.

the Krell. *Cinefantastique* called it "a film years ahead of its time, the direct forerunner of *Star Trek, Star Wars,* and the big-budget science fiction of today."[66]

The combination in the story of what Daniel D. Fineman has called "the psychological and moral tensions between past and future" is what set *Forbidden Planet* apart from other science fiction films of the fifties; he adds:

> . . . the attention to the supporting technology is what helps to distinguish the film. The sets . . . are all created with an attention to detail that gives them plausibility. This realism is complemented by the art work, which must create the impression of a new world and not, as was typical for this era, of a picture filmed in Arizona.[67]

There were four major sets in the film: 1) the Morbius' "house of tomorrow" (exterior and interior), 2) the Krell laboratory and powerhouse, 3) the spaceship (saucer exterior) and landscape **(Illustration 48)**, and 4) the spaceship interior. All were designed by Lonergan, who explained, "Very early in the preparation of the production I made a number of sketches, trying to find

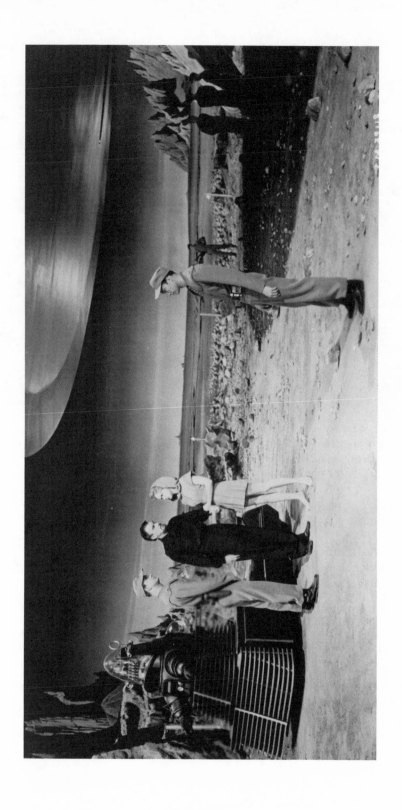

shapes that would be structurally sound and logical and yet be out-of-this world enough to be unfamiliar to the average viewer."[68]

The main sets were designed as a unit, interconnecting with one another for fluidity in camera movements. A 20' × 30' cyclorama, painted by George Gibson's scenic painting department, was placed behind the house to achieve a depth of field and to describe the eerie, desolate landscape of the planet. The house itself looks fifties modern, with touches like an interior pool and stone for some walls. Lonergan continued,

> Everything was futuristic in design. We tried to avoid using anything that would resemble an earthly appliance. I remember a frustrating moment after the set decorator had designed a special high back chair. . . . Wilcox [the director] complained that the chair blocked his view and ordered it removed. It was replaced by a regular office swivel chair. It was only after tired old Cedric Gibbons came over and interceded that the error was corrected.[69]

The most futuristic sets were the Krell lab, a model of streamlined efficiency, and the exterior of the space ship. The most effective prop in the movie was Robot Robby designed by special effects expert Buddy Gillespie, a model for all later humanistic and witty machines from Stanley Kubrick's H.A.L. 9000 computer in *2001* (1968) to robots R2D2 and C3PO in *Star Wars* (1977). At one point Robby is induced to make countless bottles of whiskey by the space ship's rummy cook (Earl Holliman). Art Department draftsmen, under Bob Kinoshita, spent eight weeks making the plans and produced 12 sheets of full-scale drawings to be followed by the construction department in their creation of Robby.

Arthur Lonergan had been working for MGM on a variety of films since 1936. He earned his degree in architecture from Columbia University and had, for a while, taught interior design and the history of architecture at New York University (1929–1935) before he came to Hollywood and took a job in the more exciting film industry.

Of working under Cedric Gibbons, Lonergan says, "He was a great critic. He always knew when something was wrong with a design." Among the new art director's first assignments was *Marie Antoinette,* the picture which, along with *Romeo and Juliet,* seems to have done more than any other to expand the Art Department.

During his decade at MGM, Lonergan had a chance to work with many directors. To get good sets from management in the days of the big studios, "the director and art director had to work as a team. There were always challenges to expenditures at production meetings, and without the director's backing, the art director had little chance of realizing his ideas."

48. *Forbidden Planet,* 1956. Arthur Lonergan, Cedric Gibbons, art directors. Leslie Nielsen, Walter Pidgeon, and Anne Francis stand with Robot Robby before a 20' × 30' cyclorama of the barren and eerie planet Altair IV in this groundbreaking science fiction film.

Lonergan considers George Cukor and Gene Kelly masters at getting the sets they wanted on their pictures. "Cukor would 'set up' scenarios with me, to take place at upcoming production meetings, in which we would trade off things we hadn't wanted in the first place."

Gene Kelly was an expert at using this technique too, Lonergan remembers.

> On *It's Always Fair Weather* (1955), which Kelly co-directed with Stanley Donen, Gene wanted a lot of big sets, including three blocks of 3rd Avenue in New York City with an elevated railway and the interior of Pennsylvania Station with large escalators running through it. At the production meeting (Arthur Freed was producing) there was a knock down fight about the sets. Talk turned, as usual, to the reuse of standing sets. Finally, Kelly began to cry. Arthur finally conceded: "Hell, give them Third Avenue and drop Penn Station." Gene turned off the faucets. This was exactly what he'd wanted all along."

"One thing that you always had to consult before building sets, was the stock warehouse," according to Lonergan. Architectural units were stored there—wall sections, doors, moldings and other details.

> The problem with using these units was that it gave a sameness to all of the sets you built, because the sections were all in standardized dimensions. But not using stock units meant your sets were sure to be challenged at production meetings.

Lonergan was at MGM when it unionized in the forties. He believes that art directors were not eager to unionize and that the studio's policies forced the issue. He can remember, before unionization, working 14 straight weeks, nights and weekends, included, on a straight salary. In the fifties, he was president of the Society of Motion Picture Art Directors (1952–1954) and editor of their publication *Production Design* when it flourished during that period (see page 39 above). Salaries improved and gross abuses discontinued under unionization, but the art director became hemmed in with regard to the things he could do on a picture; he had to be careful not to trespass on other worker's territories, especially those of the sketch artist and set decorator.

Location work, which became more and more important in the fifties when Lonergan was an independent, did much to turn things around again. He recalls:

> It was like a return to early art direction, when the art director had to get in and do everything by hand. You didn't have the studio's well-trained crews, and either you did things yourself or you taught other people (mostly in foreign countries) how to do things—how to age buildings or fake materials. Experience was really important when I became an independent. There was no one around to ask questions of anymore.

Another big change according to Lonergan was that "you spent a lot more time scouting locations. Most big studios had had location departments that helped art directors."

Lonergan very successfully made the transition to work as an independent, traveling all over the world to do pictures. Some of his most memorable films, such as M*A*S*H (1970), are from this period. He was also asked to design theme parks and television programs. Television art direction was so different from film design, that he was able, without difficulty, to do half a dozen at a time on the Goldwyn lot (including *The Loretta Young Show, Mr. and Mrs. North,* and *The Ghost and Mrs. Muir*). Like the old movie serials, television series use the same basic sets over and over, and the attention to detail is not so essential because they don't register on the small screen.

In 1942, while Lonergan was at MGM, swimming champion Esther Williams was signed up and was to be given a star build-up. For her, the studio built its only personal set—a gigantic backlot swimming pool. Just about everyone in the art department would have a chance to deck it out in various camoflague for Williams' pictures, where the aquatic numbers were designed in the Busby Berkeley tradition.

By 1962 Miss Williams had retired from films and the many great Metro stars had departed for work as independents; by 1963 MGM was in the red for the first time, to the tune of $17 million. The studio system, as it had been known in the heyday of the great art departments, was all but dead.[70]

Metro-Goldwyn-Mayer, from its foundation in 1924, produced motion pictures with fine production values. Lucky to have a strong and gifted supervising art director in Cedric Gibbons, the company gave him ample budgets and a large and able staff to accomplish the art direction on their films. Gibbons loved the details of art and architecture and insisted that the Art Department produce a perfected and polished decor that eventually became synonymous with the MGM name. But a fine eye for perfected historic styles did not prevent Gibbons and the Art Department from producing in the late twenties and thirties some of the best modern settings ever to be seen on the screen. It is not too surprising that this fastidious care in creating film decor was well suited to the meticulous Technicolor process, which had its first great popular successes with such studio classics as *The Wizard of Oz.* To today's audiences the MGM visual style may seem somewhat slick and overly polished, but such perfectionism reflected the studio's general stance toward the content of motion pictures which was both traditionalist and imaginative, reflecting a view of the world that was permeated with the optimism of the many "happy endings" of the narratives of the day.

SELZNICK INTERNATIONAL

MGM's biggest release of the thirties was, of course, the David O. Selznick production of *Gone with the Wind* (1939), filmed on the Selznick International lot. Selznick, from a second generation movie family, had made his way into independent production after having served an apprenticeship at MGM (1923–1926), first as a story editor and then as an associate producer on B pictures. He then went on to Paramount and RKO where he produced several memorable films including *King Kong* (RKO, 1933). He returned to MGM in 1933, where he helped convince Louis B. Mayer of the commercial possibilities of filming literary classics and made several that proved his theory — *David Copperfield* (1935), *A Tale of Two Cities* (1935), and the Garbo classic *Anna Karenina* (1935) — before leaving the fold again to establish himself as an independent producer (his first independent films were released in 1936).

Always a stickler for fine production values, Selznick oversaw all the details of his pictures, including costumes, sets, and script. Because of the scale of the elaborate epic *Gone with the Wind,* Selznick brought in William Cameron Menzies to design the production. He chose art director Lyle Wheeler, who had previously worked on nine other pictures with him, to be the picture's art director. Selznick even tried to persuade Richard Day, who was then leaving Goldwyn, to come into his company while the production was in progress, as he explained to his business manager in a memo on June 7, 1938:

> I had a long talk with Richard Day yesterday and got nowhere, as he has definitely decided that he wants to head a big studio's art department. If he fails to get such a job, he expressed himself as being most anxious to be here; but I feel that this is a very remote possibility, since I think he will not have the slightest difficulty in getting the post as chief art director at any one of the big studios with the exception of Metro. There is not the slightest question in my mind but that the entire industry rates the art directors as (1) Gibbons, (2) Day, (3) Menzies.[71]

Menzies drew dozens of continuity sketches for the picture, establishing both settings, in a general way, and camera position. Selznick changed directors on the picture several times, with Victor Fleming finally receiving screen credit, and through the three years in which the film was in production it was Menzies' sketches that were the backbone for the visual realization of the picture. Selznick had foreseen Menzies' important role in the picture, and had commented on it in one of his many lengthy production memos:

> What I want on *Gone with the Wind* and what has been done only a few times in picture history (and these times mostly by Menzies) is a complete script in sketch form....[72]

A comparison of the drawings of Menzies and Wheeler and the Art Department helps to clarify their roles in the making of the film (see **Illustration 15** on page 32). Menzies' sketches are abbreviated as to details; they establish in a bold fashion the position of the figures in a frame, the set, the direction of the light and the principal colors. Wheeler and his staff clarified, articulated and sometimes changed the sets (the stairway in Rhett and Scarlett's postwar home is one example) that Menzies had suggested. Wheeler's ideas, carefully rendered in drawings by sketch artists J. McMillan Johnson, Dorothea

Holt and many others, show in exacting details the type of moldings, the treatment of draperies and walls, the style and placement of furniture, and the subtleties of color.

The lush Technicolor sets for *Gone with the Wind,* especially the plantation houses Tara and Twelve Oaks **(Illustration 49),** and the Atlanta home of the Butlers, have the richness of detail and precision of period design typical of MGM films and very much subscribed to at Selznick International. Wheeler, along with set decorator Edward Boyle, tried to follow the detailed descriptions found in the 1000-page bestseller. The Selznick Art Department and the research department headed by Lillian Deighton had to turn directly to the novel's author Margaret Mitchell for help when they had difficulties finding photographic materials on Atlanta prior to its destruction by fire in 1864. She recommended that a local historian of the Civil War and painter, Wilbur Kurtz, be consulted. He was brought out to Hollywood and assisted Menzies and Wheeler with the visual details of the picture: "Kurtz . . . [gave] detailed descriptions and drawings of the city of Atlanta, farm implements, and household items; among other things, he wrote a 32-page description of a typical Southern barbecue of the pre–Civil War era."[73] Such expert assistance (usually credited as technical advisers) to art directors was common in the Hollywood studio system.

Lyle Wheeler was responsible for the solution to one of the biggest scenic and special effects problems of the picture, the burning of Atlanta. While roaming the 40 acre Selznick backlot trying to devise ways of transforming the standing sets into a faithful facsimile of Atlanta, he concluded that it would be easier and cheaper to burn down the still standing *King Kong* and *King of Kings* sets, than to tear them down, and it would serve the purposes of the film as well. Menzies concurred, and under his direction Atlanta (the old sets) was burned, with extras acting the principal roles, some of which, like Scarlett, had not even been cast.[74]

William Cameron Menzies was presented with a special Academy Award for his work on *Gone with the Wind.* No stranger to the Oscar itself, he had won it the very first time it was given, under the designation "interior decoration," for *The Dove* (1928) and *The Tempest* (1928). Selznick's early prediction of Menzies' importance to the film was correct as one of his post-production memos (October 23, 1939) makes clear:

> no one could be more gracious with people, or more generous, than Bill Menzies, who has for the past twenty years—or certainly since "Robinhood" [sic] and all the Fairbanks pictures—been far above any worry as to somebody else getting credit. But his contribution to the picture is, in my opinion, one of the greatest of all the many people who worked on it. I am giving him an extraordinary credit on the screen, and I hope to be able to do so in publicity.

49. *Gone with the Wind*, 1939. William Cameron Menzies, production designer, Lyle Wheeler, art director. Vivien Leigh descends the hill covered with lush vegetation in front of Twelve Oaks plantation. A full set of continuity sketches by Menzies as well as production sketches and models by others preceded the building of the plantations in this epic.

The term "production designer" gained credence when applied to Menzies' screen credit on *Gone with the Wind*. Harry Horner, who received his own first screen credit on *Our Town* through Menzies' good graces (he had been taken off the picture), has perceptively described the art director's approach, "His big and important theory was that designing is not a matter of simply doing backgrounds but must definitely take an active participation in the creating of the scene."[75]

The man who helped Selznick and Menzies decide on the term "production designer" was art director Lyle Wheeler. He, along with Menzies, had a long and profitable association with the producer. Wheeler, after finishing his architecture training at the University of Southern California, had worked in architectural practice and as a magazine illustrator and industrial designer, during the twenties. As he explains his entry into the movies, "the Great Depression pushed architecture right out of the window; there simply weren't enough projects."[76] Since 1929, when he began in pictures, he estimates that he has worked on some 500 pictures.

First at MGM in 1931, under Gibbons, Wheeler advanced from sketch artist to assistant art director, and in 1935 joined Selznick's production team there. Wheeler's meticulous work on Jean Harlow's *Reckless* and Ronald Colman's *A Tale of Two Cities* led to his being asked to defect to Selznick International. His first picture for that company was the Technicolor production, *The Garden of Allah* (1936); he was asked to create sets, some of them not too difficult, but some like a reflecting pool done in the quixotic conditions of the Mohave Desert were a challenge. The pool filled up with sand three times during filming.[77]

Lyle Wheeler won an Oscar for his art direction on *Gone with the Wind*, and went on to win four more for *Anna and the King of Siam* (1946), *The Robe* (1953), *The King and I* (1956), and *The Diary of Anne Frank* (1959), films done while at 20th Century–Fox where he worked for 18 years, many of them as the head of the Art Department.

Wheeler's assignment, immediately following *Gone with the Wind*, was to design *Rebecca* (1940) for the meticulous Alfred Hitchcock, himself a former art director, who was then beginning his first American film under contract to David O. Selznick. Preparation had actually begun on the picture prior to the sets being struck for *Gone with the Wind*, as Wheeler recalled, "I remember we couldn't wait to strike the Twelve Oaks hallway to make room for Manderley."[78] Manderley, the great mansion to which Laurence Olivier brings his young bride, Joan Fontaine, is almost exclusively the setting for the picture (**Illustration 50**). Wheeler and the Selznick staff tried to find a location suitable for the action, but much searching yielded nothing that fit the many prerequisites. Ray Klune, of the Selznick production department, remembered:

> So Lyle and I, and I believe Hitchcock . . . came up with the idea of several different-sized miniatures of Manderley. We figured that the only way to do it really effectively was to build probably the largest-scale miniature that had ever been built; then another miniature half that scale; and then sections of it full scale. . . . So he [Selznick] gave the go-ahead and we built the biggest miniature first. . . . It was so big and it took up so much of one of the old unsoundproofed stages that we couldn't really get far enough away from it to get a full feeling of the scale of it, so that's why we needed the smaller one . . . to show the scale of the whole estate.[79]

Wheeler had originally designed the picture for color, but found that Hitchcock wanted to film in black and white; he recalls: "We used to outline every single camera movement in the sketches. If you look at the sketches for *Rebecca*, you'll see written notes indicating where the real set ends and a painted matte should meet, and how the cameraman should move."[80]

Rebecca's Manderley became one of the most memorable settings in a Hitchcock film. Like another actor in the story, it sets the mood of foreboding

50. *Rebecca,* 1940. Lyle Wheeler, art director. The country house, Manderley, is rich in period detail. Joan Fontaine and Laurence Olivier (left) are met by the staff led by Judith Anderson (center) in a spacious room, replete with medieval fireplace, 18th century portraiture, and oriental carpet.

and tragedy inherent to the Daphne du Maurier story. Seen first in the opening shots as a crumbled relic of what it had once been, and then resurrected for the telling of the tale, it seems to hold the key to the mystery of the dead wife that is unraveled in its rooms. Wheeler was again nominated for an Academy Award for his work.

Wheeler left Selznick in 1941, and the producer used such excellent art directors as James Basevi, John Ewing, and Mark-Lee Kirk on his subsequent films. Probably the oddest experiment in art direction on a Selznick film was for Hitchcock's *Spellbound* (1945), when Salvador Dalí was called in to design the dream sequence **(Illustration 51)** in which Gregory Peck, an amnesiac, is presented clues to his true identity. Dalí and other European artists had realized their own "expressions of the subconscious" on film in Europe many years prior to the dream sequence in *Spellbound.*[81]

The art director on the film was special effects expert James Bavesi with John Ewing his associate. Hitchcock decided that he wanted to portray the dream on the screen, and related that "dream scenes in films were always done with swirling smoke, slightly out of focus.... I decided I wanted to go the other way ... to convey the dreams with great visual sharpness and clarity, sharper than the rest of the film itself."[82] After conferring with Hitchcock, Dalí

51. *Spellbound,* 1945. James Bavesi, John Ewing, art directors. Based on Surrealist Salvador Dalí's designs, this dream sequence's space contains gambling tables with legs like a woman's, and has a fictive painted space with floating eyes and a path that leads into infinity.

was commissioned to paint the dream images and supervise their realization as film decor. To fully actualize Dalí's ideas as built sets would have cost almost $150,000, too high for Selznick until Hitchcock rescued the project with his conception — that minimal sets and miniatures could be used along with projections of Dalí's images.

In the film, as Peck begins to tell his dream, a glimmering light appears by his eye, it is transformed into the eye of a cat, dozens of eyes are then seen painted on over-hanging draperies in a gambling house. People are set out at large intevals from one another in an ambiguous space, card-playing is done over a vast table whose legs are shaped like a woman's, then an argument erupts between the winning player and a masked man. The scene switches abruptly to another Dalí composition, more disorienting than the first, it includes a large, block-like house with a roof and chimney. In the final action, a minuscule Peck flees over a vast tilted space, streaked with light and with the shadow of great wings slowly embracing it in darkness.

The brief sequence is one of the most gripping in the film, but apparently no one on the production found it satisfactory. William Cameron Menzies was called in, as he was so often by Selznick, to vitalize the conception, but did not much change the original idea. Despite Selznick's dissatisfaction with the dream sequence in *Spellbound,* it proved a groundbreaking use of contemporary painting in American film decor, and paved the way for many other similar uses of modern art in movies.

Selznick International Studio did not innovate stylistically. Rather — reflecting Selznick's own taste and his avowed admiration for Cedric Gibbons — his films perfected production values similar to those associated with MGM. Selznick International decor was always stylish, imaginative, well-researched, suggestively illuminated and in the service of a carefully crafted screenplay.

5

Warner Bros.

Warner Bros. was never known in the movie industry for its great technical departments. Only one Academy Award for art direction ever went to the studio in the period from the inception of the Oscar in the twenties until 1960 (to Carl Jules Weyl for *The Adventures of Robin Hood,* 1938). Partly this must be attributed to the tight-fisted economic policies of Jack Warner, the studio head in the thirties and forties. The Art Department, unlike those at MGM and Paramount, never had a powerful supervising art director who might have fought for bigger budgets and higher quality settings. In fact, unlike other studios Warners did not even have a supervising art director. Yet exceptional art direction was regularly accomplished at the studio by imaginative and inventive art directors who learned to capitalize on the meager resources at their disposal.

Warner Bros. was not a giant of the silent era and narrowly averted bankruptcy at times in the early twenties. The brothers, Sam, Harry, Albert, and Jack had firmly established themselves in the film business in 1903 when they opened the Cascade Theatre in Newcastle, Pennsylvania, screening rented films. They quickly moved into the lucrative motion picture exchange business, the distribution end of the industry. They bought films and exchanged them between theatre owners on a circuit that ran along the east coast from Pennsylvania to Georgia.

The brothers' flourishing exchange, the Duquesne Amusement Supply, was forced out of business by the Motion Picture Patents Company (Edison's Trust). This powerful monopoly had been formed by the major film producers (Edison, Vitagraph, Selig, Essanay, Biograph, Lubin, Kalem, Pathé, Gaumont, Méliès) in 1908 to monopolize the movie business based on the patent rights held by the members, primarily those of Thomas Edison.

Undaunted the Warner brothers decided to turn to the making of films. This proved to be an unmitigated disaster, and by 1912 they had decided to try the exchange business again, but this time on the West Coast where they were farther away from the Trust. As in the past, the company made and lost money, never hitting it big. By 1918 they were producing an inaugural feature length film, *My Four Years in Germany*. The following year, with the infusion of a capital loan of $25,000, they built their first studios, covering 10 acres at Sunset and Bronson Avenue.[1]

The early twenties were a formative period, with 1923 a banner year. The studio was refurbished and among the successful films was *The Gold Diggers* (1923), based on a David Belasco Broadway hit. Its theme of poor girls chasing rich boys was to be the durable bases for a series of musicals bearing the same title that were produced during the Depression thirties.

The same year saw the emergence of one of the Warners' first big motion picture stars, the German import Rin-Tin-Tin. The dog had been rescued from the trenches in World War I, brought to the States, and trained for stunt work in movies. An enormous star in silents, he went on to make 18 subsequent films for the studio and eventually earned $1,000 a week. Rin-Tin-Tin easily survived the transition to sound. And it was sound that finally made Warner Bros.

Sam Warner had heard the newly developed sound-on-disc system at the Bell Laboratories and at his urging the brothers signed an exclusive contract for the system with Western Electric in 1926, creating the Vitaphone Corporation.[2] The new sound system was tried out with a feature film in August of 1926 when a synchronized musical score was added to John Barrymore's *Don Juan* and introduced at the newly acquired Warners Theatre in New York. A success, it paled by comparison to the sensation caused by the next Warner Vitaphone production, the part-talkie *The Jazz Singer,* a musical melodrama starring Al Jolson who sang and uttered a few words of ad-libbed dialogue. *The Jazz Singer* besides its captivating use of sound also included sequences in color; this proved to be a popular and recurring feature in the string of musicals that were soon to emerge from the studio.

Even the Warner brothers were surprised at the appeal the new sound system had for the moving picture audience. The success of *The Jazz Singer* and the other sound films that were immediately rushed into production boosted the company to the top of the motion picture industry. The studio, which had posted a loss of $279,096 in 1926, was showing a net profit of $14,514,628 just three years later,[3]—a leap in profitability that *Variety* called "the highest increase ever reported for a picture company or any other concern for that matter."[4]

Vitaphone sets of the early sound period are witness to the limitations of the sound equipment (see **Illustration 52**). It had to be kept stationary, and was frequently hidden in or behind some element in the set. An urn in a garden setting, as seen here, could be the repository of the cumbersome microphone. Settings tended, in many cases, to be rather shallow, because sound could not be heard from the far reaches of a set. On the other hand the equipment picked up the whirring of the camera and the movement of the dolly. Almost immediately the camera was encased and muffled in some sort

52. *Early Vitaphone Set,* circa 1930. With early sound equipment the microphone had to be stationary; usually hidden in part of the scenery, it limited the action to its close proximity.

of box, and eventually, until sound equipment became more sophisticated, the box was put on wheels so moving shots could be made.

The movie musical was to prove one of the most successful of sound film genres, and in the forties to become the forte of MGM. But it was at Warners in the thirties, with the birth of sound film and the genius of dance director Busby Berkeley, that the musical came into its own.

Warner Bros. immediately followed up their success with *The Jazz Singer* with other musicals, including another Al Jolson film, *The Singing Fool* (1928), and *Sally* (1930), starring Ziegfeld star, Marilyn Miller. None of these films were particularly innovative in terms of set design, although some oddities were in evidence, like the human chandeliers in the 1929 *Show of Shows.*

Warners was not to distinguish itself for musical film decor until Busby Berkeley appeared on the scene to direct the dance sequences for the 1933 smash hit *42nd Street.* A former actor, Berkeley had become an acclaimed Broadway director in the twenties. His staging of shows like the Earl Carroll Vanities of 1928 prompted Samuel Goldwyn to acquire his services to direct the musical sequences of the filmed version of *Whoopee* (1930), which allowed Eddie Cantor to recreate his stage success. At this stage, Berkeley credits art director Richard Day with helping him find a movie style when he totally lacked confidence behind the camera:

> The art director of *Whoopee*, Richard Day, happened to notice me looking at a camera with obvious puzzlement and gave me a great piece of advice that helped me greatly. "Buzz, they try to make a big secret out of that little box, but it's no mystery at all. All you have to remember is that the camera has only one eye, not two. You can see a lot with two eyes but hold a hand over one and its cuts your area of vision." This was simple advice but it made all the difference. I started planning my numbers with one eye in mind.[5]

His confidence mounting as the film progressed, Berkeley decided to do away with the four camera set-ups that were typical for dance routines in the period:

> ...during my entire career in films I have never used more than one camera on anything. My idea was to plan every shot and edit in the camera.[6]

Berkeley's films, filled with beautiful girls doing precision routines, were a direct carry-over from his stage work, but prior to *42nd Street* none had electrified film audiences. Art director Jack Okey's sets for the film combine gritty realism in the backstage scenes with fantasy in the production numbers staged by Berkeley. Okey and Berkeley worked closely on the dance numbers where the sets are integral parts of the routines — particularly on a railway sleeping car in "Shuffle Off to Buffalo" and Manhattan's 42nd Street and skyscraper profile in the final number to the title tune (Illustration 53). Berkeley reveals that he didn't always know what he was going to do with a set when he ordered it:

> Since it was a honeymoon song, I had them build me a Pullman train carriage, one that would split down the middle as I moved my camera into the interior. I was stuck for an idea on what to do once I got inside. I sat for three days in front of that set, and then during a lunch break it came to me, and what you see on the screen — the action inside the Pullman — was staged that afternoon.[7]

Berkeley credits Darryl Zanuck, then head of Warners' production, with giving him carte blanche on the sets after having seen his plans, "Give Berkeley whatever he wants in the way of sets, props, costumes. Anything he wants, he can have."[8] The elaborate "42nd Street" set in that production number is revealed behind star, Ruby Keeler, when she jumps down from a taxicab on which she's been tap dancing and singing. Berkeley's camera wanders through the set as the street fills up with people and vignettes of "naughty, bawdy" life along it are revealed. Parts of the set were built — the inside of a barber shop and of an apartment where violence erupts — the rest consists of expert scenic painting; real neon signs hang from the prop buildings. And, in the final climactic moments of the number another entire set is used. This idea of multiple sets within a single number, became a repetitive element of Berkeley's

53. *42nd Street,* 1933. Jack Okey, art director. This part of the musical finale's multipart set had a central stair on which Ruby Keeler (shown here) danced while Manhattan's skyscrapers swayed to the rhythm of the song.

style. In this case Okey built a broad stairway on which dancers could sway holding up realistically painted depictions of New York's famous skyscrapers while Keeler continues dancing to the song. It seemed like all of Manhattan had caught the beat of "42nd Street."

In comparison to the sets of Warners' earlier musicals, Okey's sets are simpler and more relevant to the musical theme. The sets for *The Gold Diggers of Broadway* (1929) by Max Parker seem lumpy and contrived in comparison to those of *42nd Street.* In that film's musical production number, "Tiptoe Through the Tulips" (**Illustration 54**), shapely girls stand on tiers in front of a painted backdrop of a green house, their legs protruding from flower pots and their heads encased in tulip petals. Much of the action happens in front of the set rather than in it; the set is passive and the "Tulip" number is essentially theatre staged.

The new cinematic style introduced by Berkeley in *42nd Street* is credited with reviving the moribund musical genre, and Warners rushed two more musicals into release in the same year, *Gold Diggers of 1933* and *Footlight Parade;* both proved critical and financial successes.

Designer Jack Okey had worked at First National in the twenties and then become a part of the amalgamated company in 1925 when Warners absorbed their competitor; he remained at the studio throughout the thirties. He had designed several notable silent films for director Maurice Tourneur (*Torment*, 1924, *The White Moth*, 1924, and *Old Loves for New*, 1926) while at First National and prior to his efforts on Warners' musicals Okey had helped to establish the studio's claim to the social realism genre with his design for *I Am a Fugitive from a Chain Gang* (1932).

Hungarian film producer and director Alexander Korda later, in 1934, invited Okey to London to select the site and design his large Denham film studios. In the forties and fifties the art director went over to RKO, and sometimes worked on films directed by Jacques Tourneur, Maurice Tourneur's son (*Experiment Perilous*, 1944, and *Out of the Past*, 1947).

On *Footlight Parade*, Okey was teamed with Anton Grot, the artist who dominated art direction at Warner Bros. beginning in the twenties until his retirement in 1948. They worked with director Lloyd Bacon and dance director Busby Berkeley on another backstage musical, this time starring Jimmy Cagney as a harassed producer of "prologues," musical stage numbers to precede films.

"By a Waterfall," running 15 minutes, is the film's biggest production number. It has a multipart set and uses the Berkeley techniques of dancers in patterns, overhead shots, and a single moving camera. It opens with scantily clad female swimmers and divers cavorting about a huge forest waterfall, replete with five water slides. A water ballet is staged with synchronized diving and swimming. The scene then changes to another mammoth set **(Illustration 55)**, a rectangular Roman Bath pool where the acquatic ballet continues in more intricate kaleidoscopic patterns which are shot from every angle, including overhead and underwater. At the pool's far end, against an abstract Art Deco background, a hydraulic fountain spouting water rises to become a tower of human figures reflecting in the water, for the grand finale. The entire number was later to be reprieved in infinite variation for the Esther Williams pictures, some of them with sequences directed by Berkeley (*Million Dollar Mermaid*, 1953 and *Easy to Love*, MGM, 1953).

On *Gold Diggers of 1933* Anton Grot was the sole designer, and if Berkeley's numbers are as memorable as usual, the sets are even more so. As John Hambley and Patrick Downing have remarked, "the numbers 'We're in the Money' and 'Remember my Forgotten Man' ... owe as much to Grot's designs as they do to Berkeley's choreography."[9]

Ginger Rogers, Joan Blondell, and Ruby Keeler, dressed in bras and g-strings made of coins, open the movie to the tune of "We're in the Money"

54. *The Gold Diggers of Broadway*, 1929. Max Parker, art director. The "Tiptoe Through the Tulips" number had a more static, theatre-derived type of set than those soon to be used by Busby Berkeley.

55. *Footlight Parade,* 1933. Jack Okey, Anton Grot, art directors. A circular fountain with tiers of bathing beauties rose before an Art Deco background and was reflected in a swimming pool as part of the "By a Waterfall" number.

(**Illustration 56**). The decor is composed of mammoth coins, tipped on end in the background and serving as cantilevered platforms for the chorines in the foreground. The number is fast paced, the costumes suggestive, and the gold diggers theme established in song and set.

The film's production of the song *Shadow Waltz* (**Illustration 57**) has one

Gold Diggers of 1933, 1933: 56. (Top) Anton Grot, art director. In the middle of the Depression, dancers cavorted to "We're in the Money" among gigantic coins tipped on end, stacked, and cantilevered into platforms. 57. (Bottom) The elegant curves of the spiraling stair in the "Shadow Waltz" number is a classic musical film set in its abstraction, economy, and functional spaciousness.

of the most successful sets in film musical history and one of the most influential. It is classic for its abstraction, its economy, its ample open space, and its shining bakelite floor. As the song begins, 60 women in futuristic spiraling white hoop skirts and skull caps are seen playing white violins on a spiraling staircase. The girls slowly dance in flower-like progressions. The subdued (for Berkeley) ending is an overhead shot where one large violin is formed by the dancer's many, now illuminated (note the extension cords right and left in Illustration 57), smaller violins which glow in the darkness.

Another film classic, the "My Forgotten Man" number, is something of an anomaly in the Berkeley repertoire; it is a number with an emotionally powerful, social conscience message. It centers on the theme of the World War I veteran who finds himself jobless in the America of 1933. As the song begins, Joan Blondell speaks and partly sings the moving lyrics in the low-key setting of a barren street corner, the camera then travels to the windows of a tenement revealing a black woman who continues the song. The sequence shifts to telling vignettes of the vets' former and present lives—the glorious march off to war and finally the breadlines to which they have been reduced. Grot's set for the final scene is unforgettable: a huge wheel is illuminated from behind, inside of it uniform clad soldiers rigidly posed with rifles on their shoulders march in alternate directions on three levels. In front of the wheel, on broad stairs, the men from the breadlines kneel before Joan in a circle raising their arms in a gesture of supplication. The mechanistic set, matched to the mechanistic rhythm of the song, and the marching, powerfully suggests that the men are caught in some terrible machine (society) over which they have little control.

Anton Grot, the film's designer and the most formidable art director at Warner Bros., came to the United States from his native Poland at the age of 25 in 1909, changing his name from Antocz Franciszek Groszewski. (See Illustration 58.) Grot had studied at the Cracow Academy of Arts and then gone to Koenigsberg in Germany where he attended the Technical College to further his studies in interior design and illustration. Nothing is known of his activities as a designer in Europe or until 1913, when he was hired by Sigmund "Pop" Lubin, who had seen some of his oil paintings displayed in Wanamaker's Department Store, to design sets for his Philadelphia based Lubin Company. Grot apparently worked with Lubin until his motion picture company folded in 1917, at the same time doing films for Vitagraph (*The Mouse and the Lion*, 1913) and for Pathé.[10]

At Pathé, George Fitzmaurice, one of their busiest directors, used Grot's sets for five pictures between 1916 and 1918, as did Louis Gasnier for his 15 part serial *The Seven Pearls* (1917). Grot went on to design several other serials at Pathé with George B. Seitz as their director. It was during this time that Grot must have worked out several of his distinctive design techniques. His efforts of these years have been described by cameraman, Arthur Miller:

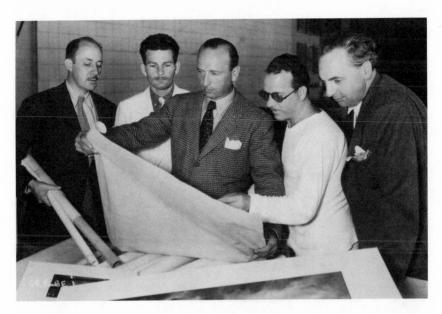

58. (Left to right) Dwight Franklin, Sherry Shourds, Michael Curtiz, Anton Grot, and Hal Mohr looking at some sketches in the Warner Bros. Art Department circa 1940.

> Grot was the first art director that I had the opportunity of working with who hadn't come up through the ranks from the construction department. Anton Grot was a gifted and talented artist who made beautiful charcoal drawings . . . of the set before it was constructed. All his compositions showed a full shot of each set, with all the delicate tones and shadings that suggested ideas for lighting and, in general, were of great help to me as a cameraman. This new experience gave me an opportunity to consult and suggest breaks in the set to make it convenient for lighting and, in a practical sense, afforded me with the opportunity to continue studying composition, with instructions from Anton.[11]

Miller's appraisal of Grot's contributions in this period suggests the close collaboration between designer and cinematographer which had been necessary since Wilfred Buckland began to refine lighting and sets.

Grot continued to make his careful charcoal and ink sketches, in all sizes, throughout his career (see **Illustration 59**). He preferred charcoal for black and white pictures, but used color in his sketches later when he designed color films.[12] As Miller indicates they were developed for each set in the entire film and were, he says, mathematically calculated considering the camera's angle and the use of a 40mm lens.

> The set, when constructed, duplicated his drawings in camera angle as well as showing sizes of objects in their proper relative proportions when photographed. . . . For his own use, he had made what he referred to as a "diminishing chart." . . . By measuring the distances from the floor plan on the set and using his diminishing

59. Townscape, charcoal sketch, Anton Grot, 1930 (for *Svengali*, 1931?). A brooding, semiabstract Central European townscape with towering sculpted figures, peaked roofs, planar surfaces, this sketch recalls German expressionist work in both painting and film.

chart as an overlay while making his drawings, they would match exactly when the camera was set on the long shot.[13]

Grot's technique of presenting in sketches the film's sets in sequence passed on into general usage among art directors, particularly through his association with William Cameron Menzies who served as his assistant on the 1917 Fitzmaurice film *The Naulahka*. Later both Grot and Menzies added the actors and action to many of their sketches.

Grot came to Hollywood in 1922 to assist Wilfred Buckland with the tremendous sets being erected for Douglas Fairbanks' *Robin Hood*. He remained to work as art director on Mary Pickford's *Tess of the Storm Country* (1922) and *Dorothy Vernon of Haddon Hall* (1924). In a role reversal, he worked as Menzies' assistant on *The Thief of Bagdad* (1924), for which he did a marvelous publicity poster. At the same time Grot began an association of several years with Cecil B. DeMille productions; he helped design, with Paul Iribe and others, several films including the epic biblical film *The King of Kings*. In 1927, a well-established figure in Hollywood art direction, Grot signed a contract with Warner Bros. where he remained to design 80 films, mostly solo, before his retirement in 1948.

Grot's contracts, in the legal files of the Warner Bros. Collection at the University of South California, indicate the fortunes of the art director. The terms of his June 1929 one-year contract with First National Productions Corporation were that Grot would be "art director, artist and designer" under an exclusive agreement, allowing them to lend him out to other studios and to lay him off for up to eight weeks during the year. He was paid $250 a week.[14] By way of comparison, at about the same time, in 1932, some on-screen stars like James Cagney were making $1,750 a week at Warners, but others, like Joan Blondell, were making the same amount as Grot, despite their starring roles.

By 1939 Grot was on a two-year contract with Warner Bros. and was earning $450 a week; he designed only two pictures that year, the big-budgeted *Juarez* and *The Private Lives of Elizabeth and Essex,* down from the record 11 productions released in 1934 which he had designed single-handedly. (In the same year independent art director William Cameron Menzies working on *Gone with the Wind* was receiving $1,000 a week.) But Grot's salary had only gone up to $500 by 1947 when the company was showing the largest net profit of its history. Grot had the security of a steady pay check, but like most art directors in the studio system, did not earn as much as many of his colleagues in other departments (not as much as the musical director or the top paid screenwriters).

Grot was the only Warner art director repeatedly nominated for Academy Awards in the thirties and forties (for *Svengali,* 1931, *Anthony Adverse,* 1936, *The Private Lives of Elizabeth and Essex,* 1939, and *The Sea Hawk,* 1940), but he only won once, an honorary award in 1940 for the invention of a ripple machine first seen in Michael Curtiz' *The Sea Hawk,* which he had patented. At Warners in the forties, Grot worked on fewer pictures, but those he did design, like the Joan Crawford films *Mildred Pierce* (1945) and *Possessed* (1947), were done with the same professionalism and with a fine eye for location shooting.

An interoffice memo of March 22, 1948, states, "We will not take up the option on Anton Grot. He will continue on a week-to-week basis." Grot is credited with only one picture after 1948. He retired and turned to painting during the remainder of his life. Grot died at the age of 90 in 1974. His work was prominently featured in a BBC-TV show on art direction in Hollywood shown in 1979, but the high caliber of his work has not been much appreciated or discussed in America.

It was Grot's second film at Warner's, *Noah's Ark* (1929) (see **Illustration 60**), that brought him into collaboration with Jack Warner's recent discovery, Hungarian director Michael Curtiz. Grot was to design 15 subsequent films for the director. The biblical epic, one of the studio's most expensive and longest (135 minutes) pictures to date, retold the story of the flood relating it to a World War I romance; each of the principals played dual roles. In theme and production values it resembled such films as *Intolerance.*

Profitting from his experience on DeMille's *King of Kings,* Grot con-

60. *Noah's Ark,* 1929. Anton Grot, art director. Noah's barge-like ark in the distance
was seen through rocky crags while rainwater streamed over dead trees and bodies in
an image that recalls Michelangelo's and Nicholas Poussin's painted images of the same
story. Three extras died in the filming of this scene.

structed dozens of sets in all dimensions for *Noah's Ark,* from a thoroughly
detailed European tavern interior, to the ark with animals two-by-two, and vast
temples built to collapse during the flood. Cameraman Hal Mohr resigned
when he heard that the temples were going to fall not only to the ground but
on the extras. The temples did little harm, but the flooding scenes became too
realistic when several extras were drowned. Curtiz, with little experience of
"dump tanks" of water, did not graduate the load sufficiently and 15,000
gallon sluices opened directly onto the set.[15]

In the thirties, Curtiz and Grot teamed on such memorable pictures as
Captain Blood (1935) and *The Private Lives of Elizabeth and Essex* (1939). Grot
is considered instrumental in the development of Curtiz's style in these years,
and some writers (John Hambley, Patrick Downing, and John Everson) would
go farther:

> Warner Bros. in the early 1930s made films almost on the assembly-line system.
> Directors were unable to give much preparation time to films when they were mak-
> ing five or six full length features a year. Sometimes, and this was certainly the case

PROD. NO | 602-00
PROD. NAME | SVENGALI
SET NO | 602 04
SET NAME | BILLYS
DATE 1-26 | at STUDIO

61. *Svengali,* 1931. Anton Grot, art director. Some of Grot's most stylized art direction is seen here; floors undulate, stairs splay outward, fireplaces are yawning maws, and walls slope radically (back) suggesting the unbalanced mind of Svengali.

with Curtiz, the first they saw of the sets was when they were ready to begin shooting. (John) Everson believes that as a result Curtiz has been given credit for a style that was largely Grot's: Production teamwork may have given a certain uniformity to Warner product, but it was often a creative and certainly an efficient uniformity. Other art directors assigned to work on upcoming Curtiz' projects knew how well the Grot design had worked for him and did their best to copy it. Cameramen, aware of the unique 'look' of the Curtiz-Grot films, knew what Curtiz liked or was used to, and likewise copied the lighting style for which Grot's sets had been designed. As a result, Curtiz' films acquired a specific visual style that, understandably, came to be regarded as his personal style.[16]

Grot's drawings provide ample evidence that, at the very least, there was a close collaboration on visual style between director and art director (see **Illustrations 64–67** on pages 134–135).

For *Svengali* (1931), directed by Archie Mayo, an inspired John Barrymore recreated the villainous music teacher and mesmerizer in some of Grot's most stylized settings, for which he received his first Academy Award nomination. Grot's Paris, with its angular walls that tilt precariously inward and which twist into far distances, set the picture's mood and suggest the evil, twisted mind of Svengali **(Illustration 61)**. They owe much to German-Expressionist silent films but are more substantially built. The *Svengali* sets should be considered among Grot's masterworks and indicative of his imaginative range, yet the art director was rarely called upon at Warner to do such stylized decor. Grot did manage to employ modified expressionist techniques, at which he was so expert, on some other films he designed, particularly the rare horror fantasies that came out of the studio in the thirties, like *Doctor X* (1932) and *The Mystery of the Wax Museum* (1933).

A *Midsummer Night's Dream* (1935) was an anomaly among Warner Bros. films, and gave Grot a chance to create film decor of an unexpected and fantastic sort. This was the seventh film Grot designed for director William Dieterle (who had taken over the production from his less film oriented mentor Max Reinhardt). The production was lavish, and Grot's dense forest setting for the Shakespearean comedy was built on two large sound stages in Burbank, with real leaves individually glued to each tree **(Illustration 62)**. Indeed the forest was so deep and realistic that when Jack Warner saw the rushes he complained that he couldn't see the actors for the trees. Cinematographer Hal Mohr was brought in and he chopped away at Grot's exquisite forest, thinning it and adding aluminum paint and shellac to the leaves. He explains:

> And where the set had been to the eye, a beauty of nature, it suddenly became a very bad Christmas card, to the eye it looked that way, it didn't photograph that way.[17]

Mohr may have redone the forest but Grot's interior sets and props were magnificent throughout and garnered praise from others in the industry, as did the extravagant costumes by Max Ree. Despite the visual effects, the production received mixed reviews from the critics and from the public. Warner Bros. did not attempt another homage to the Bard.

Among the many successful films that Grot designed for director William Dieterle in the thirties were several biographies, *White Angel* (a life of Florence Nightingale, 1935) *The Life of Emile Zola* (1937) and *Juarez* (1939); each had highly polished period settings. Except for the Errol Flynn adventure

62. *A Midsummer Night's Dream*, 1935. Anton Grot, art director. **Dancers cavort in a thick forest whose leaves were individually glued to the trees and then given a coat of aluminum paint and shellac to project a magically illuminated fairy kingdom.**

pictures, bio-pics were the closest Warners usually came to historical narratives.
The studio had begun producing biographies in the twenties when they acquired the services of George Arliss for the 1929 *Disraeli*. Arliss was a tireless
(albeit tiresome) winnower of the biographical fields at Warners and
elsewhere.

The Life of Emile Zola garnered Warner Bros. its first ever best picture of
the year award from several sources, the Academy of Motion Picture Arts and
Sciences, the *New York Times,* and the New York film critics; it also earned
Grot his third Oscar nomination. Paul Muni, giving an intense performance
in the lead, donned the cloak of bio-king that Arliss had cast down only in the
same year.

Warners poured out its resources on the Zola film, proving once again that
when they wanted to, their production values could be as fine as any in the
industry. This time Grot's recreations of nineteenth century Paris were without
mannerism; Zola's study, the jail and the courtroom where he defends Dreyfus
are realistic and detailed.

Desiring the same sort of authenticity they had achieved in *The Life of
Emile Zola* for *Juarez,* Warners built an entire Mexican village on the backlot.
It was to do frequent service in their films and those of other studios
throughout the forties. Considering these filmed biographies their "class"
efforts, Warners again budgeted a large sum, $1,750,000, for the production.
Lavish sets were constructed, with the art department producing over 7,000
blueprints for them. But while the Mexican villages succeeded in providing a
convincing background for the story of Benito Juarez, the other characters,
Brian Aherne as the misguided Emperor Maximilian and Bette Davis as the
Empress Carlota, languished in more stylized settings.

In the film's beginning, Claude Rains in his role of French monarch
Napoleon III, is seen overacting in a royal palace which is done as "Rococo"
writ large. The details are doughlike and have nothing of the delicacy of the
original style. Likewise, an extremely dry rendering is given the Mexican royal
palace whose location is established by a few lonely cactuses (probably thriving
in the setting) in a garden seen beyond the windows. A feeling for the pomp
and pageantry of court life is captured by Grot: in the throne room, where
Maximilian's monogram is emblazoned behind elevated thrones, and at an
elaborate dock **(Illustration 63)** where the background is minimal — one gigantic triumphal arch festooned with flags strongly projects against a cloudless sky.
These sets, semiabstract in character, clash with the extreme realism of the
Mexican village sets, giving Grot's art direction of the film an uncharacter-
istically jumpy character, which underscores the real world of the peasants and
the irreal, fantasy world of the Emperor and Empress.

With the fictionalized historical narrative *The Private Lives of Elizabeth
and Essex* (1939), Grot seemed again to find his *métier*. Directed by Michael
Curtiz as a series of tableaux rather than as an action film, the principal sets

63. *Juarez*, 1939. Anton Grot, art director. Bette Davis and Brian Aherne are greeted by Donald Crisp (center) on their arrival in Mexico against a monumental triumphal arch. The court decor was in a semiabstract style; the peasant village was realistically depicted.

may be seen at leisure. Foremost among them are the interiors of Elizabeth's medieval and Tudor royal residences seen in a seductive Technicolor (see Illustrations 64–67). Grot's continuity sketches for the film remain; done in color, they are executed with his usual authority, and an added vitality which seems indicative of a special enjoyment in the job. Monumental architecture is rendered without a lot of detail, but with Tudor stucco and beamed ceilings indicated, and the light sources carefully delineated. Grot suggests the placement of a few pieces of furniture within the cavernous spaces; he often frames the actors within an image in a fragment of architectural detail. Grot's only indication of abundant ornament is in the costumes, which project beautifully against his restrained backgrounds.

The handling of color in the film was rich and was singled out for comment at the time and later:

A frequent feature of lighting for Technicolor, which persisted for decades, first appeared in *The Private Lives of Elizabeth and Essex* (1939) as lit by Sol Polito and

The Private Lives of Elizabeth and Essex, 1939: 64. (Top) Color continuity sketch by Anton Grot, art director. Grot's sketches established not only the setting, but how the action would take place in it, and the camera angle. 65. (Bottom) Director Michael Curtiz followed Grot's continuity sketch closely in this military parade led by Errol Flynn as Essex.

The Private Lives of Elizabeth and Essex, 1939: 66. (Top) Color continuity sketch. Anton Grot, art director. Elizabeth's cavernous Gothic throne hall and its lighting were illustrated by Grot in this forceful, economical sketch. 67. (Bottom) Only minor details (like the torchères) were added to Grot's original intention for this scene which has the soldiers guarding the dungeon stair as Errol Flynn confronts Bette Davis.

W. Howard Greene. This was the practice of splashing areas of amber light and blue light on the backgrounds of "period" interior scenes without regard for any consistency with possible sources, the actors being lit with white light.[18]

Grot's sketches indicate that it was his intention to wash color onto walls. This treatment of light had already occurred, to a lesser extent, in the previous year's *The Adventures of Robin Hood* with sets by Carl Jules Weyl, where blue light is frequently splashed onto the grey stone walls of the interior of Sir Guy of Gisbourne's castle, especially in the night scenes.

In the thirties and forties Warner Bros. counted on the reliable performances of such fine actors as Gary Cooper, Barbara Stanwyk, and Humphrey Bogart, and on interesting stories to hold the audience in their A pictures. They also specialized in making low-budget programmers, the B end of the double-bill. Working on both ends of the bill in this period were art directors Carl Jules Weyl, Robert Haas, Max Parker, Hugh Reticker, Esdras Hartley, John Hughes, Charles H. Clarke, Charles Novi, Stanley Fleischer, Leo Kuter, Douglas Bacon, Ted Smith, Ed Carrere, with the indefatigable Grot.

In the thirties, Warner Bros. settled into producing a steady fare of crime films, women's stories, social conscience melodramas, and adventure stories, losing ground to 20th Century–Fox and MGM in the production of musicals and historical dramas. Warners had early laid claim to certain of these genres, particularly crime and social consciousness films, and these in particular became identified as the "Warner picture." Both of them depended on realistic, contemporary settings, 95 percent of them in an urban milieu.

Earlier films like the 1928 *Tenderloin* (*Lights of New York,* 1928, was another) were already beginning to show the stylistic hallmarks of the later cycle of gangster movies, although thirties films would invariably have a male central character. *Tenderloin,* with Warner's Michael Curtiz directing (art director uncredited), starred Dolores Costello as a dancer accused of theft and hounded by the police. Her tale of woe unfolds in dank little rooms, police stations, nightclubs, speakeasies and on the rain splattered city streets. As photographed by Hal Mohr, all the expressive possibilities are gotten from the meagre surroundings.

Many of the same scenic values were to recur in Warner's now classic crime films of the thirties like *Little Caesar* (1931) or in the same year *The Public Enemy,* both directed by William Wellman. The latter starred James Cagney and Jean Harlow and had sets by art director Max Parker. Laid in shabby lower-class interiors and on city streets, the drab sets are consistent with the character's circumstances. Much of the picture is shot in close-ups and medium shots with the actors consuming most of the frame, so that in many scenes the sets hardly seem to exist. This is due, in part, to the fact that in 1930 the only Hollywood company still using the "ice box" type of sound-proof booth was Warners; the others had gone on to their own improvised version of a muffled camera. At Warners, both cameraman and camera were encased in a booth, and despite the fact that several of these booths had wheels, camera movement was extremely limited. When, periodically, the camera draws back for a long shot in *The Public Enemy,* as in the robbery of a fur company, the scenic values are scant and the sets have a wooden look with a minimum of detail. The lighting is often the most interesting factor in the *mise-en-scène* of Warner Bros. crime films, with many scenes set at night. Darkness helped to hide the paltry quality of the architectural setting.

This niggardly approach to setting is usually blamed on the economic strictures imposed at Warners, particularly in the early thirties when the company suffered heavy financial losses. The other major studios had quickly caught up with Warners in the use of sound and the 1929 stock market crash had been felt by the company, in terms of ticket sales, almost immediately. Jack Warner used his art directors to cut costs. Anton Grot, who designed *Little Caesar,* had to be mindful of the picture's low budget; as one writer has commented:

> many of Grot's storyboards were produced to serve the Warner studio economy, ensuring that only minimum necessary elements of a set were built and as a result limiting directors to the camera positions and angles he visualized.[19]

Grot's economical style seemed to thrive rather than suffer under budgetary stricture; his big budget films like *Anthony Adverse* (1936) and *A Midsummer Night's Dream* (1935) can sometimes become overly detailed and less successful than his bare-bones style.

Little Caesar traces the rise and fall of small-time gangster Caesar Enrico Bandello. Grot sets the gangsters in spare rooms with his characteristically low ceilings, in a realistic diner, then in a nightclub with geometric marble floor, bland grey walls, and the latest Deco furniture and female nude statue as ornament; the detailing here is Warner's thin.

Rico starts to take on the trappings of the wealthy mobsters whom he apes. His clothes change and his surroundings change; he can afford a fancy apartment **(Illustration 68)**. Here Warner Bros.' Art Deco enters in, but is a far more pedestrian variety (but befitting the character) than what was coming out of MGM and Paramount in the same period. Rico's apartment has the requisite bare walls and marble floors, but a somewhat too detailed floral filigree around the fireplace, and a somewhat too profuse sprinkling of modern *objets d'art* around the room gives it an overstuffed look. The furniture, especially the boldly patterned Deco armchair adds to the *nouveau riche* look of the place. Betrayal starts Rico's downward fall—he's seen in a flophouse, and in the final scene (as so many Warner mobsters were to do subsequently) he dies on a lonely, dirty street in the gutter.

In Warner Bros. crime films, spot-lighting and back-lighting taken from German expressionist pictures were put to frequent use. Often the light sources would be indicated—a lonely street lamp or store window, but sometimes the

68. *Little Caesar,* 1931. Anton Grot, art director. The Art Deco apartment of Edward
G. Robinson (left, with Ralph Ince) reflects his own expensive, gaudy taste—marble
floors, gilt floral trim and a splashy floral print on the furniture respond to his spats,
vest, and diamond stick pin.

light just streams inexplicably from around the corner of a building—cutting
up the image into foreground, middle ground and background, the latter
often left in pitch darkness. Silhouettes created by cut-outs break up the stark
walls.

In time, Warner Bros. came to have a lot of the finest technical equipment in the industry, like a fog machine purchased in 1940, which could mask backgrounds and a lack of detail in the settings. After they purchased the fog machine, for about a year, every other picture found someone lost in the fog. In *The Sea Wolf* (1941) it was Edward G. Robinson and John Garfield, and in *Out of the Fog* (1941) it was Garfield accompanied this time by Ida Lupino, and, unforgettably, fog shrouded the airport in the final scene of the slightly later *Casablanca* (1943).

Economy was evident in the running time of Warners' pictures too. Usually averaging 75 minutes, they were as Clive Hirschhorn suggests,

> brilliantly edited, with dissolves, wipes and quick cuts keeping the action constantly on the boil.... Every shot counted, every line of dialogue advanced the narrative. Waste was not tolerated. The good guys as well as the bad spoke like machine-gun fire.[20]

A subcategory of the crime film genre was the prison picture. Beginning with the ground-breaking social protest melodrama on the penal system *I Am a Fugitive from a Chain Gang* (1932), the studio went on to perfect the type in such pictures as *20,000 Years in Sing Sing* (1933), *Girls on Probation* (1938), and *Each Dawn I Die* (1939). The same prison cells and warden's office could be used repeatedly, and were; then they were wed to film clips of the exteriors and the interiors of different prisons.

I Am a Fugitive from a Chain Gang, which began the series, is less conventional in decor than many of the later pictures. Paul Muni played a wronged war veteran who is framed for a holdup and finds himself on a chain gang. Filmed much of the time at locations chosen by art director Jack Okey and director Mervyn LeRoy—at a rock quarry and in a prison camp, the picture achieved a semidocumentary character. In following years' productions, *20,000 Years in Sing Sing* and *Ladies They Talk About*, the action takes place mostly behind studio built prison bars. This proved a cheap and therefore a popular way of mounting such pictures at Warners. These social protest and crime films were all expertly shot in black and white which seemed to fit their subjects and the Depression era mood of desperation that many of them captured. Jack Warner understood that what the public wanted from Warners was "movies straight from the shoulder—hard-hitting and snatched from newspaper stories of the day."[21]

Besides musicals and crime films Warner's most lucrative films of the thirties were the so-called "women's pictures." Popular with all segments of the audience, they focused on women as either heroines (Bette Davis in *Dark Victory,* 1939) or fallen women (Barbara Stanwyck in *Shopworn,* 1932, or Constance Bennett in *Bought,* 1930).

These pictures were relatively cheap to make. They did not call for huge sets, but usually required the contemporary decor that Warners was excellent

at producing. Art director Robert Haas designed many of these pictures, particularly those starring Bette Davis: *Dark Victory* (1939), *Now, Voyager* (1942) and *A Stolen Life* (1946). He was also responsible for the art direction of several of Miss Davis' costume successes, including *Jezebel* (1938) and *The Old Maid* (1939).

Haas, a native of New Jersey who had taken a degree in architecture from the University of Pennsylvania, practiced architecture from 1912 to 1920 before joining Famous Players–Lasky as "art manager." In 1922 he moved to Inspiration Pictures, which put him to work both in New York and Italy. His art direction was already receiving praise at this time for such memorable pictures as *White Sister* (1923) and *Romola* (1924) made under the direction of silent film great Henry King.

Haas migrated to the West Coast in 1927, where he worked for a couple of years at the Fox Studio. Warner Bros. hired him in 1929, and he remained there, an important formulator of the Warner "Look" in the thirties and forties, until his retirement in 1950. He was nominated for Oscars twice, for *Life with Father* (1947) and for the innovative location picture *Johnny Belinda* (1948), but like most Warner Bros.' art directors, never won.

The women's films were shot almost exclusively on the studio lots. *Dark Victory* is typical; the story and powerful performance of star Davis are more important then the decor, whose primary purpose is to create the genteel upper-class milieu against which the star can perform her role as a tempermental, rebellious sophisticate, who eventually goes blind and dies. The drawing rooms, doctor's office, and country cottage are professionally done, serviceable, and don't interfere with the emoting of the principals.

Less typical, but still studio-bound, is the art direction of *The Letter* (1940), a product of the talented and versatile Carl Jules Weyl who was a mainstay of the Warners' Art Department in the thirties and forties. The "L Rubber Company, Singapore, Plantation No. 1" is the principal setting for the story of adulterous Leslie Crosbie, played by Bette Davis, who in the picture's first scene shoots her lover on the front steps of her plantation home **(Illustration 69)**. The handling is typical of the dramatic way that light and setting will be manipulated throughout the film. Light pours out from the doorway silhouetting Bette's figure against it, the house is barely discerned in the light of the moon, a witness to the crime which casts an eerie light on the murder scene and then unexpectedly goes behind a cloud. Similar patterns of light and silhouette recur in the final moments, a coda which parallels the opening — in the moonlit garden Gale Sondergaard, as the Eurasian widow of the slain lover, avenges him by stabbing Bette to death.

69. *The Letter*, 1940. Carl Jules Weyl, art director. Bette Davis' plantation house was subtly tropical with wide verandas and shuttered windows set in a lush garden lit by the moon and a shaft of light from the interior in this violent scene.

Weyl's plantation house with wide veranda is subtly detailed and convincingly foreign; the "green" sets are lush and exotic in a distilled semiabstract style as they are seen several times at night. Weyl's sets aid immeasurably in the telling of the story and more than most, they create a pervasively sensuous mood for this tale of love and retribution.

Carl Jules Weyl, a native of Germany, had had an architectural practice in California in the twenties before he began working for Warner Bros. in 1935. He remained there until his death in 1948. Like all important art directors he was adept at producing the decor for many types of films; in 1940, besides *The Letter,* he was also responsible for the settings of such memorable pictures as *Dr. Ehrlich's Magic Bullet* and *All This and Heaven Too.*

Anton Grot's late career centered on a series of films with powerful female leads, but falling more within the genre of *film noir* than of "women's" pictures: *Mildred Pierce* (1945), *Deception* (1946), *Nora Prentiss* (1947), and *The Two Mrs. Carrolls* (1947). Grot brought all of his accumulated expertise to these films, which seemed thematically to mesh with his dramatic style of drawing and lighting. As Hambley and Downing have commented, "no-one was better equipped than he to produce sets and storyboards for the cynical slice-of-low life Forties dramas that were to become known as *film noir.* He had been designing that kind of film throughout his career."[22]

Grot's continuity sketches for *Mildred Pierce,* as usual starkly contrastive, are composed two to a page (see **Illustration 14** on page 31). In bold print Grot specifies the angle of the shot for director Michael Curtiz, and then carefully delineates it in a small sketch just beneath his description. In the dramatic opening at a beach house, gunshots ring out, a mirror shatters as a man calling "Mildred" drops to the floor, dead. All the *film noir* elements of darkness, male-female conflict, and violence are established in the first few seconds of the film. Grot's beach house is full of shadowy darkness and from darkness a woman emerges onto an ocean pier, in the next sequence. It is Mildred (Joan Crawford), contemplating suicide. Grot's written explanations of each frame, following the script, indicate exactly how the set will function to establish the mood and promote the action: "Shot over Mildred's shoulder. Show sea heaving and billowing greyly in the moonlight, wind whipped, cold and evil."[23] The next frame will show Mildred's response to the "cold and evil" sea in close-up, an angle shot, that still gives half of the frame to the turbulent sea behind the figure. There follows a long shot of the pier, a single streetlight picking out a policeman coming toward Mildred (**Illustration 70**), who finally, in the next frame, responds to his shouts and his beating on the dock's railing she clutches. Grot instructs, "Close on Mildred as impact of policeman's club on railing stings her hands, she reacts violently and looks in his direction." While Grot's sketches do not include all details, like the magnificent fur coat worn by Mildred, they are remarkably powerful, evoking the sense of despair and death that are the scene's themes.

70. *Mildred Pierce,* 1945. Anton Grot, art director. Joan Crawford seen on a lonely pier that closely parallels Grot's continuity sketch of the action (see Illustration 14 on page 31). Grot's sketches helped Warner Bros. keep filming on schedule and economized on the building of sets.

The story then unfolds in flashbacks as it is told by Mildred to the police. It opens in Grot's convincing middle-class bungalow with Miss Crawford in fussy patterned dress rather uncomfortably performing the role of industrious housewife baking cakes and pies so that she had enough money to further spoil her already monstrously selfish daughter, Veda. The house is carefully lit, although not with the chiaroscuro lighting of the opening scene, to throw shadows across the rooms and faces, and illuminate the not very auspicious furnishings.

Mildred becomes a waitress, opens her own restaurant, and then a chain of restaurants. Mildred's restaurant, in which much of the action of the middle of the picture takes place, is done in a forties "California modern" style with walls of plate glass windows contrasting with stone; sleek and trim, it is like Mildred's new man-tailored suits. The mansion of Monte Baragon, whom Mildred weds to give Veda the proper social connections, is conveniently upper-class, suiting the character's claim to old-money ties.

The film moves out of the studio at periodic intervals, onto California highways as Joan searches for a location for her restaurant, and outside in the beach house scene; Grot's matching of the interiors with these locations are extremely well-done. Grot seldom needed to use matte shots in these later pictures, but when he does they seem apt if also a little out-of-place, like the matte and miniature shot showing the opening of Mildred's new restaurant with tiny cars gathering beneath a brassy neon sign.

Both Carl Weyl and Robert Haas also worked on the many *noir*, mystery and intrigue stories that Warner produced in the forties, most of them featuring their fine contract players Humphrey Bogart, Peter Lorre, and Sidney Greenstreet. Haas designed *The Maltese Falcon* (1941) and Weyl's most famous and one of his best sets was the interior of Rick's Café Américain for *Casablanca* (1942). Its cavernous interior is characterized by a semiabstraction derived from Moroccan architecture; this set helps enormously in establishing the "foreign" ambiance of the story **(Illustration 71)**. Using an arch system, stuccoed and painted white, Weyl suggests the depths of the cafe while providing intimate spaces for the private conversations that develop the main and the subplots of the film. The white wall surfaces also provide backgrounds for the multitude of soft-focus closeups that director Michael Curtiz uses to construct the basic fabric of the film. The interior is punctuated by hanging brass lamps, carved screens, and plants, and is filled with delicate looking chairs and tables lit by small fringed lamps.

Warner Bros. did not have any directors like Paramount's Lubitsch and Von Sternberg who emphasized and elaborated on the symbolic aspects of setting. In *Casablanca* the cafe's arches momentarily frame Ingrid Bergman as she first enters, and later when she is talking to Humphrey Bogart in his rooms the shutters cast a cage like shadow over her face, alluding perhaps to her feelings of entrapment in the relationship with Paul Henreid (her husband), but by and large Curtiz does not manipulate the physical setting for symbolic purposes.

If Warners' directors seldom pushed the symbolic aspect of decor, they were among the best in the business at getting everything they could out of their sets. In *Casablanca* — with essentially one principal set — we see Rick's Café Américain from every conceivable angle. Each portion of the set is isolated and then seen from a distance as part of the integral whole in another part of the film. The bar and bandstand appear in their entirety in the long shot when "La Marseillaise" is being sung, the bar is seen in a medium shot with people mulling around it, and in a close-up when Rick demands a drink. The set is a companion to the story, and at the end one knows it intimately.

The same is true of John Huston's *Key Largo* (1948) **(Illustration 72)**. Leo K. Kuter's recreation of the interior of the Key Largo Hotel is on the screen in almost every scene of the film (the Victorian exterior seen during the hurricane was a miniature). At the film's beginning, Huston visually opens up the

71. *Casablanca,* 1942. Carl Jules Weyl, art director. Rick's (Humphrey Bogart, right) Café Américain was a cavernous white interior based on Moroccan architecture. Its stuccoed arches, tiled floor, and brass, wood and rattan furnishings provide the film's exotic ambiance.

picture with some second unit location shooting done in Florida—a bus carrying Humphrey Bogart hurries across a causeway to the Keys. At intervals during the picture he moves the action to the ocean (the studio tank), but when the dramatic conflicts begin, we are inside the interior of an off-season tropical hotel, vintage 1900. Kuter's set, like Weyl's in *The Letter,* has just the right tropical touches (rattan furnishing, fish mounted on the walls, shuttered windows). Likewise it has its important subdivisions: bar, lobby, halls, and separate rooms. Most of the spaces visually interpenetrate, so that you can see from one to the other, adding possibilities for spatial complexity in individual frames of the film.

Huston, like Curtiz, uses every nook and cranny of the set, and, moreover, he focuses attention on it by periodic isolation in a frame without action or actors. Most often this occurs when he is changing scenes. In the early part of the picture the bus deposits Bogart at the hotel; we see him approach the door, then from the interior, for just a second, the lobby and door are

72. *Key Largo,* 1948. Leo K. Kuter, art director. The main set, an off-season, slightly seedy, tropical hotel, vintage 1900, where fishing memorabilia outfitted the bar (seen here Edward G. Robinson, Claire Trevor, Lionel Barrymore in wheelchair, Thomas Gomez, Humphrey Bogart, Lauren Bacall, and unknown actor).

viewed alone. This creates a momentary pause before the narrative continues, much like turning a page in a book.

In the earlier *The Maltese Falcon* (1941), Huston frequently manipulated Robert Haas' realistic studio-built streets and sets in a manner that seemed to entrap the characters. Suggestive of how much at odds they were with one another, Huston placed the figures within the sets in shallow triangular compositions, their actions inhibited. The lighting in the film was hard and unattractive, giving the cluttered sets an edgy quality, corresponding to the edginess of the figural compositions. Many shots were taken from a low angle, particularly of Sidney Greenstreet, looking up over his corpulent seated figure which appeared to be wedged into a narrow angle of the room. In the most significant exterior sequence, Sam Spade (Bogart) is seen from below looking down a ravine at his partner Miles Archer's slain body: he seems perilously trapped between the hillside and the buildings behind it.

Warners continued to produce *films noirs* in the fifties when more of the action was moved out-of-doors, and the films lost the claustrophobic character they often had in the forties. Alfred Hitchcock's suspense films fluctuated between the closed single set mystery *(Rope, Rear Window)* and the open type *(North by Northwest, Vertigo)*. His Warner Bros. release of 1951, *Strangers on a Train,* has an open character. Edward "Ted" Haworth, just beginning a career in art direction, designed the sets. Filmed in black-and-white, the action moves restlessly from trains, to exteriors and interiors in Washington, D.C., to tennis courts and an amusement park. Although most of the decor was studio built, it tended to look less so because of the now more advanced film technology (like lacquers that in the forties gave black and white prints an added brilliance and sheen over the grainy ones of the thirties) and also because of the frequent and fast cuts that characterize much of this film.

At Warner Bros. in 1935, Errol Flynn, recently arrived from England, became a star in another type of picture, *Captain Blood.* Flynn's enormous, instantaneous popularity launched a series of costume/adventure pictures from the studio that allowed the actor to show off his considerable charm and his swashbuckling abilities. With features like *The Charge of the Light Brigade* (1936), *The Adventures of Robin Hood* (1938) and *The Sea Hawk* (1940), adventure films became associated with the Warner name. Flynn was periodically allowed to escape the 17th and 18th centuries to tame the Wild West *(Santa Fe Trail,* 1940 and *Virginia City,* 1940), or to help win World War II *(Objective Burma!* 1946).

Anton Grot's sets for Flynn's first success, *Captain Blood,* with their combination of abstraction and realistic detail, are among his best creations. They complement the tongue-in-cheek direction Michael Curtiz gave the picture. As is often true in a Curtiz/Grot film, the first shot sets the tone for the entire film. Here, a rider doing a comic Paul Revere imitation, is seen feverishly galloping his horse to the home of Dr. Peter Blood (Flynn) before a thin background of rolling landscape. The landscape is so patently artificial as it rolls repetitively by, that director and art director tell us unmistakably to "take this with a grain of salt."

The next set, ingenious in design, is the lamplit corner of Dr. Peter Blood's house. The jagged, abstract character of the set, with its crooked sign bearing Blood's name, is worthy of any of the best German Expressionist films. Curtiz next gives us a first, show-stopping close-up of Flynn through the grate in his front door. The interior of the house is semiabstract like the exterior, with large portions of the wall unarticulated and bold elements of the architecture and furniture played against it.

Blood is summoned to care for a wounded man in an inn. We see almost nothing of a set; the actors play the scene before a huge shadow of Blood caring for the wounded man on a background wall. This is one of the most minimal sets in a film of minimal settings.

The most serious scene in the film occurs next when Blood finds himself in a courtroom that is a study in minimalism (Illustration 73). Only the judges' elevated benches and a lectern before it delineate the room; the walls seem to have no definition. Grot's next major set is on the Caribbean island where Blood and the other prisoners have been sent into slavery (Illustration 74). The tropical backgrounds are schematic, like those of the first shots in England. The vivid acting of Olivia de Havilland (the love interest) and Flynn are somehow enhanced by this quality in the background; as they are so vividly real among the irreal.

Matte shots are frequently necessary in adventure pictures and in *Captain Blood* Grot uses them for the establishing shots of Port Royal and other islands; as always, the mattes stay on the screen for only a few seconds. Grot's intricate way of reusing sets (the prison camp, governor's house, and jungle) so that they are hardly recognizable the second time around, is accomplished by the lighting; many episodes take place at night. This technique gives the false impression that a much greater variety exists in setting than is actually the case.

The most ingenious moment in terms of set economy, and the most visually forceful scene, occurs when Flynn and his prison buddies escape their slavery on a night when Spanish pirates attack the English colony. The escapees creep through a long hall illusionistically created by light and shadow, with the battle for the town represented by giant shadows of fighting men looming in the background.

Flynn becomes Captain Blood as he commandeers one of the pirate ships and sails off. The subsequent action is mostly confined to the decks of accurately detailed sailing ships. In the final scene, which Flynn and de Havilland play as broad farce, the pair are reunited and Captain Blood is ensconced as governor of Port Royal. All of the film's improbable proceedings have been wonderfully helped by Grot's imaginative, memorable and economic sets; they are among the best in American film history.

The most spectacular sets ever built for a Flynn adventure film were those by Carl Jules Weyl for *The Adventures of Robin Hood* (1938). Warners budgeted the large sum of $1,600,000 for the film (it came in at $2 million) and opted to film in the three-strip Technicolor process just coming into use. Happily, Jack Warner cast Errol Flynn as Robin Hood rather than his original choice for the lead, Jimmy Cagney. William Keighley directed much of the film, but was replaced by Michael Curtiz when Warner thought the pace of the picture was dragging.

The film's location shooting of Sherwood Forest took place in a California state park, with action shifting back and forth during the story between the forest and the town of Nottingham and its Castle. Mattes are used only sparingly in the film, for the town of Nottingham and the abbey of the Bishop of Black Canon are seen from a distance, and they are of an exceptional quality for Warner Bros.

Captain Blood, 1935: 73. (Top) Anton Grot, art director. A minimalist approach was used by Grot in this courtroom whose main defining elements are the judges' benches and the lectern. Walls were stock sections that registered almost without definition in the background. 74. (Bottom) The large Caribbean island prison camp had several sections: treadmill (foreground), stockade (center), prisoners' sleeping quarters (background). Grot deleted all definition above the stockade walls.

75. *The Adventures of Robin Hood,* 1938. Carl Jules Weyl, art director. Following
Wilfred Buckland's powerful art direction of the silent version of this tale, Weyl has
a cylindrical tower with open spiraling stair at one end of the great hall (compare with
Illustration 81 on page 163), the scene of several action sequences; here maid Marian
(Olivia de Havilland) spies on Prince John.

The Castle interior is the picture's one vast set **(Illustration 75),** with the
great hall seen early in the picture in a long shot establishing its scale. The walls
are textured stone and the detailing of fireplace and window is writ large. The
mute grey walls set off the vivid costumes in this early segment, and in later

night scenes a vivid blue light whose source is unidentified falls over the walls and causes the room to glow with color. The most dramatic element in the interior is a cylindrical wall with an open stair spiraling down its side and leading to the dungeons (a revision of Buckland's sets for Fairbanks' 1925 *Robin Hood* (see **Illustrations 80–82** on pages 162, 163, and 164). The stair is an important scenic prop in the film, the mortal conflict between Robin Hood and Sir Guy of Gisbourne (Basil Rathbone) is staged on its steps and it serves Maid Marian as a platform from which to spy on evil Prince John (Claude Rains) and Gisbourne.

Weyl manages, as Grot had with his sets in *Captain Blood,* to make the great hall look different in different scenes: in the banqueting scene it is illuminated by scores of candles in iron chandeliers, colorful banners flutter from its walls, and servants roast pigs on spits in the hearth, so that it only remotely reminds one of the empty cavernous space of the earlier scene. Later in the coronation episode, when John attempts to have himself crowned king, the room is again transformed by Weyl, this time through the simpler devices of an elevated throne and wall hangings.

The exterior action sequences are all memorable, especially the archery tournament staged by Prince John to capture Robin Hood where Weyl's tents and standards form an enclosure around the open tournament field achieving a colorful sense of medieval pageant. For *The Adventures of Robin Hood,* Carl Jules Weyl became the first and only art director at Warner Bros. to win an Oscar for art direction in the heyday of the Studio.

Infrequently the Art Department was called upon to produce a stylized modern set; this task fell to Ed Carrere for the Gary Cooper film *The Fountainhead* (1949), the story of an idealistic modern architect, Howard Roark. The sets were to be emphatically modern, with Ayn Rand, the novel and the screenplay's author, insisting that they resemble those of Frank Lloyd Wright. This dictate certainly created difficulties for designer Carrere as hero Roark wants to build skyscrapers, while Wright was first and foremost an architect of houses. Roark's (Carrere's) imaginary buildings, the Enright (see **Illustration 76**) and others, are based loosely on skyscrapers of the pioneering Bauhaus architects, like Mies van der Rohe and Walter Gropius, whose style was only then finding a receptive audience in post-war America. (Gropius and van der Rohe both emigrated from Germany to the United States.)

The Fountainhead's many striking visual effects were achieved by mattes, miniatures and models, much more so than was usual for Warners, and the film is extremely contrastive in terms of mattes, sets, and locations. The large built sets, like the architects' offices are, because of the film's architectural theme, aggressively modern and so large that the actors seem to be lost in them at times (as they do likewise in Rand's turgid screenplay). The drawings of a large house that Roark does for his patrons the Wynands most resembles Wright's work, specifically his "Falling Water" of the 1930s.

76. *The Fountainhead,* 1949. Ed Carrere, art director. Architect Roark (Gary Cooper, right, with Ray Collins) gazes at a photo montage of his Enright Building. Carrere's architectural designs for the film ranged through the work of Frank Lloyd Wright and the Bauhaus architects.

Ed Carrere's career flourished at Warners in the forties and fifties and he designed films like *White Heat* (1949), which had James Cagney's explosive good-bye to his "Ma" and the world from the top of an oil tank; *Dial M for Murder* (1954), another of Hitchcock's one set pictures, with a set that is not as stylish as Paramount's for *Rear Window;* and the threadbare English seaside resort hotel for *Separate Tables* (1958, with Harry Horner).

The forties saw director Frank Capra, with his own production company, making some of his best films at Warner Bros., including *Meet John Doe* (1941) and *Arsenic and Old Lace* (1944). For the latter, Capra used in-house art director Max Parker, but for *Meet John Doe* he brought in Stephen Goosson, who had helped formulate the Capra style at Columbia where he was Supervising Art Director.

In *Meet John Doe,* as in all Capra films, the sets play an important role in defining place, as does the useful Main Street in *It's a Wonderful Life* (RKO, 1946, art director Jack Okey), that so accurately places the story in small town middle–America. The sets for *Meet John Doe* move the tale, of idealism versus cynicism in the Depression, along smoothly. Warners was the perfect place to render the realistic newspaper offices, hotel rooms, and train stations that accommodate Cooper as "John Doe," Barbara Stanwyck's confection of the common man, as he moves around the country establishing do-gooder clubs.

The last scenes involving the convention of the John Doe Clubs and Cooper's attempted suicide are the most cinematically inventive. A vast convention stadium is illusionistically realized through mattes, lighting effects, and sections of bleachers containing extras. Capra's quick crosscuts between the parts give the scene vitality and dramatic appeal.

In the final sequence, a desperate and discredited Cooper contemplates jumping from the top of a skyscraper. For this scene, Goosson built a roof terrace, a superb backdrop for the action and the best set in the picture **(Illustration 77)**. The snow-covered terrace consists of huge fluted piers that dwarf the protagonists in the medium shots. In the close-ups the piers are a granite backdrop for Cooper's drawn and haggard face, as he does some of the most moving acting of his career. Goosson designed a sort of noble and ancient-looking setting for the ancient truths about honesty and morality that Capra is expounding in this, the movie's summary scene.

Like all of the other studios, Warners patriotically dug in to give the country its fair share of war pictures. *Air Force* (1943), *Action in the North Atlantic* (1943), *Destination Tokyo* (1944) were but a few. These pictures called for a replication of military establishments and equipment: submarines, tanks, barracks, and enemy territories. Art directors were frequently offered consultant services from the War Department to insure authenticity. Newsreel footage added to the overall realism of the films, which in the usual Warner manner moved along briskly with exciting stories.

The fifties saw Warners releasing almost as many pictures per year as in the forties (a total of 246 for the decade as compared with 274 for the forties), but often they were of indifferent quality. The Studio's great contract players, both stars and secondary leads, began departing the Studio in the forties. Independent producers were contracting space on the lot, among them John Wayne, Alfred Hitchcock, and Doris Day, and very often, like Frank Capra earlier, they brought their own personnel with them, including favorite art directors. This, together with the fact that by 1950 Warner's contract art directors, Anton Grot, Carl Jules Weyl, Robert Haas and others, had left the Art Department, meant that its glory days were numbered.

The recognizable "Warner picture" became harder to discern, and by 1956 the Studio had so little regard for the old product that they sold off their entire film library to television for $21 million. Paramount and 20th Century–Fox joined Warners in dismantling their libraries in the decade, but for larger sums. Only RKO did worse monetarily, when Howard Hughes sold the Studio's 740 titles for $15.2 million.[23] Considering the revenues these films

77. *Meet John Doe,* 1941. Stephen Goosson, art director. A snowy skyscraper roof terrace provides a monumental setting for the climactic scene in which Gary Cooper contemplates suicide (left, with Barbara Stanwyck). The group (right) is led by Edward Arnold.

have generated for television, the sale sums do not seem large today, but in a decade that saw RKO and Republic Pictures cease production altogether and Warner's net profit dwindle each year, Jack Warner saw the sale as offering the Studio viable alternatives in terms of profitability.

Warners did release fine films in the fifties, including *A Star Is Born* (1954), *A Streetcar Named Desire* (1951), and the James Dean pictures, *East of Eden* (1955), *Rebel Without a Cause* (1955) and *Giant* (1956). They also tried, as did the other majors to compete with television by producing blockbuster epics *(Helen of Troy, The Land of the Pharaohs, The Silver Chalice),* but with less success.

Although filmed in Cinemascope and Warner Color rather than the gritty black and white the studio had been known for, *Rebel Without a Cause* still had the old Warner topicality and social commentary as principal components. Designed by Malcolm Bert (he also collaborated with Boris Leven on the design of *Giant*), the contemporary fifties sets, props, and carefully chosen locations present classic examples of decor working to advance the main themes and subtly commenting on them.

Shot both on location in southern California and in the studio, the film is seamless; there are no obvious breaks between what is done in studio and on the street. This is not true of all fifties films. Some of them still cultivated an artificiality in their interiors which was highly contrastive with the exterior work. The Doris Day and Rock Hudson films for Universal, for instance, make these abrupt changes.

In *Rebel Without a Cause,* the principals (three adolescents and their parents) are introduced in a police station (James Dean, one of the teenagers, has been briefly glimpsed previously, drunk on a city street), and the entwinement of their lives begins as we hear of their "crimes." The story then moves into the physically comfortable milieus in which the teenagers live their uncomfortable psychological existences. They are out of place in the police station (Are they really criminals?), but equally out of place in their affluent parents' homes.

Action then focuses on the high school; it is Dean's first day. Again the setting is conventional as is the character's costume; he will change to a tougher blue jeans image in subsequent sequences. The unconventional begins to appear as the school group is seen on an excursion to the Art Deco Griffith Park Observatory. Director Nicholas Ray skillfully manipulates the action into and around the Observatory, which is posed frightening overhead as a fight erupts between Dean and Buzz (Corey Allen), and he is challenged to play "chicken" that night to settle it.

The field of honor, dramatically lit by car headlights, overlooks a steep cliff, which Buzz accidentally drives over to his death in the "chicken" contest. The action moves quickly from place to place from this point onward, most of them familiar, except for a deserted mansion where the three teenagers (Dean, Natalie Wood, and Sal Mineo) who have by now formed bonds of various kinds, hide from the police. Mineo flees to the Planetarium in the morning hours, where the aura of menace surrounding the building is finally realized as he is slain by the police.

There is nothing particularly new here in terms of film decor, but it definitely looks different in color and Cinemascope. Art director Malcolm Bert manages to fill the screen without losing the actors in vast and unmanageable spaces, and the contemporary story comes alive through Dean, Wood, and Mineo's performances and Ray's carefully structured handling of the camera. It is almost a recognizable Warner Bros. picture.

But by the mid-fifties, although the name was to remain on the studio, the brothers were themselves pulling out of the company they had founded. The studio went on to new success in the sixties and beyond, but now the personnel on each picture was contracted independently, and this included the art director.

Looking back today at the work of the Warner Bros. Art Department, one can't help but be struck by the rich variety of inspired art direction that came out of the studio despite the frequent economic strictures, and perhaps because of them. Warner's art directors, especially Anton Grot, got to design some of the most original decor in the history of Hollywood film of the Classic period. Grot's use of minimal and German Expressionist principals for settings went far beyond what Hollywood was usually willing to allow. His early insistence (in the teens) on the sketch as a key to setting up the visual continuity of a picture, his manipulation of light, and his tendency to establish even the camera angle gave Grot a control over the finished motion picture that few other art directors had at that time.

6
Paramount

The Paramount Pictures Corporation was founded by the little known W.W. Hodkinson in 1914 as a film distribution company, but he had little to do with molding it into a giant corporation, one of the "big five" of the Hollywood studios. Hodkinson did invent the company's name and its logo, the snow-covered mountain peak — the result of a bit of doodling and reminiscing about his ancestral home in Utah. Paramount Pictures was to become the "most successful and important of the silent era film production companies"[1] through an amalgamation of the ideas of several pioneers of the motion picture industry: Jesse Lasky, Adolph Zukor and Cecil B. DeMille.

For his new distribution company, Hodkinson had signed up the Jesse L. Lasky Feature Play Company as one of his clients. At that time the company's partners: Jesse Lasky, a vaudeville musician and theatrical entrepreneur, his brother-in-law Samuel Goldfish (later Goldwyn), former glove salesman, and Cecil B. DeMille, an actor and struggling playwright (his play *The Return of Peter Grimm* had been produced by David Belasco on Broadway), had little product to offer him.[2] They had not yet released their first film, which was then in production, and would be the colossally successful *The Squaw Man* (1914) directed by DeMille and Oscar Apfel in Hollywood, the first feature film ever shot there. The idea that had prompted the formation of the Lasky Company was that the public would buy feature length films based on plays familiar to them from the stage.

In 1914, the biggest coup of Hodkinson's Paramount Company was the acquisition of the rights to distribute the films of Adolph Zukor's Famous Players Film Company. It was two years old, well established in comparison to the Lasky Company, with films to distribute, among them those of the popular Mary Pickford.

Zukor had made his first impression on the fledgling American film industry with his distribution of the French film *Queen Elizabeth* starring Sarah Bernhardt. Its success had convinced Zukor that what the movie going public wanted was to see "famous players" and he pursued personalities as varied as stage actors James O'Neill and the youthful John Barrymore for membership in his company.

By 1916 Zukor and Lasky merged into a single organization, Famous Players–Lasky, now dedicated to presenting "famous players in famous plays." It only took them one year to swallow up 12 smaller production companies; Famous Players–Lasky Corporation was on its way to the big times. They next set their sights on Hodkinson's Paramount distribution company and acquired it in the same year. Budd Schulberg has explained how his father B.P. Schulberg, then working for Zukor, perceived the objections to Hodkinson:

> Regrettably, in controlling all of the Paramount exchanges across the country. . . . He could tell them (Zukor and Lasky) how many comedies he wanted, how many dramas. . . . It was not only a case of the tail wagging the dog, Hodkinson was trying to take over our bark.[3]

The distributor's uninviting personality was apparent in the annual meeting that saw his departure. Schulberg continues,

> Before the s.o.b. Hodkinson knew what hit him, there was a vote of hands and he was out of office. He was a silent, unfriendly man, cold and abrupt in his dealing with all of us, even Mr. Zukor. When he saw his control of Paramount, and therefore of Famous Players, disappear like *that,* he didn't say a word. He simply reached for his hat and walked out.[4]

As the company evolved, Zukor handled the business and financial end of Paramount, Lasky found the plays to be produced, and DeMille and others directed the films. In late 1916, Goldfish was eased out of the company in a power struggle between the partners.

For authenticity the Lasky Company's *The Squaw Man* was to be shot by DeMille and Apfel in Arizona. It was a "feature play," following the credo of the Company. DeMille has described the feelings of the partners at that time:

> I was convinced that the future lay with . . . "feature plays"; pictures several reels long, telling a well-constructed story, well acted, and intended not as conglomerate items on the daily changing programs of the nickelodeons or as "chasers" in the vaudeville houses, but precisely as "feature" attractions which could stand on their own merits. . . .[5]

It was scenic values that prompted the partners to send a small company to Arizona to film *The Squaw Man* and it was on account of those values that DeMille made a spur-of-the-moment decision on a railroad platform in Flagstaff not to make his film there.

> In 1913, the only location department we had was our imagination. We had blithely assumed that the West was, after all, the West. Our story was laid in Wyoming. We knew that, in the fall of the year, Arizona was warmer and sunnier than Wyoming, so we had come to Arizona. It was warm. . . It was sunny. But some of us had been in Wyoming. . . .[6]

The directors and company reboarded the train and set out for the end of the line, Los Angeles, and, they hoped, a closer approximation of Wyoming. Hiring a vacant barn at the corner of Vine Street and Selma Avenue, DeMille proceeded to make his western, starring Dustin Farnum and Indian actress Red Wing. Shot out-of-doors in the California sun, the sets were detailed for the period, particularly the western saloon, papered with dozens of printed notices. **(Illustration 78.)** The story of love and devotion between Indian and white man was to become a favorite with the public; DeMille remade the film two times, in 1918 and 1931.

However, the California sun soon began to bother DeMille. Full light in every scene made films look monotonous, he thought. At the time, even night scenes were shot with sunshine beaming in through the windows.

To achieve more refined effects Lasky and DeMille took the momentous step of bringing Broadway stage designer Wilfred Buckland to Hollywood in 1914. Buckland was one of David Belasco's set designers and was well known for his innovations in lighting. Buckland and DeMille had met at the American Academy of Dramatic Arts in New York City when the latter was a student and Buckland was on the faculty teaching make-up. In his *Autobiography* DeMille gives few details of their work together despite a rather grand declaration:

> Set design today is one of the most important elements in motion picture production. If anyone is ever inclined to catalogue contributions I have made to motion pictures, I hope that my bringing Wilfred Buckland to Hollywood will be put near the head of the list.[7]

Buckland's experiments with lighting soon became known throughout the industry and were emulated by others. At first what came to be called "Lasky Lighting," the use of klieg lights to modulate the light in both indoor and outdoor scenes, created waves with the Paramount front office. DeMille recalled that when Sam Goldfish saw the first print of *The Warrens of Virginia* (1915) he sent a wire:

> Didn't we know that if we showed only half an actor's face, the exhibitors would want to pay only half the usual price for the picture? . . . Jesse [Lasky] and I wired back to Sam that if the exhibitors did not know Rembrandt lighting when they saw it, so much the worse for them. Sam's reply was jubilant with relief: for *Rembrandt lighting* the exhibitors would pay double![8]

Along with "Rembrandt" lighting, Buckland hung black velvet outside the windows, so that DeMille could finally have a dark night.

By 1917, with *Joan the Woman* designed by Buckland (see **Illustration 8** on page 17), DeMille was forging his style as a director of historical pictures, many of them conceived of as spectacles but with intimate personal stories interwoven with the epic events. For this film Buckland created brightly lit medieval exteriors rich in detail, like the timber-work town square where Joan

78. *Squaw Man,* 1914. Wilfred Buckland, art director. Dustin Farnum and Red Wing appeared in the first feature filmed in Hollywood amid realistically detailed sets.

is burned at the stake, and abstracted interiors where stark chiaroscuro lighting sent dramatic patterns over walls.

Although DeMille preferred making pictures that Lasky dubbed the "spectacle stuff," he soon was a specialist at handling the sort of sophisticated contemporary stories loaded with sexual innuendo that Paramount became known for in the teens and twenties. It was Lasky who pushed for this sort of fare. He told DeMille in January, 1917: "What the public demands today is modern stuff with plenty of clothes, rich sets, and action. Nothing prior to the Civil War should be filmed, until such time as the artists among our audiences shall comprise more than the present 10 percent."[9]

DeMille's early success with such contemporary themes came in 1915 with *The Cheat* designed by Buckland and starring Fannie Ward and Sessue Hayakawa. Ward, a society woman, is seen in luxurious settings, especially the home of wealthy Hayakawa whom she eventually shoots among his collection of Oriental vases and shrines **(Illustration 79)**. For one of these contemporary films, *Old Wives for New* (1918), DeMille invented a bathtub scene. Such scenes, with their exotic bathroom sets, were to become a trademark of the

79. *The Cheat,* 1915. Wilfred Buckland, art director. The home of Sessue Hayakawa (here with Fannie Ward) was luxuriant, with silken wall coverings, painted screens, gilded and porcelain shrines and oriental lanterns.

director's films, even the biblical ones. Wilfred Buckland did the rich and modish sets for several of these films in which DeMille groomed Gloria Swanson for stardom—she eventually reigned as queen of the Paramount lot in the twenties. Her costumes in this period were usually designed by Mitchell Leisen, who later became an art director and then a successful Paramount director.

Although they teamed for nine films, Buckland and DeMille were at odds with each other from the beginning. Buckland intruded too much into territory that the director considered his own, like grouping the actors.

Buckland's finest achievement outside of the Paramount films was his work as supervisory art director on Douglas Fairbanks' production of *Robin Hood* (1922). Working with art directors Irwin J. Martin and Edward M. Langley (both Anton Grot and William Cameron Menzies contributed to the film but were uncredited in the titles), Buckland provided ample opportunities for Fairbanks' acrobatics in his medieval castle, reputed to be the largest Hollywood set of the silents. Seen from the distance in a glass shot at the opening of the picture, its formidable built scale is made clear in both interiors and

80. *Robin Hood,* 1922. Wilfred Buckland, supervising art director, Irwin J. Martin, Edward M. Langley, art directors. An enormous medieval castle set (both interiors and exteriors) had sharply defined masonry walls, punctuated by arched openings from which drapery cascaded; it was lit with the dramatic Buckland touch.

exteriors as the camera moves in closer and the people are dwarfed by the height of crisply defined stone walls. **(Illustration 80.)** Buckland's renowned touch with lighting is evident throughout the picture, especially at one point when he uses shafts of light around the piers of the great hall to heighten the sense of their enormity.

81. *Robin Hood*, 1922. One end of the castle's great hall had a tower with open spiraling stair; the lighting defined masses of various shapes, the draperies provided a vehicle for some of Douglas Fairbanks' most memorable stunts.

In the great hall, an open stair spirals up a huge tower wall (**Illustration 81**). Director Alan Dwan used every part of the big, expensive set for action scenes, and at one point even has Fairbanks bounding around a parapet with the camera taking his point of view so that the set may be seen from above. The motif of the spiral stairway was to be used in Warner Bros.' later sound and color version of *Robin Hood* and in *Dracula* and other horror films.

First for Maid Marian and then for Richard the Lion Hearted's crusading troops, tents were fashioned by the art directors (**Illustration 82**). Deep folds of variously textured drapery create the walls of their exotic interiors and, like the castle, they are huge in scale with Oriental rugs strewn over floors, furniture inlaid with ivory, and brass lanterns and braziers completing their outfitting.

While Buckland was at work on the Fairbanks film, DeMille turned in 1921 to the French art director Paul Iribe who was to design (with others) six elaborate productions for him (*The Affairs of Anatol*, 1921; *Manslaughter*, 1922; *The 10 Commandments*, 1923; *The Golden Bed*, 1925; *The Road to*

Yesterday, 1925; and *The King of Kings,* 1927). Iribe was a well-known Parisian designer whose work was identified with the avant-garde. On their first picture, DeMille again quarrelled with his art director, his biographer explains:

> Lasky sent the suave and elegant Iribe to DeMille following Wilfred Buckland's inevitable resignation, with instructions DeMille use him; correcting DeMille's vulgar streak, Iribe created an ambience so dazzling, so intoxicating, that many art critics discussed the picture in serious journals.[10]

DeMille and Iribe subsequently became friends and their work on *The Ten Commandments* and *The King of Kings* proved lavish successors to D.W. Griffith's works, especially *Intolerance,* which the director greatly admired. With these films DeMille hit his stride as a producer of spectacles; they became synonymous with his name and are characterized by a visually ostentatious style with innumerable opulent settings often dwarfing the actors. Yet, whatever their faults, it is DeMille's pictures which most successfully lived up to the Paramount motto: "If It's a Paramount Picture, It's the Best Show in Town."

DeMille was a stickler for research in terms of the sets, but always leaned toward the most elaborate interpretation of any historic period (to the chagrin of Lasky and Zukor this was always the most expensive interpretation). DeMille's films demanded extremely large sets for the many extras he involved in the action shots. *Motion Picture News* gave an account of the set for *The Ten Commandments* **(Illustration 83)** as it stood in Guadalupe, Mexico:

> The big set representing the ancient walled city of Rameses was 750 feet wide and 109 feet high. It was the largest ever constructed for a motion picture [yes, it was larger than Griffith's *Intolerance* set], and was approached by an avenue of 24 sphinxes. This avenue was designed and built under the direction of Paul Iribe. . . . To make the huge set required 55,000 feet of lumber (enough to build 50 ordinary five-room bungalows), 300 tons of plaster, 25,000 pounds of nails and 75 miles of cable and wire for bracing.[11]

In the twenties as many of their big American stars and directors like Mary Pickford, Douglas Fairbanks and D.W. Griffith left Paramount, the company depended more on foreign film professionals including Marlene Dietrich, Maurice Chevalier, Ernst Lubitsch and Maurice Tourneur. Paramount's great supervising art director, Hans Dreier, was at home in this company of the emigre directors and artists gathered at the studio. **(Illustration 84.)** Born in Bremen, Germany, in 1885 and educated as an architect, he worked as an architect-engineer for the German government in the Cameroons, West Africa. In 1919, immediately after his release from the army of World War I, he entered German films, working for the Paramount subsidiary UFA-EFA in

82. *Robin Hood,* 1922. The tents were unsurpassed for luxury and sensuality; they were filled with silken coverings, oriental carpets, animal skins, brass lanterns and furniture inlaid with ivory.

83. *The Ten Commandments,* 1923. Paul Iribe, art director. The pylon gate of the city of Rameses with its avenue of sphinxes was done on a grandiose built scale that was to become synonymous with DeMille's epic productions. In them, the historic past was freely reinterpreted rather than replicated.

Berlin. His credits there include 34 films in four years. Among the eminent UFA designers he worked with in those formative years were Paul Leni (on *Lady Hamilton,* 1922) and Erno Metzner (on *Fridericus Rex,* 1923).[12]

Metzner was yet to become identified with the designs for G.W. Pabst's films. They did six pictures together in the period 1926–1933, but the native Hungarian had already designed a variety of film types in Germany since 1920, and was a polished professional able to work in modern or historic terms.

Leni's work was more expressionistic, along lines achieved by Walter Röhrig, Hermann Warm, and Walter Reimann in *Das Kabinett des Dr. Caligari* (1919), but soon went beyond that film in terms of technical sophistication. Both art directors had skills and the ability to manipulate decor for dramatic effect that were passed on to Dreier.

In 1923 Dreier joined Paramount in the United States, by 1932 he was supervising art director of the studio, a position he held until his retirement in 1950. Dreier's style as an art director is best defined by his work with two directors, Ernst Lubitsch, for whom he designed the polished sets for sophisticated comedies, and Josef Von Sternberg, for whom he designed the docks and city streets of the director's early crime films and then the sultry, evocative sets of his tales of sexual desire and intrigue starring Marlene Dietrich.

84. Hans Dreier, supervising art director, Paramount Pictures.

As supervising art director, Hans Dreier reigned supreme in the Paramount Art Department, as did Cedric Gibbons at MGM. Dreier had a gift for spotting talent and an ability to organize work, which he did in a hierarchical manner similar to Gibbons, but with a more personal touch. The gifted designer Boris Leven and others of Dreier's colleagues recall life in the Paramount Art Department with uniformly laudatory remarks about the tough but not unfeeling supervising art director.

Leven, born in Moscow and an architecture graduate of the University of Southern California began his career in films as a sketch artist at Paramount. He recalls:

> Hans Dreier was a tall man, whose posture was ramrod-straight, a real military bearing.... And he ran the Art Department at Paramount—where I began my movie career in 1933—as a kind of military hierarchy. You'd spend so many years as a private—a draftsman; then you'd become a corporal—an assistant art director; and so on.
>
> ... Every morning Dreier would walk through the entire department, stopping at each desk, making comments on your sketches or on the film in pre-production. Ernst Fegte was the finest designer in the department, and when I first worked

there I tried to copy Ernie's style. When Dreier saw my sketches he said, "I hired you because I liked *your* style. I don't need you if you're going to draw like Ernie."[13]

Leven's comment indicates how suggestive drawing was for film design and that Dreier was self-consciously seeking a variety of expressions from his art directors to pass on to the other technical departments.

Dreier was one of the first supervising art directors to try to raid talent from graduating classes of architecture and design schools, and he followed the European tradition of artist-teacher to such a degree that the art department was known affectionately as "Dreier College." Boris Leven explained that at Paramount

> it was my job to follow through with all . . . departments on whatever film I was designing. There was no assembly line at Paramount. We all did our own drawings, our own details. Paramount was the best studio for learning your craft—a crash course in Art Direction.[14]

Robert Boyle (*The Birds*, 1963, *North by Northwest*, 1959), a classmate of Leven's in Architecture School at the University of Southern California, was hired by Dreier in the midst of the Depression "when one architectural firm after another for which I worked, went broke."[15] Boyle says of Dreier, "He didn't say all that much. But you might be there working on an idea, maybe drawing a castle and he'd come by and look and he'd just say 'Nuh? Castles?' That's all. And believe me you didn't draw any more castles."[16]

Art director Robert Clatworthy (*Touch of Evil*, 1958, *Psycho*, 1960), who entered films in the forties, thought of Dreier as

> a good teacher, not only of work but of conduct—of discipline and responsibility. He was a very warm man. Socially he was absolutely charming. But he really ran the department—let's say he changed faces the minute he walked in the door. Then it was punctuality, discipline. He was a taskmaster.[17]

Tambi Larsen entered the Paramount Art Department near the end of Dreier's tenure there. Born in Denmark, Larsen trained in scene and costume design at the Yale Drama School (1934); he worked first as a scenic designer on Broadway and then following duty in World War II came into films early in 1946; he remembers his initial reception in Hollywood:

> I went to Paramount after interviews at all major studio Art Departments. At each place the reception was cordial, the remarks about my portfolio very pleasing, and the matter of employment deferred. . . .
> Paramount remained. The Supervising Art Director was Hans Dreier. . . . He saw I was a member of the United States Scenic Artists Local 829 . . . however, I wouldn't want to be a scenic artist in Hollywood. It was a far cry from doing backdrops for the stage. He couldn't use me as a draftsman because I had no architectural training. I wouldn't want to be an illustrator. That wasn't creative. . . .
> (At last an outspoken man who was saying: "Go back where you came from.")
> . . . so . . . all he could do was make me an assistant art director!![18]

Larsen became a full-fledged art director in 1953, fulfilling the promise Dreier had obviously seen in him and worked not only at Paramount but as an independent, designing several pictures for director Martin Ritt: *Hud* (1962), *The Spy Who Came in from the Cold* (1965), and *The Molly Maguires* (1968), and more recently Michael Cimino's *Heaven's Gate* (1979). He recalls how the studio art department got him ready for his long creative career:

> The major studio Art Department taught you how to do the job that ultimately would be expected of you. Not only did the supervising art director influence work procedure and even taste, but it was certainly expected of, say, the assistant art director, that he learn from simple observation in the drafting room, and on the stages, and in the workshops.... The studio Art Department was very proud of its proficiency. You wanted to belong in that company. Five or six pictures were on the boards of the drafting room at any time. It was a goldmine, all of it.

Dreier, like other supervising art directors of Hollywood, committed himself to print on the subject of art direction at periodic intervals, including a chapter on "Designing the Sets" in the 1937 volume *We Make the Movies.*[19] In it he stressed the absolute accuracy in detail that was sought in sets whether they represented "the habitat of Neanderthal man or the bedroom of Napoleon at St. Helena."[20] He then went on to give an account of the technical side of art direction, but gave little indication of his own style and approach to designing. Of all the great supervising art directors, he more than the others continued to personally design films, according to Hambley and Downing,

> When he [Dreier] was not making his departmental rounds, or holding the creative meeetings that he was wont quietly to dominate, he would be alone in his office. There, with the studio cat perched on his drawing board and surrounded by clouds of cigar smoke, he would produce his familiar charcoal-and-ink drawings on yellow paper, almost all of which have long since disappeared.[21]

Dreier is one of the few art directors who ever addressed the question of whether the studios promoted a certain stylistic "look" in their pictures. Dreier said no, that the visual appearance of a film depended on the story: "the art director is responsible for creating the reality of the backgrounds, against which the characters in the story move...."[22] Dreier himself won Academy Awards for the settings of such different looking Paramount films as Cecil B. DeMille's *Samson and Delilah* (1949 with Walter Tyler) and Billy Wilder's *Sunset Boulevard* (1950 with John Meehan).

Yet Dreier, with his background in German Expressionist film and his eye for significant detail, was to help create films redolent with style that help define both the Lubitsch and the Von Sternberg touch, which are so closely identified with the Paramount look of the thirties and forties.

In essence, what Dreier said is that there was no self-conscious planning of a style by studios; no one ever sat down and said this will be Paramount's style. But a look did emerge, principally because of the individual designers and directors at the studios and because of the tendency of companies to specialize in certain film genres.

Paramount's style under Dreier has a sophistication, a polished and witty elegance, different from the work of other studios. Locales are invariably at the service of dramatic plotting. Lighting, in all of its infinite variety, is used as a means to evoke mood and is a dominant tool of the designer. John Baxter writing on Hollywood in the thirties has described Paramount's style:

> Under the control of Hans Dreier ... the studio's product achieved an opulence of surface never equalled by others. ... If Metro's films had polish, Paramount films had a glow. The best of them seem gilded, luminous, as rich and brocaded as Renaissance tapestry. Decor in a Paramount production was seldom, as in Metro films, merely a background; settings, draperies, gowns insinuated themselves into the action, guiding and occasionally dictating the feel of a film.[23]

Dreier's first film in America was Lubitsch's *Forbidden Paradise* (1924), starring Paramount's exotic Polish import, Pola Negri. He worked on it briefly in New York and continued with it in California. Lubitsch and Dreier had been acquainted in Berlin and the director apparently invited him to join in his move to Famous Players–Lasky–Paramount from Pickford. Lubitsch's German films had included comedies, and historical and contemporary dramas, but in America comedies came to dominate his oeuvre, some of them having serious overtones, like the anti–Nazi *To Be or Not to Be* (1942).

For Lubitsch's comedic films, focusing on sexual foibles and the pursuit of wealth, Dreier was asked to design settings in which characterization and plot were often revealed in short scenes and individual shots. Details had to be telling and Dreier's rooms, of Paris, Vienna and other European capitals, were richly outfitted with the witty accoutrements of their occupant's lives.

Dreier and Lubitsch paired on 10 films. The art director even accompanied the director to MGM to make the *Student Prince* (1927).[24] Lubitsch's themes and style easily transferred to sound films, where the addition of smart dialogue only enhanced his ability to amuse the American public.

Trouble in Paradise (1932) was one of Lubitsch's early sound successes. Over 200 stills of Dreier's sets have survived and they illustrate the flair with which he worked on this film.[25] The set stills convey reams of information without benefit of actors or dialogue. The decor is eclectic. It follows the plot as it moves from Venice to Paris with two thieves (Herbert Marshall and Miriam Hopkins) as they connive to part rich perfume entrepreneur (Kay Francis) from her money. The sets evidence a luxuriant touch in everything from an ornate opera corridor to a big stylized Art Deco Parisian house for Kay Francis. The latter is filled with mirrors, chandeliers, silken upholstery and draperies, Deco clocks and other bric-a-brac. The film has been called "a stylized fantasy" partly because of the decor, but also because of the way Lubitsch uses it:

The stylistic flourishes in the decor are paralleled by the flourishes of composition and camera movement which give the film's direction an art deco feeling as well. Stylized compositions include the shot of the Major from inside the ladies' shop as he stands outside looking into the display case, his figure framed by a huge circle in the display window. Only when the camera pulls back do we find out where he is and what makes the circle [the display window].[26]

In his next film, *Design for Living* (1933) based on the Noel Coward play, Lubitsch used a set in the same manner, staging two entire scenes with the viewer looking in at a window.

In contrast to this technique, early in *Trouble in Paradise*, there is a scene at the Hotel Venezia, where Lubitsch takes advantage of Dreier's entire set by having the camera glide around and through it. Such movement through a set is remarkable at this moment near the advent of sound films, when the noise of camera movement had to be carefully camouflaged—in Lubitsch's films usually by music.

Frequently Lubitsch used decor to set out contradictions within the thematic material, some of them funny and others suggesting a more serious side. Although *Trouble in Paradise* is mostly played out in the circles of the rich, the opening scene is one of a garbage man at work in a grimy back alley, location unknown, from whence the camera pans to reveal a Venetian canal devested of its romance as the garbage is removed in a gondola.

From his beginnings in American films, Dreier was lucky enough to be working with a director for whom decor was more than a mere setting before which actors said their lines. In a Lubitsch film, sets frequently had a metaphoric quality, suggesting analogies to the characters' personalities or to the story line, as they did in *Trouble in Paradise*.[27]

Given his success with the design of light-hearted fare, Dreier might easily have been typecast as an art director. On the contrary, he began immediately to make a mark in vehicles that called on his knowledge of German Expressionist film. These films often featured dark and mysterious surroundings and dramatic lighting whose effects could cast much of the background into deep misty shadows. This technique is already evident in Dreier's second American film, Raoul Walsh's *East of Suez* (1925), starring the sultry Negri. Dreier (assisted by Lawrence W. Hitt) created tawdry backgrounds, full of atmospheric effects befitting a tale of mystery in the opium trade.

This dark style of Dreier's was to admirably suit the somber stories told by Josef Von Sternberg (*Underworld*, 1927), Maurice Stiller (*The Street of Sin*, 1928), and Billy Wilder (*The Lost Weekend*, 1945, with Earl Hedrick). While his light style suited the work not only of Lubitsch, but of Leo McCarey (the Marx Brothers films), Cecil B. DeMille, Mitchell Leisen and others.

Seldom have director and art director seemed so perfectly suited to one another as were Josef Von Sternberg and Hans Dreier. Although other eminent director/art director pairs come easily to mind (von Stroheim and Day,

Minnelli and Ames), the distinctive qualities which set Von Sternberg's art apart—his moody and arresting effects—stem directly from Dreier's decor. Together they made 12 films: *Underworld* (1927), *The Last Command* (1928), *The Drag Net* (1928), *The Docks of New York* (1929), *The Case of Lena Smith* (1929), *Thunderbolt* (1929), *Morocco* (1930), *Dishonored* (1931), *An American Tragedy* (1931), *Shanghai Express* (1932), *The Scarlet Empress* (1934), and *The Devil Is a Woman* (1935), among them some of the most important work that either was to do. Dreier did not return to Germany to participate in the making of Von Sternberg's classic *The Blue Angel* (1930) at Paramount's UFA studio in Berlin, but by then the essentials of the Von Sternberg style had been worked out in America.

Beginning with *Underworld*, a forerunner of the many successful gangster movies of the thirties, it was clear that the director and art director had a special rapport. Von Sternberg was a director who had enormous input on the sets for his films, and he became a master at integrating the action with the decor. Von Sternberg's active participation in the scenic preparation for his films came in part from his own love for it. He amassed an extensive art collection including works by Van Gogh, Brancusi and other modernists, as well as a large library of books on art.

The sets for Von Sternberg's films are actors themselves. Not only do they create the mood for each scene, but they insist upon being part of the action. They must be stepped through, seen through, they interfere with the actors. Curtains fall into faces, the camera moves with erotic intent through crevices in the wall—first blocking and then admitting the viewer. In a Von Sternberg film the surroundings engage the actors.

Viennese born Von Sternberg grew up in New York City, where as a youth he worked in a lace house on Fifth Avenue. He has explained,

> After some weeks I became familiar with the differences between Venetian lace and rose point, Alençon, Chantilly, Valenciennes, Brussels, and Swiss . . . [and] it occurs to me that this painfully acquired knowledge may have bobbed up in my films in my use of coarse fishnets to conceal some of the actors.[28]

It was actually much more than fishnets that he used to both conceal and reveal the actors; Von Sternberg's films evidence a feeling for materials and textures that has seldom been seen in films, and most of the laces he so carefully enumerated turn up somewhere in his images. His comment about concealing the actors is a crack typical of him. As Budd Shulberg has observed "Von Sternberg had a way of talking to his actors as if they were slightly retarded children."[29] On the other hand, his relationship with his art director was apparently cordial and characterized by respect.

Von Sternberg's method of working with Dreier was to describe his ideas for sets and their dressing, sometimes providing a rough sketch. Dreier used these ideas as the bases for detailed drawings, complete in all respects. Von

Sternberg corrected or approved the drawings and the sets were begun. Von Sternberg's lighting preferences: spotlit faces, back-lit hair, and often a beam from the side to soften contours were respected by the designer. The director sometimes used gauzes over the camera lens to nourish the irreality and dreamlike aspects of his films. As Von Sternberg was not a director who favored action scenes, the viewer is usually afforded ample opportunity to linger over and savor Dreier's decor.

Von Sternberg had had a bumpy road in Hollywood prior to joining Paramount in 1926. His first film *The Salvation Hunters* (1925), done on a shoestring and shot on the wharfs of San Pedro, had gained immediate attention. Von Sternberg has said that one of the principal parts in the location shooting was played by a huge crane — an early expression of a devotion to inanimate objects as purveyors of meaning in his films. Rudolf Arnheim has described what he calls a "salient characteristic" of the director's work:

> . . . the important part played by objects, inanimate things, which, by showing the effects of human actions or symbolically reflecting the human, became the most powerful means of cinematic expression.[30]

Dreier was the art director who designed or found the objects that Von Sternberg saturated with meaning.

Von Sternberg's first assignment at Paramount was the film that made a star of George Bancroft and made the director's name a household word. In *Underworld*, developed from an idea of Ben Hecht's, Von Sternberg and Dreier were, as Andrew Sarris has put it, "improvising in an unexplored subject area."[31] Episodic as finally scripted, the story follows the decline and fall of "Bull" Weed (Bancroft), with sets, not wholly realistic, depicting city streets where holdups take place, and well-dressed apartments, the reward of crime. The most cinematically rich moment in the picture is at the gangsters' ball, where Evelyn Brent, as Bancroft's girl "Feathers" McCoy, is crowned queen to the drunken revelry of the crowd. The distances of the hall are suggested through the brilliant play of light and shadows seen through streamers and clouds of confetti; Sarris concludes, "Sternberg's underworld is visually rendered as a hell of false illusions."[32]

Von Sternberg's next film, *The Last Command* (1928), starred Emil Jannings in a story suggested by Ernst Lubitsch. The convoluted plotline concerns a former czarist general, Sergius Alexander, who has fallen to the level of a Hollywood movie extra. Dreier built a gigantic set for the film representing Russian streets and interiors and also Hollywood studio offices and stages — the latter, readily available at Paramount, did not suit Von Sternberg.

For *The Docks of New York* (1928), the director again returned to an urban American milieu for a story of lust and love among the poor working class. Dreier created seedy tenement rooms, dockside dives, and in the studio tank the grimy wharfs of New York harbor, dramatically lit and shrouded in mist.

Again the director seemed to revel in Dreier's atmospherically rendered settings, allowing star George Bancroft what seem to be redundant trips through the saloon, the fishnet of the wharfs, and clutter of corridors.

Among the talented art directors working with Dreier at Paramount in the thirties and forties were Roland Anderson, Franz Bachelin, Haldane Douglas, Earl Hedrick, John Meehan, Hal Pereira, Walter Tyler, Robert Clatworthy, and Wiard Ihnen. Ihnen, an early film entrepreneur and an art director beginning in 1919, had been one of the first to work for Famous Players in their East Coast art department. Robert Haas was hired to set up the department and in turn recruited Ihnen from his job as an architect. Ihnen had known a clever office boy "by the name of Van Nest Polglase" while working in architecture and "I suggested that we hire him because I thought he was bright enough to come on as a draftsman!"[33] Polglase would become the supervising art director at RKO. In the course of his career Ihnen was to work for most of the major studios. His art direction of *Wilson* (20th Century–Fox, 1944) and of *Blood on the Sun* (Cagney, United Artists, 1945) won him Oscars.[34]

Although not given screen credit, Wiard Ihnen designed the *Blond Venus* (1932) for Von Sternberg and has left an account of his work with the director:

> On *Blond Venus* . . . I worked with Von Sternberg only. . . . Strangely, V.S. would never look at the sets ahead of time. He approved of my sketches and only saw the set on the morning of the shooting. I guess he wanted to be surprised.
>
> A side lite: one of the sets was a music hall in Paris. I designed a shot that brought Dietrich in from the street and followed her up stairs and into the box. This required the use of a boom. This piece of equipment was new at the studio. When Von S. saw it . . . he wanted to know who the hell had ordered it. I stepped forward and confessed to having done so, explaining how I had planned the shot and the set. It would have been impossible without it. He grumbled a lot but later in the day I visited the set and not only was he using it but he was actually sitting on it in the place of the camera operator!
>
> After that he rode a boom almost constantly. We got along well and later I designed the very modern dressing room built for Dietrich.[35]

Blond Venus had Marlene Dietrich playing a devoted mother, wife and former stage star who tries to support her ailing husband (Herbert Marshall) through a serious illness by returning to the stage. Set first in the couple's unassuming New York apartment, there is much spotlighting and backlighting of Dietrich. She is seen through curtains, exquisitely framed by elements in the apartment, and then as the plot leads to a lecherous agent's office she stands next to such obvious symbols as a nude statue of Venus.

Marlene's next incarnation is in the dense backstage clutter of theatres and nightclubs. In a nightclub dense with vegetation she performs a jungle "voodoo" number and emerges from a monkey suit. She has fallen for wealthy underworld figure Cary Grant, and he sets her up in a sleek apartment replete with satin sofas, flowers, and grand piano. As is also true in Von Sternberg/

Dreier films, very few special effects are used in *Blond Venus* — a couple of film clips and some back projection — but for the most part the fully-realized individual sets are lingeringly examined with almost no quick cuts to divert the viewer.

When Dietrich's husband (Herbert Marshall) returns from the cure she has financed, he finds out about her sordid life, refuses her love and demands their child. Fleeing from him she drifts south, going from bad to worse with the law at her heels. Finally, forced to give up her child, Dietrich is seen in a flop house. The tacky yet lush "Southern" interiors are entered through run-down shutters and are cluttered with lattice and plants obscuring momentarily our view of the star, who is sensuously lit and as ravishing looking as ever, despite the wear and tear.

The final scenes in the film find the now hard-bitten heroine the reigning star of Parisian nightlife **(Illustration 85)**, making lesbian gestures to members of the audience and wearing a white tuxedo. She is rediscovered by Grant in a swank but cold nightclub, whose decor is a metaphor for the changes Marlene has undergone. Her dressing room — with scalloped drapes, lace curtains, flowers, silver wine buckets, crystal goblets — is in total contrast to her drab yet vibrant dressing room at the beginning of the film.

Cary Grant still loves her, they are engaged, but seeing how unhappy she is without her child, he reunites her with the ungrateful husband. In the final scene, we are returned to the humble apartment and there is a replay of the opening sequence in which the child is put to bed by its parents to the tune of an angel music box. Throughout the film the decor has worked intimately with the plot — reenforcing and commenting on it.

Dreier's absence from *The Blond Venus* may be explained by the fact that he was designing six films single-handedly for release in 1932, including such lavish productions as Frank Borzage's *A Farewell to Arms,* Lubitsch's *Trouble in Paradise,* and Von Sternberg's own *Shanghai Express.* It is clear that, by then, Ihnen and the Paramount Art Department understood Von Sternberg's preferences as they had been worked out earlier with Dreier.

In 1934 for *The Scarlet Empress,* starring Dietrich as Catherine II with Sam Jaffe as the mad Grand Duke Peter, Dreier created his most exotic and expressionistic settings ever. Lotte Eisner in discussing German expressionist film, could have been commenting on the *mise-en-scène* of *The Scarlet Empress;* she observed that "Expressionism constructs its own universe, it does not adapt itself to a world already in existence."[36]

Dreier designed the highly stylized principal sets himself, assisted by German artist Richard Kollorsz and by Boris Leven, then working as a sketch artist, who together drew and executed the many Russian icons and paintings seen in the decor. **(Illustration 86.)** Peter Ballbusch, a Swiss sculptor, created in plaster-of-Paris the strange and tortured oversize sculpted images that people the Russian Royal Palace and Chapel.

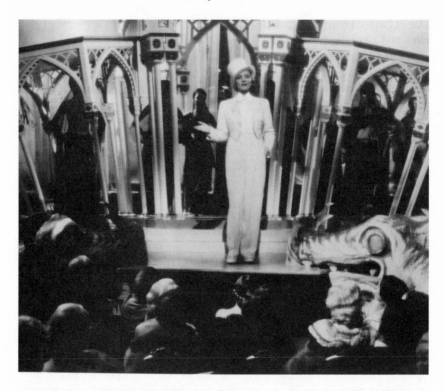

85. *Blonde Venus,* 1932. Wiard Ihnen, art director, uncredited. Tuxedo clad Marlene
Dietrich sings in a swank Parisian nightclub before pointed arches filled with harem
girls; one of several elaborate nightclub settings in the film.

Dreier, while working at UFA in Berlin, had designed the Dmitri
Buchowetzki film *Peter the Great* (1922), which dealt with a similar theme, but
it looked nothing like Von Sternberg's vision of the corrupt and erotically explicit Russian court.[37] The decor in *The Scarlet Empress* is fascinating to the
point of diversion — alternating between what seem like spaces vast in dimensions with spaces that seem crowded and small. A frequently used stylistic
device is the spotlighting of actors together with specific decorative elements.
In the reception scene, Louise Dresser as Empress Elizabeth awaits Catherine
on a broad flight of stairs in the middle ground of the image. A huge, brilliantly lit sculpted eagle hangs behind her, the reaches of the palace are dark;
eagle and Empress loom menacingly over the scene. Giant columns rise at the
side of the room, while in the foreground, back to us, a sculpture of a
seminude saint yearns heavenward with a tortured gesture. The grotesque
decorative elements entrap the human characters.

Dietrich is opulently dressed in costumes almost as suffocating as the settings.[38] The story follows her life, its erotic and power seeking side, from a

86. *The Scarlet Empress,* 1934. Hans Dreier, art director. Stylization and fantasy played a greater role in the formulation of the decor for this film than was usually permitted in American films (here expressionistic religious icons surround Marlene Dietrich).

childhood milieu where she is enmeshed in a world of mechanical toys, through her arranged betrothal, seduction by the king's messenger, to the birth of an illegitimate child and eventually the murder of the king and her ascension to the throne. At the end, the viewer realizes that she will be as despotic and corrupt as her demented and crippled husband Peter had been; she has joined the other grotesques in the royal collection.

Von Sternberg's association with Dietrich and Dreier was to end with their next film together, *The Devil Is a Woman* (1935). The director left Paramount and drifted first to Columbia and then to other studios for the remaining few pictures he was to make as his career faltered. His Paramount pictures, although most of them were critically successful, had not been consistently good box office. Dreier, in a manner analogous to that of Richard Day with von Stroheim, still had decades of fine work ahead of him when Von Sternberg's career was coming to a premature close. Von Sternberg was to work with such talented art directors as Stephen Goosson at Columbia and Boris Leven at United Artists, but his style and its finest articulation had been worked out with Hans Dreier in the Paramount years.

The thirties were not particularly happy years at Paramount — the giant of the silent era, unprepared for sound, filed for bankruptcy in the year 1933. They recovered enough to have the proceedings lifted in 1934, but were never to regain their position of the teens and twenties over the next decades.

Dreier continued to make interesting pictures with a variety of directors in the period, like Rouben Mamoulian's *Dr. Jekyll and Mr. Hyde* (1932), but he also had to work on scenically dry-as-dust films like the Bulldog Drummond series and then the Hope and Crosby road pictures that were a mainstay of Paramount in the forties, beginning with the *Road to Singapore* (1940).

A bright moment came in 1942 with *Holiday Inn,* a film on which Dreier worked with Roland Anderson. Anderson had come into art direction in the early thirties and he spent most of his career working for Paramount, collaborating with Dreier many times and then with Hal Periera when he became the head of the art department in 1950. His work includes several DeMille films, among them: *Cleopatra* (1934), *The Plainsman* (1937), and *Reap the Wild Wind* (1942). Anderson was adept at all genres and following Dreier's retirement, although it does not appear to have been his speciality, even designed realistic dramas, like the splendid period piece *Carrie* (1952 with Hal Pereira), and the low-key *The Country Girl* (1954).

Holiday Inn, a musical show-biz romance starring Fred Astaire, Bing Crosby, and Marjorie Reynolds, was shot in black and white (color would have been preferable). The settings handsomely compliment the engagingly light-hearted story as it moves from New York nightclub life, done in an exuberant Art Deco, to a rustic inn where Bing Crosby retires to mull over unrequited love. The inn is a Hollywood version of New England, combining modern features with Early American decor. The art directors obviously had a field day coming up with hilarious scenic changes for the inn's ballroom as they concocted sets for the theatrical shows given on occasions like Lincoln's and Washington's birthday and the Fourth of July.

In the forties Dreier frequently collaborated with the distinguished German art director Ernst Fegte. A native of Hamburg, Fegte had entered films in 1919. When he came to America in the early thirties he became a unit art director at Paramount, first at the Astoria, N.Y. studio and from 1932 in Hollywood. A fine draftsman, whose style was mimicked by young art directors; Fegte won an Academy Award with Dreier for the color sets of Mitchell Leisen's costume romance *Frenchmen's Creek,* an interpretation of a Daphne du Maurier story.

Robert Usher, another talented designer, often worked under Dreier's supervision on the lighter fare that Paramount was producing in the forties,

87. *Double Indemnity,* 1944. Hans Dreier, Hal Periera, art directors. In this classic *film noir,* blonde bombshell Barbara Stanwyck, among prosaic canned foods in a super-market, plots her husband's murder with Fred MacMurray.

especially the romances and comedies directed by Mitchell Leisen (Usher did a total of six films with the director).

In the same decade, Dreier once again worked with an emigre director, the Austrian Billy Wilder. Wilder had been primarily a script writer in Europe, but after coming to the States in 1934 he combined writing with directing.

Dreier worked with Wilder from the very beginning of his career as a director in America, on the Ginger Rogers' comedy *The Major and the Minor* (1942, with Roland Anderson), a piece of fluff that has Rogers impersonating a minor to save money on a train ticket. However, their work together is best represented by a series of memorable and often grimly realistic pictures like *Double Indemnity* (1944, with Hal Periera) starring Fred MacMurray and Barbara Stanwyck and *The Lost Weekend* (1945, with Earl Hedrick) and starring Ray Milland. Their last picture together, for which they both won Academy Awards was *Sunset Boulevard* (1950, with John Meehan) in which Wilder brought together in the cast such former Paramount greats as Gloria Swanson and Cecil B. DeMille.

Double Indemnity, a classic *film noir*, is set in the Los Angeles of Raymond Chandler (he did the screenplay with Wilder) and James M. Cain (who wrote the original novel). The film makes excellent use of locations, although like most films of this genre in the early forties, 90 percent of it was shot in interiors.

In the opening scene a wounded insurance salesman played by Fred MacMurray is seen in his office, where, in flashbacks, his story of desire and murder is spilled into a dictaphone on the desk. A routine matter has brought him to a brightly sunlit street in Glendale and Barbara Stanwyck's house, a Spanish-revival style place. Admitted by a maid to its interior, which is drab in comparison to its occupant, whose hair is bleached blond and who likes wearing boldly printed blouses. It soon seems clear that the house represents the stultifying taste of her much older husband. Stanwyck immediately recognizes in MacMurray the perfect vehicle for doing away with her burdensome husband and making it profitable (through the victim's life insurance).

The pair must meet surreptitiously to plot the crime and the locale chosen for this is the orderly and ordinary world of a Jerry's Supermarket on Melrose Avenue **(Illustration 87)**. As they rendezvous Stanwyck pretends complete absorption in the mundane task of selecting groceries from neatly stacked shelves as she urges MacMurray on to the eventual murder.

The sets for this film are few, and are not discursive in the earlier Dreier manner of the Lubitsch and Von Sternberg pictures. The art directors have picked up their cues for the sets from the sparsely written story itself and from the basic preferences of director Wilder, who rarely shows an interest in evocative decor.

The closest that Dreier came, in his partnership with Wilder, to the style of symbol and metaphor he had used in the twenties and thirties was in the

88. *Sunset Boulevard,* 1950. Hans Dreier, John Meehan, art directors. Playing a nar-
cissistic silent film star, Gloria Swanson dances with William Holden in an elegant,
decaying 1920s mansion crammed with her memorabilia, mainly portraits.

decor for *Sunset Boulevard.* Yet by 1950 the times had already changed
significantly. The principal set, a decaying twenties mansion, as conceived by
John Meehan with Dreier supervising, was not built in the studio. It was a real
mansion, with a swimming pool, and a winding staircase. But the mansion's
atmosphere and its interior decor were the invention of Meehan and Dreier

(with set decorators Sam Comer and Ray Moyer). (See **Illustration 88.**) Table tops, piano, every available surface in the house's grand salon was densely cluttered with photographs and memorabilia of the aging actress's (Gloria Swanson) career as a Hollywood movie star of the silent era. Her exotic bedroom is bizarrely draped; the bed is an erotic dream ship.

The interiors perfectly capture the essence of the star's persona and encapsulate her past, leaving no breathing space. They are interiors that will, almost literally, end up suffocating William Holden, the down-on-his-luck screenwriter and then gigolo who cannot seem to escape their confines. The coffin — for Swanson's pet monkey — introduced early in the film is a metaphor for this house, one that Wilder repeatedly suggests throughout the film (Erich von Stroheim as the butler/ex-husband of Swanson, plays funereally on the house's organ). The setting of *Sunset Boulevard* ranks with best the Paramount Art Department ever created.

Dreier's last prestigious film, released in 1951 after his retirement to Europe to live and travel, was George Stevens' *A Place in the Sun.* It was a brilliant revision of Theodore Dreiser's famous novel *An American Tragedy,* which had been filmed earlier by Paramount in 1931 with Von Sternberg directing (after Sergei Eisenstein had been fired from the job) and with studio built sets by Dreier. Stevens' conception was to film much of the picture on location in the Lake Tahoe area, and then to combine the location footage with several studio built interiors and exteriors.

Walter Tyler was the unit art director on the film and the settings are telling in all details. The most personally revelatory sets in *A Place in the Sun* are those for the two female protagonists, both of whom are in love with George (Montgomery Clift); the sets describe exactly the character of their lives. The rented room of homely Alice Tripp (Shelley Winters) is dull and ordinary, with the only softening touches coming from some cheap souvenirs.

Gorgeous and wealthy Angela Vickers (Elizabeth Taylor), whom George (Clift) falls in love with and wants to marry, is seen in an environment that contrasts completely with factory-worker Alice's. She is first seen by George speeding past him in a Cadillac convertible, and then later in the mansions of the rich, with their ballrooms and billiard rooms, that are her natural habitat.

The last part of the film is set mainly in the modern lakeside retreat of the Vickers' family **(Illustration 89)**. Built of splendid stone, timbers and glass, its terraces stretch out toward a manicured lawn and Lake Tahoe beyond. Besides Angela, these places are also what George covets, they are what constitutes success in America. The director's cuts between the poor and the rich

89. *A Place in the Sun,* 1951. Hans Dreier, Walter Tyler, art directors. The stylish fifties decor of the Vickers' lake house seems to overwhelm Montgomery Clift (with Sheppard Strudwick); it represents the world of his dreams of wealth and power.

90. *Rear Window,* 1954. Hal Pereira, Joseph MacMillan Johnson, art directors. An inner court of apartments is the architectural framework for this suspense film. The camera pans repeatedly around it and into its apartments as the story unfolds.

settings are riveting, and build sympathy for the weak young man's position. Who wouldn't prefer Angela's world to Alice's?

Alice's spaces are small and cramped while from the start Angela's are open and spacious—like the columned foyer of George's uncle's house where he meets her for the first time, the ballroom where they dance and fall in love, and the mountain retreat open to the landscape beyond. At the end of the film, with George's execution for murder inevitable, Angela's spaces seem to close in around her; winds rattle through the mountain retreat as winter approaches and she sits in narrow confines.

The memorable settings for *A Place in the Sun* are as emotionally charged as the screenplay, and must be part of the reason a critic like Charles Chaplin, paying tribute to director and studio, could say that *A Place in the Sun* "was the best film ever to come out of Hollywood."[39]

Dreier's tenure at Paramount was followed by that of Hal Pereira, who headed the Art Department from 1950 until it closed down in 1967–1968. Unlike Dreier, Pereira is not reputed to have been much involved in the designing of films on which he was supervising art director. Chicago born, he had studied at the University of Illinois, and joined his brother William Pereira's Chicago architectural firm in 1933 where he remained for seven years. He then turned to designing for theatre and joined Paramount as unit art director in 1942, working on a variety of films such as *Double Indemnity* and *Blue Skies* (1946). In the late forties he worked at Paramount's New York office doing special effects. Although Pereira won an Academy Award for *The Rose Tattoo* (1955, with Tambi Larsen), his work does not have the highly individualistic look that so much of Dreier's did.

When Hitchcock returned to Paramount in the fifties (he had filmed *Jamaica Inn* there in 1939) to make several films including *Rear Window* (1954) and *To Catch a Thief* (1955), Pereira together with Joseph MacMillan Johnson are credited with the settings. *To Catch a Thief* brilliantly filmed against locations in and around Monaco, mostly involved the manipulation of existing decor and the harmonizing of studio interiors with it. However, *Rear Window* was shot exclusively in the studio and largely using a single set, a claustrophobic interior court of a group of New York apartments. **(Illustration 90.)** Every portion of the set was built to accommodate the action and Hitchcock's economical direction.

The court and its inhabitants are first seen in a pan shot (pans of the court are used continually throughout the picture), and then are minutely examined as a photographer (Jimmy Stewart) spies on his neighbors while recuperating from a broken leg. A certain artificial quality in the set and its lighting abets the extreme stylization of the film, and makes what the human characters do spring vividly to life.

As Stewart looks in through his neighbors' windows, first normally and then with binoculars and camera lenses, fragments of the set are isolated and elements of the architecture, like window surrounds, frame the action. Many private worlds are revealed with the interconnected apartment houses being their principal commonality. Although a single suspense story is told in *Rear Window,* the character of the film is reminiscent of other one set pictures like *Grand Hotel,* where many stories are told within a single architectural framework.

By the time the Hitchcock films were made Paramount was becoming a service company to independent producers and directors. Independent art directors like Harry Horner were now brought in to do individual films, like his splendid Victorian period film *The Heiress* (1949) directed by William Wyler. There were still fine art directors at Paramount, but the great days of the studio, and with it the Art Department were drawing to a close. John Meehan, native Californian and member of the Paramount Art Department since 1935 left in 1950 for work elsewhere and others drifted away too. The official close of the Art Department came in 1968.

7

20th Century–Fox

The huge Art Deco trademark dramatically blazoned across the screen to the sound of a trumpet flourish declared that 20th Century–Fox was a modern movie company. Only formed in 1935, it was the sole major Hollywood company to be inaugurated in the midst of the great Depression. Its first head of production was Darryl F. Zanuck, who remained for the next 21 years, making all the principal decisions, defining the company's taste, and even dictating many of the film stories.

Zanuck had spent his formative years at Warner Bros., first as a writer, then as a producer, and finally as head of production. He brought with him from that association a penchant for social conscience, crime, and musical films. In dramas he had a preference for historical settings, so that people soon began calling the new company, 16th Century–Fox.

20th Century–Fox was an amalgamation of the larger Fox Films, founded by William Fox in the silent era, and the much smaller Twentieth Century Pictures, which Zanuck and Joseph Schenck had put together in 1933. Fox had parlayed a nickelodeon into a chain of theatres when the Motion Picture Patents Company tried to force him out of business. He courageously fought the Trust, suing them under the Sherman Anti-Trust Act, and winning a victory in 1912. William Fox first made pictures in New York and New Jersey; then in 1916 he moved to Los Angeles where he opened a studio on Western Avenue and Sunset Boulevard. By 1928 he was providing films for the 1,000 theatres he owned nationwide and by 1928 he was building a vast addition to his studio space, the Westwood Studio, in Beverly Hills; it is still the home of 20th Century–Fox despite the sell-off of the huge backlot for the commercial development of Century City.

Fox had sound-on-film developed for his company and called it Movietone (the Westwood facilities were dubbed Movietone City in the thirties); it was the sound system that other studios (Paramount, Universal, MGM, and Columbia) soon accepted, adding to the profitability of his company. Prone to overextending his resources, in 1929 Fox acquired 53 percent of Loew's

Corporation in an attempt to purchase MGM. The stock market crash squelched his scheme; Fox lost Loew's and was ousted from the company in 1930.[1]

In his first two years as head of Twentieth Century Pictures Zanuck made 18 films. All but one made money, and among the most successful were pictures drawing on history, including *The House of Rothschild, The Mighty Barnum, Clive of India,* and *Les Misérables.* The fledgling company rented studio space at United Artists and worked with a skeletal staff. This shows up in a thinness of setting for movies that featured major actors, like *Clive of India* (1935), which starred Ronald Colman. This exceptionally dull movie illustrates how even a great art director like Richard Day could be stymied by a jumpy, hackneyed story and a lack of commitment to built sets.

The plot of *Clive of India* is so schematic that a profuse number of title cards had to be inserted, as in silent films, to tell the audience where the story is placed and why. Beginning in 1748 we see Clive's rise to power, decline and rise again. Because the story flits from place to place most of the sets are fragmented and shallow. Though the film is well-lit throughout, it is difficult to miss a certain phoniness in the many matte shots (Indian cities and countryside). The call to authenticity in the sets seems never to have been raised, and interiors like an Indian prince's palace, with its illusion of polished black and white marble floors, comes straight out of the Hollywood musical tradition. One is grateful for the many times Day uses fog and mist to cover the settings which he must constantly reuse. There is no unusual or imaginative use of historical decor in this film like that in Warner's of the same year *(Captain Blood),* nor is there the attention to authentic detail that would have been put into the sets at Paramount or at MGM.

The quality of the historical pictures was to gradually improve once Zanuck was settled as head of the merged company. At first, Zanuck was preoccupied with garnering more star power for the company rather than improving the technical departments. At the time of the merger, the new studio could boast of only two big box office draws among its contract players — Shirley Temple and Will Rogers — and Rogers was to die in a plane crash during the first year of the new company's existence. Zanuck was never able to compete with MGM or Warners in the star department and seems to have realized this early on; he decided that the screenplay would be the star in his productions.

The pictures that kept 20th Century–Fox afloat in the first five years of its existence were those starring Shirley Temple. The child star topped the *Motion Picture Herald*'s box office draw category every year from 1935 to 1938. One of the best things about her films for the new company was that they were cheap to produce. Roy Pickard commented, "She didn't need an expensive co-star..., the stories were simple, brought in on time and had few sets."[2]

Whether placed in the 19th century (*The Littlest Rebel,* 1935 and *Dimples,* 1936) or contemporaneously (*Poor Little Rich Girl,* 1936, or *Little*

Miss Broadway, 1938) Shirley Temple brought such a sincere touch to the sentimental stories and such a flair for music to the production numbers, usually the only scenes with elaborate sets, that the viewer scarcely noticed the background.

Shirley Temple had proven that sets didn't matter very much when she made her first lengthy film appearance in Fox's big budgeted *Stand Up and Cheer* (1934). She sang and danced with James Dunn to the tune of "Baby, Take a Bow" and the expensive production numbers had paled in comparison. The audience was entranced by her, forgetting the marshalled rows of chorus girls, big props and sets when they went home, but remembering the girl with the bouncy curls.

Zanuck at Twentieth Century Pictures had produced a big musical before the merger, *Folies Bergère* (1935); it starred Maurice Chevalier playing a double role. It too had tried to emulate the Berkeley style with legends of chorus girls twirling umbrellas on ramps in "clouds" as Maurice Chevalier crooned to Ann Sothern in a number called "Rhythm of the Rain," one of the innumerable song-and-dance numbers done in a downpour in the twenties and thirties. This was simply a style unsuited to the child star and Zanuck reserved it for his female musical star of the thirties, Alice Faye, and later for the other 20th Century–Fox "blonds," Betty Grable in the forties and Marilyn Monroe in the fifties.

William Fox had formulated an Art Department already in the twenties, with William S. Darling joining his company in 1922 to become chief art and technical director shortly thereafter. Harry Oliver, a well known art director of the silent film, had joined Fox in the late twenties to design such memorable films as *Seventh Heaven* (1927) and *Street Angel* (1928), and Jack Schulze was a member of the Department from 1929 onward for several years before he became an independent art director.

Darling (see **Illustration 91**) was born Vilmos Bela Sanderhazi in Hungary in 1882, when it was still a part of the Austro-Hungarian Empire. Educated first in Budapest in the fields of architecture and painting, Darling then proceeded to Paris where he was a scholarship student at the École des Beaux Arts, and had a studio in the same building with fellow art student Lionel Barrymore (they worked together years later on *The Little Colonel,* 1936). He migrated to the United States in 1905 and set up shop as a portrait painter to New York City notables, including Billy Sunday and F.W. Woolworth.

Darling's first work in motion pictures was with the American Film Plant in Santa Barbara (date unknown). He then found his way into the employ of then independent producer Louis B. Mayer. Darling must have been fairly well established in his craft by the time he joined Fox on the big production of *Monte Cristo* (1922), starring John Gilbert and directed by Emmett J. Flynn.

Darling's first Academy Award and greatest celebrity while at Fox came for the design of an epic film *Cavalcade* (1933). Based on a Noel Coward stage

91. William S. Darling, supervising art director, 20th Century-Fox.

play, it traced the lives of an aristocratic British family and their servants for the first 32 years of this century. (**Illustrations 92 and 93.**) Darling had the opportunity of recreating bits of Edwardian England—an upper-class home, a pub, a music hall—and larger scenes of war, including the departure of British troops for battle in South Africa. Using a camouflaged Catalina ferryboat as the troop ship, Darling created an authentic dockside setting for the hundreds of extras acting as soldiers. Impressive in detail, the many large sets, like Trafalgar Square, were praised for their realism and for providing a telling commentary on the changing times of the early years of the century. Darling's many other outstanding pictures of later years, like *The Rains Came* (1939), *The Song of Bernadette* (1943, with James Basevi), *The Keys of the Kingdom* (1944), *Anna and the King of Siam* (1946, with Lyle Wheeler), show this same preference for carefully researched and rich detail.

In the early years of the newly merged 20th Century–Fox Studio, the Art Department was put to work on series (Charlie Chan, Mr. Moto, the Temple pics), and on films grooming the new crop of actors Zanuck was promoting, especially Tyrone Power (*Lloyd's of London*, 1936, and *In Old Chicago* and *Alexander's Ragtime Band*, both 1938), and Alice Faye (*You Can't Have Everything*, 1937).

92. *Cavalcade*, 1933. William S. Darling, art director. Outdoor stalls cram the narrow streets of one of Darling's many period sets — both upper and lower class — in this saga of the first three decades of the century.

93. *Cavalcade,* 1933. Shimmering gold cloth covered walls, decorative zigzag patterns and a modern tapestry define this elegant Art Deco dining room.

In Old Chicago was a favorite project of Zanuck's, one in which he invested $1,800,000 of the company's money, placing it among the most expensive Hollywood films of the decade. The historic settings of the Chicago of 1871, the year of the great fire, were lovingly set forth by Beaux-Arts trained Darling, assisted this time by unit art director Rudolph Sternad. Most of the fictional action takes place in their often lavish interior settings, particularly two saloons which are not destroyed until the last half of the film in one of the most spectacular fire scenes ever filmed. The special effects team of H. Bruce Humberstone, Fred Sersen, Ralph Hammeras, and Louis J. Witte prepared a fire that roared for 25 minutes of on-screen time (it had actually lasted three days on the back lot of the Beverly Hills studio and cost $750,000 to stage). As directed by Henry King, *In Old Chicago* became a disaster classic of the mid-thirties—a period that perfected the disaster film—and added to the public's impression that 20th Century–Fox despite its corporate title was most expert at producing stories anchored in the historic past.[3]

Alexander's Ragtime Band is set in the not so distant past of the present century, beginning around 1915 in a San Francisco of the ragtime era; it is one of 20th Century–Fox's best scenic efforts of the early years as designed by Bernard Herzbrun and Boris Leven. Like other of Fox films in this period when William Darling was guiding the Art Department, the settings are richly textural, so much so that one never questions their authenticity. They seem to be the very essence of movie realism.

Bernard Herzbrun had worked at Paramount beginning in 1926, and then joined 20th Century–Fox in the late thirties. He would go on to become the supervising art director at Universal in the period 1947–1954. Boris Leven was a relative newcomer to art direction in 1938; he had worked briefly as a sketch artist at Paramount in 1933, but spent much of the Depression unemployed. Never intending to abandon architecture as a profession he, like so many of his colleagues, took work in the movie industry only as a filler. Leven remained at Fox for almost a decade (1938–1947), then went to Universal for two years, before becoming a prolific freelance art director.

Alexander's Ragtime Band began production immediately after the completion of *In Old Chicago* with the same team of stars (Tyrone Power, Alice Faye, and Don Ameche) and the same director (Henry King). Conceived as a showcase for the songs of Irving Berlin, the songwriter also provided, with Richard Sherman, the rather thin plot.

The sets show the same attention to detail and aptness as did those of *In Old Chicago*. The saloons look suspiciously like their predecessors in the earlier film. Boris Leven explains the convenience of the reuse of sets:

> The joy and curse of working as an art director in the studios was that everything was *right there*. You almost never went on location; everything was shot in the studio, or on the back lot. Each sound stage had its own standing set—say, a colonial home with a beautiful curved stairway—that would be used perhaps ten times a year, slightly redressed each time. One company would move out, having taken down their decorations, and we would move in, with eighteen hours to redo the set for our own picture.[4]

Twentieth Century–Fox moved resolutely into the forties with films that were increasingly based on social issues. The greatest of these films, *The Grapes of Wrath*, on the plight of farmers in the dust bowl of middle America of the thirties, appeared in 1940, and was followed by such ground-breakers as *Gentleman's Agreement* (1947, on anti-Semitism), *The Snake Pit* (1948, on mental illness), and *Pinky* (1949, on the color barrier).

Although William Darling remained, art director Richard Day became the leading force in the Art Department at 20th Century–Fox in the early forties. He worked there from 1939–1947, serving as Supervising Art Director from 1940 until 1942 when he entered the Marines; on his return from the War he was credited in this manner on only one feature. Lyle Wheeler was named Supervising Art Director in 1944, a position he held until 1960. Day left Fox in 1947, having produced many of his most memorably designed films while at the studio, including *The Grapes of Wrath* and *How Green Was My Valley*, both for director John Ford.[5]

Day's early tenure with the perfectionist von Stroheim and his talent for realism stood him in good stead for both pictures. The art director's study of documentary styles is particularly evident in *The Grapes of Wrath*, which director Ford and cinematographer Gregg Toland cast in a semidocumentary form. The Oklahoma farmhouses for the Joad family and their neighbors were caught in swirls of dust by the second unit shooting on location; they are driven off the land and their dilapidated truck takes them down Route 66 to the promised land of California in shots reminiscent of those seen in newsreels of the period. The roadside is dotted with typical thirties architecture — gas stations, soda fountains, hotels — most of which the Joads cannot afford to enter, and with signs — "Last Chance for gas and water," "Water 15¢ gal.," "Pop 5¢," "We fix flats," which testify to life on the road during the Depression. Most of the film was shot on the company's lot, with the government camp and Hoovervilles built by Day on the backlot. Day's sets and Toland's evocative lighting work perfectly as background for the splendid ensemble acting.

In *The Grapes of Wrath*, the sets that more than any underscore the social plight of the Depression migrants are the two transient camps the Joad family encounters. The first — squalid and filled with flimsy makeshift dwellings jerry-built around old cars and trucks — shows in devastating detail, as the camera slowly moves through it, the level the pickers are reduced to by the starvation wages they are receiving for their work. By contrast, the government camp that the Joads next enter seems a paradise of hygienic, orderly dwellings; run democratically, it even has a place for socializing and dancing. Its very humaneness suggests hope for the future, against the other camp's projected despair.

Even as the Studio was producing the forties "conscience" films, it continued with more familiar products, but with several surprises — in the musical films in the guise of Betty Grable and the wonderful Carmen Miranda, the "Brazilian bomb-shell." In the history pictures there were more deeply emotional themes — the story of a family of Welsh coal miners, *How Green Was My Valley* (1941) and the story of fervent religious piety, *The Song of Bernadette* (1943), both with Academy Award winning art direction.

For *How Green Was My Valley* Richard Day and Nathan Juran built a 19th century Welsh miner's village at a valley setting called Brent's Crags (**Illustration 94**) in the Ventura Hills outside Los Angeles. The village's long street, lined with blocks of uniform workers' housing, climbed a steep hill to the colliery at the top, perched like a Gothic cathedral above the town and like a cathedral, the dominant factor in the lives of the inhabitants. The men trailing to work and returning from it on the steep hill, sometimes singing and sometimes bone-weary silent, is a motif woven through the film. The miner's houses (their lives) are built upon the hill in which they spend most of their waking hours.

Complete in every detail (set decoration was by Thomas Little), the stone chapel, houses and dividing walls project an unfriendly harshness that underscores the lushness of the valley's landscape setting. The land is the place to which the miners' families escape on occasion, and the scene in particular of many of the film's more intimate conversations, like those between the sensitive younger son of the Morgan family (Roddy McDowall) and the impoverished minister (Walter Pidgeon), who befriends and encourages him to think of life beyond the confines of the village. The valley itself undergoes a gradual transformation during the film's course, as the mine owners begin gouging profits and cutting the workers' salaries. Furthermore, disregarding the natural beauty of the place, the owners allow the mine's slag heap to spread out and cover more and more of it.

Although 20th Century–Fox was to reuse Day's and Juran's Welsh village, reclad, many times in the forties, the studio's art department was soon hard at work building a French village complete with a river coursing through its center for *The Song of Bernadette* (**Illustration 95**). The Academy Awards for art direction on this 1943 release went to James Basevi and William Darling, with Thomas Little again being honored as best set decorator.

English born Basevi stepped in as supervising Art Director at 20th Century–Fox from 1943–1944, while Day was in World War II. The distinguished naturalistic settings of *The Song of Bernadette* appear seamless as the story moves from interiors to exteriors. The studio again chose to photograph in black and white, putting the cinematography in the hands of the masterful Arthur Miller, who had likewise been responsible for *How Green Was My Valley*.[6]

The film begins in the cottage of miller François Soubirous, the father of Bernadette, the heroine and subsequent saint, of this fictionalized story based on events in a provincial 19th century France. Its rooms with low ceilings seem cramped and vaguely claustrophobic, as do several other interiors as the film progresses and Bernadette is made to repeat her story of a heavenly vision to various official personages. These interior scenes are alternated with more expansive exterior views, rich in detail, of life in the village and of the countryside and natural spring where Bernadette first experiences the vision. The black and white chiaroscuro effects of the light on the sets, are like those in engraved images of the 19th century, rich in mood and textured with nuances of greys.

The Song of Bernadette has the unity of design which is part of the recognizable Fox look in the historical films of the forties. Costumes, sets, landscapes, lighting all combine to move the viewer into the emotional texture of the film. Gone is the contrived and artificial historicism of the earlier thirties films, like *Clive of India* and the thinner realism of the Shirley Temple pictures. The time and money have been spent to create an actual physical ambience into which the story is set.

The studio did in fact put Shirley Temple in one big budgeted, big set picture, *The Blue Bird* (1940). It was her first flop. Filmed in Technicolor,

directed by Walter Lang, and with elaborate sets by Richard Day and Wiard Ihnen, the fable of the quest for the blue bird, which takes place in past and future time frames, did not allow the beloved Temple persona to shine through, as did the simpler tales.

The Blue Bird's "future" set **(Illustration 96)** filled an entire sound stage at the Westwood Studio, with the Publicity Department claiming "The set was designed after Michelangelo's Medici Chapel in Florence . . . [the] largest interior ever constructed at 20th Century–Fox, the set gives the impression of being suspended in the sky." The large set affords a view at one side through a door and transparent wall to a sailing ship; the door itself is an almost literal translation of the entry into, not the Medici Chapel, but the Medici Library (Laurentian Library) by the great Renaissance master. The rest of the set is a grandiloquent abstraction after ideas from Michelangelo, with the boat's ramp a satiric bow to the Library's famous stairway. The dozens of children in the scene are clothed in costumes that suggest the even more distant past of Greco-Roman antiquity in this "future" set.

The war years saw many imaginative musicals come out of 20th Century–Fox—*Springtime in the Rockies* (1942), *My Gal Sal* (1942), *The Gang's All Here* (1943) and *State Fair* (1945)—filled with a *joie de vivre* and peopled by a cast of characters that cheered audiences, including Rita Hayworth, Carmen Miranda, Betty Grable, John Payne, Charlotte Greenwood, and Cesar Romero. Mostly placed in contemporary settings and filmed in Technicolor, they had the usual convoluted and zany plots, updated from the thirties.

The Gang's All Here stands out as the oddest of the bunch, because of director Busby Berkeley's handling of the musical numbers, especially those featuring the electric Carmen Miranda. Berkeley's first Technicolor film, it gave him the opportunity to explore his fondness for kaleidoscopic effects in the intense colors of a real kaleidoscope.

The Gang's All Here was Alice Faye's last musical and she was clearly outdazzled by Miranda in three-inch wedgies. The big number "The Lady in the Tutti-Frutti Hat" has Miranda on a South Sea island that sports surreal banana trees with live monkeys among its silken leaves. The number opens on dozens of "native" girls in skimpy costumes lying on the sand as Carmen Miranda enters on a golden cart drawn by golden (painted) oxen. She sings, dances in her inimitable way (a sort of jet-propelled wiggle), and plays a huge circular xylophone. The chorus of native girls then performs an intricate dance partnering *gigantic* bananas. The effect is bizarre, sexually suggestive, and comic and is concluded by one of art director James Basevi's famous special effects, the sight of a distant Miranda, her fruit salad hat (it was 30 feet high) leaning

94. *How Green Was My Valley,* 1941. Richard Day, Nathan Juran, art directors. A 19th century Welsh miners' village was built in the Ventura Hills of Los Angeles; the workers' stone rowhouses climbed the hill to the colliery that dominates the village.

toward the screen, flanked on either side by a row of lush giant strawberries moving backward into infinity. The number has rightfully become a cult classic.

State Fair (1945), a musical slice of contemporary Americana, had nothing to do with the fantasy of a Berkeley film. Its charm, much dependent on the screenplay and lyrics of Oscar Hammerstein II (music was by Richard Rodgers), had to do with the elevation of the ordinary—the winning of a prize in a hog judging contest—to the extraordinary. The cast, Jeanne Crain, Dick Haymes, Fay Bainter and Charles Winninger, are perfect in this piece, as they perform such hokey songs as "All I Owe Ioway" and "It's a Grand Night for Singing."

The sets in *State Fair,* designed by Lyle Wheeler and Lewis Criber, are, in character, similar to those of many period musicals of the thirties and forties; the areas where action occurs are authentically built if a bit overly coloristic in the Technicolor manner, and everything beyond the immediate area is obviously phoney—here views out windows and barn doors, the backgrounds of farmyards and fairgrounds. These backgrounds are done with scenic drops, mattes, or miniatures which stay on the screen longer than the few seconds that is usual with such effects, and so lose their potential as illusions. This doesn't seem to be questioned by musical audiences, because the convention that has been accepted by them is not one of realism—everyone knows that real people don't break into song at the drop of a hat—but is more like that accepted by opera audiences.

The mid-forties saw 20th Century–Fox produce its usual share of dramas laid in historical settings. Art director William Darling was again at work on a lavish production with *Anna and the King of Siam* (1946), this time with Richard Day and with Lyle Wheeler, who was just beginning his long tenure as supervising art director (1944–1960) at the Studio.

Writer Dewitt Bodeen relates how 20th Century–Fox's commitment to the story began:

> When Margaret Landon wrote her best-selling biography *Anna and the King of Siam,* Twentieth Century–Fox purchased film rights from gallery proofs. The story, which was only slightly fictionalized, had all the ingredients for a beautiful big period romance, and the studio spared nothing in its lavish production, creating anew the fantastic city of Bangkok as it had been in the second half of the nineteenth century, building sixty-seven exteriors and thirty-four ornate interiors as sets.[7]

As Bodeen points out, the audiences of the war years would have tolerated no view of a mysterious East, where a romance of any sort could be played out.

95. *The Song of Bernadette,* 1943. William S. Darling, James Basevi, art directors. A provincial 19th century French village traversed by a river was built in authentic detail with stone dwellings, bridges and shrines, seen here during a religious processional. Jennifer Jones is on the litter.

96. *The Blue Bird,* 1940. Richard Day, Wiard Ihnen, art directors. Using Michelangelo's Renaissance Medici Library for inspiration, the art directors created a fantastic "future" set for this Shirley Temple vehicle. Director Walter Lang shouts through cupped hands, foreground.

By 1946, they were again ready to tolerate and indeed be intoxicated by a Siam of 1862 as conceived by Wheeler and Darling. Irene Dunne starred as Anna and Rex Harrison was the King in whose palace the story unfolds. Filmed in black and white, the screen seems to shimmer, surfaces shine throughout,

97. *Anna and the King of Siam,* 1946. William S. Darling, Richard Day, Lyle Wheeler, art directors. Irene Dunn and Richard Lyon enter the King of Siam's palace from a lush garden through a portico of polished columns.

interrupted by carved screens, and complemented by costume designer Bonnie Cashin's silken clothes. The award winning set decorators Thomas Little and Frank E. Hughes appointed the rooms with satined furniture and all kinds of exotic *objets d'art.*

The exteriors include everything from boat docks to city streets and the palace facade; the interiors — the King's audience chamber, the classroom where Anna teaches the King's many children, the harem where the wives and children of the King live, and a private garden house which Anna is eventually able to wrest from the King — are painstakingly created. This publicity still **(Illustration 97)** shows Dunne entering the multileveled royal palace through a field of columns. Behind her is a lush garden defined by elegant carved balustrades; light is filtering sensuously through them and onto the columns, throwing the pitched ceiling into shadow.

Director John Cromwell's handling of the setting is not particularly innovative, but the action is well woven throughout with the decor, so that one gets a chance to savor the foreignness of the place, a key point in this story of a remote country confronting the modern world.

Lyle Wheeler succeeded Richard Day as head of the 20th Century–Fox Art Department, becoming one of the most powerful supervising art directors in Hollywood; he worked, he says, on every Fox picture from around 1944 until his retirement from that post in 1960, although his name does not appear in the credits of all of them. In the course of his career he was to receive 29 Oscar nominations for art direction and win five.

Oddly, it was his first film at Fox that remains his favorite, despite the hundreds that followed,

> Of all the Fox films that I worked on, *Anna and the King of Siam* gave me the most pleasure and lasting pride. It was originally planned as a color picture, but the painters and carpenters went on a terrible strike. The strike lasted almost two years, from 1944–1946. Hundreds of people were out of work. The plasterers were not on strike, so I convinced Zanuck to go with black-and-white. The sets had to be built in plaster — even the doors were cast from plaster. There was a material called nicrosyn which cameramen use in sidewalks to kill excessive sunlight reflection and which looks like gunpowder. We used it to get different values from the plaster; we had shadings of gray and even black.[8]

Wheeler had begun his career in the mid-twenties, doing sketches for a picture being made by Marshall Neilan. He quit when, after working day and night on watercolor renderings of ideas for sets, the director continued to change his mind about what he wanted. Wheeler, lively, articulate, and still working in the field of art direction in his seventies, commented: "After all, I was a trained architect, and that was really what I wanted to be."[9]

Wheeler worked at MGM and Selznick International before coming to Fox. Of MGM's Cedric Gibbons, Wheeler recalls: "He had a big ego, but was diplomatic. He could tell people where to get off, without really going too far. Gibbons demanded that every inch of the set be lit, so that every detail showed, and had to be meticulously done."

The 20th Century–Fox Art Department under Wheeler was run hierarchically, as was Gibbons' department, and with a similar care for details. Wheeler is candid about the difficulties of being a supervising art director: "I usually had 16 or more art directors in the Department and, at any given moment, at least half of them thought they could do my job better than I could." A perfectionist, Wheeler demanded perfection from his art directors and says he worked best with directors, like Otto Preminger and Jean Negulesco, who shared this trait: "Negulesco had been an art student, and when he said he wanted a Renoir over the fireplace, it had to be there." Of the notoriously demanding Preminger, for whom Wheeler designed films for over two decades, he observed with pride, "Preminger wanted everything to be precisely and accurately done, down to the doorknobs. Over the years, he trusted me to the extent that he never even looked at the sets until they were built and he was ready to start shooting, even the difficult foreign locales."

Wheeler credits much of the historical accuracy in Fox's pictures to their excellent research department headed by Frances Richardson. "We had a great Art Department, and our research was the best!" he says flatly. "We knew how to do things, and a lot of that came from having done it in architecture. We built whole cities and oceans too, in a tank."

After becoming a supervising art director, working on around 30 pictures a year, he did almost no sketches, unlike his years with Selznick on *Gone with the Wind* and *Rebecca*. Indicating he was still a part of the creative process, Wheeler commented,

> Sketch artists did the drawings after ideas I gave them. I had to come up with a budget for each picture, the budget was not just handed down at Fox. And I usually read the script *before* the director did. On *Gone with the Wind,* I had to come up with the budget for sets 2 years before we went into production, but that was unusual and not the case at Fox.

Indicating that the quality of Fox's pictures depended on many factors, including construction, set dressing, properties, and costumes, Wheeler remarked: "The art director was the one who said what went into the construction of the set, and his design had to be followed exactly by the crew and the set dressers. No liberties were taken with the art director's designs." According to Wheeler,

> They wanted you to use the properties on the lot, but if you needed something specific it could be rented or bought. Fox and Metro had the best prop departments, because they did the most buying, and had built up the best collections through the years.

Costume colors were carefully coordinated with the art director's ideas about the sets, says Wheeler. "I would never tell anyone how to design a gown, that was not my job," but they had to work with the set and at Fox usually did.

Asked about scenic backdrops, Wheeler commented:

> They were very expensive, and sometimes were done by well-known artists. We had a special studio stage to accommodate them. We got quite a few of our scenic backdrops from the Coakley Scenic Art Co. It was an old company and they did excellent work. They're still gong today run by Gary, the son of the original owner. We had a whole group at Fox that did oil paintings of originals, so that we would not have to use prints on walls, but had actual paintings with texture. The portrait of Gene Tierney in *Laura* was actually painted in the Studio.

Wheeler and unit art director Leland Fuller worked with Otto Preminger on *Laura* (1944). Wheeler explains how he got Preminger to use the very effective long take at the beginning of the film that had apparently been planned by Alfred Hitchcock for the beginning of *Rebecca*,

> The first long take he [Hitchcock] devised—which I thought was great, because it showed off the set so well—was in the boathouse. Laurence Olivier is delivering his story, and the camera travels over every inch of the room. It took about a day to shoot. Unfortunately, it was cut from the final print. But four years later, I got Otto Preminger to film exactly the same shot in the opening scene of *Laura*.[9]

Wheeler was right, it is a superb way to introduce the rarified dwelling of Waldo Lydecker (Clifton Webb), the catty radio critic and film's narrator, whose taste dominates the film. First the camera slowly pans over Lydecker's collection of Oriental art, then moves to survey the vast living room with shuttered windows and views to a terrace beyond. The room is sumptuous in detail — booklined walls, antique masks, an ornate grandfather clock — objects which the boorish detective (Dana Andrews) is seen carelessly handling as Lydecker watching him from another room begins, in a voice over, the tale of his relationship with Laura leading up to her murder (we then see the story unfold in flashbacks). Lydecker's egoism dominates as he summons the detective from the living room to wait upon him in a marbled bathroom, where he sits in the tub, typewriter conveniently swung over the water on a moveable desk. **(Illustration 98.)** Noting the detective's appreciative glance at the surroundings, Lydecker comments, "It's lavish, but I call it home."[10]

The rest of the detective melodrama is set in the swank interiors of 1940s New York (expensive restaurants, apartments, Laura's streamlined office) — in this *Laura* is unlike most detective stories of the period, which tended to be played out in poorer circumstances and on the city's streets. All of the sets, exteriors and interiors, were designed and studio built by Wheeler and Fuller and carefully appointed by Thomas Little and Paul S. Fox.

Like Lydecker's dwelling, each domestic interior is conceived as a character study of the inhabitant's personality and circumstances. Mrs. Treadwell, Laura's aunt, lives in a posh apartment furnished in the Louis XV style and with a white grand piano. A swirling, curvilinear rococo shadow encircles the living room ceiling. The decor exudes an aura of wealth, artificiality, and pleasure seeking befitting the aunt, played by Judith Anderson. In the story, this is best evidenced by her relationship with callow playboy Shelby Carpenter (Vincent Price) whom she thinks should marry her instead of Laura, "because I can afford him."

Laura's refined taste, according to Lydecker molded by himself, is seen in her antique filled apartment whose living room is narcissistically dominated by her own portrait over the fireplace. It is the portrait that casts a mesmerizing spell over the police detective investigating the murder of a woman found dead in the apartment. Laura's portrait introduced the film and it, together with the setting of her apartment and the hypnotic theme music, are the chief means through which the audience comes to know and sympathize with her in the first half of the film.

Laura's apartment, more intimate than the others in the film, is broken up into small interrelated spatial units. The designers covered the windows with ruffled curtains and packed every available surface with *objets d'art*. The decorative style of the apartment changes from room to room, expressive of Laura's own search for definition. The study is done unexpectedly in a Victorian style, down to Belser sofas, and other action takes place in Laura's bedroom, which is decked in gauzy curtains and has a canopied four-poster bed.

98. *Laura,* 1944. Lyle Wheeler, Leland Fuller, art directors. Waldo Lydecker (Clifton Webb) summons detective (Dana Andrews) to wait upon him in his marble bathtub. "It's lavish, but I call it home," he remarks to Andrews' appreciative glance at the surroundings.

The apartment, as first seen, is brightly lit, but when the detective, now in love with the slain girl, returns at night it is expressively lit. He sits in the living room sipping a drink beside her portrait; he has practically moved in. For the last scene, after Laura has returned unharmed and the real identity of the dead girl, but not her murderer, has been revealed, Preminger has the camera pull back so that we again see the apartment in a moody light. In a long pan, similar to the one that opened the picture, the camera moves lovingly across the objects in the living room, tables now covered with vases of roses, to Laura's bedroom. The film's final action is a coda, resolving the story by using almost the same pictorial terms with which it began. And as Lydecker's rifle shot, meant to kill Laura, hits the clock he has given her and he is mortally wounded by the police, we again hear him in a voice over, saying, "Goodbye my love."

Seldom have settings in an American film evoked character and mood with greater subtlety than in *Laura,* and art directors Lyle Wheeler and Leland

Fuller found themselves honored with Academy Award nominations for the film. Otto Preminger, his reputation solidly established with this film, had shown his ability to dramatically manipulate a setting to tell a story.

At about the same time that *Laura* was being filmed in the mid-forties, producer Louis de Rochemont urged 20th Century–Fox to film the espionage drama *The House on 92nd Street* (1945) in the documentary style he had become famous for through "The March of Time" series (a twenty minute monthly motion picture news magazine that dramatized contemporary events). Like the news series, *The House on 92nd Street* used live actors to dramatize a story in real locations, and mixed in archival material (newsreels and still photographs). All of these elements were tightly interwoven by director Henry Hathaway to produce a thriller documenting an actual Federal Bureau of Investigation case, the "Mr. Christopher File," concerning a German spy ring attempting to steal American atomic secrets during World War II. Done with the Bureau's cooperation, it even featured footage of J. Edgar Hoover at work in his office. Hathaway had the actors, all relatively unknown, talk in flat monotones, which added to the documentary character being simulated (a technique later picked up for other docudramas including those on television, like *Dragnet*).

Begun just as location shooting was returning in a big way to Hollywood production in the postwar period, *The House on 92nd Street* was among the first films to move in greater part out of the studio. Beside the FBI Headquarters and others sites in Washington, D.C., locations in New York City—a bookstore, a beauty parlor, and the 92nd Street house—also figured prominently in the film. City street scenes shot from behind hidden mirrors seemed extremely vivid to audiences at the time. New equipment that was easily mobile, fishpole microphones and lighter weight moveable cameras, made this location work economical and the quality of it almost as good as what could be obtained in the studio. Newsreel footage was also used in the film and some was faked by using very grainy film stock. The studio-built interiors adhered absolutely to the look of wartime America in order to mesh with the locations, and art directors Lyle Wheeler and William Creber seem to have had no difficulty in accommodating themselves to de Rochemont's style. So successful was the film that Fox followed it up with several others done along similar lines, *13 rue Madeleine* (1947, also produced by de Rochemont) and *Panic in the Streets* (1950).

In the late forties, along with the neorealism of the docudramas, there was no let up in the period pictures filmed at 20th Century–Fox and the Art Department worked overtime on the many opulent sets for these films, but more enduring than them has been the modest and charming Christmas movie of the period, *The Miracle on 34th Street* (1947).

Both the original story by Valentine Davies and screenplay by George Seaton (also the film's director) for *The Miracle on 34th Street* were so filled with warmth and wit, that in combination with Edmund Gwenn's unsurpassed performance as Kris Kringle the film was both a critical and a financial success. Location shooting in this period has seldom worked to better purpose than in this movie, centered around Macy's Thanksgiving parade and the holiday season in New York City. **(Illustration 99.)** Seaton shot the footage of the parade and the other locations (interiors and exteriors) of the department store in the winter of 1946.

The locations are the uncontrived surroundings for the story of a city child (Natalie Wood) brought up so "reasonably" that she does not even believe in Santa Claus. The film opens with Gwenn walking down a New York street and stopping to correct a display of reindeers in a store window; it is a delightful and intimate way to use New York City as background, and this sense of intimacy is not lost by Seaton in the rest of the picture, even in the parade sequences, where it might easily have been. He only draws back for long views of the parade occasionally enough to convince us that we are actually there; mostly he focuses in middle and close shots on the actors and on the narrative, which is beginning the involvement of Gwenn in the lives of a mother (Maureen O'Hara), daughter (Wood) and their neighbor (John Payne).

The subsequent story is played out in the art directors', Richard Day and Richard Irvine, studio built interiors (apartments, a courtroom) and the real interiors at Macy's (offices, corridors). Day's expert eye for locations seems evident throughout the picture, and when an actual office or apartment is being used the camera points out of the window so that the buildings of New York are a constant, subtle reminder of the locale. The last scene, after Kris Kringle's trial, is set in a wintery suburban residential area, ending the film at another convincing location, a welcome change after the war years, when California passed in Hollywood films for all parts of the country.

The type of contemporary realism — mixing strong story, expert acting, location and studio settings — evidenced in *The Miracle on 34th Street* was a continuing current in the films coming out of the 20th Century–Fox in the fifties, as in *All About Eve* (1950), designed by art directors Lyle Wheeler and George Davis. Wheeler has described his work at Fox on such pictures:

> I would scout locations with the art director assigned to each picture, approve all sketches, and most importantly, work with the writer almost from the beginning of the project. I believe that the narrative is central to the success of a picture, and I was always more interested in that facet of filmmaking than in directing."[11]

The writer and director in the case of *All About Eve* was Joseph L. Mankiewicz, who provided a biting script about backstage life on Broadway. The flashback technique of the film moves the narrative from dressing rooms, to on-stage moments, to modern apartments. New York City backgrounds were shot by cameraman Milton Krasner without the principals and, unlike *The Miracle on 34th Street,* are seen only briefly in passing. Seeking authenticity for the

99. *The Miracle on 34th Street,* 1947. Richard Day, Richard Irvine, art directors. Postwar pictures were again done at distant locations. New York as a locale has seldom been fused with built interiors to greater advantage than on this film. Here, Natalie Wood and John Payne watch Macy's Thanksgiving Parade.

on-stage portions of the film, Wheeler found the old Broadway style Curran Theatre in San Francisco, saving a trip to New York City for the cast and crew.

At the same time that location shooting was gaining in popularity and frequency among directors, the big studios were still producing totally studio photographed films in the fifties. A convincing real-life story of confinement in World War II, *Three Came Home* (1950), starring Claudette Colbert, had all of the principal action shot in the studio in sets designed by Lyle Wheeler and Leland Fuller, with only a few frames given over to establishing the locale, Borneo, done on location (and without the presence of the principals).

Unlike RKO and other studios on the decline in the early fifties, Fox, partly because of Cinemascope, was still thinking in expansive terms. This thinking embraced the Art Department, which began the construction of a mammoth backlot waterway that art director Herman Blumenthal wrote about in *Production Design:*

When the proposed schedule of pictures for 1951–1952 was released by the Production Office ... a definite need for a permanent "waterways" site was seen by ... Lyle Wheeler, since many of these productions were scenically laid in localities where water was a definite part of the background. Preliminary plans for such a scheme had been studied by Wheeler for many years, and progress had been made through permanent landscape planting on a fifteen acre site at the Beverly Hills Studio....[12]

The site, as constructed in 1952, consisted of a river, lake, canals, working locks, swamp, beaches, paths, docks, and separate jungle and park areas. According to Blumenthal, "The lake can be emptied in order to build sets on its bottom, and then refilled without touching sets which are in other areas."[13] The "waterway" succeeded in getting the camera out of doors, but kept it on the lot; when combined with mattes it became innumerable notable bodies of water, including Lake Michigan in *The Snows of Kilimanjaro* (1952) (with a matte shot designed by art director John De Cuir).

By 1951, the postwar approach to location work was in place and *The Desert Fox,* designed by Maurice Ransford, exemplifies the thoroughness of it. Ransford was a trained architect; he had graduated from the University of Illinois, and worked in the profession from 1920–1930. His career as an art director was spent at 20th Century–Fox, where he designed a wide variety of films, including Alfred Hitchcock's one-set *Lifeboat* (1944), the Edwardian England of *Hangover Square* (1945) for John Brahm, and the menace-filled tourist resort of Henry Hathaway's *Niagara* (1953).

The Desert Fox was based on the book by Desmond Young, *Rommel, the Desert Fox,* and starred James Mason in the title role. The film's primary action was placed in North Africa, but there were also sequences in Germany and France. Henry Hathaway directed, and he and Ransford were particularly concerned about matching the backgrounds, to be filmed mostly in America, with the real ones, since they "were known from the personal experiences of millions of American Servicemen, the British Commonwealth, and to both German and French audiences."[14]

Hathaway took a small crew to Europe to get establishing shots of various localities — as *Production Design* reported, "process plates to be used with the actors back at the studio, and whatever research photographs would be needed to match the different buildings in which the actions took place."[15] At the same time, Ransford spent weeks searching southwest deserts for a location that closely resembled North Africa, finally deciding on Borrego Springs, California, because it was possible to shoot in all directions without interferences and because it was near an emergency Navy airfield that could double as a German Airdrome.

Since the sets shot on the desert location would be intercut with stock footage received from American, British, and captured German sources, it was the requirement of the Art Director to match as closely as possible the equipment and fortifications used by both the German and British. (for this purpose) A very fine collection of photographs shot by a German Officer . . . of Afrika Korps army life was purchased by the studio.[16]

The German portion of the film followed the sites filmed by Hathaway, including the General's house. In addition, "The widow of Field Marshall Rommel placed at Mr. Hathaway's disposal the vast collection of the photographs taken by the General on his various tours of duty."[17] From these, Ransford designed the sets that were erected at 20th Century–Fox, including Hitler's secret headquarters at Rastenburg near the eastern front where the plot to take his life, in which Rommel was involved, took place.

Using such carefully documented research, Hathaway and Ransford achieved a semidocumentary treatment of Rommel's life, without the expense of the actors' going abroad. *The Desert Fox* is virtually seamless, with the dramatic action faultlessly moving from place to place. By the mid-fifties, with the European economy and lifestyle recovered from the war and the price of labor cheaper there than in America, it would become more cost efficient to send the actors to Europe and hire European crews to film the picture.

Many consider 1945–1953 to have been the peak years for 20th Century–Fox, and they topped off their success with the introduction of CinemaScope, a widescreen process that achieved a sense of three dimensions without the awkward glasses, then the craze. But as Roy Pickard commented, CinemaScope "simply provided a bigger screen and made good films seem only adequate and bad films abysmal."[18]

The thinking at Fox was that a big screen called for a big story and production values large enough to fill the added space on the screen. Where else to turn but to the Bible, as reinterpreted by Lloyd C. Douglas in his bestselling novel, *The Robe*. CinemaScope was to launch a second cycle of filmed biblical epics in the mid-fifties—the first had been in the silent era, the period from 1915–1927.

Few of the new crop of films surpassed the success of *The Robe;* it opened on September 16, 1953, at the Roxy in New York and quickly earned over $17 million, to become 20th Century–Fox's biggest grossing picture ever. The CinemaScope process won an Academy Award for special technical achievement, and *The Robe*'s art directors, Lyle Wheeler and George W. Davis, along with set decorators Walter M. Scott and Paul S. Fox, were also honored.

The Rome of the Emperor Tiberius consisted of just about every kind of interior and exterior known to the Romans, and that meant dozens of sets, on which the entire Fox Art Department worked. **(Illustration 100.)** Like all epics, *The Robe* makes profuse use of special effects, in this case by Ray Kellogg— mattes (of Capri), miniatures (a Roman ship), scenic backdrops (behind the Crucifixion) and many others. The interiors of Roman houses, Imperial Palaces, the gladiator's coliseum are done in multicolored marbles, splashed with colored light, particularly blues in the backgrounds, so that everything is

100. *The Robe,* **1953. Lyle Wheeler, George W. Davis, art directors. Jean Simmons and Richard Burton (center) amid polished marble walls and floors. Imperial Roman emblems are emblazoned on the throne at the rear. Numerous elaborate sets were required for epic films from the teens through the fifties.**

pristine, dirt free—in other words, a big step from the reality of life in antiquity.

This is Hollywood's view of the past; it is based on historical evidence and then glamorized. Foster Hirsch, writing on movie epics, comments,

> ancient Rome or Jerusalem looks much the same in the Fifties as it did in the Twenties. Hollywood's standardized conception of epic backgrounds was a function of economics; a big budget film cannot risk challenging popular preconceptions with eccentric, revisionist visual depictions of the ancient world as savage or dangerous or truly alien.[19]

The Hollywood epic is a film genre that has been much more controlled by art directors' understanding of the history of art and archaeology than has any other genre. "The Hollywood epic," according to Hirsch,

> presents a conservative view of the ancient world. Its sense of the past is based on visual conventions borrowed from Victorian paintings, Nineteenth-century stage design, the decor in the early Italian epics and in the pioneering work of Griffith and DeMille.[20]

Although the visual formulae of the biblical epic were established early, Fox's interpretation of the past tended to be a great deal more realistic than the extremes of sanitized antiquity of the contemporary DeMille films like *Samson and Delilah* (1949).[21] Fox's big sets tend to be massive and solid looking, and to draw on the particular brand of realism they had perfected in the black and white films of the forties, like *The Song of Bernadette*. Especially in certain outdoor scenes in *The Robe,* as when the hero Marcellus (Richard Burton) approaches Jerusalem, a certain dusty authenticity prevails. At other times, the screen seems oddly empty at the sides; during Burton's rescue of his servant, Demetrius (Victor Mature), there is a fight along stretches of unarticulated Roman palace wall. For the most part, however, the hope that the grandeur of a recreated Roman Empire would engage the big screen was fulfilled, and 20th Century–Fox hurriedly began a sequel, *Demetrius and the Gladiators* (1954).

The Robe told its story of romantic love and Christian commitment in relatively static terms, director Henry Koster was not able to activate the big screen, a task that others would soon solve. On the other hand, the Art Department's sets did prove, in this first CinemaScope production, the infinite superiority of film over television to provide extraordinary visual effects to enhance stories. Television would not turn out to be an art director's medium. The very qualities of detail in decor that *The Robe* exemplified, would be totally lost on the small screen.

Fox decided not to reserve CinemaScope to any particular type of "big" story, and photographed all of its productions in the process beginning in 1954. Even "small" domestic comedies could succeed in CinemaScope the studio insisted, and this was particularly true if new star Marilyn Monroe was involved.

The Seven Year Itch (1955) put Tom Ewell and Monroe in what was an essentially one set picture. Lyle Wheeler and George W. Davis proved their versatility again with this simple set, the New York Brownstone apartment home of Ewell. His family away on vacation for the summer, Ewell is sorely tempted by new neighbor Monroe. The set consists of a single large room— entry door and stairwell to one side, glass doors to a patio opposite, walls of books and a grand piano on the other walls. Every part of the set functions at one time or another as a foil for the silliness of Ewell and the seductive comedy of Monroe: several scenes take place at the entryway, Monroe drops a plant on Ewell's patio, they talk at the piano. The art directors put interesting art objects around the room, with the great number of books suggesting Ewell's profession; he works for a publisher. The apartment is as much a lure to Monroe as is its occupant (he doesn't seem to notice this), because in the sizzling New York summer, it is air conditioned and hers is not (she improvises, though, by keeping her undies in the refrigerator).

The Seven Year Itch was taken from the stage, where the use of a single set is more prevalent than in film. Director Billy Wilder wisely stayed with the stage concept, which focuses on the actors. The intensity of Ewell's fantasies flourish in the familiar apartment, and falter during the few times he escapes it; the one exception being when Monroe's skirt blows up around her thighs as she catches the breeze from a subway grate.

While *The Seven Year Itch* had CinemaScope, it didn't really need it. Other films, particularly musicals did seem to profit from the process, *The King and I* (1956), perhaps most memorably. A remake of the studio's dramatic hit *Anna and the King of Siam*, the musical had Lyle Wheeler, one of the orignal's art directors in charge, this time working in concert with 20th Century–Fox's talented art director of the fifties and sixties, John De Cuir. De Cuir was known for his innovative designs, and the breathtaking drawings, often in watecolor, that illustrated them. His designs had a broad expansiveness that was absolutely right for the widescreen of the fifties. He bathed large areas in rich color, but included opulent detail that registered well in the blown-up close-ups of the new CinemaScope process.

A San Francisco native, De Cuir studied at the Chouinard Art School in Los Angeles, a school that has produced a number of fine illustrators for motion pictures. De Cuir joined Universal at the age of 20 in 1938 and worked there until 1949 when he joined Fox. He is still active in film art direction and in stage design in Los Angeles. De Cuir's speciality at Fox came to be large productions, like, *Call Me Madam* (1953), *3 Coins in the Fountain* (1954), and *The Agony and the Ecstasy* (1965) **(Illustration 101)** but he also handled smaller films in a realistic vein like the period melodrama *My Cousin Rachel* (1952).

For *The King and I,* the splendid Royal Palace of Siam was finally glimpsed in full color on the screen. More dazzling, less realistic than in the earlier version, the palace's shining floors, semiabstract decoration, and elaborate lighting fit the conventions of the musical. This is definitely a movie Siam. **(Illustration 102.)**

The grandeur of De Cuir and Wheeler's palace rooms was perfect for CinemaScope, and beside existing in breadth, the rooms exist on several levels separated by low tiers of stairs that lead from place to place in the very large spaces. The interiors merge with gardens, sculpture in profusion adorns the spaces, and a lotus vault covers Anna's map in the schoolroom seen here.

The king's private chamber, one of several big sets, is covered with ornate bookshelves, scientific instruments sit about to characterize the king's inquisitive nature. Everything in the room, as elsewhere in the palace—moldings, furniture, statues, a globe—has been dipped in gold. Statues of Siamese dancers, French Empire furniture and draperies fill the room. A pagoda form, seen in the base for the globe, is used again in large sculptural shapes, gold of course, that form a balustrade on the balcony. The stupas of Siam are glimpsed beyond the balcony, and their silhouettes are echoed in the shapes chosen for the piers and pilasters that encircle the room. Exotic trees and plants

101. *The Agony and the Ecstasy,* 1965. John De Cuir, production designer, Jack Martin Smith, art director. The camera-ready miniature of the Sistine Chapel used in the film is surveyed (the two men are unidentified).

102. *The King and I,* 1956. Lyle Wheeler, John De Cuir, art directors. The royal children parade through an open court in the palace toward their school beneath a flowing canopy; the wit and fantasy of the art direction was premised on large scale watercolor sketches by John De Cuir.

are seen in the landscape and enter the room in long, low planters. Color is used by the art directors and the cinematographer Leon Shamroy to change the mood of the room and to make it seem larger and smaller. At times it is an almost neutral white with blues, and at times it is shot through with gold, greens, pinks, and blues giving the decor many expressive possibilities.

The big Art Department at 20th Century-Fox continued into the sixties, longer than did those of other studios. The members of the department were given some interesting productions to design, but the quality of Fox pictures was not as high overall as it had been in the forties and early fifties. In 1960, with the departure of Lyle Wheeler at the time of the fiasco surrounding *Cleopatra* (1963), the character of the company was changing radically from the old Zanuck days. Wheeler explains,

> I stayed at Fox for eighteen years; never once was I loaned out by Zanuck or the studio. . . . If I left, it was because the old company seemed to be on the way out. Zanuck was gone, Buddy Adler was dead, Spyros Skouras had all sorts of problems

with *Cleopatra*. I was on *Cleopatra* for two years while it was a Walter Wanger production—with sets worth $250,000 already built on the lot—when Elizabeth Taylor came into the project. The film was going to be made in London, then they moved to Italy. Rouben Mamoulian was going to direct—I worked closely with him on the design—but then Joseph Mankewicz took over. With a new director my Rome—Rouben Mamoulian's Rome—didn't look at all like the gold and marble Rome you see in the finished film. We wanted a realistic Rome, closer to that of *The Robe*, earthy in color and texture."[22]

A direct result of the losses sustained by *Cleopatra* was the sell-off of the 20th Century–Fox backlot to developers. As Lyle Wheeler put it, "They bulldozed the Art Department." Gone was the "Chicago Lake" constructed for *In Old Chicago* (1938) and used in over 20 other films; gone was the plantation house built in 1934 for Shirley Temple's *The Little Colonel* and seen in *The Foxes of Harrow, The President's Lady, The Long Hot Summer,* and *Sanctuary,* along with the innumerable other familiar streets, houses, and the mammoth waterways.[23]

Still tying its hopes to big-budget, big-set pictures the studio built a last huge set, the New York City of the 1890s, for *Hello, Dolly* (1969). They assembled a top-notch art direction team: John De Cuir, Jack Martin Smith, and Herman Blumenthal to build the multiple streets seen in the film, at a cost reputed to be around $2 million. The set had to be jerry-built around office buildings at the entryway to the studio off Pico Boulevard, because there was no place else to put such a gigantic outdoor stage with the backlot gone. The public was more impressed by the sets—they are still a big tourist attraction at Fox—than by the performance of star Barbra Streisand, and *Hello, Dolly* was not the financial success the studio needed. The days of the big studio Art Department were over at Fox, too.

In the big studio days, Fox was thought of as a specialist in historic films. The studio's Art Department, one of the largest in the movie industry in the forties and fifties, became expert at recreating other centuries. The members of the department played an enormous role in establishing the visual values so important to telling stories laid in the past. They based their ideas on sound research, and then brought them painstakingly to life in drawings, models, mattes, scenic backdrops, and sets. If there is a discernible Fox visual "look"— and one is less pronounced there than at other studios—then it is most apparent in the dense packing of the visual image with accurate, historic detail.

But 20th Century–Fox produced many other types of films—social conscience, crime, musicals, and comedies, and today these pictures are prized over the historical ones, which are no longer in vogue. It is the "smaller" films of the studio, like *Miracle on 34th Street, Laura,* and *The Grapes of Wrath,* that are most often seen and preferred by audiences.

8
RKO Studio

Although RKO had the shortest life span of any of the major studios prominent in the thirties and forties, 1929–1957, it was responsible for several of the greatest scenic films of the period: *King Kong, Top Hat,* and *Citizen Kane.* A case study in how not to manage a large motion picture company, RKO changed production heads repeatedly, but managed to bring in strong individuals from time to time to produce, direct, and star in their most outstanding productions.

Not even in existence in the silent era, the formation of the studio was a direct result of the success of Warner Bros. with sound. In 1929 the Radio Corporation of America, wishing to promote its own system of sound-on-film for motion pictures, purchased control of an insignificant studio called Film Booking Office of America, and then merged with the Keith-Albee-Orpheum theatre circuit to become Radio-Keith-Orpheum (RKO), a producer and distributor of sound films.

The subsequent years were to see a continual instability in upper management. The average duration of heads of the studio was around a year. But as Roy Pickard, in his book on Hollywood studios observed, "The lack of an iron hand meant also a lack of tight discipline and a chance of creative freedom not readily available at other studios."[1] Yet because of this lack of control he is led to conclude that, "it remains difficult to pinpoint a definitive RKO style," and other writers, like Richard Jewell and Vernon Harbin in *The RKO Story* agree with him:

> Throughout the 27 years of activity . . . RKO existed in a perpetual state of transition. . . . It failed to develop a singular guiding philosophy. . . . As a result, RKO's films tended to reflect the personality of the individual in charge of the studio at any given time—and since this time was always short . . . the pictures never evolved an overall style unique to the studio.[2]

Such conclusions overstate the case. During the thirties—RKO's most important decade—there is, as far as visual style is concerned, a quite recognizable RKO "look."

Lacking a strong production head, the RKO style was forged in the technical departments to an even greater extent than it was elsewhere. The personnel of these departments (Art, Music, Construction and others) were not reshuffled with every upper echelon change. They seem (at least this is true of the Art Department) to have stayed in place for about the same length of time as elsewhere, a decade. Despite, or perhaps because of, the many management changes, RKO was known as a studio in which there was a particularly high level of camaraderie among employees; this too abetted the development of an RKO "look."

Among the strongest departments at RKO was the Art Department. It was headed by one powerful supervising art director, Van Nest Polglase, from 1932–1942, the inclusive dates for the best pictures RKO was ever to produce. In the same period, the studio had six different production chiefs (Pandro S. Berman served twice, making the total shifts in power seven in number). The polished sense of style that emerges from the studio Art Department was particularly advanced by supervising art director Polglase who, according to several of his colleagues, had the first and last word on the visual look of every RKO picture during his ten years with the studio.

Van Nest Polglase's talented associates included Carroll Clark, Perry Ferguson, John Mansbridge, Allan Abbott, Maurice Zuberano and others. These art directors, set designers, and production illustrators brought a recognizable consistency to the RKO product especially noticeable on the most successful series the studio ever produced, the Astaire and Rogers musicals.

RKO was never the wealthiest of studios (they fought off bankruptcy all through the thirties) and so depended more than some of the other studios on the reuse of decorative detailing—moldings, doorways, mantles, stairways—which gives one a feeling of *déjà vu* in many of the lesser efforts of the studio.

The Brooklyn born Polglase was one of the few supervising art directors in a Hollywood studio in the thirties who wasn't a European. **(Illustration 103.)** Educated in New York City in the Beaux Arts traditions of architecture, he began his career as a member of the architectural firm of Berg and Orchard. After spending a year in Cuba working as an associate designer on the Presidential Palace in Havana, he turned to film work in 1919, not too long after pioneers like Hall, Buckland, and Ballin had entered the business.

Wiard Ihnen, a colleague of Polglase's at Berg and Orchard, asked him to join Famous-Players-Lasky. The studio sent him to Hollywood during his first year of employ and he remained there for the rest of his career. When the Lasky company merged with others to form Paramount, Polglase stayed on as a member of the new company's Art Department and rose to be its head before departing for MGM in 1929. Polglase did not receive a film credit until 1925, despite having worked on dozens of pictures—a not uncommon occurrence in the teens and early twenties.

103. Van Nest Polglase, Supervising Art Director, RKO.

While at Paramount Polglase established himself as a creative and versatile talent, with a bent for modernism, on films like *A Kiss in the Dark* (1925) and *Stage Struck* (1925). On the latter comedy, he paired off for the first time with director Allan Dwan with whom he would make a total of eight pictures, the last, *The River's Edge,* in 1957.

Stage Struck gave Polglase the opportunity to build both imaginative modern and extravagant traditional sets in which hard-working waitress, Gloria Swanson, could dream of a Cinderella transformation into a theatrical star. In one scene Swanson is seen, garbed in black satin gown with a 15 foot train, on a sweeping staircase flanked by panels of vibrantly patterned draperies. The set, consisting of only two parts, the stair and the draperies, is flamboyant, opulent, and thoroughly modern; all qualities that will reassert themselves in Polglase's RKO films.

For *The Magnificent Flirt* (1928) the art director got to create one of those fabulous marble bathrooms that were a Paramount trademark. Deco inspired, the studio's publicity called it "the latest idea in interior architecture for the modern home."[3] But with a sunken pool, sculptural water spout, and multiple floor levels defined by an ornamental ziggerat in the center, the bathroom

went far beyond most contemporary Americans' wildest dreams. Indeed, Polglase's bathroom suggests a world of luxury and pleasure that Art Deco seemed best to define for Depression era audiences.[4]

As MGM, also in 1928, was embarking on its own glittering string of Deco settings for films starring Joan Crawford, the success of *The Magnificent Flirt* seems to have figured in the invitation extended to Polglase to join that studio that came in the next year. Although again he must have worked on many films, the art director is only credited on one film, *Untamed* (1929), during his three year tenure at MGM (a credit shared with Cedric Gibbons and Richard Day). The picture starred Crawford and Robert Montgomery in contemporary settings similar to those seen earlier in Polglase's Paramount period.

In 1932 David O. Selznick, in a 13 month tenure as head of RKO, raided other studios to bring a host of talented people including Katharine Hepburn, Fred Astaire, George Cukor, and Merian C. Cooper into that company, and among them was Polglase, whom he hired as supervising art director. Selznick was determined to overhaul the quality of RKO pictures, and there is an appreciable change for the better in the decor of the studio's films after Polglase's arrival. Most noticeable stylistically is a whole-hearted acceptance of the modernist vocabularies of Art Deco and the Streamlined Modern for the contemporary musicals, women's melodramas, and comedies that mark the output of the studio in the decade.

After arriving at RKO in 1932 Polglase's name is frequently, although not always, listed with a unit art director's credit appended. Most often that name is Carroll Clark, with whom the supervising art director teamed on 23 films, including all of the important Astaire-Rogers musicals of the thirties. The gifted Clark had worked at Pathé before being hired by Selznick, like Polglase in 1932. Maurice Zuberano, production illustrator for 16 years at RKO, explained Clark's position in the Art Department: "He was the unit art director who was given all the best pictures." In the 1950s with the gradual decline of RKO, Clark departed to become supervising art director of the Disney Studio's live action films, with credits for such successes as *Mary Poppins.*

In its very first three years of existence RKO did not attempt many big scenic films, but when they did, had tremendous success. In the first year of production, the lavish musical *Rio Rita* (1929) was brought to the screen after a year's run on Broadway; its large cast and spectacular sets and costumes (designed by Max Ree) impressed the public. **(Illustration 104.)** The finale, staged on and before Ree's extravagant river barge, was shot in two-strip Technicolor. The set (directly facing the audience with curtains above and at the sides) and performance recall the theatre. Handsomely garbed chorus girls

104. *Rio Rita,* 1929. Max Ree, art director. The musical finale was staged on an extravagant river barge and filmed in two-strip Technicolor. The theatre type set showed only one elevation to the audience.

paraded and posed on the barge's curving steps in the usual tiered wedding cake arrangement, while others danced energetically in front of it.

The epic western *Cimarron,* a filmed version of the Edna Ferber novel, proved the triumph of 1931 for the new studio. Costing a whopping $1.5 million, *Cimarron* is probably best remembered for its actions scenes staged by director Wesley Ruggles. The 1889 Oklahoma land rush in the early part of the film featured hundreds of extras, wagons, and horses and was shot over a three day period by over a dozen cameras placed everywhere—in trenches, on trucks and in airplanes. What money was left over from the budget after these scenes was used by Ree for a careful, realistic depiction of Ferber's Oklahoma town of Osage over the forty year period covered in the story. His depiction of the growth and weathering of Osage is remarkable, as is Ernest Westmore's comparable weathering of Irene Dunne, the film's heroine, from a sixteen-year-old bride to a fifty-six-year-old grandmother. *Cimarron* won RKO its one and only best picture. Oscar and Max Ree picked up its only best art direction award.

Ree, a native of Copenhagen, had worked on important films for Nordisk Films before coming to the United States. He served as supervising art director at RKO between 1929 and 1932, until his replacement by Polglase. Ree's work often encompassed the design of costumes, as did that of other art directors of the twenties. The exact reasons for Ree's departure as supervising art director after his recent triumphs with *Rio Rita* and *Cimarron* are unknown, but Selznick was probably looking for a designer with more flair for contemporary design, suitable to the trendy dramas and comedies then becoming the RKO stock and trade. Ree also seems to have preferred costume design.

The Polglase and Clark influence is seen in the RKO films of 1932. Clark first designed elegant sets for *A Woman Commands,* the film RKO hoped would make a talking picture star out of silent great Pola Negri. It didn't. Polglase received sole credit on *The Animal Kingdom,* an adaptation of a Philip Barry play dealing with contemporary marriage and mores. Cast in the lead was Leslie Howard, who tried earnestly throughout the film to decide whether he was in love with Ann Harding or Myrna Loy. A wordy picture, the minimal action is all staged by director Edward Griffith in front of Polglase's sets, in the manner of a Broadway production. The sets are sleek and well lit throughout and their detailing refined. Much of the early action takes place in Leslie Howard's country house; an upper-class ambiance with woodwork paneling supplying a rustic touch.

Ann Harding's apartment provides the best evidence of the Polglase touch. It is an edgy set with walls less detailed than in the country house, and with a prominent door surround of curved wood. Polglase loved showy door surrounds; they are seen later, at their flamboyant best, in the Astaire-Rogers musicals. Harding's apartment, despite its odd assortment of conventional furniture, is filled with Polglase's elegant details—like the giant lilies in crystal vases. These add a touch of class (Polglase's speciality), as does the door surround, to what would otherwise be an ordinary interior. At night a bridge with twinkling lights is viewed from the apartment's windows (a cut-out, this bridge recurs in innumerable night scenes at RKO in subsequent years).

David O. Selznick considered *The Animal Kingdom* important enough to screen at the dedication of the new RKO Roxy Theatre in Radio City. Not a big budgeted extravaganza, it had fine performances by the principals, despite Barry's verbiage, and excellent complementary settings by RKO's new supervising art director, who was again proving his great sense of style in contemporary decor.

According to art director Robert Boyle, Polglase continued to do drawings on his pictures even as a supervising art director, something that other art directors like Lyle Wheeler and Cedric Gibbons gave up after becoming department heads. Boyle relates,

> Van used to make these very strange drawings with a T-square and an Eagle drafting pencil, a very soft pencil, and they got very smudged because if you draw in that way and get involved in your work it finally looks a mess. But evidently it worked because then he would turn these drawings over to the art director or set designer and they would be translated. Sometimes not even that; I understand some of them went right on to the floor and were constructed.[5]

During Polglase's first year at RKO, *King Kong* became a pet project of his boss David O. Selznick. Selznick's belief in the film allowed directors Merian C. Cooper and Ernest B. Schoedsack to let out all stops in having artwork made for the film which was released in 1933.

King Kong is an extremely cinematic film, just the opposite of *The Animal Kingdom*, which was a filmed play. Art directors Carroll Clark and Al Herman were assigned to create the physical settings of Kong's Skull Island and the special effects artists, headed by chief technician Willis H. O'Brien, were let loose on the creation of Kong and the other mammoth creatures inhabiting the island.

King Kong is essentially a special effects, a "trick" picture,[6] and detailed drawings were prepared by Art Department members Mario Larringa and Bryon L. Crabbe for the action sequences involving the animals. Sharply contrastive in terms of black and white, they indicate the kind of chiaroscuro lighting employed in the film. This moody lighting resulted from a study of Gustave Doré's 19th century prints, which the members of the Art Department poured over while working on the film. The drawings were used as a selling tool by the picture's directors as they induced Selznick to sink more money into the production. They succeeded; the picture ended by going $300,000 over the original budget.

The effects in *King Kong* are a combination of actual settings, miniatures, glass shots, and scenic paintings. Carroll Clark took over Stage 11 at the RKO-Pathé lot in Culver City and had built

An eerie swamp, man-made cliffs, a waterfall and a ravine bridged by a fallen tree
were dressed with authentic tropical trees and undergrowth. . . . [The elements of
the sets were so designed] that they could be rearranged to create a variety of
different settings. With the addition of glass art by Larrinaga and Crabbe and atmospheric effects by Harry Redmond, Jr., the total set became, as far as the camera
could discern, a vast jungle. . . ."[7]

Al Herman with his crew worked over the massive outdoor set that was
left standing after the completion of Cecil B. DeMille's biblical epic *The King
of Kings* (1926). Consisting of huge cliffs, boulders, a 75 foot high wall, with
remnants of columns and steps, it became, through the addition of jungle
foliage and sculptural carvings, the island's scary lost village (**Illustration 105**).
In this night scene, the wall, its huge wooden door surmounted by a strange
hieroglyph is seen partially covered with scaffolding. Beside the stairs,
fragments of columns are overgrown with vegetation as the jungle encroaches
on them and on the village in the foreground.

More than most pictures *King Kong* depended on glass shots and
miniatures. (**Illustration 106.**) Miniatures were made of the animals, and also
of portions of Skull Island, the ship, and the New York Elevated Railway. Glass
paintings were used for the background of the miniature settings, like the
views of New York City in the final scene with Kong atop the skyscraper.

The final mesh between the built settings and the special effects was a
landmark in films of the early thirties. Despite the fact that these techniques
have been infinitely improved upon since that time, *King Kong* still amazes
for its visual audacity. If the film doesn't bear the stamp of a studio "look,"
it is doubtful whether it would have done so anywhere. It is a unique film; the
work of creative people given license to do something daring.

In 1933 beside the sets for *King Kong,* the RKO Art Department was
called on to design 40 other pictures, including such oddities as *Emergency
Call.* The sets for this tale of malfeasance among doctors included a completely
furnished 16 room hospital put together by art directors Van Nest Polglase and
Al Herman (the versatile Herman was a mainstay of the Art Department from
the thirties into the fifties). Irene Dunne films also kept everyone busy in this
period, and in 1933 *Ann Vickers* (art direction by Polglase and Charles Kirk)
had stylish sets (judge's chambers, a model detention home, domestic interiors) suitable to the actress' always stylish performances. Charles Kirk came
to RKO in the early thirties after a distinguished career in silent films; he was
D.W. Griffith's art director for many of his features in the period 1921–1926,
among them, *Dream Street* (1921), *Orphans of the Storm* (1921), and *America*
(1924). The authenticity of his decor of France at the time of the Revolution
for *Orphans of the Storm* is considered a classic of American silent films. The
RKO Art Department was never as big as some of the other studios, but with
strong, imaginative art directors like Herman and Kirk managed to compete
successfully with other studios, especially when given adequate budgets.

King Kong. 1933. 105. (Top) Carroll Clark, Al Herman, art directors. The massive outdoor remains of a Cecil B. DeMille film became the backbone of Skull Island where the jungle encroaches on the huge wall that separates villagers from a world of mammoth creatures. 106. (Bottom) This composite shot utilizes glass painting, live actors and miniatures, which were all essential to this "trick" film.

Aside from *King Kong* the single most important event at RKO in 1933 was the beginning of the Astaire-Rogers pairing in the musical *Flying Down to Rio*. This began the well-known series, which included *The Gay Divorcee, Roberta, Top Hat, Follow the Fleet, Swing Time, Carefree,* and *The Story of Vernon and Irene Castle.* Incomparable, this was to be the best RKO series ever and also the most identifiable in terms of visual style.

All of the Art Department must be credited for designs that included the Deco Venice of *Top Hat,* the sleek nightclubs of *Swingtime,* and the grand hotel of the *Gay Divorcee.* The official credits on the first five of these films go to Van Nest Polglase and Carroll Clark, who were the Art Department's creative mainstays for the productions. They were ably assisted by others like set designer Allan Abbott and illustrator Maurice Zurbarano. The series contains some of the most dazzling Art Deco and Streamlined Modern sets of an era renowned for them.

Flying Down to Rio opens in the modernistic kitchen of a Miami hotel where Gene Raymond's band (Fred Astaire is its accordionist and Ginger Rogers the singer) are about to be fired by the hotel's manager. The crisp modernity of the set suggests that this quality will dominate the design of the film, but it does not. Wild period touches alternate with modern touches throughout the film, the real (background footage of Rio) alternates with the unreal (the "Carioca" set).

The action changes to the hotel dining room where the band is performing; it is a melange of Spanish tiles, tropical vegetation, and vases. Raymond pursues the film's other star, Delores Del Rio (Astaire and Rogers are only featured players), on the dance floor and, smitten, offers to fly her to her native Brazil in his own airplane. When they must force land on an island he consoles her with a serenade of "Orchids in the Moonlight" accompanying himself on the piano with which his plane is conveniently equipped. The glamour of air travel is, putting it mildly, exaggerated here. But who cares? This whole musical series is predicated on exaggeration and glamour.

Raymond's band has been signed to open Del Rio's father's Hotel Atlantico in Rio. As the plot thickens (Del Rio is already engaged and gangsters are trying to take over the hotel), we see the Hotel Atlantico's courtyard, an uninteresting historiated exterior with a garden, and Del Rio's bedroom, the first of a long line of inspired boudoirs, the rest of which will belong to Rogers. The most unremittingly modern set is the Aviator's Club in Rio, which has open steel stairs like those on a steamship, sleek floors, and incongruously a doorman in 18th century livery.

The most exciting set in the film is the Club Carioca, scene of the big production number, where Astaire and Rogers first dance together on film. The Brazilian nightspot is rustic, set among trees, and exotic, decked out with gigantic illuminated butterflies, mock obelisks, and plants that dangle from every part of the terraces that make up the vast set. The spacious central dance floor is traced with butterfly patterns and tables are placed above it on the surrounding terraces.

The dozens of "Carioca" dancers are dressed in elaborate, even fussy costumes, all based on Latin motifs. For the only time in this series, the costumes, designed by the great Walter Plunkett, seem to seriously clash with the set. The big numbers will, in future, have simplified costumes, complementary to the setting.

At one side of the Club Carioca, the old theatrical device of semicircular stairs is revised to provide a focal point in the set. Between the stairs, a circle of eight white pianos is perched on a revolving platform. It is on their tops that Astaire and Rogers, showing the Latinos "a thing or three," perform their version of the theme dance. (**Illustration 107.**)

Flying Down to Rio contains almost every one of the set types that will recur continually throughout the series: hotels, nightclubs, boudoirs, and natural settings (the jungle island). Although not unremittingly modern as will be the best decor in the series, some of the sets, especially the Club Carioca, have that flamboyance which leaves an indelible impression in future films, and seem so perfectly suited to the fantasy implicit in the dancing of Astaire and Rogers.

The Gay Divorcee, 1934, truly inaugurates the series; directed by Mark Sandrich, it belongs to the dancing pair, now playing the leads. Astaire is an American dancer traveling in Paris and views of the "city of lights" are the introductory moments of the film; we know it will be a romance. The first numbers takes place in a lavish Parisian nightclub, but this is all prelude to the meeting of Astaire and Rogers in a boat terminal in England. He falls in "love at first sight," while she, seeking a divorce from a philandering husband, is antagonistic to his advances.

The rest of the film takes place almost entirely in hotels, first in Fred's London suite for the number "Needle in a Haystack." He ponders the difficulty of finding Ginger in the vastness of London, in a number that brilliantly integrates the furtherance of the plot with song and dance. It is one of Astaire's many famous "prop" dances, where he dances alone but where the objects and furniture and items of apparel in the room are essential elements in the dance. The room interior eclectically combines historic period styles, and has those extraordinary touches that Polglase and Clark always insert to make the decor "simply reek of class," as Astaire will later sing in the song "Top Hat" — in this case a Tiger skin on the floor and chair, a bust of a Roman Caesar on the carved Adam mantle, and French Empire motifs (the × shape) in the room's detailing).

Fred is clad at the beginning of the dance in a silk dressing robe, which he casually tosses to his valet as he leaps over couch and chair, nonchalantly changing attire and tipping his hat as he exits in a quest that we know will eventually discover Rogers.

107. *Flying Down to Rio,* 1933. Van Nest Polglase, Carroll Clark, art directors. The Club Carioca is a melange of the rustic, exotic and modern. Semicircular stairs surrounded a circle of white pianos; the background featured giant butterflies and sculpted filials.

Believe it or not, the couple accidentally meet again at the Bella Vista Hotel in the seaside resort of Brightbourne. The hotel's seaside pavilion is the site of a humorous number by Edward Everett Horton and Betty Grable, and later of the haunting "Night and Day," a duet performed by the principals. The pavilion is pure Polglase-Clark; a circular space with contrastive white iron detailing, again in French Empire style patterns, ×'s and scallops, with a gleaming dark floor with radiating white rib pattern. A vista to the moonlit sea is seen from a terrace at the back of the room; the furniture is again (as in *Flying Down to Rio*) in a white iron Thonet pattern. Totally airy and modern, the pavilion is a polished example of the kind of set that perfectly suits the dancers, never interfering with our appreciation of them, as had the busier "Carioca" set.

The exterior facade and terraces of the Bella Vista Hotel are the film's big-white-set built for the captivating 17 minute "Continental" production number. (**Illustration 108.**) Big, to hold the nearly 100 dancers accompanying

108. *The Gay Divorcee,* 1934. Van Nest Polglase, Carroll Clark, art directors. The Bella Vista Hotel, with Astaire and Rogers dancing to the "Continental," was Streamlined Modern, with flowing balconies and frescoed dolphins on the facade.

Astaire and Rogers; white and modern, because white is the color of early modernism, and they are a modern pair (she is even obtaining a divorce). This is one of the finest sets ever conceived by Polglase and Clark for the series. It is Steamlined rather than Deco, in that its lines are crisp and machine inspired, like those of fast trains or steamships designed by Raymond Lowey and without historical allusions. Art Deco almost always contains a decorative allusion to some historical moment, whether it be from Ancient Egypt, Pre-Columbian art, or the Rococo.

This set owes much to the architectural thinking of pioneering modernists like Le Corbusier, Walter Gropius and others. Built up three full stories on three sides of the sound stage, it has balconies on the upper levels, from which some of the action takes place. The lobby level has a glass curtain wall with revolving doors in the center. It is reached via a broad horizontal band of steps which stretch the entire length of the facade. The steps function beautifully to silhouette the dancers in certain portions of the number. The revolving glass doors serve as foils for Rogers and Astaire, and are also seen as backdrops for close-ups of the women dancer's faces.

Directly above the lobby entrance a balcony traces the length of the facade connecting to the lateral balconied rooms. On the middle of this vast wall painted dolphins playfully leap from the surf. Blossoming trees and plants soften the hotel's contours, as do paintings of sea horses on the walls at the ends of the lobby level.

Curves are injected into the composition on the sides through a semicircular built story of the hotel and through a ground floor terrace with tables. The pattern of the floor has a circular medallion with radiating ribs (the same as in the pavilion set); the art directors always have the highly polished dance floors carry some pattern in these films.

Walter Plunkett's costumes are a marvel of elegance in black and white, with some of the dancers pairing in like costumes and some having costumes that are half dark and half white. The costumes have the usual Plunkett richness, but are completely complimentary to the spare modernism of the set.

At different moments in the long dance, Sandrich cuts to the actors and dancers in various parts of the set. Every portion of the monumental set is seen from a variety of angles. The open central space serves the intricate maneuvers of the chorus, while the stairs, and even the tables and chairs come in handy for the duets that Astaire and Rogers perform as they do Spanish, Hungarian, Viennese and jazz versions of the "Continental."

For many people *Top Hat* is the quintessential Astaire-Rogers musical of the series. Dance critic Arlene Croce writes,

> In the class-conscious Thirties, it was possible to imagine characters who spent their lives in evening dress — to imagine them as faintly preposterous holdovers from the Twenties, slipping from their satin beds at twilight, dancing the night away and then stumbling, top-hatted and ermine-tangled, out of speakeasies at dawn. It was a dead image, a faded cartoon of the pre–Crash, pre–Roosevelt Prohibition era, but it was the only image of luxury that most people believed in, and *Top Hat* revived it as a corrected vision of elegance.[8]

The sets for *Top Hat* are the most wildly extravagant and fantastic of any of this RKO musical series. If the Bella Vista Hotel of *The Gay Divorcee* might have appeared in the built environment, and did in the Streamlined South Beach district of Miami Beach, no one in the Thirties could have imagined seeing the Venice of Polglase and Clark in their own surroundings (Post-Modern architecture has changed that and it is not so difficult to imagine these structures as built architecture after having seen the Louis Armstrong Park in New Orleans or the Pioneer Square in Portland).

The plot of *Top Hat* is even more specious than that of the other dance musicals in the series. However, composer Irving Berlin attended all of the script conferences, and the resultant integration of the songs and dances with what there is of the plot, makes this one of the most excellent Astaire-Rogers films.

The Polglase and Clark sets, beginning with the opening in the Thackeray Club in London, like the songs, seem absolutely perfect for this romance that unfolds in dance. Astaire, ensconced behind a newspaper in a wing-back chair, rattles his paper disturbing the staid Club members. A period room, the huge ornate overmantel of the fireplace is the sole element to betray the RKO touch.

When next Astaire is seen, he has joined Edward Everett Horton in one of those imaginative Moderne (Moderne is a term which embraces early modern but with decorative additions) hotel suites that the picture's designers could produce with such facility. The walls have what has become a Polglase-Clark signature, silhouette frescoes, like those used on the hotel in *The Gay Divorcee,* this time of cloud formations, and of trees, animals and riders. The room is filled with the angular, blond furniture of the period—sofas, round tables glass topped, an oval mirror, low blond cabinets on which Astaire taps a beat. Indirect lighting falls over white ceramic busts, some standing in niches, some on their own pedestals. Doors, always important to Polglase's definition of a room, have painted silhouette portraits like those found on ancient Greek vases.

Astaire's tap dancing on the parquet floor disturbs a sleeping Rogers in the room below. We see her awaken in a large satin cradle of a bed, placed horizontally to the screen. It's a dream of a bed, a stylization based on the elegance of French Empire style furniture, which along with the Rococo seems to be Polglase's and Clark's favorite point of departure.

The couple's first dance together, with Rogers in equestrian costume, takes place in a park shelter to thunder claps and the tune of "Isn't This a Lovely Day, to Be Caught in the Rain." No little wooden affair, the shelter reprises the elegant white iron-work of the Bella Vista hotel pavilion, but with odd perversions of classical motifs, like the upside-down Acanthus leaves serving as a ceiling border. The characters are in a natural setting, but with a touch of man-made elegance in the pavilion to match the elegance of their dancing.

Astaire opens his London show (he is, of course, a dancer, this time being backed by Horton) with the number "Top Hat, White Tie and Tails" in a classically minimal set, as is often the case for his big solo numbers (the "Bojangles in Harlem" number in *Swingtime* and the "Shall We Dance" number in *Shall We Dance*). Using his cane as a prop, Astaire dances across a shiny bakelite floor, before a background drop showing a diminishing line of street lamps and a stencil outline of the Eiffel Tower and of clouds. Menaced by a line of top hat clad rivals, Astaire systematically shoots them down with his cane.

One of the biggest ever big-white-sets next appears. It is a resort hotel on the Lido of Venice, where Astaire and Rogers again meet and eventually unravel the case of mistaken identity that plagues their romance. **(Illustration 109.)** Although it photographed as contrastive black, greys, and whites, the set actually had a red bakelite floor, was painted in bright colors, and canal water that was dyed black. Always used on the floors in these pictures, bakelite is a synthetic resin, whose main virtue was that it was shiny and good for dancing;

its major drawback was that it had to be reworked after each take because of scuff marks.

Croce suggests that director Mark Sandrich came up with the idea of using Venice as the setting for the big-white-set:

> Actually, there was no reason why the locale had to be Venice—it could have been Cannes or Tangier or Monte Carlo—except that, once the art department got hold of the idea, it would hear of nothing else. Venice is itself a stage set, and Polglase's designers needed little prompting to get into the right spirit. The Big White Set normally occupied the largest share of the physical costs of production.... Two adjoining sound stages were flung open, a winding canal was built across both of them....[9]

The Lido set, built up two stories, was used for much of the action of the second half of the picture, with the dances to "Cheek to Cheek" a duet, and the big production of "The Piccolino" performed on it. The set is four-sided, rather than the usual three, with terraces surrounding the canal that wanders across the sound stages. Two arched step bridges, vaguely recalling the Rialto, cross over it at one end and a flat bridge spans the other. Ornate gondolas glide through this witty, make-believe semi-abstraction of Venice. The planar walls and bridge surfaces of the set are in a slightly darker tonality than the gigantic detailing: columns, pilasters, moldings, bull's eye openings, window and door surrounds, canal moorings, and giant lanterns, mostly done in white.

The entire set had to be built above ground level because of the canal. The terrace on which "Cheek to Cheek" is performed is ten feet above the water, adding an unusual perception of depth to the set. For this number the art directors again enclosed Astaire and Rogers in their own elegant spatial co-coon for the private amorous dance (as they had been enclosed by the hotel pavilion in *The Gay Divorcee* and the park shelter in the earlier part of this picture). As the dance begins, Astaire guides Rogers across a bridge and onto a circular terrace covered with a striped awning. It is surrounded by columns at the front and has a low back wall punctuated by an opulent grilled door. Beyond this a garden and distant view to the domed churches of Venice is seen.[10] As their private dance ends—it has embraced all of the space of the pavilion—Rogers walks through the wall gate while the camera turns, so that we see her with the canal and Lido once again, as the world again intrudes on the lovers' privacy.

The film's denouement occurs in the bridal suite of the Lido Hotel. This is another big-white-set consisting of three separate rooms: an ultra-modern bathroom, an opulent sitting room with foyer at the rear, and the bridal chamber itself. The sort of modern/traditional mix found in the bridal suite

109. *Top Hat*, 1935. Van Nest Polglase, Carroll Clark, art directors. The big-white-set was the semiabstract Lido of Venice with its hotel, dining terraces, bakelite dance floor, and canals with bridges.

was sometimes seen, although without the same element of extravagance, in the more swank built environments of New York and other large American cities in the same period. Such a well-known design modernist as Russel Wright used many of the same romantic and historiating elements in his New York home, illustrated in detail in the *House Beautiful* of June, 1934. In a bedroom, white half-columns stood before chocolate brown painted walls adorned with shell sconces, while both French Rococo and Empire inspired furnishings designed by Wright filled the room.

From a set still (**Illustration 110**), the *Top Hat* bridal chamber looks like a traditional proscenium stage set. Yet, it doesn't read that way on film because director, Mark Sandrich, keeps the camera moving capturing only fragments of the decor in individual shots. The doorway, surrounded by shelves laden with porcelain bric-a-brac, is classic Polglase and Clark. The opposite wall holds a regally appointed vanity, while the room's large central space is furnished with pieces inspired by the French Rococo including a satin chaise placed on a furry circular rug.

The focal point of the bridal suite is the circular bedchamber placed in an alcove. Much of the action near the picture's end occurs on the steps to the bedchamber, which is raised in the manner of a royal bed of the 18th century. Diaphanous floor-to-ceiling curtains are theatrically draped at either side of its entry, underscoring the bed as central to the plot. The bed itself is a satin covered circle, the walls of the chamber are covered in drapery, a crystal chandelier hangs overhead. Vases filled with roses enhance the theme of romantic love made explicit in the playfully erotic symbolism of the wall paintings flanking the outside of the bedchamber. In this set, Polglase and Clark have perfected their vision of the bedchamber as a paradise and as the goal of the lovers, an idea not always fully expressed in the dialogue of this series.

Another type of set essential to the RKO dance musical was the modern twenties and thirties nightclub, and *Swingtime,* which revolves almost exclusively around nightlife, is the main film of the series for inventiveness in this type of set. The art direction credits go to Van Nest Polglase and Carroll Clark, but at Jerome Kern's suggestion (he did the score) John Harkrider, who was designing costumes for Universal's *Show Boat,* was brought in to do the costumes for Astaire's "Bojangles of Harlem," a tribute to Bill Robinson. The set for that number was built on a separate sound stage from the other big sets, the Silver Sandal Club and the Club Raymond, and is also Harkrider's work.[11]

Other than clubs, the film's most remarkable set, is the Streamlined Modern Mr. Gordon's Dance Studio, where in an early comedic scene Rogers attempts to teach Astaire to dance. The central space is circular and bordered

110. *Top Hat.* The bridal chamber, in Rococo Deco, had a circular bed in a circular alcove surrounded by diaphanous draperies. The theme of romantic love was made explicit in the playful erotic symbolism of the wall paintings.

with a low railing, plate glass windows, chrome trim, and the ubiquitous linear horizontal strips of the Streamlined are present everywhere. After faking naivete, Astaire shows his dancing prowess as he and Rogers use the entire dance studio, including the furnishings (the low railing serves for athletic pull jumps back and forth by the pair), for one of their fastest and most exciting dances.

The Club Raymond, one of two big-white-sets in the film, is built on several levels that separate out the club's activities; gambling is seen on the upper level, an orchestra plays at an intermediate level, and a dance floor is at the bottom. There are lots of mirrors, shiny chrome fittings, and, alluding to the Rainbow Room in Rockefeller Center, a huge window opening onto a snow scene.

The Silver Sandal Club, of *Swingtime,* is a variation on many other RKO musical sets (see *Flying Down to Rio*) and musical sets in general prominently featuring stairways. The principal architectural element in the Silver Sandal Club is a double curving stairway that looks like it is covered with black lacqueur **(Illustration 111).** Entry to the Club is through double mirror doors onto a circular platform, the nightclub's upper level. Tiers at the sides of the stairs hold tables covered in gold lame and cellophane and laid out with champagne glasses and orb lamps. The band plays between the curves of the stairs. A vast dance floor, delineated with Art Deco chevrons, is at the bottom front of the set. The smooth semicircular back walls of the club are dark and covered with tiny glittering stars. In the crowd scenes, the women guests are all garbed in slinky low-backed white dresses, while the men are in white or black tie tuxedos.

In a deserted Silver Sandal Club Astaire and Rogers dance to the melancholy "Never Gonna Dance."[12] Astaire, who is responsible for the principal choreography of the great duets he does with Rogers, knew the dimensions of the sets, but not all of the details, before he began working on each dance. In some cases Astaire dances in front of the set, but in "Never Gonna Dance" the concept of the dance is intimately connected to the set, particularly the stairs. They serve to underscore the lovers' separation and alienation by isolating them from one another in certain parts of the dance. as he sings the lyrics of the song to her she slowly ascends the stairway, then as he finishes she turns and descends to the dance floor; they walk around the floor until their movements finally flow into a dance that recapitulates their entire relationship. The dance ends with each one moving separately up one of the staircases and Rogers exiting alone.

There has been much discussion as to who actually designed the sets for the Astaire and Rogers pictures. The brilliant Carroll Clark was the principal designer in charge, but given his expertise with modern settings Van Nest Polglase must also have played an important part in the process. His hand is evident throughout in detailing which is so reminiscent of that found earlier in films he executed by himself.

111. *Swing Time,* 1936. Van Nest Polglase, Carroll Clark, art directors. The Silver Sandal Club's curving stairs surrounded the band and had lateral terraces for tables covered in cellophane; tiny stars twinkled on the walls.

Others were involved. Allan Abbott was a chief set designer at the time at RKO and played a part in the execution of the sets. The set decorator on five of the films was the talented Darrell Silvera, who sometimes had as many as 100 or more men working under him (furniture men, drapery men, carpet men) on a picture.

John Mansbridge was an art director at RKO at the time and he indicates that each of the major sets usually required its own art director working under Clark. Mansbridge recalls that, "Polglase, after picking the unit art director, periodically checked the sets during the course of construction. The creative choices were often made by him."[13]

Mansbridge picked up much of his art direction expertise from Polglase, and more particularly from Carroll Clark, who may have been more accessible to a beginner than was the supervising art director. **(Illustration 112.)** Mansbridge is one of the RKO Art Department's success stories. He rose up the corporate ladder: beginning as a messenger in 1933, he advanced to blue print boy, to draftsman (junior), draftsman (senior), assistant art director, art director. Mansbridge stayed on at RKO until it closed its Art Department in 1957, then went on to work at 20th Century–Fox, designing, among others, three films for Samuel Fuller, including *China Gate* (1957) and *Forty Guns* (1957). He later became supervising art director for live feature films at the Walt Disney Studios.

Mansbridge admired Carroll Clark's style: "He didn't like to make things square. He liked curves and designing in depth. You often got views from one room to the other. He used frequent breaks, nooks and crannies, for lights. The opulence of those settings in the thirties was due to the times being hard. They wanted to give people an uplift."

The Astaire-Rogers pictures were among the principal money makers for RKO in the thirties and it is clear that the full resources of the Art Department were poured into them.[14] The sets celebrated glamorous, modern romances being told through an artistic medium—the dance—and provided a visual counterpart to the dance that was provocative, and no matter how fanciful, seemed fitting.

The many Art Deco and Art Moderne interiors in the series appealed to the Depression decade audiences' desire for a better world—more modern, more glamorous than the one they were inhabiting. If Astaire and Rogers could leave the audience thinking that perhaps they too could dance, Carroll Clark and Van Nest Polglase left them believing they too might someday exist in luxuriant, modern settings.

The RKO sets are wittier and lighter in concept than the new architecture most people saw around them in the thirties, when skyscraper construction (the Empire State Building) and WPA projects (the Hoover Dam) that were heavy and monumental in concept got a lot of attention as representative of modern tendencies in architecture and design. Only a few corporations, the Greyhound Bus Company and Coca-Cola, were smart enough to use Streamlined aesthetics to define their identities as modern companies. Many department stores and shops also grasped the fact that in the thirties, the public was ready to accept modern design principles. Interestingly, builders of huge movie palaces in the twenties had mostly ignored modernity for the exotic vocabularies of Moorish, Renaissance and Baroque and only a relatively few movie theatres in the thirties were built in the Deco or Moderne (the Radio City Music Hall is, of course, one of them).

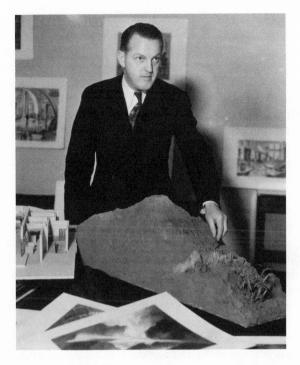

112. Carroll Clark, RKO art director, and supervising art director of Disney live-action films.

There is no doubt, that film art directors Polglase, Clark, Day, Pye, Gibbons, Dreier (Paramount was a pioneer), and others, were leading the public away from historicism in design, and that pictures like the Astaire-Rogers series did much to revolutionize American thinking. The Second World War, when there was little building activity, slowed up the acceptance of modernism, but the postwar era saw it flourish again. But after the War, it was not the Deco and Streamlined that were to remain popular. Instead the modernism of the International Style, especially involving the look provided by the angular glass curtain wall (Mies van der Rohe's 1954 Seagram Building is a seminal building in this regard) came to dominate.

Oddly, it is in the fifties that the Polglase and Clark movie interiors were to receive their finest (their last?) apotheosis in the glamorous hotels built by Morris Lapidus in Miami Beach — the Fontainebleau and the Eden Roc Hotels. Lapidus is one of the few modern architects who has admitted that he was influenced by film decor, especially of the thirties.[15]

Although not RKO's forte, period films were infrequently produced in the thirties, and the Art Department rose to the occasion for memorable pictures like *Little Women* (1933), *The Little Minister* (1934), *Gunga Din* (1939), and *The Hunchback of Notre Dame* (1939). Always conceived as prestige films at RKO, period films were given a better budget and more Art Department personnel were set to work on them than for the usual contemporary picture. *Little Women*, set in Louisa May Alcott's New England of the Civil War era, was finely tuned in terms of the details of Victorian middle-class interior decor by art directors Polglase and Hobe Erwin. The sets are truer in terms of authentic evocation of the period than the much more expensive sets that MGM was to mount for its 1949 Technicolor version of the story. All of the major studios of the era seem able to produce distinguished period decor, which is understandable given their Beaux Arts–trained art directors, who in these pictures are bringing to bear their strict earlier training in the historical styles.

Katharine Hepburn, who starred as rebellious sister Jo in *Little Women*, was frequently to head the case of the period pictures at RKO. She teamed with John Beal for *The Little Minister*, RKO's most expensive film of the next year. Van Nest Polglase and Carroll Clark designed the countryside of a small Scottish township with great authority basing their ideas upon period photographs and engravings of Scotland.

Among the real triumphs in RKO scenic films of the thirties were the period pieces, *Gunga Din* (1939), the most expensive film ($2 million) RKO had ever made, and *The Hunchback of Notre Dame* (1939), costing nearly as much. The locations for *Gunga Din*, a story freely adapted after the sonorous Rudyard Kipling poem set in India, were shot in the countryside near Long Pine, California. The sets are not merely exotic background in this George Stevens' film, as they often are in adventure pictures, but partner the wonderful action sequences at the heart of the film. The *Gunga Din* sets—a British colonial house, army barracks, Indian temple and town—just about all end up demolished by the battling British Lancers (Cary Grant, Victor McLaglen, Douglas Fairbanks, Jr.), the heroes of the piece. We are introduced to the threesome as they throw assorted things and persons through an Indian screen from an upper story window. In another scene an elephant assists Cary Grant in escaping from the stockade by pulling out a window and accidentally bringing down the entire building.

Much of the budget for the picture was put into Polglase and Perry Ferguson's sets and into hundreds of extras who take part in the battle scenes. (Illustration 113.) A small Indian village, geometric and white, was built up against a mountain and in the arid terrain. Few mattes or special effects were used in the picture (a notable exception is the canyon and swinging bridge [a miniature] leading to the golden temple). Even the roofs of the village were built, so that fights and daring leaps could be staged there. Dramatic overhead shots onto the village's streets done at different times of the day and evening add immeasurably to the foreign atmosphere of the film.

The decor for William Dieterle's *The Hunchback of Notre Dame* is a classic in historic recreation in films, with sets representing Victor Hugo's Paris

113. *Gunga Din,* 1939. Van Nest Polglase, Perry Ferguson, art directors. The Golden Temple, a forbiddingly tiered sculptural mass, was one of assorted large sets erected in a rugged area near Lone Pine, California, for this action film.

of the time of King Louis XI. Van Nest Polglase was the supervising art director, and seems to have done much of the designing himself; the unit art director was Al Herman. Given the scale of the sets, most of the Art Department must have been involved in some capacity on this film. The set decoration is again credited to RKO's talented Darrell Silvera.

Charles Laughton starred as Quasimodo, the deformed bellringer of the famous cathedral. Producer, Pandro S. Berman, insisted that the epic be filmed as a tremendous spectacle of late medieval life following the tradition of the Lon Chaney (1923) silent version.

The enormous sets were built in the San Fernando valley on the ranch RKO had purchased in 1929. The main studio facilities at 780 Gower Street were crowded up next door to Paramount and could provide no room for backlot expansion.

Polglase's and Herman's cathedral and square, the heart of 15th century Paris, are alive with period detail. The vast rectangle of the square is surrounded by half-timbered and stone buildings, with high peaked tiled roofs and crooked chimneys. The facade of Notre Dame figures prominently in the story and much of it was built, including mammoth details of the giant tower and belfry over which Laughton scrambles in his rescue of Esmeralda, the beautiful gypsy girl who is about to be executed. A narrow spiraling stair and the interior of the belfry with its huge bells, playfully rung by Laughton with his feet, were also built, but the church's nave and high altar were done as mattes.

Director Dieterle hardly backs off from the set enough in the first part of the picture for it to be seen, but beginning with the flogging of Quasimodo he succeeds in using its vastness for poetic and dramatic purpose — as after the flogging when the Hunchback drags himself across an almost empty square, the crowd parting before him as if he were a leper. Later during the awful and unnecessary battle between the Beggar King's army and Quasimodo, the action takes place over all parts of the square, the several streets leading into it, and the built cathedral facade, where Quasimodo pours molten metal down onto the crowd from the roofline gargoyles. In the haunting last shot, Quasimodo squats next to one of these gigantic gargoyles, matching him in ugliness, as he wishes, "I too were made of stone."

The RKO Studio became a pioneer in the use of color with their production of the first full-length Technicolor feature, *Becky Sharp* (1935). Yet, RKO's name was not to become closely associated with the color process, partly because of the high cost of the process. One thing *Becky Sharp* proved to the industry, was that color could be artfully done in film to underscore thematic material. Robert Edmond-Jones, a lighting and color expert from the Broadway stage, worked together with the director Rouben Mamoulian to etch tonal variations in the sets and costumes that played on the action and mood of the picture. At the Duchess of Richmond's ball, held on the eve of the Battle of Waterloo, the guests' growing anxiety about the events unfolding is expressed by color shifts from cool greys, greens and blues to hot tonalities of red and orange. Mamoulian and Edmond-Jones (with associate art director Wiard Ihnen) achieved their effects through cuts from figures in paler costumes to those in rich color as the dance proceeds, and by bathing the background in different colors and lights.

There are scarcely any memorable RKO films in color after *Becky Sharp* (it had cost the financially ailing company a million dollars to produce), and color does not really become established until MGM's double triumph in 1939 with *The Wizard of Oz* and *Gone with the Wind.* But black and white film was well suited to RKO's needs in the mid-thirties as it served up its own brand of realism in such gritty melodramas as *The Informer* (1935), *Winterset* (1936) and in 1941, a variation on the theme, *Citizen Kane.* These were dark films, owing more to the German school of film design, with moody lighting and minimal but telling decorative elements, than did most RKO films. Done on small budgets, necessity was the mother of daring inventions by art directors in all of these films.

The Informer, designed by Van Nest Polglase and Charles Kirk and directed by John Ford, is a taut drama of betrayal and murder set in a fog shrouded Dublin of the 1920s. Victor McLaglen starred as the cowardly, loutish informer who furtively makes his way through impoverished interiors and atmospherically menacing streets, streaked with rain and dramatically raked with light, attempting to escape the retribution that will be his due. Done on a small budget ($200,000) and filmed in less than three weeks, *The Informer* became a classic of its genre and proved what the Art Department could do when pressed for time and money.

Winterset, from a play by Maxwell Anderson, is another dark tale, in a dark setting. The minimal sets are by Polglase and Perry Ferguson, following along lines put forward in the stage set by Jo Mielziner. A son (Burgess Meredith) trying to clear his dead father's name of a crime he did not commit is led to a tenement and street in the shadow of the Brooklyn Bridge. **(Illustration 114.)** All studio built, the gloomy, ominous street is dominated by stone stairs and a looming embankment closing off one end. It is atmospherically lit and photographed from many different angles, so that the single set seems surprisingly varied.

The experience gained on *Winterset* (he had only joined RKO a year earlier) helped prepare Texas born Perry Ferguson for the much more complicated, but related task, of designing *Citizen Kane* for Orson Welles. Van Nest Polglase was again listed as art director, but on this one, Polglase seems, according to both Welles and photographer Gregg Toland, to have served in a supervisory capacity.

Citizen Kane began filming in July, 1940, but had been in pre-production for some months. Almost from the first it began to go over-budget. In early June the projected budget was over a million dollars; Welles had only been promised $500,000 by RKO to make the film. As Robert Carringer relates, "Budgetary realities led to sweeping changes in all areas of production ... art director Perry Ferguson, and cinematographer Gregg Toland were by this time (mid–June) the creative nucleus of the production, and they jointly managed the budgetary crisis."[16] One of the places Ferguson cut was in the building of entire sets, although there are some of those, like the breakfast room of Kane's home with his first wife and the interiors of the newspaper offices. For the rest of the film, and its most inspired decor, Ferguson invented memorable

114. *Winterset,* 1936. Van Nest Polglase and Perry Ferguson, art directors. This studio-built foggy tenement street beneath the Brooklyn Bridge (background), atmospherically lit and photographed from many angles set the gloomy mood for a dark tale.

fragments—giant fireplaces, huge stairs, ornate Gothic windows—especially for Kane's castle, Xanadu. These were put together with mattes, prop shots (newspaper clippings, posters, newsreel footage) and special effects processes (multiple exposures, miniatures) so that there seems to be no paucity of setting, just the opposite, the sets are rich and redolant with meanings and symbols relevant to the story.

The opening sequence is indicative of the way effects, camera focus and angle will be used in the film. In a close-up, a "No Trespassing" sign looms out of the mist, the camera swings up over it and over a fence terminating in barbed wire to a huge K imbedded in an iron gate. Gondolas bob on an unseen canal, fog shrouded Indian arches deny the sense of known place as a castle emerges at the top of a hill, its entry radiating light. Cut to a bedroom whose only perimeters, other than darkness, are the outlines of Gothic tracery windows with a muted light ebbing around them. In a double exposure a mouth whispering "Rosebud" is seen in a field of snow. The warped image of a nurse enters the room as a glass snow bubble crashes to the floor.

115. *Citizen Kane,* 1941. Van Nest Polglase, Perry Ferguson, art directors. One of several excellent mattes, this one was used in the opening sequences of the film, presenting Xanadu, "the costliest monument a man has ever built to himself."

In the entire opening sequence, the only completely built set (the wall and door through which the nurse enters) have occupied only a second of screen time. Xanadu, the "costliest monument a man has ever built to himself" has been created by mattes (the castle exterior) **(Illustration 115)** isolated built fragments (the Gothic windows), and lighting effects (on the gondolas, behind the windows, on the profile of the bed). Without dialogue, except for the spoken "Rosebud," every element has worked to visually evoke the enigma and mystery of Charles Foster Kane's persona.

There then occurs an abrupt injection of newsreel footage; Kane is dead. It is Xanadu in the bright light of day, large, gauche, eccentric, repulsive, destitute of its earlier seductive qualities. This Xanadu is achieved mostly through newsreel footage of real places which are then juxtaposed to acted vignettes in partial settings (Kane visiting Hitler). The rest of the movie recapitulates Kane's life story, all of which has been set out in skeletal form in the newsreel.

A reporter sets out to find the missing links in Charles Foster Kane's life. His first break comes from the reading of Kane's lawyer Thatcher's diary, at the solemn library bearing his name. One of Perry Ferguson's (with Toland's excellent lighting) most powerful sets: it suggests the austerity of Thatcher's personality and what must have been the bareness of Kane's boyhood, when he was deprived of his mother's love.

Gregg Toland's use of set light, hard and soft light which is combined to add gradations of shade to the sets, is telling in this and other scenes. A hard, bright light rakes over the scene, usually at a 90 degree angle so that sharp shadows appear where there are textures and shapes in the built portion of the set.

The Thatcher Library first appears in a shot to a large ceiling skylight, the camera then tracks downward to a bare wall fragment and a dedicatory pedestal. The reporter is led into the vault-like reading room where a sole ray of bright light penetrates the pitch darkness. It illuminates a long table where he sits to read the specific pages allowed him, an unseen clock ticking ominously and a guard hovering in the blackness. There is an abrupt cut, as the content of the diary is revealed, to a snow scene viewed through the window of Kane's Boarding House (originally seen as a painting in the newsreel). In its realistic interior the story of Kane's separation from his parents is played out.

The front of the boarding house materializes in a snowstorm, revealing young Charles playing with his sled. Because of the snow little can be seen of the set except for the front porch. Weather is frequently invoked by Ferguson to justify the lack of a full set; it rains incessantly in the next portion of the film, blurring what is outside windows and establishing the melancholy mood of the film as the reporter interviews Kane's past associates.

However, there doesn't always have to be a good reason for the exclusion of a set. When the newsreel ends in the early moments of the film, we are left in the unexpected darkness of the editing room, the viewing screen still glowing with light. No other lights come on as the scene unfolds. No faces are seen. Thus, the reporter sent out on the Kane story fails to be personalized; the effect is to put the audience in his place as the unseen interviewer. Such radical and expressionistic elimination of setting had been tried before—mainly in European films; but Polglase and Ferguson's decor together with Welles' direction and Toland's photography on *Citizen Kane* represented a radical departure for American films of the early forties.

On the other hand, several sets (the interiors of The New York Inquirer office) were built in full and realistic detail including the ceilings, for which the camera shows a peculiar fascination. Ferguson's Inquirer exterior, seen in a sketch executed by C. Gillinparter, was built below and was a matte in the uppermost stories. The built sets were redressed and reused continuously throughout the film. The newspaper's office is first seen as Kane idealistically takes over the small operation, later a party for all the reporters he has swiped from other papers is set out before the long wall of windows of the interior with confetti and balloons added, still later it recurs when his influence is dwindling as in disgrace he loses the election for governor and then, still later, loses his integrity as he pushes his second wife's singing career in the now dim, lamp-lit interior.

In another built set, the breakfast room, Kane's first marriage is seen to deteriorate in brief vignettes enacted while they sit at table. It is a shallow set built on three sides. Through changes in the position of the figures (they first sit together and then at either ends of the table), in costumes (six changes), and in decor their estrangement is etched. The room has lancet windows at the back; the wall behind Kane is covered by plants, flamboyant palms among them, that becomes sparser with the passage of time (indicated by a slide pan), the wall behind his wife is partially obscured by a silver tea service and a candelabra with knife-like hanging crystals that become prominent in the last vignette as they sit in silence, she reading a rival newspaper.

The campaign sequence is likewise masterful in telescoping action and using a minimum of built set together with special effects. Newspaper headlines again proclaim the facts, then in a live action sequence the camera moves in swiftly over crowds in pinpoints of light packed into a vast auditorium (a miniature) to Kane and his cronies on a platform standing before a huge campaign poster of his shifty looking features. Campaign rhetoric pours from the candidate's mouth, as the camera pulls back to reveal his arch enemy, Boss Gettys, in the high rafters of the building, and in a reverse shot Kane, the size of an ant on the platform below. With the poster almost the only built element of the set, Kane's story has been forwarded, but also something of the dark power behind all of the mass political rallies of American politics has been suggested by the miniature people and the giant politico of the poster.

Not all of the settings were as carefully calculated as was the one for the campaign rally. Joseph Cotten recalls how he was telephoned one evening with the news that Welles had hurt his ankle and would not be able to act the next day, thus putting him on call for a scene that wasn't supposed to come up for another several weeks. He had overnight to prepare to play Kane's ex-friend, a drama critic, now aged and confined to a wheelchair in a nursing home. As Welles, himself in a wheelchair because of his ankle, directed the scene, Cotten recalls, "We shot until lunch with an improvised set. It was meant to be the roof garden of a hospital. All they did was lower a big section of street and put a low wall and a wheelchair in front of it. Nothing more. It was just thrown together in a hurry."[17] As it appears on the screen, with Cotten giving a moving performance in a shadowy foreground, the low wall is in the distance as are two men in wheelchairs, unmoving and deathlike in a raking white light. It is a haunting and surreal image, reminiscent of an Edward Hopper painting. Ferguson's set doesn't look like it could have been much more improved on even with the additional several more weeks of planning that Cotten says were intended. This dark scene, laced with macabre overtones, leads directly into the brightly lit and, at first, upbeat breakfast scene.

Throughout the film, the places where Kane has once been happy and active are drawn out in the most realistic terms (the interior of the Kane Boarding House, the interior of the Inquirer, the interior of the breakfast room), while the places where his life has been unhappy and unrealized, the opera houses of his second wife's aborted career and Xanadu, are the most unrealistic and fragmented.

Kane first meets his paramour, Susan, on a rain wet street corner, where he accepts her invitation into the dowdy, cluttered Victorian apartment that is now her home. Later, this new wife's singing career unfolds in set fragments suggestive of the vast expanses of opera houses. A few props with her singing are superimposed on newspaper copy and suffice to tell the sad tale of her brief career.

The embittered couple retire to their fairy-tale castle, a place stuffed with the things Kane has plundered from the art warehouses of Europe. In this place of escape from the forces he can no longer control, Kane ages terribly. He cannot even control Xanadu; it is never finished and is deteriorating even before his death. And he cannot control his wife, who leaves him.

The main interior of Xanadu is a great hall defined by a towering stone stairway, a gigantic fireplace and huge statues — often the couple's only company. (**Illustration 116.**) Kane's wife plays with a mammoth jigsaw puzzle — everything about the place is too large. In this respect *Citizen Kane* is referential to the great horror films, like *Dracula* (1931), done earlier at Universal and designed by Charles D. Hall. Mrs. Kane sits in the corner of the hearth next to a bellows that is almost as tall as she is. He sits isolated in a throne, a king with a failed principality, Gothic windows again filter light into a vast space where darkness provides much of the definition of walls.

When the action closes in on Susan packing to leave, her room, a sort of exquisite doll's house, is built in its entirety including the ceiling, and is filled with fluttery draperies and curtains. Shelves and tables are cluttered as they had been in her little Victorian apartment, but this time with precious porcelain statuettes. She departs through a perspectival series of Moorish doorways that appear to be a long progression of rooms. Kane, furious, demolishes her room. He pulls off the satin bedcover, hurls the bric-a-brac to the floor, keeping only the glass snow-filled orb, as he utters "Rosebud." Kane departs

116. *Citizen Kane.* Xanadu's great hall is filled with antique sculpture and cumbersone carved furniture; Kane's wife (Dorothy Comingore) gazes across the vast inhuman expanse of the hearth toward Kane (Orson Welles, right).

the ravished room, past the exotic Moorish decor, and past a mirror reflecting his solitary image as he exits the frame. The illusive image of Kane has been frequently seen through glass and reflected in it—through the window of his mother's boarding house, in the windows of his newspaper office, and now a fading hulk in a mirror of his castle.

In the famous final sequence, the camera comes down from a great height onto Xanadu's stairway, with Kane's belongings—in a sea of crates—filling the formerly empty space around it, to settle on the sled "Rosebud." Next with smoke rising from the furnace into which the sled has been thrown, the camera retraces the opening shot, ending on the "No Trespassing" sign that has originally warned us against prying too deeply into unknown places.

The art directors, Polglase and Ferguson, seldom mentioned by those who write about *Citizen Kane,* should be credited for the part they played in making this landmark American film. They had dug into the Expressionist bag of cinematic effects, and come up with some of the most inventive and emotionally moving settings in the history of American films.[18]

117. *The Magnificent Ambersons,* 1942. Mark-Lee Kirk, art director. Agnes Moorehead and Tim Holt confront one another in a Victorian stairwell; its blocky shape, turned balusters, and stained-glass windows were to be seen frequently in RKO films.

Citizen Kane and Welles' next production, *The Magnificent Ambersons* (1942, designed by Mark-Lee Kirk) **(Illustration 117)** were highpoints in the history of art direction at RKO. Although many fine pictures were to emerge from the studio in subsequent years, the stylish and inventive period of Van Nest Polglase's tenure as supervising art director were over. He left the studio in 1942. Polglase continued to design pictures at Columbia and independently until 1957, including *A Song to Remember* (1945) and *Gilda* (1946, with Stephen Goosson), but is best remembered for those great years at RKO.

Polglase was succeeded as supervising art director by Albert D'Agostino, a New Yorker, who began his career in 1915. He had been trained at the Mechanics' Institute and Columbia University, and first worked as a stage designer for scenic studios in New York City. He worked for various companies in the twenties, including MGM in New York and Selznick Pictures, in Fort Lee, New Jersey. D'Agostino organized a business called Tec-Art Studios in 1923, then in 1925 he joined Universal, where he remained for much of the thirties. He was at RKO from 1939 until his retirement in 1958 at the time of the demise of the company.

At RKO, D'Agostino's name is most intimately associated with the small, creative group of people surrounding producer Val Lewton; he and Walter E. Keller designed for them most of the small budget horror pictures which have subsequently become prized examples of the genre: *The Cat People* (1942, with Keller), *I Walked with a Zombie* (1943, with Keller), *The Leopard Man* (1943), *The 7th Victim* (1943, with Keller), and others.[19]

Cat People (1942), the first of the series and arguably the best, was filmed on the modest budget of $134,000. Then head of production at RKO, Charles Koerner, had decided to form the special unit in 1941; as supervisor he hired Val Lewton, a former story editor for David O. Selznick.

The basic premise of these pictures, often filmed in the most ordinary of settings, was to build a feeling of terror in the audience through the gradual unfolding of a story involving the supernatural. As written by DeWitt Bodeen and directed by Jacques Tourneur, *Cat People* succeeded through the most economic of means to scare people out of their wits.

As was so often the case, D'Agostino and the RKO Art Department continued to face austerity budgets. Writer DeWitt Bodeen, recalls that because of wartime emergencies *Cat People* was filmed almost in its entirety on the RKO lot in Hollywood and on the back lot in Culver City,

> Only one sequence, the swimming pool scene, was shot off the lot at a swimming pool in a once-swank residential hotel in the Alvarado district of Los Angeles; the cat cages at Central Park Zoo, the transverse walk through the park, and the street scenes were all filmed on studio stages. The largest interior setting, Alice's apartment, was the upper floor of the same brownstone front building that had been used in *The Magnificent Ambersons* (1942). The four-storied stairway in the entrance hall was redressed to lend the film a richness it could not otherwise have afforded on its limited budget.[20]

The story set in Manhattan, involves a Yugoslavian girl, Irena (Simone Simon), one of the cat people, who, according to the lore of her country, can transform themselves into dangerous large cats and kill their loved ones under certain circumstances. The studio built Central Park Zoo figures prominently in the story which opens there with Irena sketching a black leopard in his cage and ends there with her being killed by him.

The story unfolds in the relatively bland settings of apartments, pet store, and offices. The very blandness of the settings serves to heighten the audience's perception of the strange, exotic, and feline character of Irena. Subtle clues as to the nature and activity of the cat people are given in the decor. In one instance, an innocent looking Irena stands before the painting by Francesco Goya of *Don Manuel Osorio de Zuñiga and His Pets* [c. 1787], which shows an innocent-looking child with two wide-eyed cats menacing a pet bird at his feet—an analogue in the story to Irena frightening to death her own pet bird and then feeding him to the panther in the zoo.

In the second half of the picture, under cloak of darkness, the startling terror-filled action scenes begin to erupt in more dramatic settings than have been previously seen. The cat woman begins to stalk her prey (a woman friend of her husband's, who has provoked her jealousy). Unseen, but to the accompaniment of the insistent sound of paws on pavement and cat snarls, she terrorizes the woman, first in a dark Central Park with rings of light from streetlamps the only illumination, and then in a lonely indoor swimming pool where shadows play in dreadful, ominous ways over the walls and ceiling. The darkness of the last part of the picture adds an extra dimension of menace to the *mise-en-scène* that evokes evil through eerie lighting, and through sound effects.

The horror cycle designed by Albert D'Agostino and Walter E. Keller has its own recognizable "look" as did the Astaire/Rogers series, and the decor is sometimes more involving than the plot of the picture. This is the case in the sequel, *The Curse of the Cat People,* directed by Gunther V. Fritsch and Robert Wise. It has nothing of the menace and suspense of the original, and is even somewhat at odds with it in the overlay of sentimentality in the plot concerning a little girl and her imaginary friend, a benign Irena. The settings are again backlot ordinary, with most of the narrative taking place in the suburban home and yard of the child and her parents (the father was Irena's husband and the mother the coworker who had roused Irena's jealousy). Whenever Irena appears to the chid in the yard, it is magically transformed, marvellous effects occur—trees rustle, leaves fall in darkness that becomes light. These gripping effects are more engaging than the plot, which goes nowhere, and one simply waits for them to occur again. This is a case of art direction surpassing, unintentionally, a tired narrative.

In 1937 with *Snow White,* Walt Disney began distributing his films through RKO, and in the forties Sam Goldwyn and other independent producers and directors, also entered into distributing or coproduction contracts with the company. The RKO art directors were not involved with the Disney animation films, but several of them, Carroll Clark and John Mansbridge in particular, joined Disney when RKO folded and Disney began to do live action films. Art directors at RKO were often called on to work on Goldwyn productions; Perry Ferguson helped design the award winning *The Best Years of Our Lives* (1946), but Sam Goldwyn was also fond of finding new talent and brought Broadway designer George Jenkins to Hollywood to work with Ferguson. Their ingratiating and realistic portrait of postwar America perfectly suited those same characteristics in the picture's story.

In the same year, Frank Capra, as a part of Liberty Films, released one of his finest pictures, *It's a Wonderful Life* (1946), through RKO. But RKO has also produced memorable films throughout the forties on its own, although they became fewer. After 1948, when Howard Hughes acquired controlling interest in the company and, for economy reasons, began the reduction of studio personnel which quickly reached 75 percent, they became far apart.

The early forties saw clever comedies, *The Devil and Miss Jones* (1941), and melodramas, *The Little Foxes* (1941), and the middle years produced audience pleasers like the sentimental Ingrid Bergman and Bing Crosby *The Bells of St. Mary's* (1945). The late forties are best remembered as the Robert Mitchum years at RKO. His pictures, many of them *film noir,* and built around the star, bear the distinguishing marks of the RKO visual style of the decade. Films like *Out of the Past* (1947) and *The Big Steal* (1949) were photographed in the crisper black and white film available, and are characterized by contrastive, shadow-filled interiors (studio built) and much more location shooting than had been seen in the war years.

Albert D'Agostino was supervising art director on both *Out of the Past* (with Jack Okey) and *The Big Steal* (with Ralph Berger), and must be given credit for honing this style. In *Out of the Past,* Mitchum plays a detective who falls in love with the *femme fatale* (Jane Greer) he is sent to Mexico to find. Told in flashbacks, we learn how Mitchum tracked Greer to Mexico. Mexico was becoming a favorite locale for mystery stories; it was foreign, exotic in places, and not far from Hollywood. Director Jacques Tourneur deftly weds the foreign with the domestic scenes in this fast paced film. One particularly good setting is the luxurious Lake Tahoe lodge seen in the last scenes, which fills with lengthy shadows as the villainess confronts and kills a former lover.

The Big Steal, also shot in Mexico, is a detective-action picture laced with *noir* overtones. Built around a chase motif, director Don Siegel deftly propels the action through Mexican back streets and rutted roads, making the countryside a much more important ingredient in the film than it was in the Tourneur film. In the story, Mitchum and Jane Greer are trying to capture the thief of an Army payroll (for which Mitchum is being blamed); they are in turn chased by William Bendix. Respectively referred to in the studio's publicity for the film, as "A Man of Ice," "A Woman of Fire," and "A Guy with a Gun," they are followed through studio built interiors (army offices, apartments, hotel rooms), and exteriors in the Mexican countryside. Siegel stages much of the action in the exteriors, along roadsides, on small village streets (the dusty

Mexican streets, so different from even the most exciting studio built replicas, add the proper note of desperation to the chase), and especially at a high-class Mexican resort hotel where he takes every advantage of the desert vegetation, the driveways, and the swimming pool.

The year after Hughes took over and began dismantling RKO, it was still producing memorable and ground-breaking films like the first feature by director Nicholas Ray, *They Live by Night* (1949). Designed by Al Herman, this claustrophobic film focused on two doomed young lovers caught in a web of crime and criminality not entirely of their making. They drift across country through cheap motor courts and diners which are grinding in their poverty.

But RKO's glory days were past by this time, and the studio that had never found a strong head to manage it, now found in Hughes one strong enough to mismanage it out of the motion picture business. The studio ceased making motion pictures in 1957, selling its buildings on Gower and Melrose to Desilu for the production of television programs. The Art Department was considered part of the plant and was dismantled; most of the files, drawings, stills and other archival materials were thrown out.

Despite the management turmoil at RKO, the art direction of their pictures, done under Van Nest Polglase's supervision, was among the best in the business. All black-and-white, it was black and white with one hundred nuances. Polglase, an early modern stylist in motion pictures, carried his sense of style into the most distinctive of the studio's series, the Astaire and Rogers pictures. He also allowed talents like Carroll Clark and Perry Ferguson to experiment with scenic values using vocabularies as far afield as Streamlining and expressionism. Because of a laxity in management supervision, the RKO technical departments must be given a high degree of credit for the many innovative pictures that came out of the studio, from *Citizen Kane* to *Top Hat*. They did much to delineate the RKO style, and if any studio had it, RKO pictures had "style."

9
Columbia

Columbia Pictures is the house that Harry Cohn built, and the regal symbol he chose for the studio, a statuesque female garbed in white holding a torch aloft, was a far cry from his own *modus operandi*. A crude, foul-mouthed studio boss who enjoyed picking on his employees, he had old-fashioned horse sense, fashioned on New York's Lower East Side, when it came to making motion pictures.

Columbia began as C.B.C. Film Sales Company in 1920, formed by three former employees of Universal's Carl Laemmle, the brothers Harry and Jack Cohn and Joseph Brandt. It was one of the "poverty row" studios that existed around the neighborhood of Sunset Boulevard and Gower Street, and made two-reel quickies hoping for a large profit on a small investment. C.B.C. soon became known by the deprecatory nickname "Corned Beef and Cabbage," eventually prompting Cohn to change the name in 1924 when Columbia Pictures was officially born.

The C.B.C. product included such early movie fan shorts as *Screen Snapshot,* which purportedly revealed the off-screen lives of the stars. In 1922, C.B.C. began the production of feature films with a six-reeler, *More to Be Pitied Than Scorned,* whose title said it all.

In those days C.B.C. worked on minimum budgets and Harry Cohn imposed cost-cutting measures everywhere, Rochelle Larkin reports:

> Every operating economy, every cost-cutting trick was employed, and that practice was to carry over even to Columbia's expansive, money-making golden era. Even lavish production numbers in the musicals to come would be mounted on sound stages a fraction of the size used by the major studios. All the skills that go into making a movie were finely honed to super-technique by the people who wanted to remain on the Cohn payroll. The result was a finished product, polished by crack professionals in every area, that stood up to anything produced by the majors...[1]

This high level of professionalism prevailed in the Columbia Art Department, which worked hard for high production values following unusual practices dictated by Cohn: "Usually, scenery was painted on one side, used and discarded.

255

Cohn decreed that both sides of the boards be utilized, and cut down half of Columbia's lumber costs."[2] The technical values in Columbia's pictures improved greatly in the thirties, mostly on the insistence of important directors like Frank Capra.

Cohn did not believe in the star system, and Columbia never built a large stable of well-known contract players. Cohn summed up his attitude: "We get 'em on the way up or on the way down."[3] This wasn't always the case though, and in the thirties Columbia's reputation rested on star director Frank Capra, who pulled the studio out of its lowly "poverty row" status with his robust American comedies and social dramas. In the forties, Columbia depended on a bona fide movie star, actress Rita Hayworth.

Harry Cohn reserved his highest regard for writers, praising their efforts for all to hear, but he treated them brusquely. One time he handed his writers a dozen titles, telling them, "Here, go write pictures for these."

The early silent years at Columbia were marked by a variety of scripts, mostly of the adventure and comedy/romance type. Things began to pick up for the studio, when in 1927 director Frank Capra, a former Mack Sennett gagman, was hired. By the next year Capra was making seven films annually, low budget quickies; his first, *That Certain Thing,* was in the can in six weeks, and that included writing. Cohn showed his faith in the new director later in the year when he picked him to take over *Submarine,* the first A production Columbia had attempted; it was budgeted at $250,000, a sum unheard of on poverty row. Filmed partly on location at San Pedro, the art direction was left to Harrison Wiley, who produced the navy barracks and other requisite interiors in the rather wooden fashion of the period. Capra was his own special effects man, rigging the underwater rescue by putting a toy submarine in an aquarium he had found in the prop room, and filming the whole thing in slow motion. When *Submarine* turned out to be the studio's biggest hit yet, Capra was given a raise and gradually gained a high level of artistic control over his movies.

In 1929 succumbing to pressure from the New York office, Cohn put Capra in charge of Columbia's first all-talkie, a mystery called *The Donovan Affair.* Because they cost so much, Cohn refused to make Columbia's first talkie a musical as many studios were doing. The picture was filmed at a rented studio that had only interior sets, so all the action takes place in what is supposed (thanks to art director Harrison Wiley) to be a country house. He had little to do except dress the sets in appropriate contemporary "country" garb, which actually looked a lot like "city" garb—heavy stuffed furniture, fringed lamps, and pictures featuring sailboats on the walls.

These early sound years at Columbia also saw the introduction of actors and actresses who would become more or less regulars on the lot, Barbara Stanwyck in particular; she appeared in Capra's *Ladies of Leisure* in 1930, and emerged a star. Also appearing regularly in Columbia pictures of the thirties

118. Stephen Goosson, supervising art director, Columbia Pictures.

and forties were Cary Grant, Jean Arthur (the biggest star to be under contract to the studio), James Stewart, Irene Dunne, Rosalind Russell, and Rita Hayworth. Practically the only one for whom Cohn tailor-made vehicles was Hayworth. Often he borrowed stars, some were lent because they were being "punished" by their own studios — this was the case with MGM's Clark Gable and *It Happened One Night* (1934).

Frank Capra stayed at the studio for over a decade, not leaving until 1939 after the release of the very successful *Mr. Smith Goes to Washington*. But it was only in 1932 that he began to examine the type of material which has become associated with his name — themes of hard work in depression times, and of virtue triumphing over vice in the context of American democratic institutions. *American Madness* (1932), his first venture along these lines, cast Walter Huston as a bank president whose basic honesty is tested amidst a society in which foreclosures and widespread unemployment are rampant.

Harrison Wiley, Capra's art director in the late twenties, was replaced in the early thirties by Stephen Goosson, who designed this film. Goosson was to be Columbia's most enduring art directorial talent, and to be its supervising art director for 25 years. **(Illustration 118.)** Born in Michigan, Goosson was an

119. *Little Lord Fauntleroy*, 1921. Stephen Goosson, art director. The sets for this Mary Pickford (left on stairs) film had to be built oversized to accommodate the adult actress; the stair risers were twelve inches high.

architect in Detroit before coming into pictures as an art director for Lewis J. Selznick (David O. Selznick's father) in 1919. Goosson then worked for Mary Pickford Productions, Frank Lloyd, DeMille Pictures and Fox before coming to Columbia, where he remained for the rest of his career.

Goosson's official Columbia biography says that he is credited for the art direction on 1,300 motion pictures, was nominated five times for the Academy Award (he won for Capra's *Lost Horizon,* and later won a Photoplay Award for *The Jolson Story*). Always a draftsman and painter, some of Goosson's pencil and wash drawings from films as early as the twenties have survived: those for *Blind Youth* (1920) are on thin tracing paper and are bold, abbreviated, and energetic.[4]

For one of his early films, *Little Lord Fauntleroy* (1921, United Artists, directed by Alfred E. Green and Jack Pickford), which starred Mary Pickford, Goosson fashioned an elegant environment. Later commenting on it, he recalled (**Illustration 119**):

120. *American Madness,* 1932. Stephen Goosson, art director. An American bank in the Depression era with tall marble piers and bronze fittings was a spacious set designed to hold the crowd action scene pivotal to the film.

> I thought when it was completed that it wasn't too bad. You see, I hadn't been an Art Director very long — only two years — and the materials needed to do the right job didn't exist. So we devised them — some of which are still being used. The sets we built oversized. Stair risers were twelve inches, the railings in proportion to them. The sets were designed very much like stage scenery so that they could be lighted from the sides, with Cooper Hewetts in the wings and overhead. The over-all set covered an area of about 100′ × 250′ and it included the great hall, the stair hall, library, and dining room plus connecting corridors. Some of the floors were wooden boards varnished, where others were cement cut up to appear like stone. The camera work on these sets took weeks. . . .[5]

The art direction for *Little Lord Fauntleroy,* especially the Gothic mansion, that Goosson describes, with its multiple lancet and round arches was exceedingly rich in detail for its time. In the mansion's library, Goosson used a very high medieval wooden vault to convey enormity of scale, and it appropriately made Miss Pickford look diminutive as Little Lord Fauntleroy.

For Frank Capra's *American Madness,* Goosson devised an Art Deco Bank (Illustration 120). An elaborate set, it is scrutinized in every detail, even to its massive storage vault, by the director's camera in the opening reel of the film. Its piers are sleek squares covered in veined marble; its heavy bronze doors and grills are ornate Roman replicas, typical of thirties banks. The massive central customer lobby was designed to accommodate the almost inevitable Capra crowd scene on which the film's action pivots.

Every detail in the bank was researched by Goosson and authentically rendered by the builders. In this regard it is much like the meticulously done United States Senate chamber designed by Lionel Banks for the later *Mr. Smith Goes to Washington* (1939) **(Illustration 121)**, which serves the same purpose as Goosson's bank; it is a symbol of the institutional process the film is examining and functions practically as a place where a lot of the important action takes place.

Goosson and Capra again teamed for the romantic comedy *It Happened One Night* (1934). Unlike *American Madness,* it has no "big" sets at all. *It Happened One Night* was a contemporary, traveling picture, showing a thirties America in the most intimate terms. It remains, along with *The Grapes of Wrath,* one of the most memorable thirties road pictures. The plot centers around bus travel, and beside the Atlantic Greyhound bus (both a real bus and a studio mock-up were used), we see the roadside signs and stores, the auto courts, lunch counters, and bus depots of the period, as reporter Clark Gable and runaway rich girl Claudette Colbert encounter them on their way from Miami to New York City. *It Happened One Night,* like *The Grapes of Wrath,* perfectly combined locations with studio built sets. The bus depots, auto camps and the roadside of the famous hitchhiking scene (which Capra wrote on the way to the site), were all authentic locales. The cabin interior with its twin beds, and flouncy flowered curtains, where the "Battle of Jericho" is first lost and then won, was realistically built by Goosson on the Columbia lot.

Stephen Goosson did not have to strive for authenticity on his grandest and most controversial design for Capra, the Shangri-La for *Lost Horizon* (1937), which was to earn the art director an Oscar. **(Illustration 122.)** He had warmed up for this task, on a futuristic musical oddity, *Just Imagine,* done in 1930 at Fox. **(Illustration 123.)** Directed by David Butler, the plot involved a romance between people living in a New York City of 1980, who only know each other by serial numbers. At one point a trip to Mars discovers the inhabitants to be sets of twins wearing metal costumes. All of this pleasurable nonsense allowed Goosson's, and fellow art director Ralph Hammeras', imaginations to roam freely, and their set of New York City is a futurist's dream. *Just Imagine* used a huge miniature of illuminated skyscrapers, elevated freeways, suspension bridges, and hanging pedestrian walkways. It seems to have been closely modelled on the famous skyscraper futurism found in *King's Views of New York* (published in 1911/12 and 1915), updated with ideas projected by Hugh Ferris in his innovative book *The Metropolis of Tomorrow* (1929).[6] According to studio publicity it took over 200 engineers and technicians

121. *Mr. Smith Goes to Washington,* 1939. Lionel Banks, art director. Director Frank Capra and Jimmy Stewart confer before a detailed replication of the United States Senate Chamber inspired by photographs.

five months to build the Goosson and Hammeras "Gotham" at an astonishing $168,000 price tag; it earned the art directors Academy Award nominations.

Goosson was again given a big budget on *Lost Horizon,* Columbia spent two million dollars on the film, close to half of its yearly production budget, and every penny of its shows on the screen, particularly in the mountainous, Tibetan lamasery, inhabited by a 200-year-old High Lama (Sam Jaffe). A mammoth miniature of the temperate Valley of the Blue Moon, with stone terraces, streams, and fields was built, and surrounded by the story's nearly impassable Himalayan mountains. **(Illustration 124.)**

Beside the miniature, massive built sets rose during the course of several months to over 90 feet tall at the Columbia ranch in Burbank. Goosson's luminous white High Lama's residence, rising above the other dwellings in the valley, is modern looking, with references to Frank Lloyd Wright's work, particularly his Imperial Hotel in Tokyo and modern style houses of the twenties and thirties. There are also historic allusions in the fabric — in the many

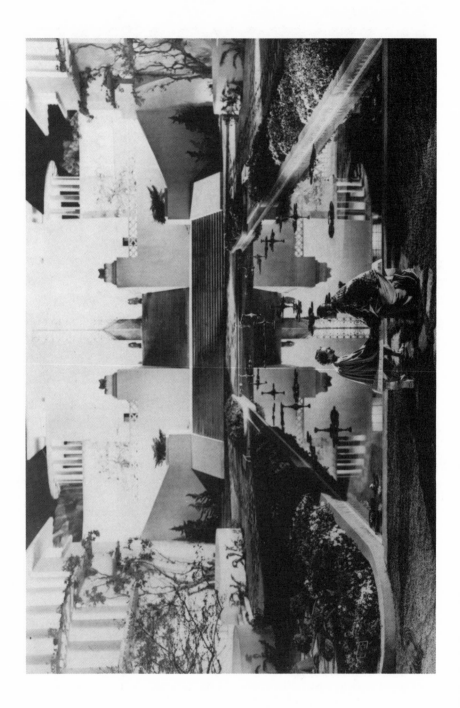

(Opposite) 122. *Lost Horizon,* 1937. Stephen Goosson, art director. The serene pool of Shangri-La (with Jane Wyatt and Ronald Colman) reflects the modernistic exterior of the lamasery which rises, white and pristine, on terraces surrounding it. (Above) 123. *Just Imagine,* 1930. Stephen Goosson, Ralph Hammeras, art directors. A futurist conception of New York City was created in this camera-ready miniature based on *King's Views of New York* (1911 & 1915).

124. *Lost Horizon,* 1937. Stephen Goosson, art director. A mammoth camera-ready miniature of the Tibetan Valley of the Blue Moon with its lamasery, included a valley with fields and river and the Himalayan Mountains in the distance.

colonades and in the plan which is a symmetrical, Beaux Arts derived circle. The palace's site rises through stepped terraces to a mammoth entry door, with wings, suggestively lit, surrounding a central garden and quiet reflecting pool.

The interiors are more eclectic than the exterior. The excuse for this in the plot is that the lamasery is the repository of civilization's knowledge and treasures. The interior walls, columns and doorways follow the patterns set out by Goosson on the exterior, but the furnishings part company with modernity; there are rococo tables, Oriental bric-a-brac, renaissance oil paintings and 18th century sconces on the walls. It certainly looks "no place like home," which was the main idea.[7] Some critics found the story ponderous, others found the sets ponderous, and *Lost Horizon* was not the commercial hit that Columbia had hoped it would be.

During the mid-thirties, screwball comedies were becoming a studio specialty, and Howard Hawks was on hand to direct *Twentieth Century* (1934), starring Carole Lombard and John Barrymore as stage star and director who take their professional and romantic problems on a cross country excursion aboard the super-sleek 20th Century Limited.

Columbia had been since the days of *Submarine* heavily involved in the production of adventure dramas revolving around some form of modern transportation technology—topics fascinating to thirties audiences, who were still enthralled with the idea that machines could make life better, or at least more thrilling. The Studio had reused the rescue plot essentials of *Submarine* over again for *Flight* (1929) and *Dirigible* (1931), both Frank Capra films, and the thirties also saw Hawks make his contribution to this genre with *Only Angels Have Wings* (1939). In the latter, daredevil fly boys, Cary Grant among them, are marooned in South America trying to make a living with a third-rate airline. Lucky for them, Jean Arthur and Rita Hayworth are stuck there too.

In this sort of picture, the special effects, here the superb aerial photography, always took precedence over the sets. The art director (Lionel Banks in this case) usually had to do little more than provide probable contemporary interiors, which left them with valuable time to design the film's huge props (dirigibles, etc.), that will ordinarily be demolished by the last reel.

Lionel Banks joined Columbia sometime in the thirties and his name appears on many of the studio's best films in that decade and the forties, sometimes alone and sometimes with other art directors (Stephen Goosson, unlike other supervising art directors, did not put his name on every film that was released by his studio). Banks was often nominated for Academy Awards (seven times), but never managed to snag one.

Banks' award nominations include one for *Holiday* (1938, with Stephen Goosson) and one for *The Talk of the Town* (1942, with Rudolph Sternad); they are indicative of his forte—the design of handsome contemporary sets. *Holiday* had the particular "look" of Columbia comedies of the thirties, they are not as flashy or resolutely Streamlined as were those at other studios (except for Howard Hawks' *Twentieth Century,* 1934), particularly RKO, nor do they have the over-designed look of some of MGM's Deco productions. They are simple, well-crafted, and without affectation.

Most of the action in the romantic comedy *Holiday* takes place in the upper-class dwelling of Cary Grant's would-be fiancée (Doris Nolan). The mansion is divided into two separate parts, one belonging to the stuffy family (including the fiancée), and the other belonging to a sister (Katharine Hepburn), a free spirit more in tune with Grant's character.

Grant is so overcome with surprise when he first enters his rich fiancée's traditional home, with its dazzling art, antique paintings, statuary, tapestries, that he does a back-flip. Hepburn's upper-floor—she calls it a "playroom"—where Grant eventually finds a retreat, is totally different. It is warmer, modern, and filled with games, toys, and family mementos. Banks and Goosson succeeded in making the two settings summations of the entire plot—the conventional versus the unconventional.[8]

Columbia's bread-and-butter pictures of the thirties were not prestige productions like *Holiday,* but rather the B programmers that they turned out, along with Universal and Republic, for the second half of the double-bill. The type of story told was usually a comedy, western, soap opera, or adventure yarn.

Columbia's other speciality was the production of serials (stories told in multiple parts) and series (the same character appearing in a series of closely related films). There were dozens of them produced over the years from the thirties through the mid-fifties, when they were finally discontinued. These included favorites like Superman, Batman, Captain Video, Blondie, the Three Stooges, Boston Blackie and Crime Doctor. Among the western stars appearing in popular series were Ken Maynard, and the legendary Gene Autry, who appeared 32 times in Columbia pictures in his late career. Columbia used its Burbank backlot, with its standing western and urban sets for these pictures. They did not get much redressing from picture to picture, so that Superman suddenly appeared interminable times in front of the same columned bank and the same newspaper office. Sometimes no art director was listed in the credits of these serials and series, and sometimes the same reliable, talented people working on major productions, like Lionel Banks and Paul Palmentola, were credited, only proving once again that art directors had to be ready to do any sort of production in the days of the big studios.

The forties were the Rita Hayworth years at Columbia, with many of the prestige productions mounted around her persona. Lionel Banks and Cary Odell designed the sets for *Cover Girl* (1944), Hayworth's most memorable musical. Gene Kelly costarred and Charles Vidor directed the lavish production, which Harry Cohn hoped would put Miss Hayworth over the top as a first-rank star; it succeeded and did the same for Kelly.

Cover Girl was an innovative film in several respects. Although filmed on Columbia's small sound stages (in comparison to the large ones used for musicals elsewhere), it had a fresh, open look not achieved elsewhere until *On the Town* in 1949 took the musical out-of-doors. *Cover Girl* had the usual anemic backstage plot, but it wasn't allowed to get in the way of the musical numbers, some choreographed by Gene Kelly in the brash, athletic style that was to become his hallmark.

Lionel Banks had created the decor for Hayworth's earlier musicals, *You'll Never Get Rich* (1941) and *You Were Never Lovelier* (1942), in which she had teamed with Fred Astaire, and so was no stranger to the art direction of musicals. The story centers on would-be-star Rusty Parker (Hayworth) and nightclub owner Danny McGuire (Kelly), with early action set in his small Brooklyn club, furnished simply with upright piano, round tables and bentwood chairs. The most unusual visual aspect of these scenes is that they are drenched in bright Technicolor, something rarely used in a Columbia picture.

125. *Cover Girl,* 1944. Lionel Banks, Cary Odell, art directors. Spiraling stairs (compare Illustration 57 on page 123) and ramps proved a lasting dance musical prop—here Rita Hayworth, amid confetti, dances up a ramp pursued by chorus boys.

The pair hang out with buddy Phil Silvers at a local restaurant-bar, warmly decorated by Odell and Banks in stripes and checks: the walls, bar, floor, even Miss Hayworth's costume are a variation on a similar motif. As the trio sings and dance to Jerome Kern and Ira Gershwin's "Make Way for Tomorrow," they swing through the restaurant, exiting onto the Studio's Brooklyn street where they exuberantly engage other people and props in their dance.

The "big" sets were, as usual, reserved for the production numbers. In one Miss Hayworth, golden gowned and hair cascading down bare back, dances her way up an enormous curving ramp **(Illustration 125)** followed by a legion of chorus boys, while from overhead clouds and confetti drift downward. The sheer size and simplicity of the set, which borrows from Anton Grot's great ramp for Busby Berkeley's famous "Shadow Waltz" number, serves well the purpose of showcasing the ravishing star.

Rita Hayworth not only danced her way through the forties, she played in several noteworthy melodramas, among them, *Gilda* (1946) and *The Lady from Shanghai* (1948), that are among the best-looking films to come out of Columbia in the decade.

Gilda is an in-house picture, filmed on two big sets, one an Art Moderne gambling casino and the other an opulent Buenos Aires mansion shared by Hayworth and husband (George Macready). The sets are unexpectedly swank and sophisticated, attributable to Van Nest Polglase's participation in their design. Polglase's stamp is apparent on all of the detailing of the principal sets, the doors especially have his signature carved branches. Polglase had parted company with RKO and was free-lancing in the mid-forties, and *Gilda* was a picture perfectly suited to his talents, which Supervising Art Director, Stephen Goosson, who is also credited on the picture, must have appreciated.

All is modern, painted white, and with shining chrome accessories in Polglase's gambling casino. The space is divided into a nightclub lined with padded leather booths, a circular bar which separates the dance floor from a foyer, and a curving stairway leading to an upper-level office. Decoration is Tropical Deco, etched glass and mirror doors support palm trees, a reminder that the locale is Buenos Aires. In this white-on-white setting, Hayworth as Gilda, in a black satin gown, warms the climate up to match the tropical motif with her famous "strip tease" to "Put the Blame on Mame, Boys."

The mansion has two stunning rooms, a foyer-stairhall, and Miss Hayworth's bedroom. The foyer is a vertical set, narrow on the ground floor, with a stairway in its center. The stair begins as a sensuous curve, off of the central axis, rises to a landing and then straightens out to reach the bedrooms above. The stair is atmospherically lit, in a manner unusual at Columbia, and again suggests outsider Polglase's influence. Director Charles Vidor underscores the desire and possessive jealousy of the main protagonists by their placement in the foyer and on the stair during pivotal scenes, giving the setting a powerful dramatic purpose. Glenn Ford, the husband's "friend" and employee, who has found out about his employer's (George Macready) recent marriage, enters the foyer to return the house key inexplicably in his possession; then he is forced to mount the stairs to meet the new bride in her boudoir — it is Hayworth, who was Ford's former lover.

Later, when the three characters face off in a final confrontation and the husband realizes the extent of the former lovers' passion for one another, they are carefully manipulated in the stairhall by Vidor; Macready plays the entire scene in dark silhouette in the foreground at the foot of the stairway, Ford is at the right in shadows by the door, with Hayworth, brightly lit, on the stairs, above and between the two men.

While *Gilda* was in release, production began on the Orson Welles–directed *The Lady from Shanghai*, starring his then wife — Rita Hayworth. Cinematically more complex than Vidor's *Gilda*, it has a plot even more convoluted than the earlier film (Harry Cohn reportedly offered a thousand dollars to anyone who could explain it to him).

The Lady from Shanghai was filmed in late 1946 in Mexico and in Hollywood. It is not a seamless effort, either dramatically or scenically. The studio's backlot exteriors look artificial in comparison to the marvellous black and white exteriors photographed on location by Charles Lawton, Jr. Harry Cohn was so displeased with Welles' effort that much of the picture was reshot, reedited, and patched together so that one does not know who to blame for the film's inconsistencies.

Art directors Sturges Carne and Stephen Goosson came up with several powerfully imaginative interior sets, most memorably the amusement park funhouse with its huge slide, comic masks, and mirror maze where the shoot-out at the end of the picture takes place.

The early part of the picture is set in a studio-built Central Park and New York City where Welles, playing the naive sailor/narrator, is sufficiently tempted by Rosalie (Hayworth) to be talked into crewing on her husband's (Everett Sloan) yacht for a trip to Acapulco. At this point, when the location photography begins, the film takes off visually. The yacht is seen sailing to the Caribbean, moored at rocks, and in a moonlight harbor while the boating company drinks and verbally assault each other on the beach. The camera draws back far enough so that the image of native boaters and torchlight may be seen as Welles suggests that the backbiting company remind him of mad-dened sharks who tasting blood, turn on themselves, so that none survive.

Marine imagery forms the leitmotif for the film. It was begun with the credits seen over ocean waves, and it ends with the sailor walking toward the ocean away from the scene of murder in the amusement park. At one point Welles and Hayworth meet surreptitiously in an aquarium, where sharks and eels in the background swim ominously in tune with their conversation. The scene was shot with a wide angle lens and the background was a traveling matte (a matte that changes in each frame with the action in the foreground) used to achieve the eerie synchronized effects.

In another powerful sequence shot on location, Hayworth, speaking fluent Chinese, chases Welles through San Francisco's Chinatown in a blur of rich visual images—shops, banners, Chinese calligraphy—into a theatre where a performance is in progress. The locales, here as elsewhere in the film, add a visual density to the picture that even a well made in-house picture like *Gilda* did not have.

Columbia, along with other smaller less well equipped studios, were among the first to move out of doors to location shooting in the postwar era. *The Lady from Shanghai* was essentially a location picture, and Columbia followed it with a stunning string of hits shot mostly away from the studio: *All the King's Men* (1949), *From Here to Eternity* (1953), *The Wild Ones* (1952), *On the Waterfront* (1955) and *The Bridge on the River Kwai* (1957). All of them won the Oscar for best picture except *The Wild Ones*—ending a dry spell for the studio that went back to 1934 and *It Happened One Night*.

In the fifties, Harry Cohn spent his time searching out original screenplays and best-selling novels for material that would lure a declining motion picture audience back into the theatres. Swimming against the current, Cohn took chances on controversial material and didn't turn to either Technicolor or the wide screen for a quick fix. He cast actors—Broderick Crawford, Judy Holliday, Marlon Brando, Alec Guinness—whose names were not household words in major parts. So while other studios, like Universal, were producing mostly sugary pap in the fifties, Columbia was embarking on a neorealist path, and producing films closer to the many European films being shown in the "art" cinema houses of the period. These pictures have survived with considerably more vigor and screen viability than many others from the period.

All the King's Men, one of this brand of new picture, was produced, written (from a novel by Robert Penn Warren) and directed by Robert Rossen; his art director was Sturges Carne, who had done the excellent job for Welles on *The Lady from Shanghai.* In the story, reporter Jack Burden (John Ireland) follows the rise and fall of political populist turned demagogue Willie Stark (Broderick Crawford) through the backwoods of a Southern state. Carne's believable, realistic sets look like they have been drawn from Dorothea Lang's Depression era photographs; Willie's humble dwelling, the Southern mansions of his opponents, fairgrounds hung with bunting and banners blaring "Hear Willie Stark" are played off against actual locations—stone courthouses, legislative buildings, and state capitol—as Willie bulldozes his way from rags to riches capturing the governor's mansion as his prize. Rossen filmed in a gritty black and white, and the picture reads like newspaper print.

The fifties saw directors, like Rossen, and powerful producers, like Sam Spiegel, at Columbia and at other studios gain more personal control over films, and the influence of studio bosses, like Cohn, was diminished. With *On the Waterfront,* Spiegel and director Elia Kazan managed at the contract stage to completely freeze Cohn out of the artistic phases of the film's production.

Fred Zinnemann, although not going as far as Spiegel and Kazan, nonetheless maintained strong directorial control throughout the filming of the James Jones' novel *From Here to Eternity,* which could not have been easy, as it involved Columbia's largest budget to date. The picture, filmed at Hawaii's Schofield Military Barracks, capped Columbia's other successes with location shooting.

Art director Cary Odell, who only the year before had created the sets for Zinnemann's densely atmospheric *The Member of the Wedding,* worked with cinematographer Burnett Guffey to evoke the island of Pearl Harbor Day. Perhaps because the viewer is so familiar with the newsreel reportage of the devastation of the Japanese bombing of the harbor, Hawaii of this period always looks more authentic in black and white than in color (another excellently designed vintage 1941 black and white Pearl Harbor is that seen in Otto Preminger's *In Harm's Way,* whose art direction was by Lyle Wheeler).

In *From Here to Eternity,* the early sequences focus on Private Prewitt (Montgomery Clift), who is joining Company G at Schofield. Zinnemann's establishing shots pull back to reveal the vast scale of the military establishment: barracks, offices, training fields, and military clubs. The camera again takes advantage of the locale in long shots of luxuriant tropical beaches, the scene of a passionate encounter of clandestine lovers (Deborah Kerr and Burt Lancaster) later in the story. Yet, most of the many confrontational sequences occur in tighter quarters: bars, barracks, and a prostitute's room given slice-of-life reality by art director Odell to match James Jones' descriptions.

The evocation of place is equally as strong, in Kazan's *On the Waterfront,* which went even farther in its seamy realism by using workers from the docks of New York as extras in the film about labor and management racketeering. These faces form a human tapestry pressing in behind the principals in important scenes, commenting on them like a Greek chorus. Kazan added to the dreariness of the setting by shooting sullen skies that hang low over the riverfront settings. Shot in the alleys (**Illustration 126**), tenements, rooftops of the worker's district, scarcely any sign of nature is seen except for the cold river and some barren trees in the wintery square in front of a church.

Independent art director Richard Day carried off yet another Oscar for *On the Waterfront.* Day, long expert at finding locations, had come up through the various schools of realism that held sway in Hollywood, and was uniquely prepared to interpret the new brand of street realism forwarded by Kazan and other directors in the decade.

Many of the next generation of art directors, those who would spend most of their working lives as independents, were just coming into the business in the postwar years; some of them, like Harold Michelson, after training on the G.I. Bill. Michelson broke into the business at Columbia in 1949, after attending the Art Students League in New York City. The art director and production illustrator, whose later films would include *Star Trek, the Motion Picture,* and *Terms of Endearment,* began as an illustrator and continuity artist at Columbia and cut his teeth on films like *From Here to Eternity* and *Miss Sadie Thompson* (1953).

Also working at Columbia in the fifties were veteran art directors, including Rudolph Sternad, Robert Peterson, Carl Anderson, and Sturges Carne. Carl Anderson ably handled many routine and not so routine films for Columbia in the forties and fifties. He was the art director on *Miss Sadie Thompson,* which cast Rita Hayworth and Aldo Ray in the remake of *Rain,* the steamy Somerset Maugham story about the fallen woman and the preacher caught in transit on a Pacific isle. Indulging in the decade's preoccupation with faraway places, there is some second unit location shooting, but the principals stayed close to Carl Anderson's studio-built exteriors and interiors. Harry Cohn was not ready to put every film on the road.

Photographed in a pleasing, not overly contrastive Technicolor, Anderson

126. *On the Waterfront*, 1955. Richard Day, art director. Shot on location at the New York dockside, the carefully orchestrated locations and sets (here Marlon Brando and Eva Marie Saint in an alley) established the character of the workers' lives.

found warm unsaturated tones for the decor of *Miss Sadie Thompson*. The principal set is an island guest house with veranda and several interconnecting rooms. Sadie (Hayworth) settles into a back storeroom (cleaned up by her G.I. friends), while the preacher and other guests use the rest of the place; the action is neatly woven through the spaces by director Curtis Bernhardt. Art director Anderson's guest house and the local bar, where Sadie manages to down a few and even sing a song, are convincingly "native," showing no taint of Hollywood glitz even though the scenic backdrops look a little tired at times. The sets follow along the same lines as Columbia's earlier pictures with contemporary settings rather than the new neorealist path of the films done on location and without Cohn's supervision.

Carl Anderson, who says he was "practically a grammar school dropout," began working at Columbia in 1938 and stayed for more than a decade.[9] He had studied mechanical drawing in high school and recalls, "A friend of mine was working as a draftsman at MGM. He suggested I come over and meet the chief draftsman." Anderson is still working as an art director, with more recent credits on *Lady Sings the Blues* (1971), for which he received an Academy Award nomination, and Robert Aldrich's *All the Marbles* (1980).

Columbia closed out the decade with one last Oscar winner, *The Bridge on the River Kwai*, directed by David Lean and produced by Sam Spiegel. The film was largely a foreign production, which brought in British art directors Daniel M. Ashton and Geoffrey Drake. Stars William Holden, Alec Guinness, and Sessue Hayakawa and a production company of hundreds were packed off to the tropical jungles of Ceylon (in the story it is Burma), and the crew put to work building an actual camp and bridge there. This type of production, done mostly without the collaboration of Columbia's personnel, rang the death knell for the great studio art departments.

Columbia always maintained something of its "poverty row" image in the movie industry, and the company under Harry Cohn did not often put large sums of money into decor. But the Art Department of the studio, if significantly smaller, was as proficient as elsewhere. Particularly when strong directors like Capra were around demanding memorable scenic values, the Art Department could come up with them. The members of the Department were frequently busied with work on pictures and serials done in contemporary settings, and when, in the fifties, Columbia accepted many independent producers and directors onto the lot to do innovative location films, the Columbia Art Department got a last chance to do challenging art direction along contemporary lines, already their forte.

10
Universal

Universal employed some of the best art directors in Hollywood in the period from its formulation in 1912 through the fifties—Charles D. Hall, Jack Otterson, John B. Goodman, Alexander Golitzen, Bernard Herzbrun, Albert D'Agostino—yet, it is one of the most difficult studios to identify in terms of a certain "look." Partly, this is because the studio was under almost continuous economic constraints. Sets were often cheap and looked it. And, despite initially having been built on the star system, Universal was one of the few studios in the big studio days without a large stable of star contract players. This meant they did not feel obliged to mount lavish productions around players to keep and enhance their drawing power. Early on, Universal's management made the decision to concentrate on easily marketable B pictures. In the thirties and forties, Universal was a factory for double-bill "programmers."

The studio had its speciality genres; some said they were genres no one else wanted—the horror film and the weepie. It is around these genres that the Art Department could and did develop an identifiable "look"—the studio management was willing to invest in sets they were sure could be reused in a sequel, *Frankenstein* and *The Bride of Frankenstein,* for instance, or *Dracula* and *Dracula's Daughter.* When Universal sunk money into a big production, an example being *All Quiet on the Western Front* (1930), their settings were as fine as any in the business, but they retrenched to a familiar pattern of B pictures immediately after such ventures.

Another Universal speciality was the production of series, among them the Cohens and the Kellys, Sherlock Holmes, Flash Gordon, Abbott and Costello, Francis the Talking Mule, and the Ma and Pa Kettle hillbilly comedies. When the studio got a good thing going they seldom gave up on it until the public was completely apathetic. Cheap to make, requiring character actors rather than glamor stars on bloated salaries, and reusing the same sets from picture to picture, these series were perfect programmers.

Even the few stars that Universal did manage to acquire, like the 15-year-

old Deanna Durbin, a top box office draw of the late thirties and reputed to
have saved the studio from bankruptcy, seemed to fit into the serial mode. Her
pictures showcased her singing talent, fresh good looks, and a cultivated
naivete, with stories set in contemporary, urban settings.

In the forties, the studio got heavily into an Arabian Nights' phase, with
exotic looking players like Turhan Bey, Maria Montez, Yvonne DeCarlo, and
Jon Hall. These films made heavy use of diaphanous draperies, satin cushioned
beds, and moonlit balconies and revived much of the vocabulary of the twenties adventure films in foreign settings, like those starring Valentino.

Despite the often less than distinguished product of the Univeral Studio
of the early years, it is still thriving in Hollywood today, a true survivor. Universal maintains one of the few active art departments, working along lines
modified from those of the heyday of the big studios, but involved now
with television as much as with film. The glory days of Universal belong to the
sixties and beyond, when their name became associated with such blockbuster
pictures as *The Sting* (1973), *Jaws* (1975), and *E.T. the Extra-Terrestrial*
(1982).

The foundation and early policies of the company were formulated by
that fascinating movie pioneer, Carl Laemmle. Not having made his fortune
in haberdashery by the age of 40, Laemmle decided to try something new. That
something was nickelodeons; within a year (1906) he had two, and before the
end of the next he had opened his own movie exchange business. Typically,
for the time, the Motion Picture Patents Company tried to close him down.
But the dynamic five-foot, two-inch German immigrant was feistier than many
and fought back. Laemmle incorporated a film production company, Independent Moving Picture Company of America (IMP), and released weekly one-
reelers to satisfy his exchange's needs. With other independents, Laemmle
went to court over the "Trusts"' monopolistic practices and won.

Laemmle was not the first to recognize film star power, but he was the first
to credit the stars by name, thus capitalizing on their popularity, and making
public creatures of them. In a masterly move he hired Florence Lawrence, then
being billed as "The Biograph Girl," away from that company. Laemmle
transformed her into "The IMP Girl" and told the public her name. Soon
Biograph's Mary Pickford followed Lawrence into the IMP fold. As Pickford's
fame accelerated she argued over salary with Laemmle and left the company.
The financial squabble he had with several of his early stars eventually turned
Laemmle against the system he had fostered. Universal had few major stars in
the thirties and forties. They had no number one box office attraction between
the peak Deanna Durbin years and the mid-fifties, when Rock Hudson gained
the title of top box office draw in the nation.

At first, IMP production studios were like everyone else's in New York and
New Jersey, but Laemmle soon saw the possibilities inherent in a California site
and in 1911 he purchased property at Sunset and Gower for his studio; in 1912

he bought additional space in Edendale. The Universal Film Manufacturing Company was formed on June 8, 1912, through a merger of IMP with several other companies: Powers Motion Picture Company, Rex Motion Picture Company, Champion Film Company, Nestor Film Company, and the New York Motion Picture Company. Laemmle, after early disputes with his partners, was elected president of the expanded company, a position he retained until he was forced out in 1936 at the age of 69.

One of Laemmle's earliest coups as new president, and one considered a folly by pundits at the time, was the purchase of the Taylor Ranch, a 230-acre spread in the San Fernando Valley for the consolidation of his two-coast production operation. He opened Universal City, an incorporated municipality, for the production of motion pictures on March 15, 1915, to unparalleled hoop-la among a crowd estimated to be 20,000 strong, with Thomas Edison, Henry Ford, and Buffalo Bill Cody in attendance. It is hard to see how anyone could have resisted the invitational advertisement announcing the opening; it read:

> See how we blow up bridges, burn down houses, wreck automobiles and smash up things in general in order to give the people of the world the kind of pictures they demand. See how buildings have to be erected just for a few scenes of one picture then have to be torn down to make room for something else. See how we have to use the brains God gave us in every conceivable way in order TO MAKE THE PEOPLE LAUGH OR CRY OR SIT ON THE EDGE OF THEIR CHAIRS THE WORLD OVER.[1]

Universal City was said by some to be too distant to be a practical studio site (it is five miles north of Hollywood). Bought for $165,000, the studio has expanded to 420 acres today, has 36 rather than the two original production stages, and maintains the biggest backlot still in existence. Its waterfalls, lakes filled with artificial snapping sharks, city streets and entire towns have become a familiar tourist attraction.

"Papa" Laemmle, as he liked to be called by employees, many of whom were related to him (70 it was estimated at one time), foresaw the lure of "movie magic" from the beginning, and is the father of the present Universal tour. He kept a zoo on the property from the earliest days, including chickens left over from the Taylor Ranch (reputedly, he sold the eggs). Laemmle opened it all to the public for 25 cents. A gallery was built at the side of an open-air stage so that spectators could watch the actors during filming. Laemmle only discontinued this "open to the public" practice with the advent of sound.[2]

The first Universal feature film was *Traffic in Souls* (1913), a sensationalized story of white slavery made for $5,700; it grossed $500,000. On the basis of this success, a commitment was made to produce feature films, but shorter films would continue as a mainstay of Universal into the thirties.

There were some lavish productions at Universal Pictures in the teens. Director Stuart Paton's *20,000 Leagues Under the Sea,* an adaptation of the

Jules Verne novel, was one of them. It was filmed in Bermuda, using a new underwater camera developed for the movies. Watery views filled with action, including a fight with an octopus, alternated with scenes played out in Indian rajah Captain Nemo's opulent quarters. The *20,000 Leagues Under the Sea* was a big budgeted "Jewel" production. The studio issued few of these prestige films, many more were of the middle-line "Bluebird" category, with the preponderance of Universal films being what were called the "Red Feather" line, low-budget quickies. The classification code served distributors, letting them know what to expect. Universal, unlike the other majors, never owned a large chain of theatres. Instead, they marketed their product to many small theatres, often in small towns, another factor accounting for the conventionality of their product.

Universal's most memorable silent films were those of the twenties, when the quality of the productions and especially the scenic values were fostered by individuals like producer Irving Thalberg and director Erich von Stroheim. Thalberg got his start as Laemmle's secretary and protégé, while von Stroheim produced his first major pictures at the studio, including *Blind Husbands* (1919) and *Foolish Wives* (1922). Always a stickler for details, von Stroheim demanded more and more elaborate decor and costumes in his pictures. This paved the way for the development of the technical departments at Universal, and more grandiose and effective settings began to be seen in other pictures, particularly those starring the studio's man-with-a-thousand-faces, Lon Chaney: *The Hunchback of Notre Dame* (1923) and *The Phantom of the Opera* (1925).

The credits for *Foolish Wives* read: "Setting and design by Captain Richard Day and Erich von Stroheim"; the "Assistant Architect" was Elmer Sheely. The "Costumes and Uniforms" are also attributed to Day and von Stroheim. The elaborate sets for this film became a *cause célèbre* in Hollywood, for their scale, authenticity, but particularly for their cost. Carl Laemmle, who had a knack for capitalizing even on mounting expenses, publicized *Foolish Wives* with the slogan "The First Million Dollar Picture."

The film's principal set was the Place Centrale in Monte Carlo, with the block-long Hôtel de Paris flanked by the Café de Paris to the right and the Casino of Monte Carlo on the left. (**Illustration 127.**) A camera was placed on a hillock facing the three-sided set to pan over the huge Place, which von Stroheim filled with dozens of extras. Built of timber and stucco, the set's detailing was painstakingly rendered. Von Stroheim, an Austrian by birth, brought a credibility to his European sets that he termed "realistic," a quality he insisted upon from the start.[3]

Von Stroheim's film decor, predicated upon hard realism, often focused in lingering takes on details in the sets to draw attention to their significance for a character or for symbolic purposes. Day's apprenticeship years with von Stroheim served him well, and his name has become associated, somewhat too

127. *Foolish Wives,* 1922. Richard Day, Erich von Stroheim, Elmer Sheely, art direction. The Place Centrale in Monte Carlo, with its block-long Hôtel de Paris, was an expensive set for Universal. Built in timber and stucco, it was painstakingly detailed.

exclusively, with realism in films. Day's highly diversified production over the course of his long career was to include Art Deco sets like those discussed earlier that he designed with Cedric Gibbons for *Our Dancing Daughters* and the recreation of World War II Hawaii for his last film, *Tora! Tora! Tora!* (1970), designed with Jack Martin Smith.

Day's work on *Foolish Wives* gave him the opportunity to recreate diverse other settings: a villa, a sporting club, the Royal Palace of Monaco, an inn, a hut, back streets of Monte Carlo, an ocean promenade, and a firehouse. He scouted the locations for the film which was shot all around southern California — at the cliffs of La Jolla, at Exposition Park in San Diego, and in the resort town of Del Monte in northern California, where facades were erected on the coast to create a Mediterranean ocean promenade.

The authenticity of von Stroheim's films left an indelible mark on American film decor, and through his fostering of Day's talent he bequeathed to it a major art director who would continue to be a force in motion pictures long after his own career was over. Von Stroheim had begun working in Hollywood as a lowly assistant in charge of wardrobe, for which he showed an uncanny interest in details. He next spent time as an assistant to D.W. Griffith on *Intolerance,* a film unrivalled in American film history up until that time for its huge and extravagant sets. With his own first film *Blind Husbands* (1919), von Stroheim had showed an interest similar to Griffith's in the settings in which his narratives unfolded. For that film he had Day and the Universal crews build a backlot Alpine village, like those remembered from his childhood. The director oversaw every element in the sets and insisted on verisimilitude. The desire for authenticity was to permeate Day's approach to film design throughout his career, as his son later remembered:

> ...his ability to read and absorb was probably the thing that made him such an outstanding success in his profession. When assigned a picture, he would totally absorb himself in the literature pertaining to the period and the plot. He built up a tremendous personal library in this way...[4]

Von Stroheim, a former Austrian army officer and always interested in things military, may originally have found this a common ground to be shared with Day, who had recently returned from service in World War I. It would account for the lingering use of the title "Captain" in Day's screen credits on the von Stroheim films (he was called "Cap Day" around the lot, a nickname he disliked). The art director became simply Richard Day in the post–Stroheim years. Day was to serve in the military again in World War II, despite his advancing age, while von Stroheim for reasons largely beyond his control, did not serve in either war.

In these early years at Universal the Art Department was run by Charles D. Hall, who with Elmer E. Sheeley, Sidney M. Ullman and Ben Carré designed the inspired settings for *The Phantom of the Opera* (1925). Besides the unforgettable underground catacombs and dungeons attributable to Carré, these settings included a replication of the Paris Opera House auditorium with five balconies to physically hold 3,000 extras. The Opera House figured in Universal pictures for several decades, even being refurbished for the Technicolor remake of the film in 1943.[5]

To the film, Ben Carré, who had himself worked at the Paris Opera as a scenic designer, brought expertise from his years as a stage and then film designer in Europe and America. Carré had made 24 master drawings of the underground world of Erik, the Phantom. These conceptions of his netherworld were so powerful that the script was changed to incorporate Carré's ideas.[6] Working closely with the Gaston Leroux novel, the art director recreated an eerie world of cavernous arches whose transverse segments and piers were as gloomy as those found in Piranesi's 18th century prints of prison interiors.

The Phantom of the Opera is dominated by the menacing performance of Lon Chaney, but the settings come in a close second to it. Together, they make this picture one of the most memorable horror films of the silent period, paving the way for Universal's dominance of the genre in the thirties.

Charles D. "Danny" Hall, Universal's chief art director, was born in Norwich, England in 1898. He studied art, worked in an architect's office, and did stage designs for the Fred Karno Shows before migrating first to Canada, and then to America. From 1912 onward, Hall worked in the film industry; first hired to do scenic painting, he gradually took on the responsibilities of art director. His brother Archer, who had accompanied him to America, joined Universal at the same time to build sets; he eventually became head of the Construction Department, when Hall was head of the Art Department.[7]

An early challenge for Danny Hall came in 1923 when he was called on to devise the enormous cathedral setting for *The Hunchback of Notre Dame,* Irvin Thalberg's favorite project during his tenure as head of production at Universal. This was followed by an association with Charlie Chaplin that began in 1925 with *The Gold Rush,* and continued through three more films: *The Circus* (1928), *City Lights* (1931), and *Modern Times* (1936).

Chaplin, along with other physical comedians, especially Buster Keaton, had exact requirements for his sets and props, one good example being the cabin that Hall designed to teeter at the edge of an icy precipice in *The Gold Rush.* Chaplin spent 14 months preparing *The Gold Rush,* much of it in Nevada where snow locations were shot. But much of the film's most hilarious action takes place in the unpretentious miner's cabin built by Hall.

Hall's settings, particularly the factory, for *Modern Times* (a 1936 United Artists release) were among the most complicated and effective ever created for a Chaplin film. **(Illustration 128.)** Chaplin had gotten the idea for the picture from a report he heard about "a factory-belt system . . . a harrowing story of big industry luring healthy young men off the farms who, after four or five years at the belt system, became nervous wrecks."[8] Hall and unit art director Russell Spencer came up with all the visualizations for the film, including the many intricate props, like the maniacal feeding machine that the working man must survive.

Modern Times opens to mattes of a large factory, as workers swarm in

(sheep to the slaughter, in an analogy concretely presented). The interior of the factory is a built set, the largest ever created for a Chaplin film, and a huge foil for his comedy. First seen is the boss' modern office; it is futuristically equipped with a monitoring screen so that he can observe the workers' every movement. The metallically glistening, relentlessly turning wheels of the factory's machinery are gigantic in scale. Chaplin is seen working on one of the conveyor belts, wrenches flying, so much a part of the mechanism that he can't seem to stop his motions even when he wants to take a break.

Chaplin becomes a guinea pig for a new feeding machine that will eliminate the need for the workers to take a lunch break. The machine goes wild, a twirling piece of corn-on-the-cob threatens to annihilate him, soup is thrown over him, and in a final cannibalizing moment the machine attempts to eat its own mechanical parts. Next the assembly line is speeded up and Chaplin, working feverishly, falls into its wheels, cogs, and rollers, his body flowing through it, back and forth. Undeterred he never stops turning bolts.

In the latter part of the film Chaplin and his girlfriend (Paulette Goddard) find themselves in a department store, complete with escalators down which Chaplin roller skates. Eventually the couple find their way to a waterfront shack (a close relative of the cabin in *Gold Rush*); "Paradise," he exclaims as he accidentally slides out of an open door, landing in water. Here Hall and Spencer have created the typical comedic "prop" house. Its every board seems determined to do him in; he is bopped by planks, chairs fall in when he sits down, and doors find ways to defeat his every purpose. Surviving it all, at film's end, the pair can still walk happily into the sunset.

At Universal around 1925, there was a major influx of European trained filmmakers (there was always a minor influx of Europeans, given Laemmle's tapping of his German relatives for positions at the studio). Hired in the mid-twenties were directors Paul Leni, Paul Fejos, Karl Freund, Edgar G. Ulmer, and E.A. Dupont. They brought with them a heightened sense of cinematic style, appreciation of scenic values, and sensitivity to the subtleties to be achieved by lighting. Although most of these Europeans stayed at Universal fewer than five years, they came at exactly the right time to encourage the development of these identical values already on the rise at the studio, and manifest in such fine productions as *Foolish Wives* and *The Phantom of the Opera*.

Both Leni and Ulmer had worked as art directors, and in particular brought to their work an eye for significant decor. Leni's suspenseful and highly successful German film *Das Wachsfigurenkabinett (Waxworks)* of 1924, which he directed and designed, had so impressed Carl Laemmle that he

128. *Modern Times,* 1936. Charles D. (Danny) Hall, Russell Spencer, art directors. The heartless mechanization of "modern times" were epitomized in the intricate machines of the film's factory, which frequently ensnarled and attacked Charlie Chaplin (right).

brought him to Universal. There Leni continued his short career (he died in 1929 at age 44), directing such silent suspense films as *The Cat and the Canary* (1927), *The Chinese Parrot* (1927), and *The Last Warning* (1928).

The Cat and the Canary involved an heiress (Laura La Plante) who must spend the night in an old mansion among a group of people all of whom would profit from her death. Leni's visual style excited the audience, his use of clutching hands (they encircle the slumbering heroine's neck), sliding panels, and an unknown killer lurking behind a hideous mask, have become set pieces in scary "old house" thrillers to the present day. Leni was himself borrowing upon techniques already tried in German films of terror, like *Warning Shadows* (1922): these techniques were soon widely used at Universal. The art director responsible for the design of all of Leni's films at Universal was Charles D. Hall, who by the end of the twenties had become the resident expert in all manner of creepy architectural settings, whether Transylvania or Pennsylvania.

By the end of the decade Universal, along with the other Hollywood studios, was ready to embark on a little toney modernity in the vocabulary of Art Deco. Although the use of this idiom was never to be widespread at Universal, unlike the case at Paramount, RKO, and MGM, Charles Hall put it to good use for the musical *Broadway* (1929). **(Illustration 129.)** He created one of the largest Deco nightclubs ever invented for the screen, in an era that loved nightclubs, on screen and off. As Howard Mandelbaum and Eric Myers have commented:

> According to Hollywood, nightclubs were vast modern temples where passion and pleasure could be played on a grand scale. Here, love affairs began and ended; fortunes were made and lost with a spin of the roulette wheel. Human lives might collapse, but the orchestra kept playing and the crowds kept dancing on and on. . . .[9]

The use of sound lengthened the duration of nightclub scenes, which had been brief in silent films. *Broadway* was Universal's first assay into the all-talking picture. A stage hit by Philip Dunning and George Abbot, *Broadway* had originally been set in a sleazy New York nightclub, but for the motion picture Charles D. Hall created a daring and vast set, so big that a special crane had to be invented in order to get shots that would encompass it.[10] The movie was budgeted at $1 million and much of this went into the set—a rare happening at Universal.

Hall's nightclub was described in the studio's publicity as a "perfect example of ultra-modern cubistic art," which doesn't half do it justice.[11] The set consists of several levels: on the ground floor, tables surround a shiny dance floor where the elaborate musical numbers were staged; on the right a stair leads to an overhanging balcony, covered with angular geometric patterns, where more tables are arranged, another balcony overhangs the left side of the set. Gus

129. *Broadway,* 1929. Charles D. (Danny) Hall, art director. The model for the elaborate Art Deco nightclub that was built for Universal's first all-talking picture.

Arnheim and His Cocoanut Grove Ambassadors serenaded the audience from the sidelines. The background consisted of three huge stepped towers, reminiscent of skyscrapers, surmounted by lights beaming fragmented ray patterns onto the ceiling (they are like the facets of glass or metal on the contemporaneous Chrysler Building by architect Willem Van Alen). Between the huge towers there are painted images of modernity, signs and background were changed for each musical number, with one sign saying simply "Moving Pictures." All of Danny Hall's background imagery responds to the urbane, pulsating, and dynamic image of New York City that was accepted by audiences during the thirties.

Universal followed up *Broadway* with *King of Jazz,* a musical revue with lavish sets, in a variety of styles, by art director Herman Rosse. Rosse's designs won for the studio its only Academy Award for art direction during the first 16 years the awards were given (rather unfairly, no Universal films were even nominated for the next five years). Rosse was primarily a stage designer and teacher of design. A native of Holland, he had migrated to the United States from England in 1908, having studied at the Kensington School of Art in London. His art direction at Universal in the thirties included films like *Frankenstein* (1931, uncredited) and *Murders in the Rue Morgue* (1932).

The *King of Jazz* was filmed in two-tone technicolor by director John Murray Anderson. Rosse's challenge, typical for revue type musicals, was to produce backgrounds for the many individual numbers, performed by such varied talents as the Rhythm Boys, the Brox Sisters, Bing Crosby (in his film debut), and George Gershwin conducting the "Rhapsody in Blue," all strung together under the pretext that Paul Whiteman was explaining how he had come to be known as "the king of jazz."

Some of Rosse's sets were resolutely modern, like the background "Paul Whiteman Scrap Book," which introduces the numbers; others were period pieces, like that for "The Bridal Veil" number featuring Jeanette Loff. The *King of Jazz* cost Universal well over a million dollars, but the public was tiring of musicals, and even the novel Technicolor process did not save the film from fizzling at the box office. The same was not true of the Studio's other prestige production of 1930, *All Quiet on the Western Front,* which won both critical and audience accolades, and saved the company from financial collapse.

All Quiet on the Western Front (sets by Charles D. Hall and W.R. Schmitt) has become an American film classic. It tells the story, in unremittingly realistic terms, of trench warfare in World War I. Seen from the German side, the story stresses the humanistic theme of the horrors of war, as it follows a group of naive students who enlist in the army at the urging of their jingoistic schoolmaster and end up maimed or dead.

The picture opens on the small flourishing German town that is the boys' home. Hall and Schmitt's town covered over four acres; its comfortable gabled houses, church, and streets suggest a quieter time, but the opening scenes are thronged with marching troops. The camera pulls back to the interior of the schoolhouse, where the street noise intrudes upon the classroom. The art directors have placed large windows on the street and the autocratic schoolmaster stands between them as he eggs his students on to enlist.

The rest of the film is set on the grim frontline of the war. Universal built a huge field of trenches in which, like rats in a maze, the weary, dirty soldiers move. The camera probes every area of the front line trenches, many times in the glare of exploding shells. Also built were several crumbling buildings, where the troops find refuge, and a stone church that serves as a hospital. Director Louis Milestone's use of the sets is varied and effective. Sometimes they seem flat, one dimensional—as in the scenes of the boys' early discussions of the war. At other times he uses them three-dimensionally, when, for instance, troops and equipment keep rolling past a hole in the wall of a bombed building in which the boys are billeted.

When the main protagonist, Paul Baumer (Lew Ayres), returns to his hometown during the war, he finds it disfigured. Stores are closed and boarded up, the people drab and unhappy, the direct opposite of what has been seen in the beginning of the film. The radical alteration in the town reflects the actualities of the war, and underscores how much Paul has changed himself.

The tenderest and most provocative moments in *All Quiet on the Western Front* are those that focus on the human tragedy in intense visual images—the passing on of a dead boy's boots from soldier to soldier as one after another dies; the French girl who stuffs her mouth with food as Baumer timidly kisses her hair in his first romantic encounter; Baumer stabbing to death an enemy soldier in a trench and then saying he's sorry. This is a film in which the settings far from dominate, but are the essential fabric upon which the story is hung.

In the thirties, Universal was kept afloat not by prestige productions like *All Quiet on the Western Front,* indeed there were considerably fewer of them, but by the horror films and weepies which were abundantly, and sometimes excellently produced. *Dracula* (1931) inaugurated the cycle, with *Frankenstein* (1932) following fast on its heels. Universal was fortunate in hiring the fine character actors Bela Lugosi and Boris Karloff for these roles. In addition, they had in Danny Hall a resident art director who thrived on this genre, producing for them an endless variety of cobwebbed halls, frightening stairs, and creepy cemeteries.

In *Dracula,* most of the dastardly blood-drinking deeds are done offscreen, so that much of the sense of evil and horror in the film had to come from the main performer, Lugosi, and the decor. In later horror films much more nastiness will actually be seen on screen and so the burden of proof shifts.

Together, Tod Browning, the film's director, Danny Hall and cinematographer Karl Freund developed the visual concepts for *Dracula.* The beginning of the film alternates between mattes of the Transylvanian mountains, the Count's castle exterior, and built settings. The first overwhelming impression of evil comes from Hall's unforgettable castle interior. Three female "corpses," Dracula's brides, arise from their coffins in a cavernous vault. Count Dracula is then seen slowly descending a long, crumbling stone stairway to greet a visitor in a vast entry hall. **(Illustration 130.)** The stair is L-shaped, and light filters lugubriously onto it through Gothic lancet windows at the right. The entire room—every stair, baluster, and pier—is covered with cobwebs; large ones form a veil over the entire motion picture screen at certain moments. There is a suffocating feeling of decay as tree branches are seen invading the interior through the windows. Wolves are heard howling outside, and the Count remarks, "Children of the night, what music they make."

The lighting is manipulated so that it burns brilliantly on Dracula's face as he speaks to the visitor, inviting him to venture further: "I'm sure you will find this part of my castle more inviting." This "inviting" part of the castle

turns out to be an incomprehensibly large room, its back wall dominated by three-story windows and a giant fireplace (long before the same motifs occur in *Citizen Kane,* where too, they evoke a house of horrors). The door, the wooden desk, the armor decorating the walls, the candles burning in torcheres around the room are all inhumanly scaled. Man is minuscule, the presence of evil is palpable.

The Count's dreadful brigade (now including the crazed visitor) travel in their coffins to a fog shrouded Victorian London. The settings become conventional, a theatre, living rooms and bedrooms of a wealthy dwelling, until Count Dracula finds a new abode—nothing less than an abandoned abbey. Luckily it is next door to a sanatorium with a ready supply of victims to satisfy the Count's nocturnal proclivities.

Minna (Helen Chandler), the Count's candidate for his next "bride," is brought to the abbey, whose cavernous rooms she wanders with him. She descends the film's second spectacular stair, an open spiral falling several stories into an arcaded lower room. As a dreadful reminder of the earlier image in the Transylvanian castle, the stair is seen through a filter of cobwebs. The shot of Minna descending the spiral stairs is done in a long take, allowing ample time for the decor to work its malevolent spell. This technique is seen in all of the principal photography of the big sets on *Dracula,* and is due, partly, to its being an early sound film. Cumbersome recording equipment could not pick up voices from a great distance, so when Browning wanted the whole set in the frame the camera steps back and there is no dialogue. The actors are seen passing through the set, as here, creating long moments of pure visual concentration familiar from earlier silent films.

Variations of themes found in the decor of *Dracula* recur with regularity in subsequent Universal horror films, and Danny Hall's cannibalization of his own ideas is not out of keeping with the spirit of the plays. Beside the Count and the Baron, Universal regularly regaled the public with the misadventures of the Mummy, the Invisible Man, and the Wolf Man. Yet in the eyes of the public, the others were not quite so winning as the original two: the Count as the personification of evil, and Frankenstein's monster as the inarticulate and horrible creature of man's vanity.

Because the grosses on *Dracula* had been Universal's largest in 1930, the production budget on *Frankenstein,* $250,000, was sufficient for Hall to again design imaginative full-scale sets, this time for director James Whale. The locale, as usual with this genre, is Central Europe, a small Bavarian town (the *All Quiet on the Western Front* town redressed), and the exteriors are stark

130. *Dracula,* 1931. Charles D. (Danny) Hall, art director. Count Dracula (Bela Lugosi) greeted Renfield (Dwight Frye) in the crumbling stone entry hall of his Transylvanian castle, where a tree grew in through the window and cobwebs covered every surface.

and barren. The film opens on a funeral in a lonely, dark cemetery set in a desiccated landscape. With the exception of one scene, naturistically rendered, in which the monster plays in the sunshine with a little girl beside a lake (before he drowns her in it), Hall's exteriors are economical, sometimes to the point of surreality.

The major interior set is Dr. Frankenstein's laboratory; it is housed in an ancient, decaying tower. **(Illustration 131.)** There the doctor conducts his grisly experiments, dissecting and grafting together parts from corpses that he and his ghoulish assistant have stolen. Unlike the tower's crumbling exterior, the laboratory is a marvel of modern electrical equipment — conductors, switchboards, huge incandescent bulbs. It is dominated by a central operating table suspended from chain cables so that it can be lifted heavenward to capture the force of electrical storms that will, Frankenstein thinks, give life to his creation. Eventually, in a chilling scene, the monster is reanimated in such a storm; it is a highpoint in horror film special effects.

For the final scene — the death of the monster — Danny Hall built a huge windmill silhouetted against a leaden studio sky. As the mill becomes an incendiary torch, the monster hurls Dr. Frankenstein groundward and is himself consumed by the flames.

When *Frankenstein* grossed $12,000,000, Universal sensibly decided that the monster hadn't really perished in the conflagration, but had only been hurt. Then, premised on Boris Karloff's sensitive portrayal of the monster, which had made him a semitragic figure who could feel pain, the studio decided that in a human way he would want a "bride." *The Bride of Frankenstein* (1935, director James Whale) followed with essentially the same characters playing the leads, but with Elsa Lanchester added to the cast in the dual role of author Mary Shelley and the bride-to-be of the monster.

The Bride of Frankenstein uses a favorite opening for Universal horror films — lightning crackling over a gloomy castle. In its interiors Mary Shelley begins the tale of what really happened to Frankenstein and the monster at the burning mill. Part of the scenic formulae of Universal's horror films is a vastness of scale — furniture, fireplaces, wall ornaments, shadows on walls all must be oversized. In such interiors Dr. Frankenstein, we are told, has been revived after the fire. The doctor's bedroom, one of Danny Hall's best creations, is expressive of his twisted personality; its bizarre ornate canopied bed is topped by a feather crown, at a massive fireplace lit by cathedral windows he reveals, not surprisingly, that he still yearns to be a "creator."

At the burnt-out mill, rising starkly skeletal against a leaden sky, the monster is revealed arising from the rubble (his same old self, he immediately

131. *Frankenstein,* 1932. Charles D. (Danny) Hall. Dr. Frankenstein's laboratory, a marvel of modern electrical and mechanical equipment, was housed in a decaying stone tower.

kills two peasants). Frankenstein's monster soon meets the nefarious Dr. Pretorius, whose upper-room laboratory (he too makes creatures) is a study in angularity and filled with scientific apparatus. Pretorius has grown creatures, now housed in jars, and he confides, "science, like love, has her little surprises."

Frankenstein's monster wanders off into a forest; at first it is naturalistic with a waterfall, but becomes, as he is pursued by hunters, an expressionistically barren place against an electric sky. The monster is finally captured and flung into a dungeon. Not a big set, it is nevertheless the embodiment of entrapment, as a crowd peers down into it through a narrow stone shaft, to taunt the monster who struggles with his chains. The monster escapes, wreaking carnage as he goes, and returns to the stoney lair that is Dr. Pretorius' lab.

In a highly effective scene, kites conduct electrical current into the bride's not yet living body during an electrical storm. The explosive character of this reanimation is even greater than in the original *Frankenstein,* but the birth of the bride is not quite as poignant. Lancaster is effective in her own way in a flowing white gown, "static"/punk hairdo, with birdlike gestures as she awakens. But the monster correctly discerns at first shriek that, "She hate me." He proceeds to send Hall's big set up in flames (a good horror film ending) taking along (or does he?), himself, his bride, and Dr. Pretorius.

What director James Whale was to Universal's production of horror films, John Stahl was to the many "women's pictures" they turned out in the thirties. Stahl directed *Back Street* (1932), *Imitation of Life* (1934), and *Magnificent Obsession* (1935); his long term contract with the Studio assured him a relatively free hand and an ample budget to mount his romantic narratives, which starred fine actresses like Irene Dunne and Claudette Colbert.

The thirties weepies were so popular that Universal remade them repeatedly from the forties to the sixties, changing little except the stars. Typical of the way this genre was handled, is the second version of *Back Street* (1941), which starred Margaret Sullavan and Charles Boyer. This story of a selfish banker's illicit love affair is set in Cincinnati and New York at the turn of the century, places which are seen in plentiful scenic backdrops. The humble dwelling of the "back street" woman and a portion of the banker's house were built sets, designed by Jack Otterson and Richard H. Riedel. But for the most part, director Robert Stevenson chose to ignore the setting and filmed almost the entire picture in close-ups (the heroine's in soft-focus) or medium shots. The most decorative element in this film is the music by Frank Skinner; it underscores every dramatic moment between the lovers with resonant orchestral vibrations so that the viewer won't miss the points made by the all too obvious plot.

In 1936 with *Three Smart Girls,* Deanna Durbin began a series of what might be called "young adult" musicals for Universal, like those being produced at MGM with Mickey Rooney and Judy Garland. They were to include

One Hundred Men and a Girl (1937), *Mad about Music* (1938), *That Certain Age* (1938), films that made her a star attraction. While keeping budgets very small on their programmers, Universal invested more in the Durbin pictures, although the case seems similar to that of Shirley Temple at 20th Century–Fox; the audience was coming to hear Durbin's lovely coloratura voice and be charmed by her wholesome good looks, rather than to see big production numbers, or for that matter, be told believable stories.

Universal continued to be short on first rate acting talent throughout the decade, but by its end they had lured one great comedian, W.C. Fields, onto the lot. Fields' hilarious features, *You Can't Cheat an Honest Man* (1939), *The Bank Dick* (1940), and *My Little Chickadee* (1940) were long on laughs, but short on sets. Fields was a verbal comedian, who loved a good prop, but for whom settings were relatively unimportant. Those for his pictures usually came straight out of the studio's storage bins.

The best designed comedy of the thirties at Universal was *My Man Godfrey* (1936), starring Carole Lombard and William Powell. It was also one of the funniest. The sets by Charles D. Hall were among the last he did at Universal. In the late thirties he moved to the Hal Roach Studios, working there on the comedies of Laurel and Hardy; after 1944, he freelanced. Patrick Downing and John Hambley have tried to summarize Hall's character and contribution,

> Of the art directors to whom the description "great" can be applied, it is modest Charles D. Hall who seems closest to the ordinary, the full-time art director who was the backbone of Hollywood studio design. He had no pretensions to power or glory, but simply turned in a thoughtful and professional performance for an enormously wide range of films and directors over thirty years.[12]

This seems an accurate, if overly restrained estimation of Hall's accomplishments. His sets were frequently inspired, and one has only to see again the factory in *Modern Times* to be reminded of this.

Jack Otterson replaced Hall as supervising art director at Universal in 1936 and maintained that position until 1943. Otterson had studied architecture at Yale in the twenties and then worked as an architect, at one time helping to design the decoration for the Empire State Building. He joined 20th Century–Fox as a sketch artist in 1932, soon moving up to art director.[13]

In the forties, Universal did not depart from its formula productions, but added to them a greater number of crime films, many of the *film noir* variety. Alfred Hitchcock, perambulating as usual among major studios, filmed *Saboteur* (1942) and *Shadow of a Doubt* (1943) at Universal. Robert Boyle in his first major art directorial effort (with Jack Otterson the supervising art director) recalls the days of making *Saboteur* among the new austerities brought on by World War II:

> We couldn't get materials, because the war had really begun. So we had to put together the picture with limited, very limited means. It was all done on Universal's

stages, with only some second unit work done on location. Hitch didn't like to take the principals on location. He used doubles for the location action stuff. We used just about every "trick" effect we had in this picture: mattes, back projection, scenic paintings, everything.[14]

Boyle, who liked to sketch, had so much to do on this picture that he needed assistants—sketch artists, like his University of Southern California classmate, Dorothea Holt. "She made the most fantastic wash drawings, which everyone admired, but never could copy. You could stand right behind her when she was doing them, and still not figure out how she got those effects." Boyle continues,

Hitch did crude early sketches, rough—he showed me what he wanted. His sketches were ideas. Then we stuck close to the sketches I had made for the sets. Today I see many pictures where the camera is not making a statement. This didn't happen with Hitchcock; he knew what he wanted in every shot.

The earliest stages of the planning are particularly vivid to Boyle,

I remember sitting across the table from Hitchcock one Sunday morning in December of 1941, and he had formalized some of his ideas already. He asked me what I thought; he was kind of testing me. The door opened and an air raid warden in a hard hat came in and asked us what we were doing there. "Pearl Harbor's been bombed," he said and slammed back out of the room. We didn't comprehend a thing and went back to work. Later Hitch asked, "What was that guy doing in that funny hat?"

Saboteur opens in an aircraft factory.

For this scene we used a Universal sound stage with a painted backing, lit from behind, the ceiling was a painted flat. The scene of the truck driving through the desert used a process shot of the desert and then in the close action of a small section of the road was built and a painted backing used for the desert.

Hitchcock did not go on location either for the scene at a ranch. According to Boyle, "When the action moved to the ranch, a second unit location shot was used in establishing shot, and then when the narrative picked up we were on a studio built patio and swimming pool."

The most memorable sequences in *Saboteur* are those near the end at the Radio City Music Hall and when the saboteur is trapped and falls to his death from the Statue of Liberty.

We built only enough of the Music Hall to cover the people in the shot, the audience. We used several mattes for the rest, one is a matte shot with a real movie going on in its center.

When the saboteur heads for Bedloes Island, the ferry ride is all done with process plates made in New York. The process shots were back-projected with only a little portion of the ferry's railing built in the studio. In those days nobody would have thought of going on the real ferry boat. Much of the Statue of Liberty sequence was mattes. I built the crown of the statue inside and out, matching it exactly with the real thing, and I also built the hand that holds the torch, which was the most expensive set on the picture. I found a wonderful production illustrator, named John De Cuir, who did the continuity sketches for the Statue of Liberty sequence.

For the saboteur's [Norman Lloyd] fall from the Statue, Hitch used a matte shot. He put the actor on a black swivel chair . . . we had black cloth below it, everything was black. They spun him around in the chair and had the camera on a sort of elevator, and pulled it upward to 40 feet and then optically reduced it, piecing the entire sequence together to create a long fall. You could conceivably do that until he was a mere dot. Everything seen in the shot around the actor was a matte.

Hitchcock was the only director I ever worked with who could absolutely visualize the scene in his head. There was no floundering when we began shooting. He wanted the emotional impact of a scene, even if the technical side wasn't absolutely perfect. He liked to involve the audience in ideas presented in a clear film language, and knew that how you tell a story must be visual.

When I started out, we were mostly influenced by silent films, which in some ways we were still doing. Some French and Russian films (like Eisenstein), we also admired. This is a visual medium, and the visual side cannot be neglected.

At Universal, especially innovative in the forties was the work of a resident director Robert Siodmak, whose *film noir* classic, *The Killers* (1946), followed upon such mystery melodramas as *Christmas Holiday* (1944), *Lady on a Train* (1945), and *Uncle Harry* (1945). Typical of Siodmak's work (although he filmed better stories) was *Christmas Holiday,* a Somerset Maugham tale, in which he cast against type, a nondancing Gene Kelly, as a pathological gambler and killer, and an almost nonsinging, sultry Deanna Durbin, as his obsessional wife.

The film's exterior and interiors, designed by John B. Goodman and Robert Clatworthy and photographed by Woody Bredell, are almost all domestic, and were, typically for early *film noir,* completely studio built. There is a nicely cluttered Victorian house where Kelly and Durbin live with his possessive mother (Gale Sondergaard), but the mood of the film, its visual presence, is established more by the Germanic lighting, heavy with shadows, than by the decor. A full palette of contrastive sidelighting and backlighting is used. Often a lamp is seen in the room to provide an artificial source for the light, and it can glare directly into the camera. The lighting appears artificial almost all of the time, whether a source for it is given, or not.

Siodmak's inventive choice of camera angles is indicative, like his lighting, of his German film training; the director had only recently, in 1940, emigrated to the United States. Frequently in *Christmas Holiday,* Siodmak chose bird's eye angles, capturing the action and the set from the vantage point of a character who is above it looking downward. Early in the film Durbin, from her second story bedroom, watches her husband and mother-in-law in conspiratorial conversation through high bay windows in the kitchen; later from the same vantage point she sees his bloodstained pants being thrown into an incinerator. Siodmak imaginatively reverses this viewpoint too, choosing low camera angles that look directly up stairs or up into a balcony. These often jarring camera positions, menacing lighting, and the abrupt editing that accompany them are part of Siodmak's distinctive visual style and set his thrillers apart from the ordinary Universal studio product.

Christmas Holiday's art directors, John B. Goodman and Robert Clatworthy were part of the Universal Art Department in the forties. Goodman did a short turn as supervising art director in the years 1943–1946, until he was replaced by Bernard Herzbrun in 1947. Clatworthy had only just come to Universal in 1943; he was to remain for 19 years. He was also the art director on Siodmak's *Phantom Lady* (1944), and relates that he almost became its director:

> At Universal, I considered directing a film, as most everyone who enters the business does. Joan Harrison [the film's producer], a very bright woman who was Hitchcock's associate producer for a long time, thought I would be a good director for *Phantom Lady*. Then it turned out to be a co-director job, and I decided it wouldn't really work.[15]

Beside Siodmak, another German filmmaker, Fritz Lang joined Universal briefly in the forties to make a *film noir* landmark, *Scarlet Street* (1945), which starred Edward G. Robinson as the hen-pecked cashier who falls for an unsavory Joan Bennett. The film, its evocative settings designed by Alexander Golitzen, contains the requisite *noir* dark streets (Greenwich Village this time), where the film begins and ends. Again, all studio built, the sets have a contained claustrophobic presence and are filled with the sort of telling detail Golitzen, like Paramount's Hans Dreier, was expert at including. Foster Hirst, generalizing on *film noir* environments, could have been describing Golitzen's *Scarlet Street* sets,

> They create closed worlds from which a sense of the flow of life has been rigorously excluded. There seems to be no world outside the frame, and there are almost no other people on view besides the principals. These stories of obsession and self-destruction are enacted in a deliberately created vacuum — a sealed-off environment of airless rooms, and of threatening, lonely streets.[16]

There are a limited number of sets in *Scarlet Street*, often the case with *noir* films. There are three principal interiors: Robinson's over-stuffed apartment, dominated by a portrait of his wife's first husband, where he is allowed to pursue his hobby, painting, only in the cramped confines of the bathroom; his office, where he sits entrapped in a cashier's cage; and the apartment he rents for Bennett with money embezzled from his company. In direct contrast to his own dark dwelling, it is uncluttered, white, with a skylight that provides brilliant light under which he can work freely on his art.

Alexander Golitzen (**Illustration 132**) was already an Academy Award

132. Alexander Golitzen, supervising art director, Universal Studios, and Joseph Wright with their model for the backlot "European Street," which was built to their specifications (1962).

winner for his settings for the remake of *The Phantom of the Opera* (1943) when he began working with Lang on *Scarlet Street*. A native of Moscow, he worked remarkably well with other Europeans, including Max Ophuls for whom he designed the marvellous *fin-de-siècle* Vienna for *Letter from an Unknown Woman* (1948), and Alfred Hitchcock, for whose *Foreign Correspondent* (1940, United Artists, with William Cameron Menzies, Richard Irvine, Edmond Bernoudy) he helped build a huge Amsterdam square, a windmill in the Dutch countryside, and a section of London.

Alexander Golitzen left the Soviet Union at the age of 16, graduated in architecture from the University of Washington in 1931 and entered the motion picture business as an illustrator at MGM in 1933. After a stint at Goldwyn/United Artists, where he worked under his mentor Richard Day, Golitzen became an art director at Universal with *Eagle Squadron* (1942). He worked primarily on Walter Wanger productions, and then when Wanger left the studio he stayed on to eventually become supervising art director in 1953 (he had served on and off in that capacity since 1952 when Bernard Herzbrun became ill), continuing in that position until his retirement in 1976.

One of Golitzen's best known films, done with art director Robert Clatworthy, was Orson Welles' *Touch of Evil* (1958), set in a tacky Mexican border town. In the fifties and sixties, Golitzen and Clatworthy both excelled in the art direction of pictures made on location. Clatworthy explains the location choice,

> Of the shows I worked on at Universal, the one I most enjoyed was *Touch of Evil*. . . . It was shot in Venice, California, because part of the town resembled the covered walkways in Tijuana. On the night we did the opening shot — the three-minute-long take that follows a white car through the streets and to the Mexican-American border — Welles had eleven generators working. Eleven! That's a lot of generators to light a night scene.[17]

Golitzen's and Clatworthy's handling of the location decor is overpowering. No traces of a Hollywood built environment are in evidence, despite the fact that the entire location had to be reworked to turn it into Los Robles, the tough border town policed by corrupt Hank Quinlan (Welles). Every locale in the film oozes sleaze; walls are cracked, paint peels from them; dusty windows are packed with advertisements of the "good" life in the town.

Honeymooning Mexican narcotics official Mike Vargas (Charlton Heston) is drawn into the investigation of a murder, and moves through the underworld of Los Robles, the bars, flea-bag hotels, bordellos, all populated with low-lifes. He has to stow his bride (Janet Leigh) somewhere to wait for him, and settles on a motel outside the town. For evil presence this deserted place is bested not even by Clatworthy's later creation, the motel in *Psycho*.

The lighting contributes to the sense of menace at every turn. The mastery of expressionistic lighting, seen in the Universal films of Siodmak, Lang and Whale, is evidenced with unsurpassed effect under Welles' direction and Russell Metty's atmospheric cinematography. Strong directors, with their own sense of style, like Welles, could get anything they needed from the Art Department at Universal.

By the late fifties, the days of B pictures and serials, long mainstays of Universal, were coming to an end. In 1946 Universal had merged with International Pictures, becoming Universal-International, and had acquired an aggressive new management that was determined to upgrade the quality of the

Studio's output.[18] The fifties saw Universal pouring more money into their productions generally, the average budget rose to over a million dollars and the Studio began using Technicolor widely, where previously it had been avoided as too expensive. Ross Hunter productions, many of them remakes of the popular weepies of the thirties, were given prestige budgets, with large investments made in sets. The production values desired by Hunter were of a slick, Hollywood elegance that usually repressed individualization in the decor, and ended up looking expensive, but often bland.

The remade *Imitation of Life* (1959), starring Lana Turner, is typical of this genre. Ross Hunter never allowed a hair on mannequin-perfect Turner's head to be out of place, nor a remotely imperfect interior to appear. Even the tenement, where the story first places Turner, is not realistically detailed. It is, however, color coded in grey. Color coding is a key to all Hunter productions: grey means poverty and meanness, white and brighter colors (pink bedrooms) means affluence and well-being. As art director Golitzen (Richard H. Riedel was unit art director) put it, "Ross loved a big white set." The audience can tell who the good and bad guys are simply by watching the colors; the lecherous agent's office is grey; the amorous playwright's apartment is grey, but with gold leaf, he is only partly bad (he lets novice actress Turner tell him how to rewrite his play).

Such an abrupt change in assignment for Alexander Golitzen, given his work of a year earlier with Clatworthy on *Touch of Evil*, underscores the fact that art directors have to be versatile in their approaches, and able to bend to the preferences of powerful directors or producers, and to the dictates of the story. Ross Hunter films do have a definite "look," one basically attributable to the tastes of the producer. The definitive set in a Hunter production was frequently the elegant home (his pictures are precursors of the 1980s television soap operas like *Dynasty* or *Dallas*, the latter looking particularly like a Ross Hunter fifties production).

In *Imitation of Life* the "big house set" is Turner's country home, the main room with high cathedral ceiling is all-over white, set off by walls of books, a *de rigueur* stone wall with fireplace, and a large bar with counter and stools stand to one side. Outside the large picture windows a luxuriant rolling countryside (scenic paintings) may be seen. Fittingly, against such a background, Lana Turner is heard to emote the unforgettable line, "But, I'm not acting."

The same slick production values spill over into the Hunter-produced Doris Day and Rock Hudson comedies which began in 1959 with *Pillow Talk*, where they are used with more flair and effectiveness. Richard H. Riedel is given sole credit for the *Pillow Talk* decor. Riedel had been working at Universal since the thirties; his career was cut short the following year when he died in an automobile accident outside Rome while scouting locations for Hunter's remake of *Back Street*.

The *Pillow Talk* interiors—fifties chic—are filled with witty nuances by Riedel; rather than serving merely as bland and suitable backgrounds for the action, they abet the plot and comment on the main characters. Doris Day is an interior decorator in the picture, so the art director could be more trendy than usual with the sets; modern art even appears on the walls. In particular, Riedel had fun with an apartment Day shapes into a flamboyant, multicolored seraglio for womanizer Hudson; it is a nightmare in purples and red, cushions and spangles everywhere, and his "seduction props"—phonograph player, automatic door locks—are given prominent place. The split-screen technique used by director Michael Gordon throughout the film, showing Hudson and Day simultaneously on the telephone in bed and bath, gave Riedel the chance to characterize the rugged he-man Hudson character and the independent career woman Day with playful props.

Science fiction films were another important part of Universal's production in the mid-fifties, as they were at other studios. Partaking in the 3-D fad, efforts like *It Came from Outer Space* tried to scare people in the way the earlier horror films had (the horror cycle was then being spoofed in Universal films like *Abbott and Costello Meet the Mummy,* 1955, and thrived as much on special effects, matte work, and outstanding make-up. For *It Came from Outer Space* art director Robert Boyle and Universal's special effects people created an irradiating extraterrestrial object that lands on the Arizona desert in full view of a scientist (Richard Carlson).

The Creature from the Black Lagoon (1954), *The Mole People* (1956) and *The Deadly Mantis* (1957) all had scaly or otherwise creepy creatures menacing mankind. One of the best of the science fiction series, *The Incredible Shrinking Man* (1957), depended heavily on screen trickery and clever sets for its chilling effects. Grant Williams starred as the man who is shrunk to a tiny two inches by a radioactive fog while he is innocently boating. Effects experts Clifford Stine, Roswell A. Hoffman and Everett H. Broussard did the shrinking and Robert Clatworthy designed the sets and huge props which menaced the man. In one case he clings to an enormous pencil to keep from being swept into the sewer, and in another he barely escapes the household cat who attacks the doll house in which he is reduced to living. **(Illustration 133.)** In contrast to most science fiction films, the shrinking man is menaced by ordinary objects, which gives this film its special sense of pathos.

While the scaly creatures, fiery outer-space vehicles, and contrived plots often seem artificial and even silly to contemporary audiences, they engrossed audiences in the fifties, in the predawn of the Sputnik era. Such films, despite their dated quality, are the cinematic precursors of the later, seventies and eighties, cycle of more technically sophisticated films, such as *E.T. the Extra-Terrestrial* (1982), also a Universal film featuring a scaly creature.

Alfred Hitchcock's *Psycho,* one of the films to end the decade (released in 1960), was shot mostly on the Universal lot. Art directors Robert Clatworthy

133. *The Incredible Shrinking Man,* 1957. Robert Clatworthy, art director. The household cat attacked the doll house (background) in which the shrinking man (Grant Williams) is reduced to staying in this special effects shot.

and Joseph Hurley provided singular visual images for Hitchcock's tale of a psychopathic killer.

Although there are other sets in the film, none of them are memorable in comparison to the lonely clapboard motel run by Norman Bates, and the establishment of his "mother" on the hill above it. **(Illustration 134.)** Hitchcock's isolation of each building at certain moments in the film makes them seem utterly menacing. Clatworthy recalls,

> *Psycho* was a little quickie picture for Hitchcock: only four weeks to prepare and shoot. Hitchcock had decided to do a picture that would cost less than a million— it came in at $830,000, I think—so it had to be shot in black-and-white. Certainly it worked better in black-and-white; so did *Touch of Evil.* Color tends to brighten things up too much; I always try to take the color out. Hitchcock is a great planner. He knows precisely what he wants to do. Sometimes he could read a newspaper while he's making a movie, he's that sure of himself. Joe Hurley and I designed the motel and the Bates house.... And for the roof, we borrowed parts from the rooftop of the house that was built, ten years earlier, for *Harvey!*[19]

134. *Psycho,* 1960. Robert Clatworthy and Joseph Hurley, art directors. The Bates
house, a Victorian Gothic Revival mansion, loomed in stark silhouette against the sky
above the drab motel of much of the film's action.

Hitchcock, a former art director, always got the best out of his art directors, and his method of visualizing each shot prior to shooting comes out of
the methods of art direction already practiced when he entered films. In
Psycho, his art directors Hurley and Clatworthy punctuate the drabness of the
motel with evidence of taxidermist Norman Bates' (Anthony Perkins) work: in
the office an enormous stuffed moose head looks down on the seemingly timid
motel proprietor, pictures on his walls (and on those in the drab motel room
given Janet Leigh) are all of birds.

The ornate Gothic Revival mansion is in exceptional contrast to the or-
dinariness of the motel: the two don't seem to belong to one another. The
mansion is one of the long line of "haunted" houses from Universal horror
films, most of whose exteriors had only been seen in mattes. The ample porch
on the Bates house leads into a handsome foyer, whose large stairway is complete with intricate carved newels and stained-glass windows; the stairs provide
the perfect site for one of Norman's stabbing murders. The several levels of the

large house are revealed on the first floor landing, eventually to be explored by Hitchcock in every nook and cranny, all of them holding some new terror.

The sixties were just the beginning of the golden years for Universal. The studio had survived by holding on to a large portion of the second-bill market over decades, by producing entertaining serials and series, by economizing at every turn, and in the fifties knowing when to divest and to turn resolutely to production for television. Today, through mergers and diversification, Universal remains one of the strongest studios in Hollywood (the only one that still has a sizeable Art Department, although it operates differently from the old days), ballyhooing its product in ways that founder Carl Laemmle would roundly approve.

Universal was the sole studio to have many supervising art directors in the period considered here. Their most definable motion pictures, for their "look," were those done under Danny Hall's direction, the horror and early woman's pictures, and those done under Alexander Golitzen's supervising art direction, the suave, urbane pictures of the fifties. Like the rest of the majors, Universal gave its Art Department plenty to do, both of the highly imaginative and of the pedestrian sort; they still do today.

References

Introduction

1. Andrew Sarris, *Interviews with Film Directors*, Indianapolis: Bobbs-Merrill, 1967; 458.

2. Cedric Gibbons, "Art Direction," *Theatre Arts Monthly*, October, 1937; 793.

3. *Ibid.*, 791.

4. Alec Guinness, "The Guinness Book of Records," *Film Comment*, March, 1986; 37.

5. Louis Giannetti, *Understanding Movies*, Englewood Cliffs, N.J.: Prentice-Hall, 1972; 268, discusses modifiers for the term realism.

6. Cedric Gibbons, "The Art Director," in Stephen Watts, ed., *Behind the Screen*, New York: Dodge, 1938; 46.

7. *Ibid.*

8. William Cameron Menzies, "Pictorial Beauty in the Photoplay," in Richard Koszarski, *Hollywood Directors, 1914–1940*, New York: Oxford University Press, 1976; 245.

9. *Ibid.*, 244.

10. Harry Horner Seminar, American Film Institute, Feb., 1970, (transcript) and also, Norman Gambill, "Harry Horner's Design Program for *The Heiress, Art Journal*, Feb., 1983; 223–230.

11. James W. Palmer, "An Extension of Reality: Setting as Theme in *The Servant*," *Mise-en-Scène*, Spring, 1980; 68.

1. Early Art Direction

1. Paul Hammond, *Marvellous Méliès*, London: Gordon Fraser, 1974; 47.

2. Frank Beaver, *On Film*, New York: McGraw-Hill, 1983; 63. Also, for discussion on early art direction, see David Bordwell, Janet Staiger, Kristin Thompson, *The Classical Hollywood Cinema*, New York: Columbia University Press, 1985; 147–149.

3. Budd Schulberg, *Moving Pictures*, New York: Stein and Day, 1981; 15.

4. Robert Henderson, *D.W. Griffith: His Life and Work*, New York: Oxford University Press, 1972; 167.

5. Karl Brown, *Adventures with D.W. Griffith*, New York, 1973; 152.

6. Karl Brown, "SPFX 101: An Introductory Course," *American Film*, Sept. 1985; 55.

7. "Here's the Chaldean Who Built Babylon," *Photoplay*, Feb., 1917; 83.

8. Henderson, 170.

9. Henderson, 85.

10. Alfreda Cohn, "The Art Director," *Photoplay*, Aug., 1916; 43.

11. *Ibid.*, 45.

12. *Ibid.*, 177.

13. Frank H. Webster, "The Art of the Art Director," in Ruth Wing, ed. *The Blue Book of the Screen*, Hollywood, 1923; 371.

14. Buckland, at age 80, killed his mentally ill son and then committed suicide. John Hambley and Patrick Downing, *Thames Television's, The Art of Hollywood*, Thames Television, London, 1979; 13ff, has a brief biography of Buckland's life. This is an excellent catalogue written to accompany an exhibition at the Victoria and Albert Museum, London, that was held in conjunction with Thames Television's series on Hollywood.

15. Julian Johnson, "Joseph Urban, Art Director," *Photoplay*, Oct. 1920; 32. Urban was the subject of an exhibition at the Cooper-Hewitt Museum, New York City, in 1987–1988, but work from his film career was not included.

16. "Central Park Casino, Joseph Urban Architect," *The Architectural Record*, 66, no. 2, Aug. 1929; 97–108.

17. "New School for Social Research, New York City, Joseph Urban Architect," *The Architectural Record*, 67, no. 4, April 1930; 305–309.

18. Kevin Brownlow, *The Parade's Gone By*, New York: Alfred A. Knopf, 1968; 109.

19. *Ibid.*, 239.

20. Kenneth MacGowan, "The New Studio Art," *Motion Picture Classic*, March, 1919; 18.

21. *Ibid.*, 66.

22. "Earle's Latest Affinity," *Photoplay*, 14, Nov., 1918; 47.

23. *Ibid.*

24. *Motion Picture Studio Directory and Trade Annual*, published by *Motion Picture News*, Hollywood, 1921; 279–283.

25. Arthur Lonergan interview with author, summer, 1984.

26. Eugene Lourie, *My Work in Films*, Harcourt Brace Jovanovich, New York, 1985. Ben Carré, Oral History, University of California, Los Angeles, Special Collections (unpublished).

27. Mary Corliss and Carlo Clarens, "Art Direction," *Film Comment*, May/June, 1978; 59.

28. *Ibid.*, 60.

29. Carré's drawing style is distinctive and his work has been featured in exhibitions that have been presented on Hollywood art direction, particularly those at the Victoria and Albert Museum and at the Museum of Modern Art. See Hambley and Downing and *Film Comment*.

2. Art Departments Under the Studio System

1. Brendan Gill, "Movies as Architecture," *Film Comment*, July-August, 1974; 29.

2. The research on this project was funded in part by grants from the Academy of Motion Picture Arts and Sciences, the University of South Carolina's Research and Productive Scholarship Fund, and the National Endowment for the Humanities. I am particularly indebted to the art directors who allowed me to interview them and to those others who answered my lengthy questionnaire.

3. Arthur Lonergan interview (June, 1983). My special thanks go to Mr. Lonergan who assisted and encouraged me in all stages of the work on this topic. Subsequent quotations by Mr. Lonergan in the text are taken from this interview, unless otherwise specified.

4. There were variations from studio to studio, and sometimes one or another of these sections were departments independent of the art department.

5. Gene Allen interview (June, 1983). Mr. Allen is the president of the Academy of Motion Picture Arts and Sciences and of the Society of Motion and Television Art Directors.

All subsequent quotations from Mr. Allen are taken from this interview, unless otherwise specified.

6. Lyle Wheeler interview (June, 1983). All subsequent quotations from Mr. Wheeler are taken from this interview, unless otherwise specified.

7. Harry Horner seminar transcript, American Film Institute, October 13, 1971; 20. My thanks to Anne Schlosser, head, AFI Library, and her staff for their assistance.

8. Kevin Brownlow, *The Parade's Gone By,* New York: Alfred A. Knopf, 1968; 248.

9. The Goldwyn Library is now owned by independent researcher Lilian Michelson. John Mansbridge interview (June, 1983).

10. John Bryan's sets for *Becket,* a British film, are a marvellous example of the posthistorical approach: when Becket visits the Pope in the Vatican he moves from a copy of a room which actually exists in Ravenna to one that exists in Venice, and just after his coronation as Archbishop of Canterbury he emerges from the French Cathedral of Vézelay.

11. The contract between art director Anton Grot and Warner Bros., June, 1929, states that the company has all rights to his "creations, designs, sketches, plans and ideas" (p. 3). This was standard phrasing for art directors' contracts. From, the Warner Bros. Collection, University of California, Los Angeles.

12. All of the art directors I interviewed confirmed this fact. Most do have sketches from their days of free-lancing. Lyle Wheeler said that he did virtually no sketching anyway after becoming a supervising art director and this seems to have been true for that position throughout the industry.

13. Models are practically impossible to find today in public or private collections. Some miniature models of the highly finished type were made to be photographed for use in films. A few of such expert models made by independent art director Rudi Feld are on exhibit at the Deutsches Museum in Berlin. Rudi Feld interview (June, 1983).

14. Herman Blumenthal, "Models," *Production Design,* no. 11, 1951; 16. He gives a thorough appraisal of the 20th Century–Fox model shop in this article.

15. *Ibid.,* 20.

16. *Ibid.,* 21.

17. *Ibid.,* 21.

18. Ted Perry, "Sergei Eisenstein: A Career in Pictures," *American Film,* Jan.-Feb., 1983; 46–51, on Eisenstein's use of a similar drawing technique for his films. In Hollywood films a celluloid triangle called a "camera angle" was frequently used to determine the dimensions of a set as it would be seen through the camera lens; see *Scenery for Cinema,* exhibition catalogue, Baltimore Museum of Art, Baltimore: New Process Press, 1942; n.p.

19. Howard McClay, "Pre-Production Planning," *Production Design,* Jan., 1952; 6ff.

20. Liz-Anne Bawden, ed. *The Oxford Companion to Film,* London: Oxford University Press, 1976; 37.

21. McClay, "Pre-Production," 7.

22. Fred E. Basten, *Glorious Technicolor,* New York: Barnes and Co., 1980; 54.

23. Leon Barsacq, *Caligari's Cabinet and Other Grand Illusions,* Boston: New York Graphic Society, 1976; 246.

24. Art director Henry Grace's scrapbooks indicate that sometimes sets were hardly allowed to cool down before reuse. On Grace's set stills for *To Please a Lady* (1950) which starred Clark Gable and Barbara Stanwyck he noted that the "same set redressed" was used for the Van Johnson and Kathryn Grayson picture *Grounds for Divorce* also made in 1950. Henry Grace Scrapbook, No. III, 1950–1952, Academy of Motion Picture Arts and Sciences Library. Sometimes actors appear in the set still books but usually they do not.

25. Found in the Academy of Motion Picture Arts and Sciences Library. Each photograph has a careful notation as to the time of day taken, the light conditions, and the direction of the shot.

26. Walter Pitkin and William Marston, *The Art of Sound Pictures,* New York: Appleton, 1930; 274–279. This volume lists the important standing sets at the major studios in that year. Everything from a Javanese fishing village to the New York subway could be

found somewhere in Hollywood. Dozens of large "specialty props," tram cars, dirigibles, etc. were also easy to find by that time.

27. University of Southern California has the production archives of Universal Studios. Many of such cost breakdowns are extant. I would like to thank archivist Ned Comstock for his able assistance in helping me locate materials in the University's archives.

28. Harry Stradling, "Richard Day Rides to an Academy Award," *Production Design,* Feb.-March, vol. 2, nos. 2-3, 1952; 7.

29. *Ibid.,* 7.

30. For more on this question of terminology see: Boris Leven "Production Designer vs Art Director," in *Film Comment,* May/June, 1978; 36. Also Leo Kuter, "Production Designer," *Production Design,* vol. 1, no. 3, March, 1951; 11ff.

31. Paul Goldberger, "Home Worthy of Oscar—In Hollywood," *New York Times,* Nov. 6, 1980; 24.

32. George James Hopkins, "From 'Then to Now'," *Production Design,* vol. 2, no. 5, 1952; 8.

33. "Cedric Gibbons," *Theatre Arts Monthly,* Oct., 1937; 784.

34. Beverly Heisner, "Morris Lapidus and the Architecture of the Movies," *Postscript: A Journal of Film Culture and the Humanities,* Fall, 1981; 8–17.

35. John Meehan, "Death . . . Goes to a Party," *Production Design,* May/June, 1951, vol. 1, no. 5.

36. Eugene Lourie, "The River," *Production Design,* Feb. 1951, 5ff.

3. United Artists and the Independent Art Directors

1. Leon Barsacq, *Caligari's Cabinet and Other Grand Illusions,* Boston: New York Graphic Society, 1976; 227. Revised and edited by Elliot Stein.

2. John Hambley and Patrick Downing, *Thames Television's, The Art of Hollywood,* London: Thames Television, 1979; 91.

3. *Ibid.,* 93.

4. *Ibid.,* 96.

5. *Ibid.,* 93.

6. Korda receives sole screen credit for the art direction on the film, but the design was a collaborative effort.

7. William Cameron Menzies, "Pictorial Beauty in the Photoplay," in Richard Koszarski, New York: Oxford University Press, 1976; 245.

8. Mary Corliss and Carlo Clarens, "Art Direction," *Film Comment,* May/June, 1978; 57.

9. Eugen Lourie, *My Work in Films,* New York: Harcourt Brace Jovanovich, 1985; 82–83.

10. Goldwyn released his pictures through United Artists (from 1925–1941) and then through RKO. Alvin H. Marill, *Samuel Goldwyn Presents,* South Brunswick, N.J.: A.S. Barnes, 1976; 7–23. Goldwyn ceased production in 1959.

11. Hambley and Downing, 68.

4. MGM and Selznick International

1. Louis Giannetti, *Understanding Movies,* Englewood Cliffs, N.J.: Prentice-Hall, 1982; 275.

2. Goldwyn distributed his pictures through United Artists and RKO.

3. Liz-Anne Bawden, ed. *The Oxford Companion to Film,* London: Oxford University Press, 1976; 463.

4. Gary Carey, *All the Stars in Heaven, Louis B. Mayer's MGM,* New York: E.P. Dutton, 1981; 103.

5. *Ibid.*, 53.

6. *Ibid.*, 53.

7. Mary Corliss and Carlo Clarens, "Art Direction," *Film Comment*, May/June, 1987; 39.

8. Arthur Lonergan interview (June, 1983). All subsequent quotations from Mr. Lonergan are from this interview, unless otherwise stated.

9. *Film Comment*, 39.

10. John Hambley and Patrick Downing, *Thames Television's, The Art of Hollywood*, London: Thames Television, 1979; 58. *See also:* Lindy J. Narner, "Cedric Gibbons: Pioneer in Art Direction for Cinema," M.A. Thesis, University of Southern California, 1988.

11. Vincente Minnelli, *I Remember It Well*, New York: Doubleday, 1974; 122.

12. *Ibid.*, 122.

13. *Film Comment*, 25ff.

14. *Ibid.*

15. *Ibid.*

16. Stephen Watts, ed., *Behind the Screen: How Films Are Made*, New York: Dodge, 1938; 41–52.

17. *Ibid.*

18. *Ibid.*

19. Carey, 145.

20. Thames Television, 54.

21. Kevin Brownlow, *The Parade's Gone By*, New York: Alfred A. Knopf, 1968. He describes the film's course in detail.

22. *Ibid.*

23. *Film Comment*, 40.

24. *Ibid.*

25. *Queen Kelly* was released in a truncated version in Europe and is now being restored.

26. Thomas Curtiss, *Von Stroheim*, New York: Farrar, Straus and Giroux, 1971; 163.

27. *Ibid.*, 163.

28. *Ibid.*, 164.

29. Von Stroheim's later films were not distributed by MGM so Day must not have had an exclusive contract with them.

30. Thames Television, 68.

31. *Ibid.*

32. Carey, 80.

33. Harry Beaumont Scrapbooks, Lincoln Center Library, newspaper, Washington, D.C., no paper name, no date.

34. *New York Telegram*, March 9, 1929, n.p.

35. *The Spectator*, August 30, 1930, n.p.

36. *The Morning-Telegraph, Talking Picture Magazine*, New York, June, 1930; 6.

37. *The Morning Telegraph*, New York, Aug. 4, 1930, n.p.

38. Watts, 40.

39. University of California, Los Angeles, Special Collection, (interview, 1968).

40. *Ibid.*, 14.

41. Frank Beaver, *A History of the Motion Picture*, New York: McGraw-Hill, 1983; 247.

42. I am indebted in this section to the following sources: Miles Kreuger, ed., *The Movie Musical from Vitaphone to 42nd St.*, New York: Dover, 1975; Ted Sennett, *Hollywood Musicals*, New York: Abrams, 1981; and Jane Feuer, *The Hollywood Musical*, Bloomington: Indiana University Press, 1982.

43. Kreuger, 67.

44. *Ibid.*, 171.

45. John Eames, *The MGM Story*, New York: Crown, 1982; 119. The Academy of

Motion Picture Arts and Sciences Library has a fine collection of photographs of John Harkrider's film designs, both for custumes and sets.

46. I owe the very apt phrase "overstuffed" for this set to Ted Sennett, *op. cit.*

47. Barsacq, 215.

48. Aljean Harmetz, *The Making of the Wizard of Oz,* New York: Alfred A. Knopf, 1977; 210–211.

49. *Ibid.,* 221.

50. *Ibid.,* 218.

51. *Ibid.,* 212.

52. *Ibid.,* 214.

53. "Cedric Gibbons," *Theatre Arts Monthly,* Oct., 1937; 783–798.

54. Merle Armitage, *Warren Newcombe,* New York: E. Weyhe, 1932, gives a rhapsodic appraisal of Newcombe's eclectic style of painting.

55. Beth Genne, "Vincente Minnelli's Style in Microcosm: The Establishing Sequence of 'Meet Me in St. Louis'," *Art Journal,* Fall, 1983; 247–254.

56. Preston Ames, *Production Design,* Nov., 1951, vol. 1, no. 11.

57. *Ibid.,* 6.

58. *Ibid.,* 7.

59. *Ibid.,* 8.

60. Minnelli, 240.

61. Minnelli, 282. Other Ames/Minnelli films are among both artists' finest work and include *The Band Wagon* (1953, with Oliver Smith), *Brigadoon* (1954), *Kismet* (1955), *The Cobweb* (1955), *Lust for Life* (1956), *Designing Woman* (1957), *Gigi* (1958), *The Bells Are Ringing* (1960), and *Home from the Hill* (1960).

62. Bosley Crowther, *The Lion's Share: The Story of an Entertainment Empire,* New York: E.P. Dutton, 1957.

63. Thames Television, 54.

64. My thanks to Mr. Duell, who consented to a taped interview conducted by Marshall Duell (spring, 1985). All quotations are from this interview.

65. Several other art directors, particularly those at Disney Studios had been involved in the design of theme parks. However, no individual film designer gained such prominence in this field as did Randall Duell. See Tim Onosko, *Funland U.S.A.,* New York, 1975, 60–67.

66. A double issue of *Cinefantastique* (by Frederick Clarke and Steve Rubin, vol. 8, nos. 2 & 3, 1979; 6–67) was devoted to this film. Although Cedric Gibbons was consulted about design matters on this film, he does not appear to have had a great deal of direct involvement with its creative side.

67. Frank N. Magill, ed., Daniel D. Fineman, author, "Forbidden Planet," in *Magill's American Film Guide,* 2, 1980; 1125.

68. *Cinefantastique,* 18.

69. *Cinefantastique,* 25.

70. Today only Universal Studios has an art department on anything like the scale of MGM's or the other big studios in the thirties and forties, and it produces work mainly for television.

71. This memo and others cited by date may be found in the Selznick Archive, University of Texas, Austin.

72. I am indebted in this section to the monograph by Ron Haver, *David O. Selznick's Hollywood,* New York: Alfred A. Knopf, 1980; 246. All unfootnoted quotations from Selznick's memos were found in the Selznick Archives, University of Texas.

73. *Ibid.,* 247.

74. *Ibid.,* 254. Menzies acted as second unit director throughout the film.

75. Harry Horner Seminar, American Film Institute, Feb., 1970 (transcript).

76. *Film Comment,* 56.

77. Haver, 184.

78. Haver, 319.

79. Haver, 319–321.

80. *Film Comment*, 57.

81. Haver, 346.

82. Dalí's own well known films, done in collaboration with Luis Buñuel, are *Un Chien Andalou* (1929) and *L'Age d'Or* (1930).

5. Warner Bros.

1. Clive Hirschhorn, *The Warner Bros. Story*, New York: Crown Publishers, 1979; 8–16.

2. *Ibid.*, 30. Warners absorbed Vitagraph in 1925 and later did the same with First-National in 1929, becoming Warner Bros.–First National. In that year they moved to the latter's more substantial operating facilities in Burbank.

3. *Ibid.*, 66.

4. Roy Pickard, *The Hollywood Studios*, London: Frederick Muller Ltd., 1978; 212.

5. Tony Thomas and Jim Terry, *The Busby Berkeley Book*, New York: New York Graphic Society, 1973; 25.

6. *Ibid.*, 25.

7. *Ibid.*, 54.

8. *Ibid.*, 51.

9. John Hambley and Patrick Downing, *The Art of Hollywood*, London: Thames Television, 1979; 33.

10. *Ibid.*, 29–34.

11. *Ibid.*, 29.

12. Donald Deschner, "Anton Grot, Warners Art Director," *The Velvet Light Trap*, no. 15, Fall, 1975; 18–22.

13. Hambley and Downing, 20.

14. Warner Bros. Collection, University of Southern California, Los Angeles, All subsequent references to Grot's contracts are also from this source.

15. Marshall Deutelbaum, ed. *"Image" on the Evolution of the Film*, New York: Dover, 1979; 224. *Also:* John Baxter, *Stunt*, Garden City, N.Y.: Doubleday and Co., 1974; 102–103.

16. Hambley and Downing, 31–32. Grot's drawings make their arguments convincing.

17. Deutelbaum, 224.

18. Barry Salt, "Film Style and Technology in the Thirties," *Film Quarterly*, vol. 30, no. 1, 1976; 31.

19. Hambley and Downing, 93.

20. Hirschhorn, 82.

21. Pickard, 104.

22. Hambley and Downing, 34.

23. Grot is, of course, following the wording of the script closely; see Ranald Mac-Dougall's screenplay in *Mildred Pierce*, ed. by Albert J. LaValley, Madison: University of Wisconsin Press, 1980; 73. It is probably an earlier version of the screenplay that Grot is actually quoting, as MacDougall's version was only completed 10 days before shooting began, and the art director must have had his designs for settings on the drafting tables before that date.

24. Hirschhorn, 281 and 322.

6. Paramount

1. Frank Beaver, *On Film*, New York: McGraw-Hill, 1983; 128.

2. Donald Hayne, ed. *The Autobiography of Cecil B. DeMille*, Englewood Cliffs, N.J.: Prentice-Hall, 1959; 62.

3. Budd Shulberg, *Moving Pictures,* New York: Stein and Day, 1981; 71.

4. *Ibid.,* 72. The adoption of the single name Paramount for the company evolved in the course of the thirties.

5. Hayne, 76.

6. *Ibid.,* 78.

7. *Ibid.,* 47.

8. *Ibid.,* 115. Cameraman Alvin Wyckoff must also be credited with the development of this kind of lighting in DeMille's pictures in this early period.

9. *Ibid.,* 212.

10. Léon Barsacq, *Caligari's Cabinet and Other Grand Illusions,* Boston: New York Graphic Society, 1976; 217.

11. I.G. Edmonds and Reido Mimura, *Paramount Pictures and the People Who Made Them,* San Diego: A.S. Barnes, 1980; 115. Indicative of the neglect of the art director in films is the fact that neither Dreier, Iribe or Buckland are mentioned in this volume.

12. Barsacq, 222 & 228.

13. Mary Corliss and Carlo Clarens, "Art Direction," *Film Comment,* May/June, 1978; 48–49.

14. *Ibid.,* 49.

15. Barsacq, 199.

16. John Hambley and Patrick Downing, *The Art of Hollywood,* London: Thames Television, 1979; 38.

17. *Ibid.*

18. Letter to author, spring, 1985. All other quotations by Mr. Larsen in the text are from the same source.

19. Nancy Naumberg, ed., *We Make the Movies,* New York: W.W. Norton, 1937; 80–89.

20. *Ibid.,* 80.

21. Hambley and Downing, 38.

22. Naumberg, 89.

23. John Baxter, *Hollywood in the Thirties,* 46.

24. The other films Dreier and Lubitsch made together are *Forbidden Paradise* (1924), *The Patriot* (1928), *The Love Parade* (1929), *The Smiling Lieutenant* (1931), *The Man I Killed* (1932), *One Hour with You* (1932), *Trouble in Paradise* (1932), *Design for Living* (1933), *Angel* (1937 with Robert Usher), *Bluebeard's 8th Wife* (1938 with Robert Usher).

25. The set stills for *Trouble in Paradise* are in the library of the Academy of Motion Picture Arts and Sciences, Hollywood.

26. Frank N. Magill, ed., *Magill's American Film Guide,* Englewood Cliffs, N.J.: Salem Press, 1983; 3452.

27. William Paul, *Ernst Lubitsch's American Comedy,* New York: Columbia University Press, 1983, for more on the Lubitsch style.

28. Andrew Sarris, *The Films of Josef von Sternberg,* New York: Museum of Modern Art, 1966; 5.

29. Schulberg, 242.

30. Peter Baxter, ed., *Josef von Sternberg,* London: British Film Institute, 1980; 37.

31. Sarris, 15.

32. *Ibid.*

33. Barsacq, 245.

34. Ihnen was married to costume designer Edith Head. See Chapter 1 for more on his work on early color productions.

35. Barsacq, 247.

36. Lotte Eisner, *The Haunted Screen,* Berkeley: University of California Press, 1969; 153.

37. Baxter, *Von Sternberg,* 113, comments on the director's vision: "To him, the Russian court was a combination of the rustic and the luxurious, part dacha, part palace, with

a hint of the church, a blend suggesting the confused allegiances of Russia's rulers. He conceived the sets as a number of movable "flats" resembling walls of log, interspersed with vast staircases, and enormous doors manufactured from normal double doors fastened together into one panel."

38. The costumes are by Travis Banton.

39. Magill's 2622.

7. *20th Century-Fox*

1. Tony Thomas and Aubrey Solomon, *The Films of 20th Century-Fox*, Secaucus, N.J.: Citadel Press, 1979; 11ff.

2. Roy Pickard, *The Hollywood Studios*, London: Frederick Muller Limited, 1978; 439.

3. Other films perfecting the disaster flick were: *San Francisco* (MGM, 1936) and *The Hurricane* (United Artists, 1937).

4. Mary Corliss and Carlo Clarens, "Art Direction," *Film Comment*, May/June, 1978; 49. Lyle Wheeler didn't mind reusing sets he said, "One of the things at Zanuck/Fox was the fact that I could reuse sets over and over and over without the public 'catching on'."

5. There is some discrepancy between Day's and Wheeler's account of these years. Day has said that he was supervising art director in 1945–47, while Wheeler says that he was in that position beginning in 1944. According to Wheeler, "Day did one picture at 20th Century-Fox as supervising art director after he returned because of the U.S. law that a person returning from World War II must be given the same position as before he left for the War." There was apparently friction around this point and Day left the Studio in 1947, while Wheeler remained in place throughout the fifties.

6. Lyle Wheeler notes that, "At this time one had to apply to Technicolor and 'be in line' for the right to use Technicolor—sometimes this influenced whether a picture was black and white or color."

7. Frank N. Magill, editor, DeWitt Bodeen, author, "Anna and the King of Siam," in *Magill's American Film Guide*, 1980, vol. 1; 144.

8. *Film Comment*, 58.

9. Interview with Lyle Wheeler, summer, 1983. All subsequent quotations are from this interview unless otherwise stated. My thanks go to Mr. Wheeler and his wife, Donna Wheeler, who together graciously read a draft of this chapter making valuable suggestions for its improvement.

9. *Film Comment*, 57.

10. Lyle Wheeler commented on the shutters in Lydecker's apartment: "Shutters were a trademark of mine—we used them for years wherever appropriate and had a big effect on the sale of same to homeowners."

11. *Film Comment*, 57; here he means directing as a profession for himself.

12. Herman Blumenthal, "20th Century-Fox Waterways," *Production Design*, vol. 2, no. 6, June, 1952; 10–11.

13. Blumenthal, 11.

14. Herman Blumenthal, "'Desert Fox,' Maurice Ransford, Art Director," *Production Design*, 2, no. 6, June 1952; 14. Lyle Wheeler was supervising art director on *The Desert Fox, Hangover Square*, and *Niagara*.

15. *Ibid.*, 14.

16. *Ibid.*, 15.

17. *Ibid.*, 16.

18. Pickard, 448.

19. Foster Hirsch, *The Hollywood Epic*, New York: A.S. Barnes and Co., 1978; 29.

20. *Ibid.*, 29.

21. *Samson and Delilah* (1949) should be cited as the film that inaugurated the revival of epics that followed in the fifties.

22. *Film Comment*, 58.
23. Thomas and Solomon, 428.

8. *RKO Studio*

1. Roy Pickard, *The Hollywood Studios,* London: Frederick Muller, 1978; 394.
2. Richard B. Jewell and Vernon Harbin, *The RKO Story,* London: Arlington House, 1982; 10. This volume is filled with much useful material upon which I have drawn for this section.
3. John Hambley and Patrick Downing, *The Art of Hollywood,* London: Thames Television, 1979; 62.
4. *Ibid.,* 63; the authors suggest that *The Magnificent Flirt* was "among the earliest examples of really influential film Art Deco."
5. *Ibid.,* 63.
6. A detailed explanation has been provided of how the effects were achieved in the book by Orville Goldner and George E. Turner, *The Making of King Kong,* New York: Barnes and Company, 1975.
7. *Ibid.,* p. 64.
8. Arlene Croce, *The Fred Astaire and Ginger Rogers Book,* New York: Vintage Books, 1977; 56.
9. *Ibid.,* 76.
10. Beverly Heisner, "Morris Lapidus and the Architecture of the Movies," *Postscript: Essays in Film and the Humanities,* vol. 1, no. 1, 1981; 8–17.
11. Croce, 112–113.
12. Croce, 108, calls this "the supreme dramatic event of the series."
13. Interview with author, summer, 1983. All further quotations from Mr. Mansbridge are also from this talk.
14. For more on the controversy about the designer of the sets, see Léon Barsacq, *Caligari's Cabinet and Other Grand Illusion: A History of Film Design,* Boston: New York Graphic Society, 1976; 234–235, where illustrator Maurice Zuberano claims Allan Abbott did the sets. Zuberano did not come to RKO until 1935, and so was not even at the studio during the formative period of the series' style. Clearly the sets cannot be by a single hand. Croce is incorrect in her claim that Van Nest Polglase did not design any sets himself while at RKO, 77.
15. Heisner.
16. Richard L. Carringer, "Who Really Wrote *Citizen Kane?*" *American Film,* Sept., 1985; 47.
17. Pickard, 400.
18. The art directors are not mentioned by Pauline Kael in her *The Citizen Kane Book,* London: Secker and Warburg, 1971, nor are they mentioned in most film summaries.
19. The other films all designed by Albert D'Agostino and Walter E. Keller are *The Ghost Ship* (1943), *The Curse of the Cat People* (1944), *Mademoiselle Fifi* (1944), *Isle of the Dead* (1945), *The Body Snatcher* (1945), and *Bedlam* (1946).
20. Frank N. Magill, ed., *Magill's American Film Guide,* Englewood Cliffs, N.J.: Salem Press, 1983; 619.

9. *Columbia*

1. Rochelle Larkin, *Hail, Columbia,* New Rochelle, N.Y.: Arlington House, 1975; 14.
2. *Ibid.,* 14–15.
3. Roy Pickard, *The Hollywood Studios,* London: Frederick Muller, 1978; 283.

4. This biography and sketches are found in the University of Southern California's Special Collections.

5. Stephen Goosson, "Little Lord Fauntleroy," *Production Design*, April, 1952, vol. 1, no. 4, 16–19.

6. Carol Willis, "Zoning and *Zeitgeist:* The Skyscraper City in the 1920's," *Journal of the Society of Architectural Historians*, XLV, March, 1986; 47–59.

7. Architect Morris Lapidus' phrase to describe his Miami Beach hotels.

8. Lionel Banks Academy Award nominations were for *Holiday* (1938, with Stephen Goosson), *Mr. Smith Goes to Washington* (1939), *Arizona* (1940, with Robert Peterson), *Ladies in Retirement* (1941), *The Talk of the Town* (1942, with Rudolph Sternad), *Address Unknown* (1944, with Walter Holscher), *Cover Girl* (1944, with Cary Odell).

9. My thanks to Carl Anderson for responding to my questions on art direction and his career.

10. Universal

1. Clive Hirschhorn, *The Universal Story*, New York: Crown, 1983; 13.

2. Roy Pickard, *The Hollywood Studios*, London: Frederick Muller, 1978; and Richard Koszarski, *Universal Pictures, 65 Years*, New York: Museum of Modern Art, 1977; 5–7.

3. There is a somewhat greater element of freedom and fantasy evident in von Stroheim's later films, *The Wedding March* and *Queen Kelly*.

4. John Hambley and Patrick Downing, *Thames Television's, The Art of Hollywood*, London: Thames Television, 1979; 69.

5. The 1943 production won Academy Awards for designers Alexander Golitzen and John B. Goodman.

6. *Thames Television*, 23.

7. *Ibid.*, 45.

8. Charles Chaplin, *My Autobiography*, London: Penguin, 1964; 377.

9. Howard Mandelbaum and Eric Myers, *Screen Deco*, New York: St. Martin's Press, 1985; 102.

10. Paul Fejos, the film's director, is credited with the conception for the crime.

11. *Screen Deco*, 103.

12. *Thames Television*, 50.

13. Otterson's nominations were for *The Magnificent Brute* (1936, with Albert S. D'Agostino), *You're a Sweetheart* (1937), *Mad About Music* (1938); *The Boys from Syracuse* (1940), *The Flame of New Orleans* (1941, with Martin Obzina), *The Spoilers* (1942, with John B. Goodman), *Arabian Nights* (1942, with Alexander Golitzen).

14. I would like to thank Mr. Boyle for allowing me to attend several of his seminars on production design held at the American Film Institute.

15. Mary Corliss and Carlo Clarens, "Art Direction," *Film Comment*, May/June, 1978; 38.

16. Foster Hirsch, *The Dark Side of the Screen: Film Noir*, New York: A.S. Barnes, 1981; 6.

17. *Film Comment*, 38. My thanks to Alexander Golitzen for an interview given in spring, 1987. All uncredited quotations by him in the text are from that meeting.

18. Koszarski, 20–21.

19. *Film Comment*, 38.

Filmographies of Art Directors*

"With" are shared-credit art directors

Ken Adam

Helen of Troy (55); Around the World in 80 Days (56, with William Cameron Menzies, James Sullivan); Night of the Demon / Curse of the Demon (57); Gideon's Day / Gideon of Scotland Yard (58); 10 Seconds to Hell (59); The Angry Hills (59); The Trials of Oscar Wilde (60); Sodom and Gomorrah (61); Dr. No (62); Dr. Strangelove, or How I Learned to Stop Worrying and Love the Bomb (64); Goldfinger (64); Thunderball (65); The Ipcress File (65); You Only Live Twice (67); Chitty Chitty Bang Bang (68); Goodbye, Mr. Chips (69); Diamonds Are Forever (71); Sleuth (72); The Last of Sheila (73); Barry Lyndon (75).

Gene Allen

The Adventures of Hajji Baba (54, with George Hoyninge-Huene, William Cameron Menzies); A Star Is Born (54, with Malcolm Bert, Irene Sharaff); Bhowani Junction (56, with John Howell); Les Girls (57, with William A. Horning); Breath of Scandal (60); Heller in Pink Tights (60, with Hal Pereira); Let's Make Love (60, with Lyle Wheeler); The Chapman Report (62); My Fair Lady (64).

Preston Ames

Blonde Fever (44); The Hidden Eye (45); She Went to the Races (45); No Leave, No Love (46); The Show Off (46); Lady in the Lake (47); The Big City (48); Three Daring Daughters (48); The Midnight Kiss (49); The Doctor & the Girl (49); The Outriders (50); Two Weeks with Love (50); Crisis (50); An American in Paris (51, with Cedric Gibbons, Jack Martin Smith, Irene Sharaff); The Wild North (52); The Band Wagon (53, with Oliver Smith, Cedric Gibbons); The Story of Three Loves (53, with Gabriel Scognamillo); Brigadoon (54, with Cedric Gibbons); Kismet (55, with Cedric Gibbons, Daniel Cathcart); The Cobweb (55); Lust for Life (56, with Cedric Gibbons, Hans Peters); Designing Woman (57); Gigi (58, with Keogh Gleason, William A. Horning); Green Mansions (59); The Bells Are Ringing (60, with George W. Davis); Home from the Hill (60, with George W. Davis); Billy

---

* These filmographies have been gathered from several sources and reflect a work in progress. Many early art directors did not receive a credit and most reference books, even some of the most recent, do not include the art direction credit, so that gathering data has been very difficult. The author would appreciate receiving additional information on this subject.

Rose's Jumbo (62); Penelope (66); Made in Paris (66); Airport (70); Brewster McCloud (70); Lost Horizon (73); The Don Is Dead (74); Earthquake (74, with Alexander Golitzen); Rooster Cogburn (75); The Prisoner of 2nd Avenue (75).

Carl Anderson

Riders of the Northwest Mounted (43); The Black Parachute (44); Meet Miss Bobby Socks (44); They Live in Fear (44); Kansas City Kitty (44); Blonde from Brooklyn (45); Eadie Was a Lady (45); Eve Knew Her Apples (45); I Love a Bandleader (45); A Close Call for Boston Blackie (46); Gallant Journey (46); The Return of Monte Cristo (46); Tars and Spars (46); So Dark the Night (46); Her Husband's Affairs (47); Framed (47); I Love Trouble (47); The Fuller Brush Man (48); Black Eagle (48); Prison Warden (49); Shockproof (49); Slightly French (49); Tell It to the Judge (49); For Those Who Dare (49); El Dorado Pass (49); Traveling Saleswoman (49); Father Is a Bachelor (50); Convicted (50); Emergency Wedding (50); The Barefoot Mailman (51); Ten Tall Men (51); Miss Sadie Thompson (53); Lieutenant Robin Crusoe, USN (66, with Carroll Clark); 100 Rifles (68); Chisum (69); The Undefeated (69); Big Jake (70); Lady Sings the Blues (71); Bonanza (72); Mrs. Sundance (73); Culpepper Cattle Co. (74); The Lindbergh Story (75); How the West Was Won (75); Against a Crooked Sky (75); I Know Why the Caged Bird Sings (76); Quest (76); A Very Dangerous Love (77); Little Moe (78); The Reach of Love (78); The Villain (79); Haywire (79); The Cheap Detective (79); Women in Prison (80); Alexander (80); All the Marbles (80); Paper Chase (82).

Roland Anderson

A Farewell to Arms (32); This Day and Age (33, with Hans Dreier, Mitchell Leisen); 4 Frightened People (34); Cleopatra (34, with Hans Dreier); The Crusades (35, with Hans Dreier); The Lives of a Bengal Lancer (35, with Hans Dreier); Give Us the Night (36, with Hans Dreier); Lady Be Careful (36, with Hans Dreier); Yours for the Asking (36, with Hans Dreier); The Plainsman (36, with Hans Dreier); Interns Can't Take Money (37, with Hans Dreier); Souls at Sea (37, with Hans Dreier); Spawn of the North (38); The Buccaneer (38, with Hans Dreier); Disputed Passage (39, with Hans Dreier); Union Pacific (39, with Hans Dreier); North West Mounted Police (40, with Hans Dreier); Bucky Benny Rides Again (40, with Hans Dreier); Love Thy Neighbor (40, with Hans Dreier); Remember the Night (40, with Hans Dreier); The Shepherd of the Hills (41, with Hans Dreier); Skylark (41, with Hans Dreier); Holiday Inn (42, with Hans Dreier); The Major and the Minor (42, with Hans Dreier); Take a Letter, Darling (42, with Hans Dreier); Reap the Wild Wind (42, with Hans Dreier); The Crystal Ball (43, with Hans Dreier); Here Come the Waves (44, with Hans Dreier); The Story of Dr. Wassell (44, with Hans Dreier); Love Letters (45, with Hans Dreier); Masquerade in Mexico (45, with Hans Dreier); Road to Utopia (45, with Hans Dreier); California (46, with Hans Dreier); To Each His Own (46, with Hans Dreier); Blaze of Noon (47, with Hans Dreier); The Perils of Pauline (47, with Hans Dreier); The Big Clock (48, with Hans Dreier); Bride of Vengeance (49, with Albert Nozaki, Hans Dreier); A Connecticut Yankee in King Arthur's Court (49, with Hans Dreier); The Great Gatsby (49, with Hans Dreier); Captain Carey, USA (50, with Hans Dreier); Let's Dance (50, with Hans Dreier); Branded (50, with Hans Dreier); My Favorite Spy (51); The Mating Season (51, with Hal Pereira); Darling, How Could You (51, with Hal Pereira); Carrie (52, with Hal Pereira); The Country Girl (54, with Hal Pereira); Space Children (58); Breakfast at Tiffany's (61, with Hal Pereira); Love with the Proper Stranger (63, with Hal Pereira); Will Penny (67); The Sterile Cuckoo (69).

Frank Arrigo

The Topeka Terror (45); Blackmail (47); Rustlers of Devil's Canyon (47); Springtime in the Rockies (47); Marshall of Cripple Creek (47); That's My Girl (47); That's My Man (47);

Bandits of Dark Canyon (47); California Firebrand (48); Heart of Virginia (48); The Inside Story (48); Lightnin' in the Forest (48); Madonna of the Desert (48); Oklahoma's Badlands (48); Secret Service Investigator (48); The Denver Kid (48); The Plunderers (48); Son of God's Country (48); Marshall of Amarillo (48); The Wyoming Bandit (49); Sheriff of Wichita (49); Renegades of Sonora (49); The Red Menace (49); The Last Bandit (49); Duke of Chicago (49); Brimstone (49); Post Office Investigator (49); Outcasts of the Trail (49); Bandit King of Texas (49); Code of the Silver Sage (50); The Savage Horde (50); Trigger, Jr. (50); Vigilante Hideout (50); Vigilante at Large (50); Gunmen of Abilene (50); Harbor of Missing Men (50); Rock Island Trail (50); Tarnished (50); The Vanishing Westerner (50); Lonely Heart Bandits (50); The Showdown (50); Frisco Tornado (50); Prisoners in Petticoats (50); Redwood Forest Trail (50); The Missourians (50); Buckaroo Sheriff of Texas (50); California Passage (50); Rustlers on Horseback (50); Under Mexicali Stars (50); Trail of Robin Hood (50); Desert of Lost Men (51); Fighting Coast Guard (51); Oh! Susanna (51); The Sea Hornet (51); Spoilers of the Plains (51); Street Bandits (51); Utah Wagon Train (51).

Lemuel Ayers

Meet Me in St. Louis (44, with Cedric Gibbons, Jack Martin Smith).

Franz Bachelin

Bulldog Drummond Comes Back (37, with Hans Dreier); Thrill of a Lifetime (37, with Hans Dreier); Stolen Heaven (38, with Hans Dreier); Thanks for the Memory (38, with Hans Dreier); Arrest Bulldog Drummond (39, with Hans Dreier); Bulldog Drummond's Bride (39, with Hans Dreier); Grand Jury Secrets (39, with Hans Dreier); Emergency Squad (40, with Hans Dreier); The Farmer's Daughter (40, with Hans Dreier); Seventeen (40, with Hans Dreier); Henry Aldrich for President (41, with Hans Dreier); Henry Aldrich, Editor (42, with Hans Dreier); Pacific Blackout (42, with Hans Dreier); Henry Aldrich Swings It (43, with Hans Dreier); Hostages (43, with Hans Dreier); Henry Aldrich Plays Cupid (44, with Hans Dreier); Henry Aldrich's Little Secret (44, with Hans Dreier); The Hitler Gang (44, with Hans Dreier); The Affairs of Susan (45, with Hans Dreier); The Searching Wind (46, with Hans Dreier); Two Years Before the Mast (46, with Hans Dreier); Cross My Heart (47); Calcutta (47, with Hans Dreier); I Walk Alone (47, with Hans Dreier); The Imperfect Lady (47, with Hans Dreier); Welcome Stranger (47, with Hans Dreier); Beyond Glory (48, with Hans Dreier); The Emperor Waltz (48, with Hans Dreier); Miss Tatlock's Millions (48, with Hans Dreier); The Night Has a Thousand Eyes (48, with Hans Dreier); Alias Nick Beal (49, with Hans Dreier); Red, Hot, and Blue (49, with Hans Dreier); Rope of Sand (49, with Hans Dreier); Chicago Deadline (49); Dark City (50, with Hans Dreier); Copper Canyon (50, with Hans Dreier); September Affair (50, with Hans Dreier); The Lemon Drop Kid (51); That's My Boy (51); Peking Express (51); Red Mountain (51); Silver City (51); The Naked Jungle (54, with Hal Pereira); Journey to the Center of the Earth (59, with Lyle Wheeler, Herman A. Blumenthal).

Douglas Bacon

The Story of Seabiscuit (49); Tea for Two (50); Colt .45 (50); The Daughter of Rosie O'Grady (50); Dallas (50); Lightning Strikes Twice (51); I'll See You in My Dreams (51); Lullaby of Broadway (51); On Moonlight Bay (51); Inside the Walls of Folsom Prison (51); Distant Drums (51).

Hugo Ballin

(As art director) Thais (17) co-dir.; Baby Mine (17); Fighting Odds (17); Nearly Married (17); The Love of Sunya (27).

Lionel Banks

Public Hero (35, with Cedric Gibbons); One New York Night (35, with Cedric Gibbons); The Best Man Wins (35); Let's Live Tonight (35); The Whole Town's Talking (35); The Awful Truth (37, with Stephen Goosson); Murder in Greenwich Village (37, with Stephen Goosson); I'll Take Romance (37, with Babs Johnstone); No Time to Marry (38); There's Always a Woman (38, with Stephen Goosson); You Can't Take It with You (38, with Stephen Goosson); Girl's School (38, with Stephen Goosson); Blondie Meets the Boss (39); Only Angels Have Wings (39); Golden Boy (39); Coast Guard (39); Mr. Smith Goes to Washington (39); Those High Grey Walls (39); Blondie Brings Up Baby (39); Blind Alley (39); Music in My Heart (40); Cafe Hostess (40); The Lone Wolf Strikes (40); Too Many Husbands (40); The Doctor Takes a Wife (40); Island of Doomed Men (40); The Lone Wolf Meets a Lady (40); He Stayed for Breakfast (40); So You Won't Talk (40); Arizona (40, with Robert Peterson); Before I Hang (40); Glamour for Sale (40); Blondie Plays Cupid (40); Escape to Glory (40); The Devil Commands (41); The Face Behind the Mask (41); She Knew All the Answers (41); Adventure in Washington (41); You'll Never Get Rich (41, with Rudolf Sternad); You Belong to Me (41); Blondie in Society (41); Blondie Goes Latin (41); Go West Young Lady (41); Harmond of Michigan (41); Here Comes Mr. Jordan (41); Ladies in Retirement (41); The Blonde from Singapore (41); Bedtime Story (41); The Lone Wolf Takes a Chance (41); The Officer and the Lady (41); Our Wife (41); Richest Man in Town (41); Sweetheart of the Campus (41); Texas (41); Three Girls About Town (41); Tillie the Toiler (41); Time Out for Rhythm (41); Two in a Taxi (41); Two Latins from Manhattan (41); Under Age (41); The Lady Is Willing (42); The Adventures of Martin Eden (42); Atlantic Convoy (42); Bad Men of the Hills (42); Blondie Goes to College (42); Cadets on Parade (42); Down Rio Grande Way (42); Flight Lieutenant (42); Harvard, Here I Come (42); Hello, Annapolis (42); Lawless Plainsmen (42); The Man Who Returned to Life (42); Meet the Stewarts (42); My Sister Eileen (42); Overland to Deadwood (42); Parachute Nurse (42); Riders of the Northland (42); Sabotage Squad (42); Shut My Big Mouth (42); Sweetheart of Stanford (42); Sweetheart of the Fleet (42); Talk of the Town (42); The Daring Young Man (42); They All Kissed the Bride (42); Tramp, Tramp, Tramp (42); West of Tombstone (42); The Wife Takes a Flyer (42); You Were Never Lovelier (42); A Night to Remember (42); The Desperados (43); The More the Merrier (43); Appointment in Berlin (43); After Midnight with Boston Blackie (43); The Boy from Stalingrad (43); City Without Men (43); The Chance of a Lifetime (43); Dangerous Blondes (43); Destroyer (43); Crime Doctor (43); Cowboy in the Clouds (43); The Desperados (43); Doughboys in Ireland (43); Fighting Buckaroo (43); Footlight Glamour (43); First Comes Courage (43); Frontier Fury (43); Good Luck Mr. Yates (43); Hail to the Rangers (43); The Heat's On (43); Is Everybody Happy? (43); It's a Great Life (43); Klondike Kate (43); Law of the Northwest (43); Passport to Suez (43); Let's Have Fun (43); The More the Merrier (43); Murder in Times Square (43); My Kingdom for a Cook (43); One Dangerous Night (43); Pardon My Gun (43); Power of the Press (43); The Return of the Vampire (43); Redhead from Manhattan (43); Robin Hood of the Range (43); Reveille with Beverly (43); Riders of the Northwest Mounted (43); Saddles and Sagebrush (43); Sahara (43); She Had What It Takes (43); Silver City Raiders (43); Something to Shout About (43); Swing Out the Blues (43); There's Something About a Soldier (43); Two Senoritas from Chicago (43); What a Woman! (43, with Van Nest Polglase); What's Buzzin' Cousin (43); Impatient Years (44); The Cover Girl (44); Strange Affair (44); Address Unknown (44, with William Cameron Menzies, Walter Holscher); Beautiful But Broke (44); The Black Parachute (44); Carolina Blues (44); Cry of the Werewolf (44); Cowboy Canteen (44); Cowboy from Lonesome River (44, with Paul

Murphy); Cyclone Prairie Rangers (44, with Perry Smith); Ever Since Venus (44, with Cary Odell); The Ghost That Walks Alone (44, with Paul Murphy); Hey, Rookie (44, with Ross Bellah); Kansas City Kitty (44, with Carl Anderson); Jam Session (44, with Paul Murphy); The Last Horseman (44); Louisiana Hayride (44, with Walter Holscher); Meet Miss Bobby Socks (44, with Carl Anderson); Mr. Winkle Goes to War (44, with Rudolph Sternad); Nine Girls (44, with Ross Bellah); Once Upon a Time (44, with Edward Jewell); None Shall Escape (44, with Perry Smith); One Mysterious Night (44, with George Brooks); The Racket Man (44, with Walter Holscher); She's a Soldier, Too (44, with George Brooks); Riding West (44, with Arthur Royce); Sailor's Holiday (44, with Victor Greene); Saddle Leather Law (44, with Perry Smith); Secret Command (44, with Edward Jewell); Stars on Parade (44, with Walter Holscher); They Live in Fear (44, with Carl Anderson); Sundown Valley (44); Swinging the Saddle (44); Boat Prisoner (44, with Perry Smith); The Vigilante's Ride (44, with Perry Smith); Wyoming Hurricane (44, with Perry Smith); A Song to Remember (45, with Van Nest Polglase); Guest Wife (45); It's in the Bag (45); Rough Ridin' Justice (45, with Charles Clague); Return of the Durango Kid (45); Tonight and Every Night (45, with Stephen Goosson, Rudolph Sternad); Sagebrush Heroes (45, with Perry Smith); Heartbeat (46); So Goes My Love (46); Ramrod (47); Magic Town (47); The Perfect Marriage (47); Siren of Atlantis (48); Moonrise (48).

James Basevi

The Big Parade (25, with Cedric Gibbons); Confessions of a Queen (25); The Tower of Lies (25); The Temptress (26); Bardeleys the Magnificent (26, with Richard Day, Cedric Gibbons); The Mysterious Island (29, special effects); San Franciso (36, special effects dir. with Arnold Gillespie, Cedric Gibbons, Harry McAfee); History Is Made at Night (37, special effects dir. with Cedric Gibbons); The Hurricane (37, special effects and a.d. with Richard Day, Alexander Golitzen); Wuthering Heights (39, with Alexander Golitzen); The Long Voyage Home (40); Tobacco Road (41, with Richard Day); A Yank in the R.A.F. (41, with Richard Day); The Black Swan (42, with Richard Day); Son of Fury (42, with Richard Day); Moontide (42, with Richard Day); The Ox-Bow Incident (42, with Richard Day); Thunder Birds (42, with Richard Day); Dancing Masters (43); The Gang's All Here (43, with Joseph C. Wright); Hello, Frisco, Hello (43, with Boris Leven); Sweet Rosie O'Grady (43, with Joseph C. Wright, Lyle Wheeler); The Song of Bernadette (43, with William Darling); Heaven Can Wait (43, with Leland Fuller); Buffalo Bill (44); The Eve of St. Mark (44); Four Jills in a Jeep (44); Greenwich Vilage (44); Home in Indiana (44); The Keys of the Kingdom (44); Ladies of Washington (44); Pin Up Girl (44, with Joseph C. Wright); The Purple Heart (44); The Sullivans (44); Tampico (44); Roger Touhy, Gangster (44); The Lodger (44); Wilson (44, with Wiard Ihnen); Jane Eyre (44, with Wiard Ihnen); Spellbound (45, p.d. with John Ewing and Salvador Dali [designer of dream sequence]); My Darling Clementine (46, with Lyle Wheeler); Duel in the Sun (47, with Joseph McMillan Johnson p.d., John Ewing, William Cameron Menzies); Margie (46); Captain from Castile (47, with Richard Day); Boomerang (47, with Chester Gore, Richard Day); The Shocking Miss Pilgrim (47, with Boris Leven); Fort Apache (48); 3 Godfathers (48); Mighty Joe Young (49); She Wore a Yellow Ribbon (49); To Please a Lady (50); Wagonmaster (50); Across the Wide Missouri (51); Night into Morning (51); The People Against O'Hara (51); Ruby Gentry (52); East of Eden (55, with Malcolm Bert); The Searchers (56, with Frank Hotaling).

Ross Bellah

Hey, Rookie (44); Chain of Circumstance (51); Her First Romance (51).

Ralph Berger

White Zombie (32); Flash Gordon (36); False Colors (43); Hoppy Serves a Writ (43); Bar 20 (43); Buckskin Frontier (43); Colt Comrades (43); The Kansan (43); The Leatherburners (43); Lost Canyon (43); Tarzan's Desert Mystery (43); The Woman of the Town (43); Heavenly Days (44); A Night of Adventure (44); Texas Masquerade (44); The Forty Thieves (44); Lumberjack (44); Riders of the Deadline (44); Tall in the Saddle (44); Dick Tracy (45); George White's Scandals (45); Strange Voyage (45); Betrayal from the East (45); China Sky (45); The Brighton Strangler (45); Back to Bataan (45); Partners in Time (46); Child of Divorce (46); Genius at Work (46); Without Reservation (46); Honeymoon (47); Trail Street (47); Miracle of the Bells (48); Boy with Green Hair (48); If You Knew Susie (48); Return of the Bad Men (48); The Big Steal (49); Where Danger Lives (50); The White Tower (50); Armored Car Robbery (50); On Dangerous Ground (51); Macao (52, with Albert D'Agostino).

Malcolm Bert

A Star Is Born (54, with Gene Allen, Irene Sharaff); East of Eden (55, with James Basevi).

Herman Allen Blumenthal

Journey to the Center of the Earth (59, with Lyle Wheeler, Franz Bachelin); Cleopatra (63, with John DeCuir, Hilyard Brown, Elven Webb, Maurice Pelling, Boris Juraga, Jack Martin Smith); The One and Only, Genuine, Original Family Band (68, with Carroll Clark).

Carl (or Karl) Oscar Borg

The Black Pirate (26, with Dwight Franklin); The Winning of Barbara Worth (26); The Magic Flame (27); The Night of Love (27); The Gaucho (27).

Robert Boyle

Saboteur (42); Corvette K-225 (43); Gals, Incorporated (43); Flesh and Fantasy (43); Shadow of a Doubt (43); Good Morning Judge (43); It Comes Up Love (43); Two Tickets to London (43); White Savage (43); Nocturne (46); They Won't Believe Me (47); Ride the Pink Horse (47); Another Part of the Forest (48); An Act of Murder (48); For the Love of Mary (48); The Gal Who Took the West (49); Arctic Manhunt (49, with Bernard Herzbrun); Abandoned (49); The Western Story (49); Buccaneer's Girl (50); Sierra (50); Louisa (50); The Milkman (50); Mystery Submarine (50); Iron Man (51); Mark of the Renegade (51); The Lady Pays Off (51); Weekend with Father (51); Bronco Buster (52); Lost in Alaska (52); Yankee Buccaneer (52); Back at the Front (52); The Beast from 20,000 Fathoms (53); Girls in the Night (53); It Came from Outer Space (53); Abbott and Costello Go to Mars (53); Ma and Pa Kettle on Vacation (53); East of Sumatra (53); Ma and Pa Kette at Home (54); Ride Clear of Diablo (54); Johnny Dark (54); Chief Crazy Horse (55); The Private War of Major Benson (55); Kiss of Fire (55); Lady Godiva (55); Running Wild (55); Never Say Goodbye (56); A Day of Fury (56); Congo Crossing (56); The Night Runner (57); The Brothers Rico (57); Operation Mad Ball (57); Wild Heritage (58); Buchanan Rides Alone (58); The Crimson Kimono (59); North by Northwest (59, with William A. Horning, Merrill Pye); Cape Fear (62); The Birds (63); The Thrill of It All (63); Marnie (64); Do Not Disturb (65); The Reward (65); The Russians Are Coming, the Russians Are Coming (66); Fitzwilly (67); How to Succeed in Business Without Really Trying (67); In Cold Blood (67); The Thomas Crown Affair (68); Gaily, Gaily (69); The Landlord (70); Fiddler on the Roof (71); Portnoy's Complaint

(72); Mame (74); Bite the Bullet (75); Leadbelly (76); W.C. Fields and Me (76); The Shootist (76); Winter Kills (78).

Ralph Brinton

Eye Witness (50); A Christmas Carol (51); Lucky Nick Cain (51).

George Brooks

Dancing in Manhattan (44); The Missing Juror (44); Cry of the Werewolf (44); One Mysterious Night (44); She's a Soldier Too (44); I Love a Mystery (45); Tahiti Nights (45); Ten Cents a Dance (45); The Man Who Dared (46); One Way to Love (46); Talk About a Lady (46); The Unknown (46); The Corpse Came C.O.D. (47); Cigarette Girl (47); Mr. District Attorney (47); Blondie's Anniversary (47); The Crime Doctor's Gamble (47); Blondie in the Dough (48); The Return of the Whistler (48); Rusty Leads the Way (48); My Dog Rusty (48); Trapped by Boston Blackie (48); The Untamed Breed (48); The Gentleman from Nowhere (48); Blondie's Reward (48); Mary Ryan, Detective (49); Blondie's Secret (49); Bodyhold (49); Mr. Soft Touch (49); The Doolins of Oklahoma (49); Anna Lucasta (49); The Nevadan (50); Prowl Car (50); Fortunes of Captain Blood (50); The Flying Missile (50); Stage to Tucson (50); Corky of Gasoline Alley (51); The Family Secret (51); The Lady and the Bandit (51); Man in the Saddle (51).

Hilyard Brown

Citizen Kane (41, with Van Nest Polglase, Perry Ferguson); A Guy, a Gal, a Pal (45); Don't Fence Me In (45); Marshall of Laredo (45); Phantom of the Plains (45); Bells of Rosarita (45); Home on the Range (45); G.I. War Brides (46); A Guy Could Change (46); The Madonna's Secret (46); The Man from Rainbow Valley (46); The Mysterious Mr. Valentine (46); Out California Way (46); Rainbow Over Texas (46); Rendezvous with Annie (46); Song of Arizona (46); The Undercover Woman (46); Valley of the Zombies (46); The Exile (47); Calendar Girl (47); The Ghost Goes Wild (47); Northwest Outpost (47); Abbott & Costello Meet Frankenstein (48); All My Sons (48); The Fighting O'Flynn (49); Wyoming Mail (50); Flame of Araby (51); Cattle Drive (51); Target Unknown (51); The Raging Tide (51); Home Town Story (51); Has Anybody Seen My Gal (52, with Bernard Herzbrun); Take Me to Town (53); The Creature from the Black Lagoon (54); The Night of the Hunter (55); Fear Strikes Out (57); Man of the West (58); Man in the Net (59); Al Capone (59, p.d.); Ten Who Dared (60, with Carroll Clark); Cleopatra (63, with John de Cuir, Jack Martin Smith, Herman Blumenthal, Elven Webb, Maurice Pelling, Boris Juraga); Shock Treatment (64); Von Ryan's Express (65, with Jack Martin Smith); Finian's Rainbow (68); Skullduggery (70); Fuzz (73); Freebie and the Bean (74); Hustle (75).

Malcolm Brown

Slightly Dangerous (43); Bewitched (45); They Were Expendable (45); Green Dolphin Street (47, with Cedric Gibbons); The Three Musketeers (48, with Cedric Gibbons); The Bribe (49, with Cedric Gibbons); Ambush (49, with Cedric Gibbons); Malaya (49, with Cedric Gibbons); Duchess of Idaho (50, with Cedric Gibbons); It's a Big Country (51, with Cedric Gibbons, William Ferrari, Arthur Lonergan, Edward Imazu); Soldiers Three (51, with Cedric Gibbons); Vengeance Valley (51, with Cedric Gibbons); Somebody Up There Likes Me (56, with Cedric Gibbons).

Wilfred Buckland

The Squaw Man (14); The Ghost Breaker (14); Brewster's Millions (14); The Man on the Box (14); The Virginian (14); The Call of the North (14); What's His Name (14); The Man from Home (14); Rose of the Rancho (14); The Girl of the Golden West (14); The Unafraid (15); The Captive (15); The Warrens of Virginia (15); Carmen (15); The Cheat (15); The Wild Goose Chase (15); The Arab (15); Chimmie Fadden (15); Kindling (15); Maria Rosa (15); Chimmie Fadden Out West (15); Temptation (15); The Golden Chance (16); The Trail of the Lonesome Pine (16); The Heart of Nora Flynn (16); The Dream Girl (16); Joan the Woman (16); A Romance of the Redwoods (17); The Little American (17); The Woman God Forgot (17); The Devil Stone (17); The Whispering Chorus (18); Stella Maris (18); Old Wives for New (18); We Can't Have Everything (18); Till I Come Back to You (18); The Squaw Man (18); Don't Change Your Husband (18); Less Than Kin (18); For Better, for Worse (19, with Mitchell Leisen); Male and Female (19, with Mitchell Leisen); The Grim Game (19); Conrad in Search of His Youth (20); A Perfect Crime (21); The Deuce of Spades (22); The Masquerader (22); Omar the Tentmaker (22); Robin Hood (22, with Irvin J. Martin, Edward M. Langley, Anton Grot, William Cameron Menzies); Adam's Rib (23); Icebound (24); The Forbidden Woman (27, with Mitchell Leisen); Almost Human (27).

Henry Bumstead

Saigon (48, with Hans Dreier); My Own True Love (48, with Hans Dreier); The Sainted Sisters (48, with Hans Dreier); My Friend Irma (49, with Hans Dreier); Song of Surrender (49, with Hans Dreier); Streets of Laredo (49, with Hans Dreier); Top o'the Morning (49, with Hans Dreier); The Furies (50, with Hans Dreier); No Man of Her Own (50, with Hans Dreier); My Friend Irma Goes West (50, with Hans Dreier); The Goldbergs (50); The Redhead and the Cowboy (50, with Hal Pereira); Dear Brat (51, with Hal Pereira); Submarine Command (51, with Hal Pereira); Sailor Beware (51, with Hal Pereira); Rhubarb (51, with Hal Pereira); Come Back, Little Sheba (52, with Hal Pereira); The Bridges of Toko-Ri (54); Knock on Wood (54); The Man Who Knew Too Much (56, with Hal Pereira); That Certain Feeling (56, with Hal Pereira); I Married a Monster from Outer Space (58); Vertigo (58, with Hal Pereira); Cinderfella (60); Come September (61); To Kill a Mockingbird (63, with Alexander Golitzen); Father Goose (64); The War Lord (65, with Alexander Golitzen); Topaz (69); Tell Them Willie Boy Is Here (69); Slaughter House 5 (72, with Alexander Golitzen); High Plains Drifter (73); The Sting (73); The Front Page (74); The Great Waldo Pepper (75); Family Plot (76); King Kong (76); Rollercoaster (77); Slap Shot (77); Same Time Next Year (78); House Calls (78); The Concorde — Airport 1979 (79); A Little Romance (79); The World According to Garp (82); The Little Drummer Girl (84); Harry and Son (84); Warning Sign (85); Psycho III (86).

Howard Campbell

Pilot No. 5 (43); A Stranger in Town (43); Swing Shift Maisie (43); Three Hearts for Julia (43); Maisie Goes to Reno (44); Rationing (44); This Man's Navy (45); Gallant Bess (46); Merton of the Movies (47).

McClure Capps

The Pride of the Yankees (42, with William C. Menzies, Perry Ferguson); The North Star (43); The Princess and the Pirate (44); Up in Arms (44, with Stewart Chaney); Wonder Man (45, with Ernst Fegte); The Kid from Brooklyn (46, with Stewart Chaney); The Marauders (47); The Red House (47); Tarzan and the Huntress (47); Tarzan and the Mermaids (48); Sword of the Avenger (48); Tarzan's Magic Fountain (49); Tales of Robin Hood (51).

Edward Carfagno

Best Foot Forward (43); The Canterville Ghost (43); The Youngest Profession (43); Between Two Women (44); The Thin Man Goes Home (44); Our Vines Have Tender Grapes (45); The Sailor Takes a Wife (45); Boy's Ranch (46); The Secret Ranch (46); Cynthia (47); Good News (47); On an Island with You (48); The Barkleys of Broadway (49); A Lady Without a Passport (50, with Cedric Gibbons); Angels in the Outfield (51); Quo Vadis (51, with Cedric Gibbons, William A. Horning); The Bad and the Beautiful (52, with Cedric Gibbons); Julius Caesar (53, with Cedric Gibbons); Ben Hur (59, with William A. Horning, Arnold Gillespie).

Sturges Carne

Little Lord Fauntleroy (36, with Lyle Wheeler); The Garden of Allah (36, with Lyle Wheeler); It's Great to Be Young (46); Tangier (46); The Son of Rusty (47); Singin' in the Corn (47); The Lady from Shanghai (48, with Stephen Goosson); The Sign of the Ram (48); The Gallant Blade (48); Rusty Saves a Life (49); Song of India (49); All the King's Men (49); The Lone Wolf and His Lady (49).

Ben Carré

(Films done in France are not listed.) The Dollar Mark (14); Mother (14); The Man of the Hour (14); The Wishing Ring (14); The Pit (14); Alias Jimmy Valentine (15); Hearts in Exile (15); The Boss (15); The Ivory Snuff Box (15); A Butterfly on the Wheel (15); The Pawn of Fate (15); Camille (15); The Cub (15); Trilby (15); A Girl's Folly (16); The Hand of Peril (16); The Closed Road (16); La Vie de Boheme (16); The Rail Rider (16); The Velvet Paw (16); The Dark Silence (16); The Deep Purple (16); The Rack (16); The Undying Flame (17); The Whip (17); The Law of the Land (17); Exile (17); Barbary Sheep (17); The Rise of Jenny Cushing (17); The Pride of the Clan (17); The Poor Little Rich Girl (17); Rose of the World (18); The Blue Bird (18, with Andre Ibels); Prunella (18, with Andre Ibels); A Doll's House (18); Woman (18); Sporting Life (18); White Heather (19); The Life Line (19); Victory (19, with Floyd Mueller); The Broken Butterfly (19); Stronger Than Death (20); The River's End (20); In Old Kentucky (20); Go and Get It (20); For the Soul of Rafael (20); My Lady's Garter (20); Treasure Island (20, with Andre Ibels, Floyd Mueller); Don't Ever Marry (21); Dinty (21); Bob Hampton of Placer (21); Man, Woman, Marriage (21); The Wonderful Thing (21); The Light in the Dark (22); Queen of the Moulin Rouge (22); When the Desert Calls (22); What Fools Men Are (22); Wife in Name Only (23); The Red Lily (24); Thy Name Is Woman (24); The Goldfish (24); Cytherea (24); Tarnish (24); In Hollywood with Potash and Perlmutter (24); Lights of Old Broadway (25); The Phantom of the Opera (25, with Charles D. Hall, E.E. Sheeley, Sidney Ullman); The Masked Bride (25, with Cedric Gibbons); More Nostrum (26); La Boheme (26, with Cedric Gibbons, Arnold Gillespie); The Boob (26, with Cedric Gibbons); Don Juan (26); The Better 'Ole (26); My Official Wife (26); When a Man Loves (26 or 27); The King of Kings (27, with Anton Grot, Mitchell Leisen, Paul Iribe, Edward Jewell); Old San Francisco (27); Soft Cushions (27); The Jazz Singer (27); The Red Dance (28); The River Pirate (28); Air Circus (28); Iron Mask (29, with William Cameron Menzies, Maurice Leloir); The Woman from Hell (29); The Valiant (29); The Cockeyed World (29); Frozen Justice (29); Hot for Paris (29, with Charles D. Hall); City Girl (30, with Harry Oliver, William Darling); River's End (30); Woman of All Nations (31, with Charles D. Hall); The Black Camel (31); Riders of the Purple Sage (31); Sailor's Luck (33); Dante's Inferno (35, inferno scenes only with Willy Pogany); A Night at the Opera (35, with Cedric Gibbons); Let's Sing Again (36); The Mine with the Iron Door (36, with Lewis J. Rachmil); Great Guy (36); 23 Hours Leave (37). *In his late career Carré painted backdrops at MGM for such pictures as:* The Wizard of Oz (39); Meet Me in St. Louis (44); An American in Paris (51).

Edward Carrere

My Wild Irish Rose (47); Winter Meeting (48); Two Guys from Texas (48); The Lady Takes a Sailor (49); The Fountainhead (49); The Adventures of Don Juan (48); White Heat (49); The Breaking Point (50); Young Man with a Horn (50); The Flame and the Arrow (50); Along the Great Divide (51); Painting the Clouds with Sunshine (51); Raton Pass (51); Force of Arms (51); Jim Thorpe—All American (51); South Sea Woman (53); Dial M for Murder (54); Helen of Troy (55); Separate Tables (58); Camelot (67); The Wild Bunch (69).

Daniel Cathcart

As Thousands Cheer (43); The Cross of Lorraine (43); Kismet (44); Lost in a Harem (44); Week-End at the Waldorf (45); Till the Clouds Roll By (46); Two Sisters from Boston (46); Unfinished Dance (47, with Cedric Gibbons); Cass Timerlane (47, with Cedric Gibbons); B.F.'s Daughter (48, with Cedric Gibbons); Julia Misbehaves (48, with Cedric Gibbons); Take Me Out to the Ball Game (49, with Cedric Gibbons); Side Street (49, with Cedric Gibbons); That Forsyte Woman (49, with Cedric Gibbons); The Happy Years (50); Please Believe Me (50); Mrs. O'Malley and Mr. Malone (50, with Cedric Gibbons); The Toast of New Orleans (50, with Cedric Gibbons); Inside Straight (51); The Law and the Lady (51, with Cedric Gibbons); Westward the Women (51); Kismet (55, with Preston Ames, Cedric Gibbons).

Cano Chittendon

Marshall of Reno (44); My Best Gal (44); San Antonio Kid (44); San Fernando Valley (44); Storm Over Lisbon (44); Three Little Sisters (44); Trocadero (44); Tucson Riders (44); Vigilantes of Dodge City (44); An Angel Comes to Brooklyn (45); The Chicago Kid (45); Dakota (45); Flame of Barbary Coast (45); Girls of the Big House (45); Grissley's Millions (45); Oregon Trail (45); Steppin' in Society (45); Strangers in the Night (45); Swingin' on a Rainbow (45); The Catman of Paris (46); Crime of the Century (46); Gay Blades (46); Heldorado (46); My Pal Trigger (46); The Plainsman and the Lady (46); Rio Grande Raiders (46); Sioux City Sue (46); Traffic in Crime (46); Apache Rose (47); Trail to San Antone (47); Web of Danger (47); Bells of San Angelo (47); The Flame (48); Strike it Rich (48).

Charles Clague

Blazing the Western Trail (45); Both Barrels Blazing (45); Lawless Empire (45); Let's Go Steady (45); Outlaws of the Rockies (45); Rustlers of the Badlands (45); Rockin' in the Rockies (45); Song of the Prairie (45); Swing in the Saddle (45); Texas Panhandle (45); Blackie and the Law (46); Cowboy Blues (46); The Desert Horseman (46); The Fighting Frontiersman (46); Frontier Gun Law (46); Galloping Thunder (46); Gunning for Vengeance (46); Land Rush (46); Roaring Rangers (46); Singing on the Trail (46); Throw a Saddle on a Star (46); Two-Fisted Stranger (46); Texas Panhandle (46); That Texas Jamboree (46); Prairie Raiders (47); South of the Chisholm Trail (47); Sport of Kings (47); The Stranger from Ponca City (47); Bulldog Drummond at Bay (47); The Lone Hand Texan (47); Millie's Daughter (47); Terror Trail (47); Last Days of Boot Hill (48); Phantom Valley (48); Rose of Santa Rosa? (48); Six Gun Law (48); Song of Idaho (48); West of Sanora? (48); Whirlwind Raiders (48); Trail of Laredo (48); Blazing Across the Pecos (48); Blazing Trail (49); Desert Vigilante (49); Laramie (49); Quick on the Trigger (49); Challenge of the Range (49); South of Death Valley (49); Feudin' Rhythm (49); Horsemen of the Sierras (49); Arctic Fury (49); Mule Train (50); Outcasts of Black Mesa (50); Texas Dynamo (50); Streets of Ghost Town (50); Indian Territory (50); Across the Badlands (50); Raiders of Tomahawk Creek (50); Hoedown (50); Lightning Guns (50); Bonanza Town (51); Cyclone Fury (51);

Fort Savage Raiders (51); Gene Autry and the Mounties (51); Hills of Utah (51); The Kid from Amarillo (51); Pecos River (51); Prairie Roundup (51); Ridin' the Outlaw Trail (51); Silver Canyon (51); Snake River Desperadoes (51); Texans Never Cry (51); Valley of Fire (51); Whirlwind (51).

Carroll Clark

The Magic Garden (27); Hell's Angels (30, with J. Boone Fleming); A Bill of Divorcement (32); What Price Hollywood? (32); Hell's Highway (32); The Most Dangerous Game (32); King Kong (33, with Al Herman); Flying Down to Rio (33, with Van Nest Polglase); Professional Sweetheart (33, with Van Nest Polglase); Spitfire (34, with Van Nest Polglase); The Gay Divorcee (34, with Van Nest Polglase); The Fountain (34, with Van Nest Polglase); Bachelor Bait (34, with Van Nest Polglase); This Man Is Mine (34, with Van Nest Polglase); Of Human Bondage (34, with Van Nest Polglase); Roberta (35, with Van Nest Polglase); Village Tale (35, with Van Nest Polglase); Break of Hearts (35, with Van Nest Polglase); In Person (35, with Van Nest Polglase); Top Hat (35, with Van Nest Polglase); Mary of Scotland (36, with Van Nest Polglase); Swing Time (36, with Van Nest Polglase); Follow the Fleet (36, with Van Nest Polglase); A Damsel in Distress (37, with Van Nest Polglase); Shall We Dance (37, with Van Nest Polglase); Vivacious Lady (38, with Van Nest Polglase); Carefree (38, with Van Nest Polglase); Bachelor Mother (39, with Van Nest Polglase); Primrose Path (40, with Van Nest Polglase); Lucky Partners (40, with Van Nest Polglase); Suspicion (41, with Van Nest Polglase); Joan of Paris (42); Flight for Freedom (43); Gildersleeve's Bad Day (43); The Iron Major (43); The Sky's the Limit (43); Tender Comrade (43); Days of Glory (44); Gildersleeve's Ghost (44); My Pal, Wolf (44); Step Lively (44); Youth Runs Wild (44); Murder, My Sweet (45); The Enchanted Cottage (45); The Spanish Main (45); Notorious (46, with Albert D'Agostino); Cornered (46); The Bachelor and the Bobby-Soxer (47, with Albert D'Agostino); The Lone Wolf in Mexico (47); Sinbad the Sailor (47, with Albert D'Agostino); Tycoon (47, with Albert D'Agostino); Mr. Blandings Builds His Dream House (48); I Remember Mama (48, with Albert D'Agostino); Every Girl Should Be Married (48, with Albert D'Agostino); Strange Bargain (49, with Albert D'Agostino); Bride for Sale (49, with Albert D'Agostino); Holiday Affair (49, with Albert D'Agostino); A Woman's Secret (49); The Secret Fury (50, with Albert D'Agostino); The Whip Hand (51, with Albert D'Agostino); Two Tickets to Broadway (51, with Albert D'Agostino); The Blue Veil (51, with Albert D'Agostino); Payment on Demand (51, with Albert D'Agostino); Best of the Badmen (51, with Albert D'Agostino); Clash by Night (52, with Albert D'Agostino); Vice Squad (53); Second Chance (53, with Albert D'Agostino); While the City Sleeps (56); Beyond a Reasonable Doubt (56); The Great Locomotive Chase (56); Johnny Tremain (57); Old Yeller (57); The Light in the Forest (58); The Shaggy Dog (59); Darby O'Gill and the Little People (59); Toby Tyler (60, with Stan Jolley); Pollyanna (60, with Robert Clatworthy); Ten Who Dared (60, with Hilyard Brown); The Absent Minded Professor (61); The Parent Trap (61, with Robert Clatworthy); Babes in Toyland (61, with Marvin Aubrey Davis); Moon Pilot (62, with Marvin Aubrey Davis); Bon Voyage (62, with Marvin Aubrey Davis); Big Red (62, with Marvin Aubrey Davis); Son of Flubber (63, with William H. Tuntke); Savage Sam (63, with Marvin Aubrey Davis); Summer Magic (63, with Robert Clatworthy); The Incredible Journey (63, with John Mansbridge); The Misadventure of Merlin Jones (64, with William H. Tuntke); A Tiger Walks (64, with Marvin Aubrey Davis); Mary Poppins (64, with William H. Tuntke); Those Calloways (65, with John Mansbridge); The Monkey's Uncle (65, with William H. Tuntke); That Darn Cat (65, with William H. Tuntke); The Ugly Dachshund (66, with Marvin Aubrey Davis); Lieutenant Robin Crusoe, USN (66, with Carl Anderson); Follow Me Boys! (66, with Marvin Aubrey Davis); Monkeys, Go Home (67, with John Mansbridge); The Adventures of Bullwhip Griffin (67, with John Mansbridge); The Gnome-mobile (67, with William H. Tuntke); The Happiest Millionaire (67, with John Mansbridge); Blackbeard's Ghost (68, with John Mansbridge); The One and Only, Genuine,

Original Family Band (68, with Herman Allen Blumenthal); Never a Dull Moment (68, with John Mansbridge); The Horse in the Grey Flannel Suit (68, with John Mansbridge); The Love Bug (68, with John Mansbridge).

Charles H. Clarke

Dark Passage (47); The Big Punch (48); Whiplash (48); The Younger Brothers (49); Caged (50); Return of the Frontiersman (50); Three Secrets (50); Montana (50); The West Point Story (50); Pretty Baby (50); Starlift (51); The Enforcer (51); Tomorrow Is Another Day (51).

Robert Clatworthy

Bulldog Drummond's Peril (38, with Hans Dreier); Top Man (43); Sing a Jingle (43); So's Your Uncle (43); Christmas Holiday (44); Can't Help Singing (44); Phantom Lady (44); Frisco Sal (45); Easy to Look At (45); Jungle Captive (45); Lady on a Train (45); She Gets Her Man (45); This Love of Ours (45); Because of Him (46); Blond Alibi (46); Smooth as Silk (46); The Runaround (46); Variety Girl (47, with Hans Dreier); Hazard (48, with Hans Dreier); Isn't It Romantic (48, with Hans Dreier); Once More My Darling (49); Woman in Hiding (49); Come Be My Love (49); Fugitive from Terror (49); Shoplifter/I Was a Shoplifter (50); Shakedown (50); Apache Drums (51); Katie Did It (51); Little Egypt (51); Steel Town (52); Scarlet Angel (52); Horizons West (52); Because of You (52); Desert Legion (53); It Happens Every Thursday (53); Law and Order (53); Wings of the Hawk (53); Francis Joins the WACs (54); Playgirl (54); Foxfire (55); Female on the Beach (55); To Hell and Back (55); Six Bridges to Cross (55); The Second Greatest Sex (55); The Benny Goodman Story (55); The Price of Fear (56); Written on the Wind (56, with Alexander Golitzen); The Incredible Shrinking Man (57); The Deadly Mantis (57); Night Passage (57); The Female Animal (58); Touch of Evil (58, with Alexander Golitzen); Once Upon a Horse (58); Never Steal Anything Small (59); The Wild and Innocent (59); Psycho (60, with Joseph Hurley); The Leech Woman (60); Pollyanna (60, with Carroll Clark); Midnight Lace (60); Love Come Back (61); The Parent Trap (61, with Carroll Clark); That Touch of Mink (62); Forty Pounds of Trouble (63); Summer Magic (63, with Carroll Clark); Bedtime Story (64); Invitation to a Gunfighter (64); Send Me No Flowers (64); Inside Daisy Clover (65, with Dean Tavoularis); Ship of Fools (65); Guess Who's Coming to Dinner (67); How to Save a Marriage and Ruin Your Life (68); Cactus Flower (69); The Secret of Santa Vittoria (69); The Wild Country (70); Scandalous John (71); Butterflies Are Free (72); Forty Carats (73); The Castaway Cowboys (74); Report to the Commissioner (75); Car Wash (76); From Noon Til Three (76); Treasure of Matecumbe (76); Another Man, Another Chance (77).

Duncan Cramer

The Fighting Seabees (44); The Woman in the Window (44); Delightfully Dangerous (45); Abilene Town (46); A Night in Casablanca (46); The Dark Mirror (46); Copacabana (47); Fabulous Dorseys (47); Four Faces West (48); On Our Merry Way (48); Lulu Belle (48); D.O.A. (49).

Paul Crawley

The Fire Brigade (27); The Bat Whispers (30).

Louis H. Creber

The Gorilla (39, with Richard Day); Frontier Marshall (39, with Richard Day); Shooting High (40, with Richard Day); Girl in 313 (40, with Richard Day); Pier 13 (40, with Richard Day); Charlie Chan at the Wax Museum (40, with Richard Day); Yesterday's Heroes (40, with Richard Day); The Cowboy and the Blond (41, with Richard Day); Dance Hall (41, with Richard Day); Sun Valley Serenade (41, with Richard Day); Accent on Love (41, with Richard Day); Man at Large (41, with Richard Day); The Man Who Wouldn't Die (42, with Richard Day); It Happened in Flatbush (42, with Richard Day); Whispering Ghosts (42, with Richard Day); The Postman Didn't Ring (42, with Richard Day); A Haunting We Will Go (42, with Richard Day); Berlin Correspondent (42, with Richard Day); Manila Calling (42, with Richard Day); The Undying Montser (42, with Richard Day); Dixie Dugan (43, with Richard Day); Margin for Error (43, with Richard Day); Bomber's Moon (43); Buffalo Bill (44); The Purple Heart (44); Roger Touhy — Gangster (44); Wing and a Prayer (44); Winged Victory (44); The House on 92nd St. (45, with Lyle Wheeler); State Fair (45, with Lyle Wheeler); Tarzan and the Leopard Woman (46); High Tide (47); It Happened on Fifth Avenue (47); In Self Defense (47); Linda Be Good (47); Caged Fury (48); Mr. Reckless (48); Speed to Spare (48); Waterfront at Midnight (48); Bob and Sally (48); Million Dollar Weekend (48); Disaster (48); Dynamite (48); Strike It Rich (48); Manhandled (49); Special Agent (49); El Paso (49); Prejudice (49); Captain China (49); Africa Screams (49); The Lucky Stiff (49); The Lawless (50); The Eagle and the Hawk (50); Tripoli (50); Of Men and Music (50); Hong Kong (51); Crosswinds (51); Passage West (51); The Last Outpost (51).

William Creber

The Greatest Story Ever Told (65, with Richard Day); Planet of the Apes (68, with Jack Martin Smith); Justine (69, with Jack Martin Smith).

Lucius O. Croxton

The Falcon in Hollywood (44); Nevada (44); Mama Loves Papa (45); Road to Alcatraz (45); Two O'Clock Courage (45); Wanderer of the Wasteland (45); West of the Pecos (45); A Game of Death (45); Tell It to a Star (45); What a Blonde (45); Ding Dong Wiliams (46); The Falcon's Alibi (46); Riverboat Rhythm (46); San Quentin (46); Sunset Pass (46); Vacation in Reno (46); The Bamboo Blonde (46); Criminal Court (46); Dick Tracy vs. Cueball (46); Seven Keys to Baldpate (47); Beat the Hand (47); Code of the West (47); Dick Tracy's Dilemma (47); Wild Horse Mesa (47); Western Heritage (48); Michael O'Halloran (48); Belle Starr's Daughter (48); Roughshod (49); Massacre River (49); Boy from Indiana (50); Fort Defiance (51).

Albert D'Agostino

Salvation Nell (21); Ramona (28); Blood Money (33); I Cover the Waterfront (33); Finishing School (34, with Van Nest Polglase); The Werewolf of London (35); The Mystery of Edwin Drood (35); The Raven (35); Dracula's Daughter (36); The Invisible Ray (36); The Stranger on the Third Floor (40); I'm Still Alive (40, with Van Nest Polglase); The Cat People (42, with Walter E. Keller); I Walked with a Zombie (43, with Walter E. Keller); The Leopard Man (43, with Walter E. Keller); The 7th Victim (43, with Walter E. Keller); Mr. Lucky (43, with William Cameron Menzies, Mark-Lee Kirk); The Ghost Ship (43, with Walter E. Keller); This Land Is Mine (43, with Walter E. Keller); The Curse of the Cat People (44, with Walter E. Keller); Mademoiselle Fifi (44, with Walter E. Keller); None But the Lonely Heart (44, with Jack Okey); Isle of the Dead (45, with Walter E. Keller); The Body Snatcher (45, with Walter E. Keller); The Spanish Main (45); Bedlam (46, with Walter E. Keller);

The Spiral Staircase (46, with Jack Okey); Notorious (46, with Carroll Clark); Badman's Territory (46); The Bamboo Blonde (46); Child of Divorce (46); Cornered (46); Crack-Up (46); Criminal Court (46); Deadline at Dawn (46); Dick Tracy vs. Cueball (46); Ding Dong Williams (46); The Falcon's Adventure (46); The Falcon's Alibi (46); From This Day Forward (46); Genius at Work (46); Heartbeat (46); Lady Luck (46); Make Mine Music (46); Nocturne (46); Riverboat Rhythm (46); San Quentin (46); Sister Kenny (46); Step by Step (46); The Stranger (46); Sunset Pass (46); Tarzan and the Leopard Woman (46); Till the End of Time (46); Tomorrow Is Forever (46); The Truth About Murder (46); Vacation in Reno (46); Without Reservations (46); Long Night (47); Magic Town (47); Mourning Becomes Electra (47); Night Song (47); Out of the Past (47); Rifraff (47, with Walter E. Keller); Seven Keys to Baldpate (47); Sinbad the Sailor (47, with Carroll Clark); They Won't Believe Me (47); Thunder Mountain (47); Trail Street (47); Tycoon (47, with Carroll Clark); Under the Tonto Rim (47); Wild Horse Mesa (47); The Woman on the Beach (47); The Arizona Range (48); Berlin Express (48); Mr. Blanding Builds His Dream House (48); Blood on the Moon (48, with Walter E. Keller); Bodyguard (48); The Boy with Green Hair (48); Every Girl Should Be Married (48, with Carroll Clark); Fighting Father Dunne (48, with Walter E. Keller); Good Sam (48); Guns of Hate (48); Gun Smugglers (48); If You Knew Susie (48); Indian Agent (48); Let's Go to the Movies (48); Mystery in Mexico (48); Race Street (48, with Walter E. Keller); Return of the Bad Men (48); Rachel and the Stranger (48); Station West (48); The Twisted Road (48); Variety Time (48); The Velvet Touch (48); Western Heritage (48); I Remember Mama (48, with Carroll Clark); The Threat (49); Strange Bargain (49, with Carroll Clark); I Married a Communist (49, with Walter E. Keller); A Dangerous Profession (49); Riders of the Range (49); The Mysterious Desperado (49); Masked Raiders (49); Bride for Sale (49, with Carroll Clark); Holiday Affair (49, with Carroll Clark); Adventure in Baltimore (49); Brothers in the Saddle (49); The Clay Pigeon (49, with Walter E. Keller); Easy Living (49); Follow Me Quietly (49, with Walter E. Keller); Roughshod (49); Rustlers (49); The Set-Up (49); Stagecoach Kid (49); The Window (49, with Walter E. Keller); A Woman's Secret (49); The Judge Steps Out (49); The Big Steal (49, with Ralph Berger); Dynamite Pass (50, with Walter E. Keller); Rider from Tucson (50, with Walter E. Keller); Storm Over Wyoming (50); Walk Softly, Stranger (50); White Tower (50); Bunco Squad (50, with Walter E. Keller); Rio Grande Patrol (50); Never a Dull Moment (50, with Walter E. Keller); Armored Car Robbery (50); The Secret Fury (50, with Carroll Clark); Jet Pilot (50, with Feild Gray); Border Treasure (50); Born to Be Bad (50); Where Danger Lives (50); Tarzan and the Slave Girl (50); Law of the Badlands (50); Double Deal (50); The Company She Keeps (50); Gambling House (50); Hunt the Man Down (50); His Kind of Woman (51); On Dangerous Ground (51); The Whip Hand (51, with Carroll Clark); Two Tickets to Broadway (51, with Carroll Clark); The Blue Veil (51, with Carroll Clark); Payment on Demand (51, with Carroll Clark); Best of the Badmen (51, with Carroll Clark); Hot Lead (51); Overland Telegraph (51); Double Dynamite (51); Gunplay (51); My Forbidden Past (51); Sealed Cargo (51); Behave Yourself (51); On the Loose (51, with Walter E. Keller); Saddle Legion (51, with Walter E. Keller); Hard, Fast, & Beautiful (51); The Thing (51); The Racket (51); Flying Leathernecks (51); Pistol Harvest (51); Roadblock (51, with Walter E. Keller); Macao (52, with Ralph Berger); Clash by Night (52, with Carroll Clark); Angel Face (52); Second Chance (53); Run of the Arrow (57).

William S. Darling

Her Mad Bargain (21); Fig Leaves (26, with William Cameron Menzies); What Price Glory (26); Paid to Love (27); Fazil (28); A Girl in Every Port (28); 4 Devils (28, sets executed by Darling from sketches by German art directors Robert Herlth and Walter Röhrig); The Black Watch (29); City Girl (30, with Ben Carré, Harry Oliver); Men Without Women (30); Bad Girl (31); The Yellow Ticket (31); While Paris Sleeps (32); Hoop-la (33); Cavalcade (33, war scenes with William Cameron Menzies); Pilgrimage (33); Zoo in Budapest (33); The World Moves On (34); Steamboat Round the Bend (35); The Prisoners of Shark Island (37); Lloyds of London (36); Seventh Heaven (37); Wee Willie Winkie (37); Wake Up and Live (37, with Mark-Lee Kirk, Haldane Douglas); In Old Chicago (38, with Rudolph Sternad); Stanley and Livingstone (39); The Rains Came (39); Hangmen Also Die (43); The Song of Bernadette (43, with James Basevi); Keys of the Kingdom (44, with Lyle Wheeler); Anna and the King of Siam (46, with Lyle Wheeler, Richard Day).

John Datu

(Also known as John Datu Arensma) The Mark of the Whistler (44); Shadows of the Night (44); Crime Doctor's Courage (45); The Power of the Whistler (45); A Song for Miss Julie (45).

George W. Davis

The Ghost and Mrs. Muir (47, with Richard Day, Lyle Wheeler); Daisy Kenyon (47); Deep Waters (48); That Wonderful Urge (48); The Beautiful Blonde from Bashful Bend (49, with Lyle Wheeler); Dancing in the Dark (49, with Lyle Wheeler); House of Strangers (49, with Lyle Wheeler); A Ticket to Tomahawk (50, with Lyle Wheeler); No Way Out (50); All About Eve (50, with Lyle Wheeler); Mister 880 (50, with Lyle Wheeler); People Will Talk (51); Rawhide (51, with Lyle Wheeler); David and Bathsheba (51, with Lyle Wheeler); The Robe (53, with Lyle Wheeler); The Egyptian (54, with Lyle Wheeler); The 7 Year Itch (55, with Lyle Wheeler); Love Is a Many Splendored Thing (55, with Lyle Wheeler); Funny Face (57, with Hal Pereira); The Diary of Anne Frank (59, with Lyle Wheeler); The Time Machine (60, with William Ferrari); The Bells Are Ringing (60, with Preston Ames); Home from the Hill (60, with Preston Ames); Two Weeks in Another Town (62); How the West Was Won (62, with William Ferrari, Addison Hehr); Mutiny on the Bounty (62, with Joseph McMillian Johnson, Arnold Gillespie); 7 Women (66, with Eddie Imazu); Point Black (67).

Marvin Aubrey Davis

Moon Pilot (62, with Carroll Clark); Boy Voyage (62, with Carroll Clark); Big Red (62, with Carroll Clark); Babes in Toyland (62, with Carroll Clark); Savage Sam (63, with Carroll Clark); A Tiger Walks (64, with Carroll Clark); The Ugly Dachshund (66, with Carroll Clark); Follow Me Boys! (66, with Carroll Clark).

Richard Day

Foolish Wives (22, with E.E. Sheeley); Merry Go Round (23, with E.E. Sheeley, Erich von Stroheim); Sinners in Silk (24); Greed (24, with Erich von Stroheim, Cedric Gibbons); The Merry Widow (25, with Cedric Gibbons); Bright Lights (25, with Cedric Gibbons); The Only Thing (25, with Cedric Gibbons); His Secretary (25, with Cedric Gibbons); Beverly of Graustark (26, with Cedric Gibbons); Bardeleys the Magnificent (26, with Cedric Gibbons, James Basevi); The Show (27); Mr. Wu (27, with Cedric Gibbons, Merrill Pye); Tillie the Toiler (27, with Cedric Gibbons, David Townsend); The Unknown (27); Adam and Evil (27); After Midnight (27); The Road to Romance (27); Tea for Three (27, with Cedric Gibbons); The Student Prince (27, with Hans Dreier, Fred Hope, Cedric Gibbons); The Enemy (27); The Divine Woman (28, with Cedric Gibbons, A. Arnold Gillespie); The Wickedness Preferred (28, with Cedric Gibbons); Rosemarie (28); The Big City (28, with Cedric Gibbons); Circus Rookies (28, with Cedric Gibbons); Laugh, Clown, Laugh (28, with Cedric Gibbons); The Actress (28, with Cedric Gibbons); Forbidden Hours (28, with Cedric Gibbons); Our Dancing Daughters (28, with Cedric Gibbons); Excess Baggage (28, with Cedric Gibbons); While the City Sleeps (28, with Cedric Gibbons); The Wedding March (28, with

Erich von Stroheim; The Masks of the Devil (28, with Cedric Gibbons); West of Zanzibar (28, with Cedric Gibbons); Queen Kelly (28, with Harold Miles); The Bridge of San Luis Rey (29, with Cedric Gibbons); The Idle Rich (29, with Cedric Gibbons); A Man's Man (29, with Cedric Gibbons); Wonder of Women (29, with Cedric Gibbons); The Girl in the Show (29, with Cedric Gibbons); The Hollywood Revue of 1929 (29, with Cedric Gibbons); The Unholy Night (29, with Cedric Gibbons); Wise Girls/Kempy (29, with Cedric Gibbons); The Thirteenth Chair (29, with Cedric Gibbons); The Kiss (29, with Cedric Gibbons); Their Own Desire (29, with Cedric Gibbons, Harry Sharrock); Devil May Care (29, with Ulrich Busch); Untamed (29, with Cedric Gibbons, Van Nest Polglase); Anna Christie (30, with Cedric Gibbons); In Gay Madrid (30, with Cedric Gibbons); Sins of the Children (30, with Merrill Pye); Whoopee (30); Madame Satan (30, with Cedric Gibbons, Mitchell Leisen); Le Spectre Vert (30, with Cedric Gibbons); The Devil to Pay (30); The Front Page (31); Indiscreet (31); Street Scene (31); The Unholy Garden (31); Palmy Days (31); Arrowsmith (31); The Greeks Had a Word for Them (32); Rain (32); Cynara (32); The Kid from Spain (32); Hallelujah I'm a Bum (33); Secrets (33); The Bowery (33); The Masquerader (33); Roman Scandals (33); Gallant Lady (33); Moulin Rouge (34); Nana (34); The Affairs of Cellini (34); The House of Rothschild (34); Born to Be Bad (34, with Joseph C. Wright); The Last Gentleman (34); Bulldog Drummond Strikes Back (34); Kid Millions (34); Looking for Trouble (34); We Live Again (34); The Mighty Barnum (34); Folies Bergere (35); Clive of India (35); The Wedding Night (35); Les Misérables (35); Cardinal Richelieu (35); The Call of the Wild (35); The Dark Angel (35); Barbary Coast (35); Metropolitan (35); Splendor (35); Strike Me Pink (36); These Three (36); One Rainy Afternoon (36); Dodsworth (36); The Gay Desperado (36); Come and Get It (36); Beloved Enemy (36); Woman Chases Man (37); Stella Dallas (37); Dead End (37); The Hurricane (37, with Alexander Golitzen, James Basevi); The Goldwyn Follies (38); The Adventures of Marco Polo (38); The Cowboy and the Lady (38); Charlie Chan in Honolulu (38, with Haldane Douglas); The Little Princess (39, with Bernard Herzbrun, Hans Peters); The Hound of the Baskervilles (39, with Hans Peters, Thomas Little); The Return of the Cisco Kid (39, with Wiard Ihnen); The Gorilla (39, with Lewis Creber); Rose of Washington Square (39, with Rudolph Sternad); Young Mr. Lincoln (39, with Mark Lee Kirk); Frontier Marshall (39, with Lewis Creber); The Adventures of Sherlock Holmes (39, with Hans Peters); Quick Millions (39); Charlie Chan at Treasure Island (39); The Escape (39); Hollywood Cavalcade (39, with Wiard Ihnen); Pack Up Your Troubles (39, with Albert Hogsett); Drums Along the Mohawk (39, with Mark Lee Kirk); Day Time Wife (39, with Joseph C. Wright); City of Darkness (39); Swanee River (39, with Joseph C. Wright); The Honeymoon's Over (39); Everything Happens at Night (39); City of Chance (39); Little Old New York (40, with Rudolph Sternad); The Blue Bird (40, with Wiard Ihnen); He Married His Wife (40, with Joseph C. Wright); The Grapes of Wrath (40, with Mark Lee Kirk); The Man Who Wouldn't Talk (40); Charlie Chan in Panama (40); Star Dust (40); Johnny Apollo (40); Shooting High (40, with Lewis Creber); I Was an Adventuress (40); Lillian Russell (40, with Joseph C. Wright); Girl in 313 (40, with Lewis Creber); Earthbound (40); Four Sons (40, with Albert Hogsett); Manhattan Heartbeat (40); Maryland (40, with Wiard Ihnen); The Man I Married (40); Girl from Avenue A (40, with Chester Gore); The Return of Frank James (40, with Wiard Ihnen); Pier 13 (40, with Lewis Creber); Young People (40, with Rudolph Sternad); Charlie Chan at the Wax Museum (40, with Lewis Creber); Yesterday's Heroes (40, with Lewis Creber); The Gay Caballero (40, with Chester Gore); Down Argentine Way (40, wtih Joseph C. Wright); The Great Profile (40, with Joseph C. Wright); The Mark of Zorro (40, with Joseph C. Wright); Streets of Memories (40, with George Dudley); Tin Pan Alley (40, with Joseph C. Wright); Youth Will Be Served (40); Murder Over New York (40); Jennie (40); Chad Hanna (40); Hudson's Bay (40, with Wiard Ihnen, Michael Shayne); Private Detective (40); For Beauty's Sake (41); Remember the Day (41); Romance of the Rio Grande (41); Western Union (41, with Wiard Ihnen); Tobacco Road (41, with James Basevi); That Night in Rio (41, with Joseph C. Wright); The Great American Broadcast (41, with Albert Hogsett); The Cowboy and the Blonde (41, with Lewis Creber); Blood and Sand (41, with Joseph C. Wright); Man

Hunt (41, with Wiard Ihnen); A Very Young Lady (41, with Joseph C. Wright); Moon Over Miami (41, with Wiard Ihnen); The Bride Wore Crutches (41); Accent on Love (41, with Lewis Creber); Dance Hall (41, with Lewis Creber); Charley's Aunt (41, with Nathan Juran, Thomas Little); Dressed to Kill (41); Wild Geese Calling (41); Private Nurse (41); Sun Valley Serenade (41, with Lewis Creber); Charlie Chan in Rio (41); Belle Starr (41, with Nathan Juran); We Go Fast (41); The Last of the Duanes (41, with Chester Gore); Man at Large (41, with Lewis Creber); A Yank in the R.A.F. (41, with James Basevi); Great Guns (41, with Albert Hogsett); Riders of the Purple Sage (41); Weekend in Havana (41, with Joseph C. Wright); Rise and Shine (41, with George Dudley); Swamp Water (41, with Thomas Little, Joseph C. Wright); How Green Was My Valley (41, with Nathan Juran); I Wake Up Screaming (41); The Lone Star Ranger (42, with Chester Gore); Son of Fury (42, with James Basevi); Roxie Hart (42, with Wiard Ihnen); Song of the Island (42); Rings on Her Fingers (42, with Albert Hogsett); The Man Who Wouldn't Die (42, with Lewis Creber); It Happened in Flatbush (42, with Lewis Creber); My Gal Sal (42, with Joseph C. Wright); Whispering Ghosts (42, with Lewis Creber); Moontide (42, with James Basevi); The Magnificent Dope (42, with Wiard Ihnen); Through Different Eyes (42, with Chester Gore); Ten Gentlemen from West Point (42, with Nathan Juran); The Postman Didn't Ring (42, with Lewis Creber); This Above All (42, with Joseph C. Wright, Thomas Little); Footlight Serenade (42, with Roger Heman); A Haunting We Will Go (42, with Lewis Creber); Little Tokyo, USA (42, with Maurice Ransford); The Pied Piper (42, with Maurice Ransford); The Loves of Edgar Allan Poe (42, with Nathan Juran); Orchestra Wives (42, with Joseph C. Wright); Berlin Correspondent (42, with Lewis Creber); Careful Soft Shoulders (42, with Albert Hogsett); Just Off Broadway (42, with Chester Gore); Iceland (42, with Wiard Ihnen); Girl Trouble (42, with Boris Leven); Manila Calling (42, with Lewis Creber); The Man in the Trunk (42, with Albert Hogsett); Tales of Manhattan (42, with Boris Leven); Springtime in the Rockies (42, with Joseph C. Wright); That Other Woman (42, with Nathan Juran); The Ox-Bow Incident (42, with James Basevi); Thunder Birds (42, with James Basevi); The Undying Monster (42, with Lewis Creber); China Girl (42, with Wiard Ihnen); Time to Kill (42, with Chester Gore); The Black Swan (42, with James Basevi); Dr. Renault's Secret (42, with Nathan Juran); Quiet Please, Murder (42, with Joseph C. Wright); Life Begins at 8:30 (42, with Boris Leven); The Meanest Man in the World (43, with Albert Hogsett); Dixie Dugan (43, with Lewis Creber); Immortal Sergeant (43, with Maurice Ransford); He Hired the Boss (43, with Maurice Ransford); Chetniks! (43, with Albert Hogsett); Magin for Error (43, with Lewis Creber); My Friend Flicka (43, with Chester Gore); Tonight We Raid Calais (43, with Russell Spencer); Crash Dive (43, with Wiard Ihnen); Coney Island (43, with Joseph C. Wright); Up in Arms (44); The Razor's Edge (46, with Nathan Juran); Anna and the King of Siam (46, with Lyle Wheeler, William Darling); Boomerang (47, with James Basevi, Chester Gore); Miracle on 34th St. (47, with Richard Irvine); Moss Rose (43, with Mark Lee Kirk); The Ghost and Mrs. Muir (47, with George W. Davis, Lyle Wheeler); I Wonder Who's Kissing Her Now (47, with Boris Leven); Mother Wore Tights (47, with Joseph C. Wright); The Captain from Castile (47, with James Basevi); Joan of Arc (48); Force of Evil (48); My Foolish Heart (49); Our Very Own (50); Edge of Doom (50); Cry Danger (51); A Streetcar Named Desire (51); I Want You (51); Hans Christian Anderson (52); On the Waterfront (54); Soloman and Sheba (59, with Alfred Sweeney); Exodus (60); Something Wild (61); Goodbye Charlie (64, with Jack Martin Smith); Cheyenne Autumn (64); The Greatest Story Ever Told (65, with William Creber); The Chase (65, with Robert Luthhardt); The Happening (66, with Albert Brenner); The Valley of the Dolls (67, with Jack Martin Smith); The Sweet Ride (67, with Jack Martin Smith); Tora! Tora! Tora! (70, with Jack Martin Smith); Tribes (70, tv movie, with Jack Martin Smith).

John de Cuir

White Tie and Tails (46); Brute Force (47); Time Out of Mind (47); The Naked City (48); Casbah (48); Mexican Hayride (48); The Life of Riley (49); Yes Sir, That's My Baby (49);

Curtain Call at Cactus Creek (50); Half Angel (51, with Lyle Wheeler); House on Telegraph Hill (51, with Lyle Wheeler); I Can Get It for You Wholesale (51, with Lyle Wheeler); Mr. Belvedere Rings the Bell (51, with Lyle Wheeler); The Model and the Marriage Broker (51, with Lyle Wheeler); Diplomatic Courier (52, with Lyle Wheeler); My Cousin Rachel (52, with Lyle Wheeler); The Snows of Kilimanjaro (52, with Lyle Wheeler); Call Me Madam (53, with Lyle Wheeler); 3 Coins in the Fountain (54, with Lyle Wheeler); There's No Business Like Show Business (54, with Lyle Wheeler); Daddy Long Legs (55, with Lyle Wheeler); How to Be Very, Very Popular (55, with Lyle Wheeler); The King and I (56, with Lyle Wheeler); South Pacific (58); A Certain Smile (58); The Big Fisherman (59); Seven Thieves (60); Cleopatra (63, p.d. with Hilyard Brown, Jack Martin Smith, Herman Blumenthal, Elven Webb, Maurice Pelling, Boris Juraga); Circus World (64); The Agony and the Ecstasy (65, p.d. with Jack Martin Smith, a.d.); A Man Could Get Killed (66); The Taming of the Shrew (67); The Honey Pot (67); Dr. Faustus (68); Hello, Dolly! (69, with Jack Martin Smith, Herman Blumenthal); On a Clear Day You Can See Forever (70); The Great White Hope (70); Jacqueline Susann's Once Is Not Enough (75); That's Entertainment, Part 2 (76); The Other Side of Midnight (77); Love and Bullets (79); Raise the Titanic (80); Legal Eagles (86).

Ralph de Lacy

Cheyenne Roundup (43); Frontier Badmen (43); Lone Star Trail (43); She's for Me (43); All by Myself (43); Calling Dr. Death (43); Captive Wild Woman (43); Cowboy in Manhattan (43); Follow the Band (43); He's My Guy (43); Hi'Ya Chum (43); Keep 'Em Slugging (43); The Strange Death of Adolf Hitler (43); You're a Lucky Fellow, Mister Smith (43); Chip Off the Old Block (44); Hi, Goodlookin' (44); Pardon My Pass (44); The Scarlet Claw (44); Weekend Pass (44).

Frank Dexter

That's My Baby (44); The Big Show-Off (45); Accomplice (46); Bells of San Fernando (47); Buffalo Bill Rides Again (47); My Dog Shep (48); The Counterfeiters (48); Street Corner (48); Amazon Quest (49); The Gay Amigo (49).

Haldane Douglas

Wake Up and Live (37, with William S. Darling, Mark-Lee Kirk); Charlie Chan in Honolulu (38, with Richard Day); Buy Me That Town (41, with Hans Dreier); Caught in the Drought (41, with Hans Dreier); Glamour Boy (41, with Hans Dreier); Night of January 16th (41, with Hans Dreier); West Point Widow (41, with Hans Dreier); The Glass Key (42, with Hans Dreier); My Heart Belongs to Daddy (42, with Hans Dreier); A Night in New Orleans (42, with Hans Dreier); Priorities on Parade (42, with Hans Dreier); Street of Chance (42, with Hans Dreier); Sweater Girl (42, with Hans Dreier); For Whom the Bell Tolls (43, with Hans Dreier, William Cameron Menzies); The Good Fellows (43, with Hans Dreier); Henry Aldrich Haunts a House (43, with Hans Dreier); Lady Bodyguard (43, with Hans Dreier); Salute for Three (43, with Hans Dreier); Rainbow Island (44, with Hans Dreier); Hail the Conquering Hero (44); Out of this World (45, with Hans Dreier); Salty O'Rourke (45, with Hans Dreier); O.S.S. (46, with Hans Dreier); Our Hearts Were Growing Up (46, with Hans Dreier); Easy Come, Easy Go (47, with Hans Dreier); Wild Harvest (47, with Hans Dreier).

Hans Dreier

(Dreier's German films are not listed.) Peter the Great (23); Forbidden Paradise (24); East of Suez (25, with Lawrence Hitt); Underworld (27); The Student Prince (27, with Richard

Day, Frederic Hope, Cedric Gibbons); The Last Command (28); The Dragnet (28); The Patriot (28); The Docks of New York (28); The Street of Sin (28); A Dangerous Woman (29); Betrayal (29); The Case of Lena Smith (29); Thunderbolt (29); The Love Parade (29); Monte Carlo (30, with Wiard Ihnen); The Vagabond King (30); Morocco (30); Dishonored (31); An American Tragedy (31); The Smiling Lieutenant (31); Dr. Jekyll and Mr. Hyde (31); Love Me Tonight (32); The Man I Killed (32); One Hour with You (32); A Farewell to Arms (32); Trouble in Paradise (32); Shanghai Express (32, with Wiard Ihnen); This Day and Age (33, with Roland Anderson, Mitchell Leisen); Design for Living (33, with Ernst Fegte); Song of Songs (33); Duck Soup (33, with Wiard Ihnen); White Woman (33, with Harry Oliver); I'm No Angel (33, with Bernard Herzbrun); One Sunday Afternoon (33, with Wiard Ihnen); Kiss and Make Up (34, with Ernst Fegte); Ladies Should Listen (34, with Ernst Fegte); We're Not Dressing (34, with Ernst Fegte); Cleopatra (34, with Roland Anderson); Six of a Kind (34, with Robert Odell); Now and Forever (34, with Robert Usher); It's a Gift (34, with John Goodman); The Scarlet Empress (34, with Peter Ballbusch, Richard Kollorsz); Belle of the Nineties (34, with Bernhard Herzbrun); The Crusades (35, with Roland Anderson); So Red the Rose (35); Paris in the Spring (35, with Ernst Fegte); The Lives of a Bengal Lancer (35, with Roland Anderson); The Devil Is a Woman (35); Ruggles of Red Gap (35, with Robert Odell); Rumba (35, with Robert Usher); Peter Ibbetson (35, with Robert Usher); Enter Madam (35, with Ernst Fegte); Wings in the Dark (35, with Earl Hedrick); The Last Outpost (35, with Earl Hedrick); Goin' to Town (35, with Robert Usher); Hollywood Boulevard (36, with Earl Hedrick); Wedding Present (36, with Earl Hedrick); Go West, Young Man (36, with Wiard Ihnen); Desire (36, with Robert Usher); Klondike Annie (36, with Bernard Herzbrun); Anything Goes (36, with Ernst Fegte); The General Died at Dawn (36, with Ernst Fegte); The Trail of the Lonesome Pine (36); Mississippi (36, with Bernard Herzbrun); The Plainsman (36, with Roland Anderson); Poppy (36, with Bernard Herzbrun); The Big Broadcast of 1937 (36, with Robert Usher); Border Flight (36, with Robert Odell); Desert Gold (36, with Dave Garber); F-Man (36, with Earl Hedrick); Girl of the Ozarks (36, with John B. Goodman); Give Us the Night (36, with Roland Anderson); Lady Be Careful (36, with Roland Anderson); The Preview Murder Mystery (36, with Earl Hedrick); The Princess Comes Across (36, with Ernst Fegte); The Texas Rangers (36, with Bernard Herzbrun); Yours for the Asking (36, with Roland Anderson); Angel (37, with Robert Usher); Artists and Models (37, with Robert Usher); Bulldog Drummond Comes Back (37, with Franz Bachelin); Easy Living (37, with Ernst Fegte); High, Wide and Handsome (37, with John B. Goodman); Hold 'Em Navy (37, with Robert Odell); I Met Him in Paris (37, with Ernst Fegte); Interns Can't Take Money (37, with Roland Anderson); King of Gamblers (37, with Robert Odell); Make Way for Tomorrow (37, with Bernard Herzbrun); Night Club Scandal (37, with Earl Hedrick); Mountain Music (37, with John B. Goodman); Partners in Crime (37, with Robert Odell); Souls at Sea (37, with Roland Anderson); Swing High, Swing Low (37, with Ernst Fegte); This Way Please (37, with Jack Otterson); Thrill of a Lifetime (37, with Franz Bachelin); True Confessions (37, with Robert Usher); Turn Off the Moon (37); Wells Fargo (37, with John B. Goodman); The Arkansas Traveller (38, with Earl Hedrick); The Buccaneer (38, with Roland Anderson); Artists and Models Abroad (38, with Ernst Fegte); You and Me (38, with Ernst Fegte); Zaza (38, with Robert Usher); The Big Broadcast of 1938 (38, with Ernst Fegte); Bluebeard's Eighth Wife (38, with Robert Usher); College Swing (38, with Ernst Fegte); Bulldog Drummond in Africa (38, with Earl Hedrick); Bulldog Drummond's Peril (38, with Robert Clatworthy); Campus Confessions (38, with William Flannery); Give Me a Sailor (38, with Earl Hedrick); Hunted Men (38); If I Were King (38, with John B. Goodman); Illegal Traffic (38, with John B. Goodman); Prison Farm (38, with Earl Hedrick); Sing You Sinners (38, with Ernst Fegte); Sons of the Legion (38, with William Flannery); Stolen Heaven (38, with Franz Bachelin); Thanks for the Memory (38, with Franz Bachelin); Arrest Bulldog Drummond (39, with Franz Bachelin); Beau Geste (39, with Robert Odell); Bulldog Drummond's Bride (39, with Franz Bachelin); Cafe Society (39, with Ernst Fegte); The Cat and the Canary (39, with Robert Usher); Disbarred (39, with William Flannery); Disputed Passage (39, with Roland Anderson); Geronimo (39, with Earl

Hedrick); The Gracie Allen Murder Case (39, with Earl Hedrick); Grand Jury Secrets (39, with Franz Bachelin); The Great Victor Herbert (39, with Ernst Fegte); Invitation to Happiness (39, with Ernst Fegte); The Light that Failed (39, with Robert Odell); Man About Town (39, with Robert Usher); Never Say Die (39, with Ernst Fegte); One Thousand Dollars a Touchdown (39, with William Flannery); Our Neighbors, the Carters (39, with Earl Hedrick); Persons in Hiding (39, with William Flannery); Rulers of the Sea (39, with John B. Goodman); Some Like It Hot (39, with Earl Hedrick); Union Pacific (39, with Roland Anderson); Unmarried (39, with Robert Odell); What a Life (39, with Earl Hedrick); Midnight (39, with Robert Usher); The Night of Nights (39); St. Louis Blues (39); Arise My Love (40, with Robert Usher); Victory (40, with Robert Usher); Northwest Mounted Police (40, with Roland Anderson); The Biscuit Eater (40, with Earl Hedrick); Buck Benny Rides Again (40, with Roland Anderson); Christmas in July (40, with Earl Hedrick); Comin' Round the Mountain (40, with Earl Hedrick); Dr. Cyclops (40, with Earl Hedrick); Emergency Squad (40, with Franz Bachelin); The Farmer's Daughter (40, with Franz Bachelin); Golden Gloves (40, with William Flannery); The Great McGinty (40, with Earl Hedrick); I Want a Divorce (40, with Ernst Fegte); Love Thy Neighbor (40, with Roland Anderson); Mystery Sea Rider (40, with Robert Odell); A Night at Earl Carroll's (40, with Robert Odell); Opened by Mistake (40, with Earl Hedrick); Queen of the Mob (40, with Ernst Fegte); Rangers of Fortune (40, with Robert Usher); Remember the Night (40, with Roland Anderson); Road to Singapore (40, with Robert Odell); Safari (40, with Ernst Fegte); Seventeen (40, with Franz Bachelin); Those Were the Days (40, with Robert Usher); Typhoon (40, with John B. Goodman); Untamed (40, with John B. Goodman); Women Without Names (40, with William Flannery); Aloma of the South Seas (41, with William Pereira); Bahama Passage (41); Birth of the Blues (41, with Ernst Fegte); Buy Me That Town (41, with Haldane Douglas); Caught in the Draft (41, with Haldane Douglas); Glamour Boy (41, with Haldane Douglas); Henry Aldrich for President (41, with Franz Bachelin); Hold Back the Dawn (41, with Robert Usher); I Wanted Wings (41, with Robert Usher); Louisiana Purchase (41, with Robert Usher); New York Town (41, with William Pereira); Night of January 16th (41, with Haldane Douglas); Nothing but the Truth (41, with Robert Usher); One Night in Lisbon (41, with Ernst Fegte); The Shepherd of the Hills (41, with Roland Anderson); Skylark (41, with Roland Anderson); There's Magic in Music (41, with Earl Hedrick); Virginia (41, with Ernst Fegte); West Point Widow (41, with Haldane Douglas); Beyond the Blue Horizon (42, with Earl Hedrick); Dr. Broadway (42, with Earl Hedrick); The Forest Rangers (42, with Earl Hedrick); The Glass Key (42, with Haldane Douglas); The Great Man's Lady (42, with Earl Hedrick); Henry Aldrich, Editor (42, with Franz Bachelin); Holiday Inn (42, with Roland Anderson); I Married a Witch (42, with Ernst Fegte); Lucky Jordan (42, with Ernst Fegte); The Major and the Minor (42, with Roland Anderson); Mrs. Wiggs of the Cabbage Patch (42, with William Flannery); My Favorite Blond (42, with Robert Usher); My Heart Belongs to Daddy (42, with Haldane Douglas); A Night in New Orleans (42, with Haldane Douglas); Pacific Blackout (42, with Franz Bachelin); Palm Beach Story (42, with Ernst Fegte); Priorities on Parade (42, with Haldane Douglas); Reap the Wild Wind (42, with Roland Anderson); Road to Morocco (42, with Robert Usher); Star Bangled Rhythm (42, with Ernst Fegte); Street of Chance (42, with Haldane Douglas); Sweater Girl (42, with Haldane Douglas); Take a Letter, Darling (42, with Roland Anderson); This Gun for Hire (42); Wake Island (42, with Earl Hedrick); China (43, with Robert Usher); The Crystal Ball (43, with Roland Anderson); Five Graves to Cairo (43, with Ernst Fegte); For Whom the Bell Tolls (43, with Haldane Douglas, William Cameron Menzies); The Good Fellows (43, with Haldane Douglas); Happy Go Lucky (43, with Raoul Rene Du Bois); Henry Aldrich Gets Glamour (43, with Earl Hedrick); Henry Aldrich Haunts a House (43, with Haldane Douglas); Henry Aldrich Swings It (43, with Franz Bachelin); Hostages (43, with Franz Bachelin); Lady Bodyguard (43, with Haldane Douglas); No Time for Love (43, with Robert Usher); Riding High (43, with Ernst Fegte); Salute for Three (43, with Haldane Douglas); So Proudly We Hail (43, with Earl Hedrick); True to Life (43, with Earl Hedrick); Young and Willing (43, with Ernst Fegte); And Now Tomorrow (44, with Hal Pereira); And the

Angels Sing (44, with Hal Pereira); Double Indemnity (44, with Hal Pereira); Frenchman's Creek (44, with Ernst Fegte); Going My Way (44, with William Flannery); The Great Moment (44, with Ernst Fegte); Hail the Conquering Hero (44, with Haldane Douglas); Henry Aldrich, Boy Scout (44, with Walter Tyler); Henry Aldrich Plays Cupid (44, with Franz Bachelin); Henry Aldrich's Little Secret (44, with Franz Bachelin); Here Come the Waves (44, with Roland Anderson); The Hitler Gang (44, with Franz Bachelin); The Hour Before the Dawn (44, with Earl Hedrick); Lady in the Dark (44); The Man in Half Moon Street (44, with Walter Tyler); Ministry of Fear (44, with Hal Pereira); The Miracle of Morgan's Creek (44, with Ernst Fegte); The National Barn Dance (44, with Walter Tyler); Our Hearts Were Young and Gay (44, with Earl Hedrick); Practically Yours (44, with Robert Usher); Rainbow Island (44, with Haldane Douglas); Standing Room Only (44, with Earl Hedrick); The Story of Dr. Wassell (44, with Roland Anderson); Till We Meet Again (44, with Robert Usher); The Uninvited (44, with Ernst Fegte); You Can't Ration Love (44, with Walter Tyler); The Affairs of Susan (45, with Franz Bachelin); Duffy's Tavern (45, with William Flannery); Hold that Blonde (45, with Walter Tyler); Incendiary Blonde (45, with William Flannery); Kitty (45, with Walter Tyler); The Lost Weekend (45, with Earl Hedrick); Love Letters (45, with Roland Anderson); Masquerade in Mexico (45, with Roland Anderson); A Medal for Benny (45, with Hal Pereira); Miss Susie Slagle's (45, with Earl Hedrick); Murder, He Says (45, with William Flannery); Out of This World (45, with Haldane Douglas); Road to Utopia (45, with Roland Anderson); Salty O'Rourke (45, with Haldane Douglas); The Stork Club (45, with Earl Hedrick); The Unseen (45, with Earl Hedrick); You Came Along (45, with Hal Pereira); The Blue Dahlia (46, with Walter Tyler); The Bride Wore Boots (46, with John Meehan); California (46, with Roland Anderson); Monsieur Beaucaire (46, with Earl Hedrick); O.S.S. (46, with Haldane Doulgas); Our Hearts Were Growing Up (46, with Haldane Douglas); The Searching Wind (46, with Franz Bachelin); The Strange Love of Martha Ivers (46, with John Meehan); To Each His Own (46, with Roland Anderson); Two Years Before the Mast (46, with Franz Bachelin); The Virginian (46, with John Meehan); The Well-Groomed Bride (46, with Earl Hedrick); Suddenly Its Spring (47, with John Meehan); Blaze of Noon (47, with Roland Anderson); Calcutta (47, with Franz Bachelin); Dear Ruth (47, with Earl Hedrick); Easy Come, Easy Go (47, with Haldane Douglas); Golden Earrings (47, with John Meehan); I Walk Alone (47, with Franz Bachelin; The Imperfect Lady (47, with Franz Bachelin); Ladies' Man (47, with Walter Tyler); My Favorite Brunette (47, with Earl Hedrick); The Perils of Pauline (47, with Roland Anderson); The Road to Rio (47, with Earl Hedrick); The Trouble with Women (47, with Earl Hedrick); Unconquered (47, with Walter Tyler); Variety Girl (47, with Robert Clatworthy); Welcome Stranger (47, with Franz Bachelin); Where There's Life (47, with Earl Hedrick); Wild Harvest (47, with Haldane Douglas); Cross My Heart (47); Desert Fury (47); The Perfect Marriage (47); California's Golden Beginning (48); The Accused (48, with Earl Hedrick); Beyond Glory (48, with Franz Bachelin); The Big Clock (48, with Roland Anderson); Dream Girl (48, with John Meehan); The Emperor Waltz (48, with Franz Bachelin); A Foreign Affair (48, with Walter Tyler); Hazard (48, with Robert Clatworthy); Isn't It Romantic (48, with Robert Clatworthy); Miss Tatlock's Millions (48, with Franz Bachelin); My Own True Love (48, with Henry Bumstead); The Night Has a Thousand Eyes (48, with Franz Bachelin); The Paleface (48, with Earl Hedrick); Saigon (48, with Henry Bumstead); The Sainted Sisters (48, with Henry Bumstead); Sealed Verdict (48, with John Meehan); Sorry, Wrong Number (48, with Earl Hedrick); Whispering Smith (48, with Walter Tyler); So Evil My Love (48); Chicago Deadline (49); Captain China (49); Alias Nick Beal (49, wtih Franz Bachelin); Bride of Vengeance (49, with Roland Anderson, Albert Nozaki); A Connecticut Yankee in King Arthur's Court (49, with Roland Anderson); The File on Thelma Jordan (49, with Earl Hedrick); The Great Gatsby (49, with Roland Anderson); The Great Lover (49, with Earl Hedrick); Dear Wife (49, with Earl Hedrick); My Friend Irma (49, with Henry Bumstead); Red, Hot and Blue (49, with Franz Bachelin); Rope of Sand (49, with Franz Bachelin); Samson and Delilah (49, with Walter Tyler); Song of Surrender (49, with Henry Bumstead); Sorrowful Jones (49, with Albert Nozaki); Streets of Laredo (49, with

Henry Bumstead); Top o' the Morning (49, with Henry Bumstead); Dark City (50, with Franz Bachelin); Sunset Boulevard (50, with John Meehan); No Man of Her Own (50, with Henry Bumstead); Riding High (50, with Walter Tyler); Paid in Full (50, with Earl Hedrick); Captain Carey, USA (50, with Roland Anderson); My Friend Irma Goes West (50, with Henry Bumstead); The Furies (50, with Henry Bumstead); Union Station (50, with Earl Hedrick); Copper Canyon (50, with Franz Bachelin); Let's Dance (50, with Roland Anderson); Fancy Pants (50, with Earl Hedrick); Mr. Music (50, with Earl Hedrick); September Affair (50, with Franz Bachelin); Branded (50, with Roland Anderson); Appointment with Danger (51, with Albert Nozaki); A Place in the Sun (51, with Walter Tyler).

Richard Duce

The Good Fellows (43); Main Street After Dark (44); The Cockeyed Miracle (46); Up Goes Maisie (46); The Romance of Rosy Ridge (47).

Frank Durlauf

Deep Valley (47); The Cobra Strikes (48); Canyon City (48); The Spiritualist (48); Hollow Triumph (48); Trapped (49); The Big Cat (49).

George Dudley

Streets of Memories (40, with Richard Day); Rise and Shine (41, with Richard Day).

Randall Duell

My Dear Miss Aldrich (37); I'll Never Forget (37); Women Against Woman (38); Enemy Territory (38); The Chaser (38); White Collars (38); Rich Man, Poor Girl (38); Out West with the Hardys (38); Huckleberry Finn (38); Sergeant Madden (39); Marie Antoinette (38, with Cedric Gibbons, William A. Horning); Emperor's Stallion (39); Florian (40); Ninotchka (39); Secret of Young Dr. Kildare (39); Susan and God (40); Bad Man of Wyoming (40); Come Live with Me (41); The Penalty (41); They Met in Bombay (41); Where Ladies Meet (41); Women of the Year (42); Then There Were Two (41); Kid Glove Killer (42); Along Came Murder (41); Love Me Not (41); Slightly Platonic (41); Her Card-Board Lover (42); Random Harvest (42); Above Suspicion (43); White Cliffs of Dover (44); Mrs. Parkington (44); Anchors Aweigh (45); Postman Always Rings Twice (46); This Time for Keeps (47); Undercurrent (46); Song of the Thin Man (47); Kissing Bandit (48, with Cedric Gibbons); Homecoming (48, with Cedric Gibbons); A Southern Yankee (48, with Cedric Gibbons); Sun in the Morning (48); Doctor on Horseback (48); The Sun Comes Up (48, with Cedric Gibbons); In the Good Old Summertime (49); Intruder in the Dust (49, with Cedric Gibbons); East Side, West Side (49, with Cedric Gibbons); Big Jack (49, with Cedric Gibbons); Asphalt Jungle (50, with Cedric Gibbons); Pagan Love Song (50, with Cedric Gibbons); Excuse My Dust (51, with Cedric Gibbons); Bradley Mason Story (50); Behind the Law (50); Come Again Another Day (51); Rain, Rain Go Away (51); The Unknown Man (51, with Cedric Gibbons); Shadow in the Sky (51, with Cedric Gibbons); Everything I Have Is Yours (52); Singin' in the Rain (52, with Cedric Gibbons); The Girl Who Had Everything (53); All the Brothers Were Valiant (53); The Last Time I Saw Paris (54); The Prodigal (55); Blackboard Jungle (55, with Cedric Gibbons); Trial (54); The Swan (56); 52 Miles to Terror (56); The Little Leaguer (56); 10,000 Bedrooms (56); Silk Stockings (57); Jailhouse Rock (57); Bay the Moon (57); The Tunnel of Love (58); Party Girl (58); The Blessing (58).

Frank Durlauf

Deep Valley (47); The Cobra Strikes (48); Canyon City (58); The Spiritualist (48); Hollow Triumph (48); Trapped (49); The Big Cat (49).

Ferdinand Pinney Earle

Ben Hur (25, with Cedric Gibbons, Arnold Gilespie, Camillo Mastrocinque, Horace Jackson).

Leon Ericksen

Wild Angels (66); Psych-Out (68); The Savage 7 (68); That Cold Day in the Park (69); Futz (69); Medium Cool (69); The Rain People (69); McCabe and Mrs. Miller (71); Images (72); Cinderella Liberty (73); California Split (74); Mahogany (75).

Hobart Erwin

Dinner at Eight (33, with Cedric Gibbons, Frederic Hope); Little Women (33, with Van Nest Polglase).

John Ewing

Paris After Dark (43); They Came to Blow Up America (43); In the Meantime, Darling (46); The Big Noise (46); The Lodger (46); Spellbound (45, with James Basevi, Salvador Dali); Duel in the Sun (47, with James Basevi, Joseph McMillan Johnson, William Cameron Menzies); So Dear to My Heart (48).

Ernst Fegte

Design for Living (33, with Hans Dreier); Death Takes a Holiday (34); Murder at the Vanities (34); Kiss and Make Up (34, with Hans Dreier); Ladies Should Listen (34, with Hand Dreier); We're Not Dressing (34, with Hans Dreier); Paris in the Spring (35, with Hans Dreier); Enter Madam (35, with Hans Dreier); Anything Goes (36, with Hans Dreier); The Princess Comes Across (36, with Hans Dreier); The General Died at Dawn (36, with Hans Dreier); Swing High, Swing Low (37, with Hans Dreier); Easy Living (37, with Hans Dreier); I Met Him in Paris (37, with Hans Dreier); College Swing (38, with Hans Dreier); The Big Broadcast of 1938 (38, with Hans Dreier); Sing, You Sinners (38, with Hans Dreier); You and Me (38, with Hans Dreier); Artists and Models Abroad (38, with Hans Dreier); Cafe Society (39, with Hans Dreier); Invitation to Happiness (39, with Hans Dreier); The Great Victor Herbert (39, with Hans Dreier); Never Say Die (39, with Hans Dreier); I Want a Divorce (40, with Hans Dreier); Queen of the Mob (40, with Hans Dreier); Safari (40, with Hans Dreier); Birth of the Blues (41, with Hans Dreier); The Lady Eve (41); One Night in Lisbon (41, with Hans Dreier); Virginia (41, with Hans Dreier); Lucky Jordan (42, with Hans Dreier); Star Spangled Rhythm (42, with Hans Dreier); I Married a Witch (42, with Hans Dreier); The Palm Beach Story (42, with Hans Dreier); 5 Graves to Cairo (43, with Hans Dreier); Riding High (43, with Hans Dreier); Young and Willing (43, with Hans Dreier); The Great Moment (44, with Hans Dreier); The Miracle of Morgan's Creek (44, with Hans Dreier); The Uninvited (44, with Hans Dreier); Frenchman's Creek (44, with Hans Dreier); The Princess and the Pirate (44); And Then There Were None/10 Little Niggers (45); Wonder Man (45, with McClure Capps); I've Always Loved You (46); Specter of the Rose (46); Mr. Ace (46); Angel and the Badman (47); Christmas Eve (47); An Innocent Affair (48); On Our Merry Way/A Miracle Can Happen (48); The Great Rupert (49); Canadian Pacific (49); Of Men and Music (50); Destination Moon (50); Superman and the Mole Men (51); The Amazing Transparent Man (60); Beyond the Time Barrier (60).

Rudi Feld

(Feld's German films are not listed.) Voice in the Wind (44); Death of a Scoundrel (56); Hellcats of the Navy (57); Twelve to the Moon (60); Summer Storm (44); Bedside Manner (45); The Bachelor's Daughters (46); Whistle Stop (46); Fun on a Weekend (47); New Orleans (47); The Argyle Secret (48); The Vicious Cycle (48); My Dear Secretary (48); Adventures of Gallant Bess (48); Parole, Inc. (48); The Big Wheel (49); Impact (49); Guilty of Treason (50); Pickup (51); Girl on the Bridge (51); Story of a Bad Girl (52); Tender Hearts (53); Turmoil (54); The Big Combo (55); The Naked Hills (56); The Wild Party (56); Hit and Run (57); Lizzie (57); Under Fire (57); From Hell It Came (57); The Abductors (57); Korean Attack (58); Escape from Redrock (58); The Threat (60); Operation Eichmann (61); Terrified (63); The Gun Hawk (63); Paradise Road (69).

Perry Ferguson

A Bill of Divorcement (32); Chance at Heaven (33, with Van Nest Polglase); Laddies (35, wtih Van Nest Polglase); The Nitwits (35, with Van Nest Polglase); Alice Adams (35, with Van Nest Polglase); Annie Oakley (35, with Van Nest Polglase); Hooray for Love (35); A Woman Rebels (36, with Van Nest Polglase); Winterset (37, with Van Nest Polglase); Having a Wonderful Time (38, with Van Nest Polglase); Bringing Up Baby (38, with Van Nest Polglase); In Name Only (39, with Van Nest Polglase); Fifth Avenue Girl (39, with Van Nest Polglase); The Story of Vernon and Irene Castle (39, with Van Nest Polglase); Gunga Din (39, with Van Nest Polglase); Citizen Kane (41, with Van Nest Polglase, Hilyard Brown); Ball of Fire (42); The Pride of the Yankees (42, with William Cameron Menzies, McClure Capps); The North Star (43, with William Cameron Menzies); The Outlaw (43); The Best Years of Our Lives (46, with George Jenkins); Up in Arms (44); Belle of the Yukon (44); Casanova Brown (44); Song of the South (46); The Stranger (46); The Kid from Brooklyn (46, with Stewart Chaney); The Secret Life of Walter Mitty (47, with George Jenkins); The Bishop's Wife (47, with George Jenkins); Desert Fury (47); A Song Is Born (48, with George Jenkins); Rope (48); Without Honor (49); 711 Ocean Drive (50); The Sound of Fury / Try and Get Me (51); The Groom Wore Spurs (51); Queen for a Day (51); The Lady Says No (51); The Big Sky (52); Ready for the People (64).

William Ferrari

Assignment in Brittany (43); Dr. Gillespie's Criminal Case (43); The Heavenly Body (43); Barbary Coast Gent (43); The Clock (45); The Harvey Girls (46); Ziegfeld Follies (46, with Cedric Gibbons, Jack Martin Smith, Merrill Pye); Fiesta (47); Living in a Big Way (47); Sleep, My Love (48); Inner Sanctum (48); Adam's Rib (49, with Cedric Gibbons); The Reformer & the Redhead (50, with Cedric Gibbons); Dial 1119 (50, with Cedric Gibbons); It's a Big Country (51, with Cedric Gibbons); Kind Lady (51, with Cedric Gibbons); Texas Carnival (51, with Cedric Gibbons); Three Guys Named Mike (51, with Cedric Gibbons); The Time Machine (60, with George W. Davis); How the West Was Won (62, with George W. Davis, Addison Hehr); Gaslight (44, with Cedric Gibbons).

William Flannery

Campus Confessions (38, with Hans Dreier); Sons of the Legion (38, with Hans Dreier); Disbarred (39, with Hans Dreier); One Thousand Dollars a Touchdown (39, with Hans Dreier); Person in Hiding (39, with Hans Dreier); Golden Gloves (40, with Hans Dreier); Women Without Names (40, with Hans Dreier); Mrs. Wiggs of the Cabbage Patch (42, with Hans Dreier); Dixie (43); Going My Way (44, with Hans Dreier); Duffy's Tavern (45, with Hans Dreier); Incendiary Blonde (45, with Hans Dreier); Murder, He Says (45, with Hans Dreier); Sister Kenny (46); Abie's Irish Rose (46); Arch of Triumph (48); The Velvet Touch (48, p.d.); The Capture (50, p.d.); The Sun Sets at Dawn (50); Valentino (51).

Stanley Fleischer

Adventures in Iraq (43); Murder on the Waterfront (43); Make Your Own Bed (44); Christmas in Connecticut (45); Danger Signal (45); Too Young to Know (45); Beast with Five Fingers (47); Love and Learn (47); The Man I Love (47); Stallion Road (47); That Hagen Girl (47); The Woman in White (48); Smart Girls Don't Talk (48); A Kiss in the Dark (49); It's a Great Feeling (49); The Girl from Jones Beach (49); Rocky Mountain (50); Breakthrough (50); Barricade (50); Bright Leaf (50); Perfect Strangers (50); The Great Jewel Robber (50); Goodbye, My Fancy (51); Sugarfoot (51); Fort Worth (51).

J. Boone Fleming

Sorrell and Son (27, with William Cameron Menzies); Hell's Angels (30, with Carroll Clark).

Park French

The Thief of Bagdad (24, with William Cameron Menzies, Anton Grot, Irvin J. Martin); Abraham Lincoln (30, with William Cameron Menzies); The Bad One (30, with William Cameron Menzies); Be Yourself (30, with William Cameron Menzies); Dubarry, Woman of Passion (30, with William Cameron Menzies); The Lottery Bride (30, with William Cameron Menzies); Lummox (30, with William Cameron Menzies); One Romantic Night (30, with William Cameron Menzies); Puttin' on the Ritz (30, with William Cameron Menzies); Raffles (30, with William Cameron Menzies.

Leland Fuller

Heaven Can Wait (43, with James Basevi); Laura (44, with Lyle Wheeler); Where Do We Go from Here? (45); Fallen Angel (45); Centennial Summer (46); The Dark Corner (46); The Fan (49); Whirlpool (49); Three Came Home (50, with Lyle Wheeler); Fourteen Hours (51, with Lyle Wheeler); On the Riviera (51, with Lyle Wheeler); Viva Zapata (52, with Lyle Wheeler); The President's Lady (53, with Lyle Wheeler); Desiree (54, with Lyle Wheeler); Hell and High Water (54); Will Success Spoil Rock Hunter? (57).

Fred Gabourie

Our Hospitality (23); Three Ages (23); The Navigator (24); The Sea Hawk (24, designed and executed ships); Sherlock, Jr. (24); 7 Chances (25); Wild Justice (25); The General (26); College (27); The Cameraman (28); Steamboat Bill, Jr. (28).

Cedric Gibbons

(Gibbons' contract at MGM (1924–56) called for his name, as supervising art director, to appear on all films produced by the company in the U.S.A. He played a prominent part in the design of many of them. What follows is a partial list of the over 1000 films on which he received credit.) Thäis (17); The World and Its Women (19); The Woman and the Puppet (20); The Return of Tarzan (20); Madame X (20); Doubling for Romeo (21); The Christian (23); The Green Goddess (23); He Who Gets Slapped (24); His Hour (24); Ben Hur (25, with Camillo Mastrocinque, Arnold Gillespie, Horace Jackson, Ferdinand Pinney Earle); The Big Parade (25, with James Basevi); The Masked Bride (25, with Ben Carré); The Merry Widow (25, with Richard Day); Bright Lights (25, with Richard Day); The Only Thing (25, with Richard Day); His Secretary (25, with Richard Day); La Boheme (26, with Ben Carré, Arnold Gillespie); The Boob (26, with Ben Carré); Beverly of Graustark (26, with Richard Day); Bardeleys, the Magnificent (26, with Richard Day, James Basevi); The Student Prince (27, with Hans Dreier, Fred Hope, Richard Day; Anna Karenina (27, with Alexander

Toluboff); Love (27, with Alexander Toluboff); Mr. Wu (27, with Richard Day, Merrill Pye); Student Prince (27, with Hans Dreier, Frederick Hope, Richard Day); Tillie the Toiler (27, with Richard Day, David Townsend); Tea for Three (27, with Richard Day); Our Dancing Daughters (28, with Richard Day); The Crowd (28, with Arnold Gillespie); The Divine Woman (28, with Richard Day, Arnold Gillespie); The Wickedness Preferred (28, with Richard Day); The Patsy (28); The Big City (28, with Richard Day); Circus Rookies (28, with Richard Day); Laugh, Clown, Laugh (28, with Richard Day); The Actress (28, with Richard Day); Forbidden Hours (28, with Richard Day); Excess Baggage (28, with Richard Day); While the City Sleeps (29, with Richard Day); The Masks of the Day (28, with Richard Day); West of Zanzibar (28, with Richard Day); The Idle Rich (29, with Richard Day); The Kiss (29, with Richard Day); Dynamite (29, with Mitchell Leisen, Eddie Imazu); The Hollywood Revue of 1929, with Richard Day); Our Modern Maidens (29, with Merrill Pye); The Bridge of San Luis Rey (29, with Richard Day); A Man's Man (29, with Richard Day); Wonder of Women (29, with Richard Day); The Girl in the Show (29, with Richard Day); The Unholy Night (29, with Richard Day); Wise Girls / Kempy (29, with Richard Day); The Thirteenth Chair (29, with Richard Day); Their Own Desire (29, with Richard Day, Harry Sharrock); Untamed (29, with Richard Day, Van Nest Polglase); Hallelujah (29); The Sea Bat (30); Anna Christie (30, with Richard Day); In Gay Madrid (30, with Richard Day); Madame Satan (30, with Richard Day); Le Spectre Vert (30, with Richard Day); The Big House (30, with Frederic Hope); Our Blushing Brides (30, with Merrill Pye); Susan Lenox—Her Fall and Rise (31); Freaks (32, with Merrill Pye); Grand Hotel (32, with Alexander Toluboff); Kong (32); Dinner at Eight (33, with Fred Hope, Hobart Erwin); Gabriel Over the White House (33); Queen Christina (33, with Alexander Golitzen, Alexander Toluboff, Edwin B. Willis); Sailor's Luck (33); The Merry Widow (34, with Frederic Hope, Gabriel Scognamillo); Men in White (34); Anna Karenina (34, with Frederic Hope, Edwin B. Willis); David Copperfield (34, with Merrill Pye); Tarzan and His Mate (34, co-directed); Mad Love (35, with William Horning); Reckless (35, with Merrill Pye); Public Hero (35, with Lionel Banks); One New York Night (35, with Lionel Banks); A Night at the Opera (35, with Ben Carré); Mutiny on the Bounty (35, wtih Arnold Gillespie); Born to Dance (36); The Great Ziegfeld (36, with Merrill Pye, John Harkrider); Romeo and Juliet (36, with Oliver Messel, Fred Hope); San Francisco (36, with James Basevi, Harry McAfee, Arnold Gillespie); Fury (36, with William Horning); The Gorgeous Hussy (36); Camille (36, with Frederick Hope); Maytime (37, with Frederic Hope, Edwin B. Willis); Madame X (37, with Urie McCleary); Conquest (37, with William Horning); Captains Courageous (37, with Arnold Gillespie, Edwin B. Willis); History Is Made at Night (37, with James Basevi); Marie Antoinette (38, with William Horning, Randall Duell); The Good Earth (37, with Harry Oliver, Arnold Gillespie, Edwin B. Willis); The Girl of the Golden West (38); The Wizard of Oz (39, with William A. Horning, Jack Martin Smith, Arnold Gillespie); Pride and Prejudice (40, with Paul Groesse); Blossoms in the Dust (41, with Urie McCleary); Girl Crazy (43); Madame Cane (43, with Paul Grosse); Lassie Come Home (43, with Paul Grosse); Gaslight (44, with William Ferrari); Meet Me in Saint Louis (44, with Lemuel Ayers, Jack Martin Smith); Thirty Seconds Over Tokyo (44, with Paul Groesse, Arnold Gillespie); National Velvet (44, with Urie McCleary); The Valley of Decision (45, with Paul Groesse); The Ziegfeld Follies (46, with Jack Martin Smith, Merrill Pye, William Ferrari); Adventure (46, with Urie McCleary); The Green Years (46, with Hans Peters); Easy to Wed (46, with Hans Peters); The Yearling (46, with Paul Groesse); The Beginning of the End (47); The Arnelo Affair (47); Cass Timberlane (47, with Daniel B. Cathcart); Cynthia (47); Dark Delusion (47); Desire Me (47); Fiesta (47); Good News (47); Green Dolphin Street (47, with Malcolm Brown); High Barbaree (47); High Wall (47); The Hucksters (47); If Winter Comes (47); It Happened in Brooklyn (47); Killer McCoy (47); Lady in the Lake (47); Living in a Big Way (47); Merton of the Movies (47); My Brother Talks to Horses (47); The Romance of Rosy Ridge (47); Sea of Grass (47, with Paul Groesse); Song of Love (47); Song of the Thin Man (47); This Time for Keeps (47); Undercover Maisie (47); Unfinished Dance (47, with Daniel B. Cathcart); Act of Violence (48); Alias a Gentleman (48); The Bride Goes Wild (48); B.F.'s Daughter

(48, with Daniel Cathcart); The Big City (48); A Date with Judy (48); Easter Parade (48); Homecoming (48, with Randall Duell); Hills of Home (48); Julia Misbehaves (48, with Daniel B. Cathcart); The Kissing Bandit (48, with Randall Duell); Luxury Line (48, with Paul Groesse); No Minor Vices (48); On an Island with You (48); The Pirate (48); The Secret Land (48); The Search (48); Summer Holiday (48); The Sun Comes Up (48, with Randall Duell); The Three Musketeers (48, with Malcolm Brown); Command Decisions (48, with Urie McCleary); A Southern Yankee (48, with Randall Duell); State of the Union (48); Three Daring Daughters (48); Tenth Avenue Angel (48); Words and Music (48); Take Me Out to the Ball Game (49, with Daniel B. Cathcart); The Stratton Story (49, with Paul Groesse); The Secret Garden (49); Scene of the Crime (49); Neptune's Daughter (49); Madame Bovary (49); The Great Sinner (49); The Bribe (49, with Malcolm Brown); Big Jack (49, with Randall Duell); Any Number Can Play (49); Intruder in the Dust (49, with Randall Duell); That Midnight Kiss (49); Battleground (49, with Hans Peters); The Red Danube (49); Border Incident (49); The Doctor and the Girl (49); Side Street (49, with Daniel B. Cathcart); East Side, West Side (49, with Randall Duell); Ambush (49, with Malcolm Brown); On the Town (49); Malaya (49, with Malcolm Brown); Little Women (49, with Paul Groesse); Adam's Rib (49, with William Ferrari); That Forsyte Woman (49, with Daniel B. Cathcart); Challenge to Lassie (49, with Edward Imazu); Tension (49); The Yellow Cab Man (50, with Edward Imazu); Stars in My Crown (50); Summer Stock (50); The Skipper Surprised His Wife (50); Shadow on the Wall (50); The Reformer and the Redhead (50, with William Ferrari); Please Believe Me (50); The Outriders (50); The Next Voice You Hear (50); Devil's Doorway (50); Duchess of Idaho (50, with Malcolm Brown); A Life of Her Own (50); The Happy Years (50); A Lady Without a Passport (50, with Edward Carfagno); Key to the City (50); Nancy Goes to Rio (50); Mystery Street (50); The Asphalt Jungle (50, with Randall Duell); Father of the Bride (50); The Big Hangover (50, with Paul Groesse); Black Hand (50); Mrs. O'Malley and Mr. Malone (50, with Daniel B. Cathcart); Grounds for Marriage (50, with Paul Groesse); The Magnificent Yankee (50); Watch the Birdie (50); Pagan Love Song (50, with Randall Duell); Two Weeks with Love (50); To Please a Lady (50); Right Cross (50); The Toast of New Orleans (50, with Daniel B. Cathcart); Dial 1119 (50, with William Ferrari); Annie Get Your Gun (50, with Paul Groesse); King Solomon's Mines (50, with Paul Groesse); Three Little Words (50, with Urie McCleary); Kim (50, with Hans Peters); Across the Wide Missouri (51); Angels in the Outfield (51); Bannerline (51); Callaway Went Thataway (51, with Edward Imazu); Cause for Alarm (51); Excuse My Dust (51, with Randall Duell); The Red Badge of Courage (51, with Hans Peters); An American in Paris (51, with Preston Ames, Jack Martin Smith, Irene Sharaff); Showboat (51); Quo Vadis (51, with William A. Horning, Edward Carfagno); Father's Little Dividend (51); Go for Broke (51); The Great Caruso (51); Inside Straight (51); It's a Big Country (51, with William Ferrari, Malcolm Brown, Edward Imazu, Arthur Lonergan); Kind Lady (51, with William Ferrari); The Law and the Lady (51, with Daniel B. Cathcart); The Light Touch (51); Lone Star (51); The Man with a Cloak (51); Mr. Imperium (51); Night Into Morning (51); No Questions Asked (51); The Painted Hills (51); The People Against O'Hara (51); Rich, Young, and Pretty (51); The Sellout (51); Shadow in the Sky (51, with Randall Duell); Soldiers Three (51, with Malcolm Brown); Strictly Dishonorable (51); The Strip (51); The Tall Target (51); Texas Carnival (51, with William Ferrari); Three Guys Named Mike (51, with William Ferrari); Too Young to Kiss (51); The Unknown Man (51, with Randall Duell); Vengeance Valley (51, with Malcolm Brown); Westward the Women (51); Royal Wedding (51); Singin' in the Rain (52, with Randall Duell); Pat and Mike (52, with Urie McCleary); The Bad and the Beautiful (52, with Edward Carfagno); Julius Caesar (53, with Edward Carfagno); The Band Wagon (53, with Preston Ames, Oliver Smith); Lili (53, with Paul Groesse); Brigadoon (54, with Preston Ames); Kismet (55, with Preston Ames, Daniel Cathcart); Jupiter's Darling (55, with Urie McCleary); The Blackboard Jungle (55, with Randall Duell); Somebody Up There Likes Me (56, with Malcolm F. Brown); Lust for Life (56, with Preston Ames, Hans Peters); Forbidden Planet (56, with Arnold Gillespie, Arthur Lonergan); The Catered Affair (56, with Paul Groesse); High Society (56, with Hans Peters).

344   Filmographies—Gillespie

A. Arnold (Buddy) Gillespie

Manslaughter (22); Ben Hur (25, with Cedric Gibbons, Camillo Mastrocinque, Horace Jackson, Ferdinand Pinney Earle); The Road to Mandalay (26); La Boheme (26, with Ben Carré, Cedric Gibbons); The Black Bird (26); Upstage (26); London After Midnight (27); The Divine Woman (28, with Richard Day, Cedric Gibbons); The Crowd (28, with Cedric Gibbons); Eskimo (33); Tarzan and His Mate (34); Mutiny on the Bounty (35), with Cedric Gibbons); San Francisco (36, special effects, with Cedric Gibbons, Harry McAfee, James Basevi); Captains Courageous (37, with Cedric Gibbons, Edwin B. Willis); The Good Earth (37, with Harry Oliver, Cedric Gibons, Edwin B. Willis); The Wizard of Oz (39, special effects, with Cedric Gibbons, William A. Horning, Jack Martin Smith); Thirty Seconds Over Tokyo (44, special effects, with Cedric Gibbons, Paul Groesse); Forbidden Planet (56, special effects, with Cedric Gibbons, Arthur Lonergan); Ben Hur (59, special effects, with William A. Horning, Edward Carfagno); Mutiny on the Bounty (62, special effects, with George W. Davis, J. McMillan Johnson).

Harvey T. Gillett

The Devil's Playground (46); Fool's Gold (46); Unexpected Guest (46); Dangerous Venture (47); Hoppy's Holiday (47); A Double Life (47); Riders of the Lone Star (47); Buckaroo from Powder River (48).

William Glasgow

Shoot to Kill (47); The Case of the Baby Sitter (47); The Hatbox Mystery (47); World for Ransom (54); Bait (54); Kiss Me Deadly (55); The Big Knife (55); Autumn Leaves (56); Attack (56); Timbuktu (58); The 4 Skulls of Jonathan Drake (59); What Ever Happened to Baby Jane? (62); The Black Zoo (63); 4 for Texas (63); Hush, Hush, Sweet Charlotte (64); The Flight of the Phoenix (65); A Guide for the Married Man (67); The Legend of Lylah Clare (68); The Killing of Sister George (68); Whatever Happened to Aunt Alice? (69); Tick..Tick..Tick (70).

Alexander Golitzen

Queen Christina (33, with Alexander Tolubuff, Edwin B. Willis, Cedric Gibbons); The Call of the Wild (35); The Hurricane (37, with James Basevi, Richard Day); Stagecoach (39, scouted locations); Wuthering Heights (39, with Jams Basevi); Foreign Correspondent (40, with William Cameron Menzies, Richard Irvine, Edmond Bernoudy); Sundown (41); That Uncertain Feeling (41); Eagle Squadron (42); Arabian Nights (42); The Phantom of the Opera (43, with John B. Goodman); Gung Ho! (43); We've Never Been Licked (43); The Climax (44); Cobra Woman (44); San Diego, I Love You (44); Ladies Courageous (44); Hi, Beautiful (44); Scarlet Street (45); Salome, Where She Danced (45); The Magnificent Doll (46); Night in Paradise (46); Something in the Wind (47); Smash Up (47); The Story of a Woman (47); The Lost Moment (47); Tap Roots (48); You Gotta Stay Happy (48, p.d.); Letter from an Unknown Woman (48); The Saxon Charm (48); The Lady Gambles (49); Sword in the Desert (49, with Bernard Herzbrun); Bagdad (49); Spy Hunt (50, with Bernard Herzbrun); Double Crossbones (50, with Bernard Herzbrun); Frenchie (50, with Bernard Herzbrun); The Golden Horde (51, with Bernard Herzbrun); Smuggler's Island (51, with Bernard Herzbrun); You Never Can Tell (51, with Bernard Herzbrun); Up Front (51, with Bernard Herzbrun); The World in His Arms (52); Treasure of Lost Canyon (52); Duel at Silver Creek (52); Against All Flags (52); It Grows on Trees (52); Brady's Bunch (53); All I Desire (53); Glenn Miller Story (54); This Island Earth (55, with Richard Riedel); The Far Country (55, with Bernard Herzbrun); Written on the Wind (56, with Robert Clatworthy);

Tarnished Angels (57); Touch of Evil (58, with Robert Clatworthy); Perfect Furlough (58); Night Watch (58); Saddle Tramp (58); One Step Beyond (58); The Green Peacock (58); Monster in the Night (58); Step Down to Terror (58); [Playhouse 90 TV 1958]; Imitation of Life (59); Spartacus (60, with Eric Orbom); Tammy Tell Me True (61); Flower Drum Song (61, with Joseph Wright); Back Street (61); If a Man Answers (62); The Ugly American (63); To Kill a Mockingbird (63, with Henry Bumstead); Father Goose (64); The War Lord (65, with Henry Bumstead); Thoroughly Modern Millie (67, with George Webb); Coogan's Bluff (68); The Forbin Project (70); Slaughter House 5 (72, with Henry Bumstead); Earthquake (74, with Preston Ames).

John B. Goodman

It's a Gift (34, with Hans Dreier); Girl of the Ozarks (36, with Hans Dreier); Wells Fargo (37, with Hans Dreier); High Wide and Handsome (37, with Hans Dreier); Mountain Music (37, with Hans Dreier); If I Were King (38, with Hans Dreier); Illegal Traffic (38, with Hans Dreier); Rulers of the Sea (39, with Hans Dreier); Typhoon (40, with Hans Dreier); Untamed (40, with Hans Dreier); Frankenstein Meets the Wolf Man (43); Flesh and Fantasy (43); Shadow of a Doubt (43); The Phantom of the Opera (43, with Alexander Golitzen); The Climax (44); Cobra Woman (44); The Frozen Ghost (45); Good Sam (48); The Great Missouri Raid (50); The Sundowners (50); High Lonesome (50); Flaming Feather (51); Warpath (51); Flight to Tangier (53, with Hal Pereira); The Trouble with Harry (55); The Mountain (56).

Stephen Goosson

Little Lord Fauntleroy (21); Oliver Twist (22); The Hunchback of Notre Dame (23, with E.E. Sheeley, Charles D. Hall); The Sea Hawk (24); The Patent Leather Kid (27); The Wreck of the Hesperus (27); Skyscraper (28); Wild Company (30); Just Imagine (30); Movietone Follies of 1930 (30); American Madness (32); One Night of Love (34); It Happened One Night (34); Crime and Punishment (35); The Black Room (35); The King Steps Out (36); Pennies from Heaven (36); Lost Horizon (37); The Awful Truth (37, with Lionel Banks); Murder in Greenwich Village (37, with Lionel Banks); There's Always a Woman (38, with Lionel Banks); You Can't Take It with You (38, with Lionel Banks); Girls' School (38, with Lionel Banks); The Little Foxes (41); Cry Havoc (43); Swing Fever (43); Bathing Beauty (44); See Here, Private Hargrove (44); Together Again (44, with Van Nest Polglase); Kiss and Tell (45, with Van Nest Polglase); She Wouldn't Say Yes (45, with Van Nest Polglase); Tonight and Every Night (45); Thrill of Brazil (46, with Van Nest Polglase); Gilda (46, with Van Nest Polglase); The Jolson Story (46); Dead Reckoning (47); The Lady from Shanghai (48, with Sturges Carne).

Chester Gore

Girl from Avenue A (40, with Richard Day); The Gay Caballero (40, with Richard Day); The Last of the Duanes (41, with Richard Day); The Lone Star Ranger (42, with Richard Day); Through Different Eyes (42, with Richard Day); Just Off Broadway (42, with Richard Day); Time to Kill (42, with Richard Day); The Dancing Masters (43); Jitterbugs (43); My Friend Flicka (43, with Richard Day); Home in Indiana (44); The Bullfighters (45); Thunderhead—Son of Flicka (45, with Lyle Wheeler); It Shouldn't Happen to a Dog (46); Johnny Comes Flying Home (46); Smokey (46); Boomerang (47, with Richard Day, James Basevi); Street with No Name (48); Father Was a Fullback (49); Thieves' Highway (49); Sand (49); When Willie Comes Marching Home (50, with Lyle Wheeler); Two Flags West (50); The Guy Who Came Back (51).

Feild Gray

Ladies' Day (43); Lady Luck (46); The Farmer's Daughter (47); A Likely Story (47); Guns of Hate (48); Indian Agent (48); Gun Smugglers (48); Station West (48); Bodyguard (48); Rustlers (49); The Judge Steps Out (49); Brothers in the Saddle (49); Stagecoach Kid (49); Make Mine Laughs (49); Riders of the Rangers (49); The Mysterious Desperado (49); Masked Raiders (49); Storm Over Wyoming (50); Rio Grande Patrol (50); Law of the Badlands (50); Jet Pilot (50, with Albert D'Agostino); Hot Lead (51); Overland Telegraph (51); Double Dynamite (51); Gunplay (51); Pistol Harvest (51).

Victor Greene

Is Everybody Happy (43); Swing Out the Blues (43); The Return of the Vampire (44); Beautiful but Broke (44); Sailor's Holiday (44); Paris — Underground (45); The Red Pony (49); Military Academy with That 10th Avenue Gang (50); Rookie Fireman (50); Beauty on Parade (50); Counterspy Meets Scotland Yard (50); The Tougher They Come (50); Al Jennings of Oklahoma (51); China Corsair (51); Never Trust a Gambler (51); Smuggler's Gold (51); Gasoline Alley (51).

Harold W. Grieve

Prisoner of Zenda (22); Dorothy Vernon of Haddon Hall (24, with Anton Grot); Lady Windermere's Fan (25); So This Is Paris (26); Ben Hur (25, research and costume design).

Paul Groesse

The Firefly (37); The Great Waltz (38); Pride and Prejudice (40, with Cedric Gibbons); Madame Cane (43, with Cedric Gibbons); Lassie Come Home (43, with Cedric Gibbons); The Human Comedy (43); Madame Curie (43); Two Girls and a Sailor (44); Thirty Seconds Over Tokyo (44, with Cedric Gibbons, Arnold Gillespie); The Valley of Decision (45, with Cedric Gibbons); The Yearling (46, with Cedric Gibbons); Sea of Grass (47, with Cedric Gibbons); Luxury Liner (48, with Cedric Gibbons); A Date with Judy (48); The Stratton Story (49, with Cedric Gibbons); Little Women (49, with Cedric Gibbons); Annie Get Your Gun (50, with Cedric Gibbons); King Solomon's Mines (50, with Cedric Gibbons, Conrad Nerrig); The Big Hangover (50, with Cedric Gibbons); Grounds for Marriage (50, with Cedric Gibbons); Mr. Imperium (51); No Questions Asked (51); The Merry Widow (52); Lili (53, with Cedric Gibbons); The Catered Affair (56, with Cedric Gibbons); Flesh and the Devil (59, with William A. Horning); Bye, Bye Birdie (63).

Abraham Grossman

Hi'Ya Sailor (43); Moonlight in Vermont (43); Babes on Swing Street (44); Destiny (44); Enter Arsene Lupin (44); Jungle Woman (44); Marshall of Gunsmoke (44); Moon Over Las Vegas (44); The Mummy's Ghost (44); My Gal Loves Music (44); The Singing Sheriff (44); Slightly Terrific (44); Swingtime Johnny (44); Twilight on the Prairie (44); The Beautiful Cheat (45); Blonde Ransom (45); The Crimson Canary (45); The Frozen Ghost (45); Honeymoon Ahead (45); I'll Tell the World (45); I'll Remember April (45); Pillow of Death (45); River Gang (45); Senorita from the West (45); Strange Confession (45); Bad Men of the Border (46); The Brute Man (46); The Cat Creeps (46); Cuban Pete (46); Girl on the Spot (46); Gun Town (46); House of Horrors (46); Inside Job (46); Little Miss Big (46); She-Wolf of London (46); The Spider Woman Strikes Back (46); Terror by Night (46); Wild Beauty (46); Trail to Vengeance (46); Slave Girl (47); Michigan Kid (47).

Anton Grot

The Mouse and the Lion (13); Arms and the Woman (16); The Seven Pearls (17); The Iron Heart (17); The Recoil (17); Sylvia of the Secret Service (18); The Naulahka (18, with William Cameron Menzies); Bound and Gagged (19); Velvet Fingers (20); Pirate Gold (20); Tess of the Storm Country (22, with Frank Ormstrom); Robin Hood (22, with Wilfred Buckland, William Cameron Menzies, Irvin J. Martin, Edward M. Langley); The Thief of Bagdad (24, with William Cameron Menzies, Park French, Irvin J. Martin); Dorothy Vernon of Haddon Hall (24); Don Q, Son of Zorro (25, with Edward M. Langley, Harry Oliver, Harold Miles); The Road to Yesterday (25, with Paul Iribe, Mitchell Leisen, Max Parker); A Thief in Paradise (25); The Volga Boatman (26, with Mitchell Leisen, Max Parker); Young April (26); The King of Kings (27, with Mitchell Leisen, Paul Iribe, Ben Carré, Edward Jewell); The Country Doctor (27); The Little Adventuress (27); Vanity (27); White Gold (27); The Blue Danube (28); Hold 'em Yale (28); A Ship Comes In (28); Stand and Deliver (28); Walking Back (28); Yellow Lily (28, with Max Parker); The Barker (28); Show Girl (28); The Godless Girl (29, with Mitchell Leisen); Smiling Irish Eyes (29); Noah's Ark (29); Why Be Good? (29); Footlights and Fools (29); The Man and the Moment (29); Lilies of the Field (30); Her Private Life (30); Song of the Flame (30); Playing Around (30); A Notorious Affair (30); Bright Lights (30); No, No, Nanette (30); Outward Bound (30); Top Speed (30); Svengali (31); Surrender (31); Body and Soul (31); Little Caesar (31); The Mad Genius (31); Heartbreak (31); Alias the Doctor (32); Doctor X (32); Two Seconds (32); Big City Blues (32); The Crowd Roars (32, with Jack Okey); The Hatchet Man (32); Scarlet Dawn (32); Footlight Parade (33, with Jack Okey); Ever in My Heart (33); Son of a Sailor (33); From Headquarters (33); The King's Vacation (33); The Mystery of the Wax Museum (33); Twenty Thousand Years in Sing Sing (33); Lawyer Man (33); Grand Slam (33); Gold Diggers of 1933 (33); Mandalay (34); British Agent (34); The Firebird (34); Easy to Love (34); Gambling Lady (34); Upperworld (34); Side Streets (34); He Was Her Man (34); Dr. Monica (34); Six Day Bike Rider (34); The Secret Bride (34); Gold Diggers of 1935 (35, with Hugh Reticker); Travelling Saleslady (35, with Arthur Gruenburger); Stranded (35, with Arthur Gruenburger); Broadway Gondolier (35); Bright Lights (35); Dr. Socrates (35); Captain Blood (35); White Angel (35); The Case of the Curious Bride (35, with Carl Jules Weyl); A Midsummer Night's Dream (35); Anthony Adverse (36); Stolen Holiday (36); Confession (37); The Life of Emile Zola (37); Tovarich (37); The Great Garrick (37); Fools for Scandal (38); Hard to Get (38); Juarez (39, with Leo Kuter); The Private Lives of Elizabeth and Essex (39); The Sea Hawk (40); A Dispatch from Reuter's (40); Affectionately Yours (41); The Sea Wolf (41); Thank Your Lucky Stars (43, with Leo Kuter); The Conspirators (44); Rhapsody in Blue (45, with John Hughes); Mildred Pierce (45); Deception (46); My Reputation (46); Never Say Goodbye (46); One More Tomorrow (46); The Unsuspected (47); Possessed (47); The Two Mrs. Carrolls (47); Nora Prentiss (47); June Bride (48); Romance on the High Seas (48); One Sunday Afternoon (48, with Fred M. McLean); Backfire (50).

Arthur Gruenberger

Traveling Saleslady (35, with Anton Grot); Stranded (35, with Anton Grot).

Robert Haas

Sentimental Tommy (21); Fury (22); White Sister (23); Romola (24); Sackcloth and Scarlet (25); She Goes to War (29); Hell Harbor (30); Merely Mary Ann (31); Three on a Match (32); Bureau of Missing Persons (33); Lady Killer (33); The Key (34); A Modern Hero (34); Page Miss Glory (35); The Story of Louis Pasteur (36); Black Legion (37); They Won't Forget (37); The Prince and the Pauper (37); Jezebel (38); Angels with Dirty Faces (38); Dark Victory (39); The Old Maid (39); City for Conquest (40); The Maltese Falcon (41); Strawberry

Blonde (41); In This Our Life (42); Now, Voyager (42); Edge of Darkness (43); Uncertain Glory (44); Janie (44); Mr. Skeffington (44); Roughly Speaking (45); Janie Gets Married (46); Devotion (46); A Stolen Life (46); Life with Father (47); The Voice of the Turtle (47); My Girl Tisa (48); Johnny Belinda (48); My Dream Is Yours (49); John Loves Mary (49); Always Leave Them Laughing (49); Beyond the Forest (49); Inspector General (49); The Glass Menagerie (50); The Damned Don't Cry (50).

Charles D. (Danny) Hall

Smiling All the Way (21); The Lying Truth (22); Bag and Baggage (23); The Hunchback of Notre Dame (23, with Stephen Goosson); The Gold Rush (25); The Phantom of the Opera (25, with Ben Carré, E.E. Sheeley, Sidney Ullman); The Cohens and the Kellys (26); A Woman of the Sea/The Sea Gull (26); The Cat and the Canary (27, with Paul Leni); Uncle Tom's Cabin (27); The Man Who Laughs (28, with Joseph Wright); The Circus (28); Broadway (29); The Chinese Parrot (29); Hot for Paris (29, with Ben Carré); The Kid's Clever (29); The Last Warning (29); See America Thirst (30); All Quiet on the Western Front (30, with William R. Schmidt); Woman for All Nations (31, with Ben Carré); City Lights (31); Frankenstein (31, with Herman Rosse); Dracula (31); The Old Dark House (32); Back Street (32); By Candlelight (33); The Invisible Man (33); Little Man, What Now? (33); Don't Bet on Love (33); The Black Cat (34); Remember Last Night (35); The Magnificent Obsession (35); Diamond Jim (35); The Good Fairy (35); The Bride of Frankenstein (35); Show Boat (36); Modern Times (36, with Russell Spencer); My Man Godfrey (36); The Road Back (37); Swiss Miss (38); Merrily We Live (38); There Goes My Heart (38); Captain Fury (39); The House Keeper's Daughter (39); Zenobia (39); Captain Caution (40, with Nicolai Remisoff); One Million B.C. (40); Saps at Sea (40); A Chump at Oxford (40); All-American Co-ed (41); Miss Polly (41); Niagara Falls (41); Road Show (41); Tanks a Million (41); About Face (42); Brooklyn Orchard (42); Dudes Are Pretty People (42); Fiesta (42); Hay Foot (42); Calaboose (43); Prairie Chickens (43); Fall In (43); The Devil with Hitler (43); The McGuerins from Brooklyn (43); Yanks Ahoy (43); Taxi, Mister? (43); That Nazty Nuisance (43); Not Wanted (49); The Vicious Years (50); The Flying Saucer (50); Two Lost Worlds (50); Red Planet Mars (42); Japanese War Bride (52); Red Snow (52); Abbott and Costello Meet Captain Kidd (52); The Blue Gardenia (53); The Moonlighter (53); Marry Me Again (53); Appointment in Honduras (53); Duffy of San Quentin (54); Top Banana (54); The World Dances (54); Desert Sands (55); The Unearthly (57); Outcasts of the City (58).

Walter L. Hall

Intolerance (16).

Daniel Haller

War of the Satellites (58); Machine Gun Kelly (58); A Bucket of Blood (59); The House of Usher (60); The Little Shop of Horrors (60); The Premature Burial (62); The Raven (63); The Terror (63); X—The Man with X-Ray Eyes (63); The Comedy of Terrors (64).

John Harkrider

Glorifying the American Girl (29, "Ziegfeld Follies" sequence); Whoopee (30, contributor to color sequence); Roman Scandals (33, contributor); The Great Ziegfeld (36, designed numbers: "Pretty Girl," "Circus Ballet," "Bouquet of Girls," "Honeymoon Cottage," "Ziegfeld's Hit Show;" art directors were Merrill Pye, Cedric Gibbons); Swing Time (36, set "Bojangles of Harlem"); Three Smart Girls (36); 100 Men & a Girl (37); Top of the Town (37); Merry Go Round of 1938 (37).

Esdras Hartley

The Show of Shows (29); The Millionaire (31); Taxi (32); Wild Boys of the Road (33); The House on 56th Street (33); Convention City (33); Jimmy the Gent (34); Special Agent (35); The Return of Dr. X (39).

Edward S. (Ted) Haworth

Strangers on a Train (51); Invasion of the Body Snatchers (56); The Friendly Persuasion (56); Sayonara (57); The Goddess (58); I Want to Live (58); Some Like It Hot (59); Pepe (60); The Longest Day (62); What a Way to Go (64); Seconds (66); The Professionals (66); The Beguiled (71); The Getaway (72); Jeremiah Johnson (72); Pat Garrett and Billy the Kid (73); Harry and Tonto (74); Claudine (74); The Killer Elite (76).

Ben Hayne

Don Juan Quilligan (45); Blondie's Big Moment (47); Blondie's Holiday (47); Down to the Sea in Ships (49).

Earl Hedrick

Wings in the Dark (35, with Hans Dreier); The Last Outpost (35, with Hans Dreier); Hollywood Boulevard (36, with Hans Dreier); Wedding Present (36, with Hans Dreier); T-Man (36, with Hans Dreier); The Preview Murder Mystery (36, with Hans Dreier); Night Club Scandal (37, with Hans Dreier); The Arkansas Traveller (38, with Hans Dreier); Bulldog Drummond in Africa (38, with Hans Dreier); Give Me a Sailor (38, with Hans Dreier); Prison Farm (38, with Hans Dreier); Geronimo (39, with Hans Dreier); The Gracie Allen Murder Case (39, with Hans Dreier); Our Neighbors, the Carters (39, with Hans Dreier); Some Like It Hot (39, with Hans Dreier); What a Life (39, with Hans Dreier); The Biscuit Eater (40, with Hans Dreier); The Great McGinty (40, with Hans Dreier); Christmas in July (40, with Hans Dreier); Comin' Round the Mountain (40, with Hans Dreier); Dr. Cyclops (40, with Hans Dreier); Opened by Mistake (40, with Hans Dreier); There's Magic in Music (41, with Hans Dreier); Sullivan's Travels (41); Beyond the Blue Horizon (42, with Hans Dreier); Dr. Broadway (42, with Hans Dreier); The Forest Rangers (42, with Hans Dreier); The Great Man's Lady (42, with Hans Dreier); Wake Island (42, with Hans Dreier); So Proudly We Hail (43, with Hans Dreier); Henry Aldrich Gets Glamour (43, with Hans Dreier); True to Life (43, with Hans Dreier); Let's Face It (43); I Love a Soldier (44); The Hour Before Dawn (44, with Hans Dreier); Our Hearts Were Young and Gay (44, with Hans Dreier); Standing Room Only (44, with Hans Dreier), The Lost Weekend (45, with Hans Dreier); Miss Susie Slagle's (45, with Hans Dreier); The Stork Club (45, with Hans Dreier); The Unseen (45, with Hans Dreier); Monsieur Beaucaire (46, with Hans Dreier); The Well-Groomed Bride (46, with Hans Dreier); Dear Ruth (47, with Hans Dreier); My Favorite Brunette (47, with Hans Dreier); The Road to Rio (47, with Hans Dreier); The Trouble with Woman (47, with Hans Dreier); Where There's Life (47, with Hans Dreier); The Accused (48, with Hans Dreier); The Paleface (48, with Hans Dreier); Sorry, Wrong Number (48, with Hans Dreier); The File on Thelma Jordan (49, with Hans Dreier); The Great Lover (49, with Hans Dreier); Dear Wife (49, with Hans Dreier); Paid in Full (50, with Hans Dreier); Union Station (50, with Hans Dreier); Fancy Pants (50, with Hans Dreier); Mr. Music (50, with Hans Dreier); Detective Story (51, with Hal Pereira); Ace in the Hole/The Big Carnival (51); Here Comes the Groom (51); Jivaro (54).

Addison Hehr

How the West Was Won (62, with George W. Davis, William Ferrari); The Day the Earth Stood Still (51); River of No Return (54, with Lyle Wheeler).

Dale Hennesy

Under the Yum Yum Tree (63); Good Neighbor Sam (64); John Goldfarb, Please Come Home (65); Fantastic Voyage (66, with Jack Martin Smith); In Like Flint (67); Adam at 6 AM (70); Cover Me Babe (70); Simon, King of the Witches (71); The Christian Licorice Store (71); Dirty Harry (71); Everything You Always Wanted to Know About Sex (72); A Time to Run (72); Slither (73); Battle for the Planet of the Apes (73); Sleeper (73); Young Frankenstein (74); Logan's Run (76); King Kong (76); Dog Soldiers (78).

Alfred Herman

Captain Blood (24); King Kong (33, with Carroll Clark); Son of Kong (33); Long Lost Father (34, with Van Nest Polglase); Anne of Green Gables (34); Room Service (38, with Van Nest Polglase); Love Affair (39); Once Upon a Honeymoon (42); Around the World (43); Bombadier (43); Forever and a Day (43); Rookies in Burma (43); Behind the Rising Sun (43); Gangway for Tomorrow (43); A Lady Takes a Chance (43); Action in Arabia (44); The Falcon Out West (44); Music in Manhattan (44); Pan-Americana (45); Sign Your Way Home (45); Having a Wonderful Crime (45); Man Alive (45); From This Day Forward (46); Crossfire (47, with Albert D'Agostino); The Locket (47); Berlin Express (48); They Live by Night (48); The Twisted Road (48); A Dangerous Profession (49); Easy Living (49); The Company She Keeps (50); Walk Softly Stranger (50); Gambling House (50); My Forbidden Past (51); The Lusty Men (52).

Bernard Herzbrun

Skippy (31); The Devil and the Deep (32); I'm No Angel (33, with Hans Dreier); Belle of the Nineties (34, with Hans Dreier); Klondike Annie (36, with Hans Dreier); Mississippi (36, with Hans Dreier); Poppy (36, with Hans Dreier); The Texas Rangers (36, with Hans Dreier); Make Way for Tomorrow (37, with Hans Dreier); Kidnapped (38); Alexander's Ragtime Band (38, with Boris Leven); The Little Princess (39, with Richard Day, Hans Peters); Jack London (43); Cinderella Swings It (43); Lady of Burlesque (43); Knickerbocker Holiday (44); Song of the Open Road (44); The Great John L. (45); Pardon My Past (45); Angel on My Shoulder (46); Temptation (46); The Egg and I (47); Woman in Hiding (49); Undertow (49); Francis (49); Abandoned (49); Sword in the Desert (49, with Alexander Golitzen); The Story of Molly X (49); Free for All (49); Arctic Manhunt (49, with Robert Boyle); Bagdad (49); The Gal Who Took the West (49); Harvey (50); The Milkman (50); Deported (50); Wyoming Mail (50); Undercover Girl (50); Spy Hunt (50, with Alexander Golitzen); South Sea Sinner (50); Sierra (50); Shakedown (50); Saddle Tramp (50); Winchester '73 (50, with Nathan Juran); Peggy (50); Outside the Wall (50); Ma & Pa Kettle Go to Town (50); Louisa (50); I Was a Shoplifter (50); The Desert Hawk (50); Comanche Territory (50); Buccaneer's Girl (50); Abbott and Costello in the Foreign Legion (50); One Way Street (50); The Kid from Texas (50); Curtain Call at Cactus Creek (50); The Sleeping City (50); Double Crossbones (50, with Alexander Golitzen); Frenchie (50, with Alexander Golitzen); Kansas Raiders (50); Under the Gun (50); Mystery Submarine (50); Iron Man (51); Mark of the Renegade (51); Weekend with Father (51); The Lady Pays Off (51); Flame of Araby (51); Cattle Drive (51); Target Unknown (51); The Raging Tide (51); Little Egypt (51); Katie Did It (51); Apache Drums (51); The Golden Horde (51, with Alexander Golitzen); Smuggler's Island (51, with Alexander Golitzen); You Can Never Tell (51, with

Alexander Golitzen); Up Front (51, with Alexander Golitzen); Air Cadet (51); Reunion in Rio (51); Cave of Outlaws (51); Bright Victory (51); Thunder on the Hill (51); The Cimarron Kid (51); The Prince Who Was a Thief (51); The Lady from Texas (51); Ma and Pa Kettle Back on the Farm (51); Francis Goes to the Races (51); The Strange Door (51); Bedtime for Bonzo (51); Comin' Round the Mountain (51); Meet the Invisible Man (51); Tomahawk (51); Finders Keepers (51); Hollywood Story (51); The Fat Man (51); Has Anybody Seen My Gal (52, with Hilyard Brown); Abbott and Costello Meet Dr. Jekyll and Mr. Hyde (53); The Far Country (55, with Alexander Golitzen).

Ernest R. Hickson

The Ghost Rider (43); Silver Skates (43); The Stranger from Pecos (43); Detective Kitty O'Day (44); Alaska (44); Hot Rhythm (44); Lady, Let's Dance (44); Million Dollar Kid (44); Captain Tugboat Annie (45); China's Little Pearls (45); Flame of the West (45); G.I. Honeymoon (45); Sunbonnet Sue (45); There Goes Kelly (45); Fashion Model (45); South of Monterey (46); Swing Parade of 1946 (46); The Gay Cavalier (46); Black Gold (47); High Conquest (47); Stampede (49).

Lawrance Hitt

East of Suez (25, with Hans Dreier); The Wanderer (26, with William Cameron Menzies).

Hubert Hobson

Marriage Is a Private Affair (44); Meet the People (44); Dangerous Partners (45); A Letter for Evie (45); Little Mister Jim (46); The Mighty McCurk (46).

Albert Hogsett

Pack Up Your Troubles (39, with Richard Day); Four Sons (40, with Richard Day); The Great American Broadcast (41, with Richard Day); Great Guns (41, with Richard Day); Careful Soft Shoulders (42, with Richard Day); The Man in the Trunk (42, with Richard Day); Rings on Her Fingers (42, with Richard Day); The Meanest Man in the World (43, with Richard Day); Chetniks! (43, with Richard Day); Four Jills in a Jeep (44); Something for the Boys (44); Tampico (44); Mollie and Me (45); Colonel Effingham's Raid (45); Claudia and David (46); Sentimental Journey (46); Strange Triangle (46); Thunder in the Valley (47); Fury at Furnace Creek (48); Green Grass of Wyoming (48); Scudda Hoo! Scudda Hay! (48); Cry of the City (48); Yellow Sky (48); I Was a Male War Bride (49); Slattery's Hurricane (49); Broken Arrow (50); Hall of Montezuma (50); Anne of the Indies (51); Bird of Paradise (51, with Lyle Wheeler); The Frogmen (51); Let's Make It Legal (51).

Walter Holscher

Lucky Legs (43); Murder in Times Square (43); Appointment in Berlin (43); Dangerous Blondes (43); The Heat's On (43); It's a Great Life (43); Something to Shout About (43); Address Unknown (44, with William Cameron Menzies, Lionel Banks); Louisiana Hayride (44); The Racket Man (44); Stars on Parade (44); Strange Affair (44); After Midnight with Boston Blackie (44); The Fighting Guardsman (45); Rough, Tough, and Ready (45); The Jolson Story (46); Renegades (46); Meet Me on Broadway (46); The Guilt of Janet Ames (47); Best Man Wins (48); The Mating of Millie (48); Relentless (48); Thunderhoof (48); The Undercover Man (49); Miss Grant Takes Richmond (49); Jolson Sings Again (49); The Petty Girl (50); Harriet Craig (50); The Good Humor Man (50); Frightened City (50); Santa Fe (51); The Son of Dr. Jekyll (51); Sunny Side on the Street (51); Two of a Kind (51).

Theobald Holsopple

Badmen of Tombstone (48); Bomba, the Jungle Boy (49); Bad Boy (49); Rocketship XM (50); The Steel Helmet (50); Park Row (52); Daughter of Dr. Jekyll (57); Kronos (57); The Fly (58); The Bamboo Saucer (67).

Frederic Hope

The Student Prince (27, with Hans Dreier, Richard Day, Cedric Gibbons); The Big House (30, with Cedric Gibbons); Dinner at Eight (33, with Cedric Gibbons, Hobart Erwin); The Merry Widow (34, wtih Cedric Gibbons, Gabriel Scognamillo); Anna Karenina (35, with Cedric Gibbons, Edwin B. Willis); Romeo and Juliet (36, with Cedric Gibbons, Oliver Messel); Maytime (37, with Cedric Gibbons, Edwin B. Willis); Camille (37, with Cedric Gibbons).

Harry Horner

Our Town (40, with William Cameron Menzies); The Little Foxes (41); Tarzan Triumphs (43); Stage Door Canteen (43); Winged Victory (44); A Double Life (48); The Heiress (49, with John Meehan); Born Yesterday (50); Outrage (50); He Ran All the Way (51); Beware My Lovely (52, director); Red Planet Mars (52, director); Vicki (53, director); New Faces (54; director); Life in the Balance (55, director); Step Down to Terror (58, director); Man from Del Rio (56, director); Separate Tables (59); The Wonderful Country (59); The Hustler (61); Outrage (64); Fahrenheit 451 (67); They Shoot Horses Don't They? (69); Who is Harry Kellerman . . . (71); Up the Sandbox (72); The Black Bird (75); Audrey Rose (77); The Driver (78); Moment by Moment (78).

William A. Horning

Ah, Wilderness! (35); Mad Love (35, with Cedric Gibbons); Fury (36, with Cedric Gibbons); Conquest (37, with Cedric Gibbons); Marie Antoinette (38, with Cedric Gibbons, Randall Duell); The Wizard of Oz (39, with Cedric Gibbons, Arnold Gillespie, Jack Martin Smith); Quo Vadis (51, with Cedric Gibbons, Edward Carfagno); The Wings of Eagles (57); Les Girls (57, with Gene Allen); Some Came Running (58, with Urie McCleary); Gigi (58, with Preston Ames, Keough Gleason); Party Girl (58); Ben Hur (59, with Edward Carfagno, Arnold Gillespie); North by Northwest (59, with Robert Boyle, Merrill Pye); The World, the Flesh and the Devil (59, with Paul Groesse).

J. Frank Hotaling

Faces in the Fog (44); Lights of Old Santa Fe (44); My Buddy (44); Along the Navajo Trail (45); Earl Carroll Vanities (45); Gangs of the Waterfront (45); Rough Riders of Cheyenne (45); Sante Fe Saddlemates (45); Sunset in Eldorado (45); The Tiger Woman (45); Wagon Wheels Westward (45); Beyond City Lights (45); The Big Bonanza (45); Scotland Yard Investigator (45); Affairs of Geraldine (46); California Gold Rush (46); Earl Carroll Sketchbook (46); The Last Crooked Mile (46); The Magnificent Rogue (46); One Exciting Week (46); Home in Oklahoma (46); The Trespasser (47); Wyoming (47); Hit Parade of 1947 (47); Twilight on the Rio Grande (47); On the Old Spanish Trail (47); The Bold Frontiersman (48); Campus Honeymoon (48); King of the Gamblers (48); The Main Street Kid (48); Under California Stars (48); Eyes of Texas (48); Daredevils of the Clouds (48); The Timber Trail (48); Homicide for Three (48); Grand Canyon Trail (48); Night Time in Nevada (48); Sundown in Santa Fe (48); Desperados of Dodge City (48); The Gay Ranchero (48); Susanna Pass (49); Streets of San Francisco (49); South of Rio (49); Rose of the Yukon (49); Law of the Golden West (49); Hideout (49); Frontier Investigator (49); Flaming Fury (49); The Far Frontier (49); Death Valley Gunfighter (49); Down Dakota Way (49); Alias the Champ (49); San Antone Ambush (49); Ranger of Cherokee Strip (49); The Golden Stallion (49); Flame of Youth (49); I Shot Jesse James (49); Rio Grande (50); Belle of Old Mexico (50); Bells of Coronado (50); The Blonde Bandit (50); Covered Wagon Raid (50); Pioneer Marshal (50); Trial Without Jury (50); Twilight in the Sierras (50); Destination Big House (50); Unmasked (50); Sunset in the West (50); North of the Great Divide (50); Arizona Manhunt (51); Cuban Fireball (51); The Dakota Kid (51); Fort Dodge Stampede (51); Havana Rose (51); Heart of the Rockies (51); Honeychile (51); In Old Amarillo (51); Insurance Investigator (51); Million Dollar Pursuit (51); Missing Women (51); Night Riders of Montana (51); Pride of Maryland (51); Rough Riders of Durango (51); Silver City Bonanza (51); Thunder in God's Country (51); Wells Fargo Gunmaster (51); South of Caliente (51); The Quiet Man (52); The Sun Shines Bright (54); The Searchers (56, with James Basevi); 3:10 to Yuma (57); The Big Country (58); The Horse Soldiers (59).

John H. Hughes

Rafter Romance (34, with Van Nest Ppolglase); Air Force (43); Old Acquaintance (43); This Is the Army (43); The Adventures of Mark Twain (44); Escape in the Desert (45); Hotel Berlin (45); God Is My Co-Pilot (45); Rhapsody in Blue (45, with Anton Grot); Cinderella Jones (46); Night and Day (46); The Treasure of Sierra Madre (48); One Last Fling (49); Look for the Silver Lining (49).

Andre Ibels

The Blue Bird (18, with Ben Carré); Prunelle (18, with Ben Carré); Treasure Island (20, with Ben Carré, Floyd Mueller).

Wiard Ihnen

Idols of Clay (20); On with the Dance (20); Dr. Jekyll and Mr. Hyde (20); School Days (21); Peacock Alley (22); Slim Shoulders (22); The Fighting Blade (23); The Bright Shawl (23, with Everett Shinn); Potash and Perlmutter (23); Monte Carlo (30, with Hans Dreier); City Streets (31); If I Had a Million (32); Blonde Venus (32); Shanghai Express (32, with Hans Dreier); Cradle Song (33); Duck Soup (33, with Hans Dreier); One Sunday Afternoon (33, with Hans Dreier); Becky Sharp (35, with Robert Edmund Jones); Dancing Pirate (36); Go West, Young Man (36, with Hans Dreier); On Such a Night (37); Every Day's a Holiday (38); Doctor Rhythm (38); Stagecoach (39, with Alexander Toluboff); Return of the Cisco Kid (39, with Richard Day); Hollywood Cavalcade (39, with Richard Day); Maryland (40, with Richard Day); The Return of Frank James (40, with Richard Day); Johnny Apollo (40); Hudson's Bay (40, with Richard Day, Michael Shayne); The Blue Bird (40, with Richard Day); Tall, Dark and Handsome (41); Remember the Day (41); Confirm or Deny (41); Man Hunt (41, with Richard Day); Moon Over Miami (41, with Richard Day); Western Union (41, with Richard Day); Iceland (42, with Richard Day); Secret Agent of Japan (42); Roxie Hart (42, with Richard Day); China Girl (42, with Richard Day); The Magnificent Dope (42, with Richard Day); Crash Dive (43, with Richard Day); Wilson (44, with James Basevi); Jane Eyre (44, with James Basevi); Along Came Jones (45); It's a Pleasure (45); Blood on the Sun (45); Tomorrow Is Forever (46); The Time of Your Life (48); Kiss Tomorrow Goodbye (50); Only the Valiant (51); Rancho Notorious (52); A Lion Is in the Streets (53); War Paint (53); I, the Jury (53); This Is My Love (54); The Indian Fighter (55); The King and 4 Queens (56); The Gallant Hours (60).

Edward Ilou

Reign of Terror (49, with William Cameron Menzies); Port of New York (49); The Iroquois Trail (50); Under the Gun (50); Air Cadet (51).

Edward (Eddie) Imazu

Dynamite (29, with Cedric Gibbons, Mitchell Leisen); Rage in Heaven (41); Three Wise Fools (46); The Crimson Key (47); The Romance of Rosy Ridge (47); Second Chance (47); Killer McCoy (47); Hills of Home (48); Challenge to Lassie (49, with Cedric Gibbons); Tucson (49); Trouble Preferred (49); Miss Mink of 1949 (49); The Next Voice You Hear (50); Shadow on the Wall (50); The Skipper Surprised His Wife (50); Stars in My Crown (50); The Yellow Cab Man (50, with Cedric Gibbons); Watch the Birdie (50); Callaway Went Thataway (51, with Cedric Gibbons); Go for Broke (51); It's a Big Country (51, with Malcolm Brown, Arthur Lonergan, Cedric Gibbons, William Ferrari); The Tall Target (51); 7 Women (66, with George W. Davis).

Paul Iribe

The Affairs of Anatol (21); Manslaughter (22); The Ten Commandments (23); The Golden Bed (25); The Road to Yesterday (25, with Anton Grot, Mitchell Leisen, Max Parker); The King of Kings (27, with Anton Grot, Ben Carré, Mitchell Leisen, Edward Jewell).

Richard Irvine

Foreign Correspondent (40, with William Cameron Menzies, Alexander Golitzen, Edmond Bernoudy); No Place for a Lady (43); Victory Through Air Power (43); Guest in the House (44); The Three Caballeros (44); The Spider (45); Circumstantial Evidence (45); Behind Green Lights (46); The Brasher Doubloon (47); Miracle on 34th Street (47, with Richard Day); You Were Meant for Me (48); Apartment for Peggy (48); Chicken Every Sunday (48); Mr. Belvedere Goes to College (49); Everybody Does It (49); The Gunfighter (50); Mother Didn't Tell Me (50); Love That Brute (50); I'll Get By (50); For Heaven's Sake (50); Elopement (51); Follow the Sun (51); Secret of Convict Lake (51).

George Jenkins

The Best Years of Our Lives (46, with Perry Ferguson); The Secret Life of Walter Mitty (47, with Perry Ferguson); The Bishop's Wife (47, with Perry Ferguson); A Song Is Born (48, with Ernst Fegte); Enchantment (48); Roseanna McCoy (49); At War with the Army (50); San Francisco Story (52); Monsoon (53); The Miracle Worker (62); Mickey One (65); Up the Down Staircase (67); Wait Until Dark (67); No Way to Treat a Lady (68); The Subject Was Roses (68); Me, Natalie (69); The Angel Levine (70); The Pursuit of Happiness (71); Klute (71); 1776 (72); The Paper Chase (73); The Parallax View (74); Funny Lady (75); Night Moves (75); All the President's Men (76); Comes a Horseman (78); Power (78); China Syndrome (79); Starting Over (79); The Postman Always Rings Twice (81); Rollover (81); Sophia's Choice (82); Dream Lover (86); Orphans (87).

Edward C. Jewell

His Dog (27, with Mitchell Leisen); The King of Kings (27, with Anton Grot, Mitchell Leisen, Paul Iribe, Ben Carré); Red Hot Rhythm (29); Brothers (30); Tol'able David (30); The Criminal Code (31); Footlight Glamour (43); Good Luck Mr. Yates (43); My Kingdom for a Cook (43); Secret Command (44); California Blues (44); Once Upon a Time (44); Detour (45); Counter-Attack (45); Club Havana (45); White Pongo (45); The Strangler of the Swamp (45); Apology for Murder (45); Arson Squad (45); Dangerous Intruder (45); How Do You Do? (45); Sargeant Mike (45); Shadow of Terror (45); Song of Old Wyoming (45); Why Girls Leave Home (45); Avalanche (46); The Mask of Dijon (46); His Sister's Secret (46); Blonde for a Day (46); The Caravan Trail (46); Colorado Serenade (46); Danny Boy (46); Devil Bat's Daughter (46); Down Missouri (46); Driftin' River (46); Gentlemen with Guns (46); I Ring Doorbells (46); Joe Palooka, Champ (46); Junior Prom (46); Larceny in Her Heart (46); Murder Is My Business (46); Queen of Burlesque (46); Romance of the West (46); The Wife of Monte Cristo (46); The Flying Serpent (46); Her Sister's Secret (46); Secrets of a Sorority Girl (46); Wild West (46); Heartaches (47); Out of the Blue (47); Born to Speed (47); It's a Joke, Son (47); Lost Honeymoon (47); Repeat Performance (47); Bury Me Dead (47); T-Men (47); Tumbleweed Trail (48); The Strange Mrs. Crane (48); Lady at Midnight (48); Stars Over Texas (48); State Department File (48); The Daring Caballero (48); Alimony (49); One Man's Way (64).

Joseph McMillan Johnson

Duel in the Sun (46, p.d. with James Basevi, John Ewing, William Cameron Menzies); Portrait of Jennie (48); Sealed Cargo (51); Behave Yourself (51); Rear Window (54, with Hal Pereira); To Catch a Thief (55, with Hal Pereira); Mutiny on the Bounty (62, with Arnold Gillespie, George W. Davis).

Stan Jolley

Toby Tyler (60, with Carroll Clark); Witness (85?).

Alfred Junge

Junge was head of art direction for MGM in Great Britain. His British films are not listed here. Edward My Son (49); Conspirator (50); The Miniver Story (50); A Farewell to Arms (57, with Lyle Wheeler).

Nathan Juran

How Green Was My Valley (41, with Richard Day); Belle Starr (41, with Richard Day); Charley's Aunt (41, with Richard Day, Thomas Little); I Wake Up Screaming (41, with Richard Day); The Gentlemen from West Point (42, with Richard Day); The Loves of Edgar Allen Poe (42, with Richard Day); That Other Woman (42, with Richard Day); Dr. Renault's Secret (42, with Richard Day); The Razor's Edge (46, with Richard Day); Body and Soul (47); The Other Love (47); Kiss the Blood Off My Hands (48); Tulsa (49); Free for All (49); Undertow (49); Harvey (50); Deported (50); Winchester '73 (50, with Bernard Herzbrun); Thunder on the Hill (51); Reunion in Reno (51); Cave of Outlaws (51).

Walter E. Keller

Irish Luck (25); The New Klondike (26); The Cat People (42, with Albert D'Agostino); This Land Is Mine (43, with Albert D'Agostino); I Walked with a Zombie (43, with Albert D'Agostino); The Leopard Man (43, with Albert D'Agostino); The 7th Victim (43, with Albert D'Agostino); The Ghost Ship (43, with Albert D'Agostino); Fighting Frontier (43); Adventures of a Rookie (43); The Avenging Rider (43); The Falcon in Danger (43); The

Falcon Strikes Back (43); Gildersleeve on Broadway (43); Mexican Spitfire's Blessed Event (43); Petticoat Larceny (43); Bride by Mistake (44); Come On Danger (44); Girl Rush (44); Marine Raiders (44); The Curse of the Cat People (44, with Albert D'Agostino); Mademoiselle Fifi (44, with Albert D'Agostino); Radio Stars on Parade (45); Those Endearing Young Charms (45); Isle of the Dead (45, with Albert D'Agostino); The Body Snatcher (45, with Albert D'Agostino); Zombies on Broadway (45); First Yank into Tokyo (45); Badman's Territory (46); The Falcon's Adventure (46); Step by Step (46); The Truth About Murder (46); Bedlam (46, with Albert D'Agostino); The Woman on the Beach (47); Born to Kill (47, with Albert D'Agostino); Dick Tracy Meets Gruesome (47); Riffraff (47, with Albert D'Agostino); Banjo (47, with Albert D'Agostino); Desperate (47, with Albert D'Agostino); Fighting Father Dunne (48, with Albert D'Agostino); Race Street (48, with Albert D'Agostino); Blood on the Moon (48, with Albert D'Agostino); The Window (49, with Albert D'Agostino); Follow Me Quietly (49, with Albert D'Agostino); The Clay Pigeon (49, with Albert D'Agostino); I Married a Communist (49; same released as The Woman on Pier 13 [50, with Albert D'Agostino]); Dynamite Pass (50, with Albert D'Agostino); Rider from Tucson (50, with Albert D'Agostino); Never a Dull Moment (50, with Albert D'Agostino); Hunt the Man Down (50); Bunco Squad (50, with Albert D'Agostino); On the Loose (51, with Albert D'Agostino); Saddle Legion (51, with Albert D'Agostino); Footlight Varieties (51); Roadblock (51, with Albert D'Agostino); Private Hell 36 (54); Son of Sinbad (55).

Russell Kimball

Home in Wyomin' (42); Ice Capades Review (42); Some One to Remember (43); The Lady and the Monster (44); Storm Over Lisbon (44); Murder in the Music Hall (46).

Charles M. Kirk

Dream Street (21); Orphans of the Storm (21); One Exciting Night (22); The White Rose (23); America (24); Sally of the Sawdust (25); That Royle Girl (25); The Sorrows of Satan (26); Aloma of the South Seas (26); Jealousy (29); Christopher Strong (33, with Van Nest Polglase); Romance in Manhattan (33, with Van Nest Polglase); Bed of Roses (33, with Van Nest Polglase); Morning Glory (33, with Van Nest Polglase); Anne Vickers (33, with Van Nest Polglase); The Informer (35, with Van Nest Polglase); Jalna (35, with Van Nest Polglase); I Dream Too Much (35, with Van Nest Polglase); A Star of Midnight (35, with Van Nest Polglase).

Mark-Lee Kirk

Wake Up and Live (37, with Haldane Douglas, William S. Darling); Young Mr. Lincoln (39, with Richard Day); Drums Along the Mohawk (39, with Richard Day); The Grapes of Wrath (40, with Richard Day); My Favorite Wife (40, with Van Nest Polglase); Kitty Foyle (40, with Van Nest Polglase); They Knew What They Wanted (40, with Van Nest Polglase); Tom, Dick, and Harry (41, with Van Nest Polglase); The Magnificent Ambersons (42); Journey into Fear (42); Mr. Lucky (43, with William Cameron Menzies, Albert D'Agostino); The Fallen Sparrow (43); Since You Went Away (44); I'll Be Seeing You (44); Junior Miss (45); A Bell for Adano (45, with Lyle Wheeler); A Royal Scandal (45); Moss Rose (47, with Richard Day); Gentleman's Agreement (47, with Lyle Wheeler); Call Northside 777 (48, with Lyle Wheeler); The Iron Curtain (48, with Lyle Wheeler); Prince of Foxes (49, with Lyle Wheeler); Stella (50); Way of a Gaucho (52); Kangaroo (52); White Witch Doctor (53); Prince Valiant (54); The Tall Men (55); Prince of Players (55, with Lyle Wheeler); The Revolt of Mamie Stover (56, with Lyle Wheeler); Bus Stop (56, with Lyle Wheeler); The Sun Also

Rises (57, with Lyle Wheeler); The Bravados (58, with Lyle Wheeler); The Best of Everything (59, with Lyle Wheeler, Jack Martin Smith); Compulsion (59, with Lyle Wheeler).

Walter Koessler

Tarzan and the Amazons (45); Dangerous Years (47); The Invisible Wall (47); Roses Are Red (47); The Challenge (48); 13 Lead Soldiers (48); Shed No Tears (48); The Creeper (48); Red Stallion in the Rockies (49).

Vincent Korda

(Mr. Korda's work in British films is not included here.) Things to Come (36, with dir. William Cameron Menzies); The Thief of Bagdad (40, with William Cameron Menzies); Lydia (41, with Jack Okey); The Jungle Book (42, with Jack Okey); The Third Man (50).

Leo E. Kuter

Trifling Women (22); Smouldering Fires (25); Sporting Life (25); Captain Salvation (27); Juarez (39, with Anton Grot); Thank Your Lucky Stars (43, with Anton Grot); Destination Tokyo (43); Northern Pursuit (43); Hollywood Canteen (44); The Last Ride (44); The Very Thought of You (44); Pillow to Post (45); Confidential Agent (45); Pride of the Marines (45); Two Guys from Milwaukee (46); That Way with Women (47); Always Together (47); The Unfaithful (47); To the Victor (48); Key Largo (48); Task Force (49); Flamingo Road (49); South of St. Louis (49); Highway 301 (50); Storm Warning (50); Chain Lightning (50); I Was a Communist for the FBI (51); The Tanks Are Coming (51); Come Fill the Cup (51); Close to My Heart (51); Operation Pacific (51); This Woman Is Dangerous (52); Trouble Along the Way (53); The Boy from Oklahoma (54); Toward the Unknown (56); The Deep 6 (58); A Summer Place (59); Rio Bravo (59); Parrish (61); Rome Adventure (62); House of Women (62); PT 109 (63); Ensign Pulver (64).

Edward M. Langley

The Three Musketeers (21, with William Cameron Menzies); Robin Hood (22, with William Cameron Menzies, Irvin J. Martin, Wilfred Buckland, Anton Grot); Don Q, Son of Zorro (25, with Anton Grot, Harry Oliver, Harold Miles).

Tambi Larsen

Secret of the Incas (54); Three Ring Circus (55); Artists and Models (55); The Rose Tattoo (55, with Hal Pereira); The Scarlet Hour (55); Spanish Affair (57); Hot Spell (58); Wild Is the Wind (57); Rock-a-Bye Baby (58); Party Crasher (58); Geisha Boy (58); Five Pennies (59); The Rat Race (60); Pleasure of His Company (61); It's Only Money (62); The Counterfeit Traitor (62); Too Late Blues (62); Hud (63, with Hal Pereira); Man's Favorite Sport (64); The Outrage (64); Disorderly Orderly (64); The Spy Who Came in from the Cold (65); Nevada Smith (66); Color Sonics (66); Chuka (67); The Brotherhood (68); The Molly Maguires (70); The Grasshopper (70); A Gunfight (70); Pocket Money (72); The Life and Times of Judge Roy Bean (72); Where the Lilies Bloom (74); The Outfit (73); Thunderbolt and Lightfoot (74); Mohammad, the Messenger of God (74); Breakheart Pass (75); Outlaw Josie Wales (75); The White Buffalo (76); Ring of Iron (77); Heaven's Gate (80).

Robert E. Lee

The Tigress (27); The Matinee Idol (28); So This Is Love (28); That Certain Thing (28); The Great Gabbo (29); The Costello Case (30).

Mitchell Leisen

(Worked also as a costume designer and director. Listing below is for art direction only.) Conrad in Quest of His Youth (20); The Road to Yesterday (25, with Anton Grot, Paul Iribe, Max Parker); The Volga Boatman (26, with Anton Grot, Max Parker); His Dog (27, with Edward Jewell); The Fighting Eagle (27); The Angel of Broadway (27); The Wise Wife (27); Dress Parade (27); The Forbidden Woman (27, with Wilfred Buckland); The King of Kings (27, with Anton Grot, Edward Jewell, Ben Carré, Paul Iribe); Chicago (28); Power (28); Show Folks (28); Celebrity (28); Lover Over Night (28); The Godless Girl (29, with Anton Grot); Dynamite (29, with Cedric Gibbons, Eddie Imazu); Madame Satan (30, with Richard Day, Cedric Gibbons); The Squaw Man (31); The Sign of the Cross (32); This Day and Age (33, with Hans Dreier, Roland Anderson).

Maurice Leloir

The Iron Mask (29, with Ben Carré, William Cameron Menzies).

Paul Leni

Leni had a distinguished career in German films (not listed below). The Cat and the Canary (27, with Charles D. Hall); The Chinese Parrot (27); The Man Who Laughs (28); The Last Warning (29).

Boris Leven

The Milky Way (35); Alexander's Ragtime Band (38, with Bernard Herzbrun); Just Around the Corner (38); Second Chorus (40); The Shanghai Gesture (41); Girl Trouble (42, with Richard Day); Tales of Manhattan (42, with Richard Day); Life Begins at 8:30 (42, with Richard Day); Hello, Frisco, Hello (43, with James Basevi); Doll Face (45); Shock (46, with Lyle Wheeler); Home Sweet Homicide (46); The Shocking Miss Pilgrim (47, with James Basevi); I Wonder Who's Kissing Her Now (47, with Richard Day, Joseph C. Wright); The Senator Was Indiscreet (47); Mr. Peabody and the Mermaid (48); Criss Cross (49); The Loveable Cheat (49); Search for Danger (49); House by the River (50); Quicksand (50); Woman on the Run (50); Dakota Lil (50); Destination Murder (50); Once a Thief (50); The Jackie Robinson Story (50); Experiment Alcatraz (50); Chicago Calling (51); The Second Woman (51); The Prowler (51); A Millionaire for Christy (51); Two Dollar Bettor (51); The Basketball Fix (51); Sudden Fear (52); The Star (52); Rose of Cimarron (52); Invaders from Mars (53, with William Cameron Menzies); Donovan's Brain (53); The Long Wait (54); The Silver Chalice (54); Giant (56); Courage of Black Beauty (57); My Gun Is Quick (57); Zero Hour! (57); Thunder in the Sun (59); Anatomy of a Murder (59); September Storm (60); West Side Story (61); Two for the Seesaw (62); Straight-Jacket (64); The Sound of Music (65); The Sand Pebbles (66, with Maurice Zuberano); Star! (68); A Dream of Kings (69); The Andromeda Strain (71); Happy Birthday, Wanda June (71); The New Centurians (72); Jonathan Livingston Seagull (73); Shanks (74); Mandingo (75); New York, New York (77); The Last Waltz (78); Matilda (78).

Thomas Little

The Hound of the Baskervilles (39, with Hans Peters, Richard Day); Charley's Aunt (41, with Richard Day, Nathan Juran); Swamp Water (41, with Richard Day, Joseph C. Wright); This Above All (42, with Richard Day, Joseph C. Wright).

Arthur Lonergan

Black Beauty (46); Song of My Heart (47); The Tender Years (47); Intrigue (47); Pitfall (48); Man-Eater of Kumaon (48); A Life of Her Own (50); The Caribou Trail (50); The Magnificent Yankee (50); Bannerline (51); Cause for Alarm (51); It's a Big Country (51, with Malcolm Brown, Edward Imazu, Cedric Gibbons, William Ferrari); The Man with a Clock (51); Rich, Young, and Pretty (51); The Sellout (51); Ride, Vaquero! (53); The Actress (53); It's Always Fair Weather (55); Forbidden Planet (56, with Arnold Gillespie, Cedric Gibbons); On the Double (61); The Errand Boy (61); A New Kind of Love (63); Who's Been Sleeping in My Bed? (63); Robinson Crusoe on Mars (64); Red Line 7000 (65); The Oscar (66); How Sweet It Is (68); Che! (69); M*A*S*H (70); Beyond the Valley of the Dolls (70); Plaza Suite (71).

Eugene Lourie

Only the American films are listed below. Lourie is best known for his French films with director Jean Renoir. This Land Is Mine (43); Three Russian Girls (43); Sahara (43); The Imposter (44); Abbott and Costello in Society (44); The Southerner (45); The House of Fear (45); The Strange Adventure of Uncle Harry (45); The Diary of a Chambermaid (46); The Long Night (47); Song of Scheherezade (47, with Jack Otterson); A Woman's Vengeance (47); Adventures of Captain Fabian (51); The River (51); Limelight (52); The Beast from 20,000 Fathoms (53); The Diamond Queen (53); So This Is Paris (54); Confessions of an Opium Eater (62); Shock Corridor (63); Flight from Ashiya (63); The Strangler (63); The Naked Kiss (64); Bikini Paradise (64); The Battle of the Bulge (65); A Crack in the World (65); Custer of the West (68); Krakatoa, East of Java (69); The Royal Hunt of the Sun (69); What's the Matter with Helen? (71); Eliza's Horoscope (71); Burnt Offerings (76); An Enemy of the People (78); Bronco Billy (80).

Harold MacArthur

Crazy House (43); It Ain't Hay (43); Mug Town (43); Allergic Love (43); Always a Bridesmaid (43); Get Going (43); Hi, Buddy (43); Hit the Ice (43); Mister Big (43); Sherlock Holmes Faces Death (43); Follow the Boys (44); The Invisible Man's Revenge (44); Murder in the Blue Room (44); Reckless Age (44); South of Dixie (44); This Is the Life (44); The Daltons Ride Again (45); The Naughty Nineties (45); Penthouse Rhythm (45); Song of the Sarong (45); Dangerous Woman (46); Slightly Scandalous (46); Her Adventurous Night (46); The Dark Horse (46); Law of the Canyon (47); The Millerson Case (47); Keeper of the Bees (47); Key Witness (47); The Last Round-up (47); Adventures in Silverado (48); The Strawberry Roan (48); Loaded Pistols (48); Rim of the Canyon (49); Riders of the Whistling Pines (49); Riders in the Sky (49); The Big Sombrero (49); The Crime Doctor's Diary (49); The Devil's Henchmen (49); Rusty's Birthday (49); Law of the Barbary Coast (49); Air Hostess (49); On the Isle of Samoa (50); Rogues of Sherwood Forest (50); Sons of New Mexico (50); When You're Smiling (50); The Blazing Sun (50); David Harding, Counterspy (50); Customs Agent (50); Cow Town (50); Beyond the Purple Hills (50); The Big Gusher (51); Criminal Lawyer (51); Lorna Doone (51); Mask of the Avenger (51); The Texas Rangers (51).

Irvin J. Martin

Robin Hood (22, with Wilfred Buckland, William Cameron Menzies, Edward Langley, Anton Grot); The Thief of Bagdad (24, with William Cameron Menzies, Anton Grot, Park French).

Harry McAfee

San Franciso (36, with Arnold Gillespie, Cedric Gibbons, James Basevi); Air Raid Wardens (43); Presenting Lily Mars (43); Andy Hardy's Blonde Trouble (44); Nothing but Trouble (44); Three Men in White (44); Without Love (45); Faithful in My Fashion (46); The Hoodlum Saint (46); Love Laughs at Andy Hardy (46); The Bride Goes Wild (48).

Urie McCleary

Madame X (37, with Cedric Gibbons); Blossoms in the Dust (41, with Cedric Gibbons); An American Romance (44); National Velvet (44, with Cedric Gibbons); Her Highness and the Bellboy (45); Adventure (46, with Cedric Gibbons); Command Decision (48, with Cedric Gibbons); State of the Union (48); The Secret Garden (49); Any Number Can Play (49); Three Little Words (50, with Cedric Gibbons); Pat and Mike (52, with Cedric Gibbons); Plymouth Adventure (52); Kiss Me Kate (53); Young Bess (53); Jupiter's Darling (55, with Cedric Gibbons); Some Came Running (58, with William A. Horning); Two Weeks in Another Town (64); 4 Horsemen of the Apocalypse (62); The Prize (63); The Split (68); Where Were You When the Lights Went Out? (68); Patton (70).

John Victor Mackay

Manhattan Merry-Go-Round (37); Man of Conquest (39); The Dark Command (40).

John Mansbridge

Tension at Table Rock (56); Public Pigeon #1 (56); Young Stranger (56); Superman (56, 13 tv); China Gate (56); Forty Guns (57); Ambush at Cimarron Pass (57); Show Down at Boot Hill (57); Thunderjets (57); Gang War (57); Sierra Baron (58); Villa (58); Verboten (58); Alaskan Passage (58); Little Savage (58); Sad Horse (58); Here Come the Jets (59); Return of the Fly (59); Miracle of the Hills (59); Alligator People (59); Jets Over the Atlantic (59); Oregon Trail (59); Five Gates to Hell (59); The Last Rookie (59); The Third Voice (59); Young Jesse James (59); Twelve Hours to Kill (60); Desire in the Dust (60); Tess of the Storm Country (60); Little Shepherd of Kingdom Come (60); The Long Rope (60); Snipers Ridge (60); Silent Call (61); Battle at Bloody Beach (61); Teddy Bears (61); Twenty Thousand Eyes (61); Purple Hills (61); Vanishing Frontier (61); The Incredible Journey (63, with Carroll Clark); Those Calloways (65, with Carroll Clark); Monkeys, Go Home! (67, with Carroll Clark); The Adventures of Bullwhip Griffin (67, with Carroll Clark); The Happiest Millionarie (67, with Carroll Clark); Blackbeard's Ghost (68, with Carroll Clark); Never a Dull Moment (68, with Carroll Clark); The Horse in the Gray Flannel Suit (68, with Carroll Clark); The Love Bug (68, with Carroll Clark); Everyone Calls Him Smith (68); Rascal (68); The Computer Wore Tennis Shoes (69); Newcomers (69); Bed Knobs & Broomsticks (70, with Peter Ellenshaw); Rating Game (70); Million Dollar Duck (70); Scandalous John (70); Moreover (71); Now You See Him, Now You Don't (71); Snowball Express (72); The Mystery in Dracula's Castle (72); Charlie and the Angel (72); World's Greatest Athlete (72); One Little Indian (72); Super Dad (72); Herbie Rides Again (72); Island at the Top of the World (73); Alvin the Magnificent (73); The Bears and I (73); Hog Wild (73); Castaway Cowboy

(73); Escape to Witch Mountain (74); Strongest Man in the World (74); Apple Dumpling Gang (74); Gus (75); No Deposit, No Return (75); Treasure of Matecumbe (75).

John Meehan

Bring on the Girls (45); The Virginian (46, with Hans Dreier); The Bride Wore Boots (46, with Hans Dreier); The Strange Love of Martha Ivers (46, with Hans Dreier); Suddenly It's Spring (47, with Hans Dreier); Golden Earrings (47, with Hans Dreier); Dream Girl (48, with Hans Dreier); Sealed Verdict (48, with Hans Dreier); The Heiress (49, with Harry Horner); Sunset Boulevard (50, with Hans Dreier); Tarzan's Peril (51); The Marrying Kind (52); Salome (53); It Should Happen to You (54); 20,000 Leagues Under the Sea (54); Cult of the Cobra (55).

William Cameron Menzies

The Naulahka (18, with Anton Grot); Innocent (18); The Witness for the Defense (19); A Society Exile (19); The Deep Purple (20); The Oath (21); Serenade (21); The Three Musketeers (21, with Edward M. Langley); Kindred of the Dust (22); Robin Hood (22, with Edward M. Langley, Irvin J. Martin, Anton Grot, Wilfred Buckland); Rosita (23); The Thief of Bagdad (24, with Irvin J. Martin, Anton Grot, Park French); The Lady (25); Her Sister from Paris (25); The Eagle (25); Cobra (25); What Price Beauty (25); Graustark (25); The Dark Angel (25); The Wanderer (26, with Lawrence Hitt); Kiki (26); The Bat (26); The Son of the Sheik (26); Fig Leaves (26, with William S. Darling); The Beloved Rogue (27); Camille (27); Two Arabian Knights (27); Sorrell and Son (27, with Julian Boone Fleming); The Dove (27); Sadie Thompson (28); Drums of Love (28); The Garden of Eden (28); The Tempest (28); The Woman Disputed (28); The Loves of Zero (28); The Awakening (28); The Iron Mask (29, with Maurice Leloir, Ben Carré); The Rescue (29); Lady of the Pavements (29); Alibi (29); Coquette (29); Three Live Ghosts (29); The Locked Door (29); Bulldog Drummond (29); Condemned (29); The Taming of the Shrew (29, with Lawrence Irving); New York Nights (29); Abraham Lincoln (30, with Park French); The Bad One (30, with Park French); Be Your Self! (30, with Park French); Dubarry, Woman of Passion (30, with Park French); The Lottery Bride (30, with Park French); Lummox (30, with Park French); One Romantic Night (30, with Park French); Puttin' on the Ritz (30, with Park French); Raffles (30, with Park French); Reaching for the Moon (31); Always Goodbye (31); The Spider (31); Almost Married (32); Chandu the Magician (32); Trick for Trick (33); I Loved You Wednesday (33); Alice in Wonderland (33, with Robert Odell); Cavalcade (33, with William S. Darling); Wharf Angel (34); Things to Come (36, with Vincent Korda); The Adventures of Tom Sawyer (38, with Lyle Wheeler, Casey Roberts); The Young in Heart (38, with Lyle Wheeler); Made for Each Other (38, with Lyle Wheeler); Gone with the Wind (39, p.d. with Lyle Wheeler a.d.); Intermezzo (39, with Lyle Wheeler); Foreign Correspondent (40, with Alexander Golitzen, Richard Irvine, Edmond Bernoudy); Our Town (40, with Harry Horner); The Thief of Bagdad (40, with Vincent Korda); The Green Cockatoo (40); Conquest of the Air (40); So Ends Our Night (41, with Jack Otterson); The Devil and Miss Jones (41); The Pride of the Yankees (42, with Perry Ferguson, McClure Capps); King's Row (42, with Charles Jules Weyl); Mr. Lucky (43, with Albert D'Agostino, Mark-Lee Kirk); For Whom the Bell Tolls (43, with Hans Dreier, Haldane Douglas); The North Star (43, with Perry Ferguson); Address Unknown (44, with Lionel Banks, Walter Holscher); Duel in the Sun (46, with James Basevi, John Ewing, J. McMillan Johnson); Ivy (47, with Richard H. Riedel); Arch of Triumph (48); Reign of Terror (49, with Edward Ilou); Drums in the Deep South (51); The Whip Hand (51); Invaders from Mars (53, with Boris Leven); The Maze (53, with David Milton); The Adventures of Hajii Baba (54, with George Hoyninge-Huene, Gene Allen, Dave Milton); Around the World in 80 Days (56, with Ken Adam, James Sullivan).

Harold Miles

Don Q., Son of Zorro (25, with Anton Grot, Edward M. Langley, Harry Oliver); Queen Kelly (28, with Richard Day).

R. Jack Mills

Ridin' Down the Trail (48); Cheyenne Takes Over (48); Return of the Lash (48); The Fighting Vigilantes (48); Black Hills (48).

Dave Milton

'Neath Brooklyn Bridge (42); The Ape Man (43); Ghosts on the Loose (43); The Mystery of the Thirteenth Guest (43); Nearly Eighteen (43); Silver Skates (43); The Sultan's Daughter (43); The Unknown Guest (43); What a Man! (43); Clancy Street Boys (43); I Escaped the Gestapo (43); Sarong Girl (43); Spotlight Scandals (43); Spy Train (43); Where Are Your Children (43); You Can't Beat the Law (43); Black Market Rustlers (43); Charlie Chan in the Secret Service (44); Detective Kitty O'Day (44); Leave It to the Irish (44); Smart Guy (44); Army Wives (44); Atlantic City (44); Black Magic (44); The Chinese Cat (44); Enemy of Women (44); Hot Rhythm (44); Return of the Ape Man (44); West of the Rio Grande (44); Kid Dynamite (44); Voodoo Man (44); Melody Parade (44); Revenge of the Zombies (44); Allotment Wives (45); Captain Tugboat Annie (45); Come Out Fighting (45); Divorce (45); Docks of New York (45); G.I. Honeymoon (45); The Lonesome Trail (45); Mr. Muggs Rides Again (45); Saddle Serenade (45); The Scarlet Clue (45); South of the Rio Grande (45); There Goes Kelly (45); Fashion Model (45); The Jade Mask (45); Behind the Mask (46); Below the Deadline (46); Bowery Bombshell (46); Decoy (46); In Fast Company (46); Missing Lady (46); Mr. Hex (46); Red Dragon (46); The Shadow Returns (46); Gentleman Joe Palooka (46); Don't Gamble with Strangers (46); Live Wires (46); Dark Alibi (46); Wife Wanted (46); The Face of Marble (46); Sensation Hunters (46); Kilroy Was Here (47); News Hound (47); Joe Palooka in the Knockout (47); Fall Guy (47); Hard Boiled Mahoney (47); The Trap (47); Vacation Days (47); Bowery Buckaroos (47); Sarge Goes to College (47); Louisiana (47); Black Gold (47); Rocky (48); Jiggs and Maggie in Society (48); Panhandle (48); Angel's Alley (48); Campus Sleuth (48); Fighting Mad (48); French Leave (48); Jinx Money (48); I Wouldn't Be in Your Shoes (48); Smart Politics (48); Stage Struck (48); Music Man (48); The Golden Eye (48); Kidnapped (48); Shanghai Chest (48); Winner Take All (48); The Return of Wildfire (48); Trouble Makers (48); Incident (48); Mississippi Rhythm (49); Tuna Clipper (49); Sky Dragons (49); Feathered Serpent (49); Leave It to Henry (49); Forgotten Women (49); Fighting Fools (49); Joe Palooka in the Big Fight (49); Hold That Baby! (49); Henry, the Rainmaker (49); Trail of the Yukon (49); The Lawton Story (49); Hallmark (49); Jiggs and Maggie in Jackpot Jitters (40); Joe Palooka in the Counterpunch (49); Angels in Disguise (49); Master Minds (49); Black Midnight (49); Alaska Patrol (49); The Texan Meets Calamity Jane (50); It's a Small World (50); A Modern Marriage (50); Hot Rod (50); Jiggs and Maggie Out West (50); The Lost Volcano (50); Joe Palooka in Humphrey Takes a Chance (50); Joe Palooka Meets Humphrey (50); Killer Shark (50); Lucky Losers (50); Blonde Dynamite (50); Blues Busters (50); Triple Trouble (50); Silver Raiders (50); Snow Dog (50); Square Dance Katy (50); The Wolf Hunters (50); County Fair (50); Big Timber (50); Blue Grass of Kentucky (50); Father Makes Good (50); Southside 1-1000 (50); Father's Wild Game (50); Call of the Klondike (50); Sierra Passage (50); Short Grass (50); Outlaw Gold (50); The Whipped (50); Side Show (50); According to Mrs. Hoyle (51); Blue Blood (51); Bowery Battalion (51); Canyon Raiders (51); Casa Manana (51); Cavalry Scout (51); Colorado Ambush (51); Crazy Over Horses (51); Elephant Stampede (51); Father Takes the Air (51); Flight to Mars (51); Ghost Chasers (51); Let's Go Navy (51); The Lion Hunters (51); The Longhorn (51); Montana Desperado (51); Navy Bound (51);

Nevada Badmen (51); Northwest Territory (51); Oklahoma Justice (51); Outlaws of Texas (51); Rhythm Inn (51); Wanted Dead or Alive (51); Yellow Fin (51); Yukon Manhunt (51); Disc Jockey (51); I Was an American Spy (51); Abilene Trail (51); The Steel Fist (52); The Maze (53, with William Cameron Menzies); Fangs of the Arctic (53); Riot in Cell Block 11 (54); The Adventures of Hajji Baba (54, with Gene Allen, George Hoyninge-Huene); Wichita (55); The Disembodied (57); Dino (57); The Beast of Budapest (58); The Bat (59); The Hypnotic Eye (60); Hell to Eternity (60); King of the Roaring 20's (61).

Thomas Morahan

The Paradine Case (47); So Evil My Love (48); Under Capricorn (49); Treasure Island (50, p.d.).

Floyd Mueller

Victory (19, with Ben Carré); Treasure Island (20, with Ben Carré, Andre Ibels); Last of the Mohicans (20); Trust Your Wife (20 or 21); The Great Redeemer (20); The White Circle (20); Deep Waters (20); The Bait (21); Her Social Value (21); Be My Wife (21, with Max Linder); While Paris Sleeps (23).

Paul Murphy

Let's Have Fun (43); Passport to Suez (43); Silver City Raiders (43); The Chance of a Lifetime (43); Doughboys in Ireland (43); She Has What It Takes (43); What's Buzzin', Cousin (43); Cowboy from Lonesome River (44); Girl in the Case (44); Jam Session (44); The Ghost that Walks (44).

Warren Alfred Newcombe

Passion (20); Vendetta (20); Four Horsemen of the Apocalypse (21); Inside of the Cup (21); Without Limit (21).

Emrich Nicholson

Are You with It? (48); Black Bart (48); The Countess of Monte Cristo (48); One Touch of Venus (48); Johnny Stool Pigeon (49); City Across the River (49); Take One False Step (49); Ma and Pa Kettle (49); The Story of Molly X (49); Undercover Girl (50); Ma and Pa Kettle Go to Town (50); The Desert Hawk (50); The Kid from Texas (50); The Sleeping City (50); Kansas Raiders (50); The Cimarron Kid (51); The Prince Who Was a Thief (51); The Lady from Texas (51); Ma and Pa Back on the Farm (51); Francis Goes to the Races (51).

C.P. Norman

Night and the City (50); The Mudlark (50); No Highway in the Sky (51); I'll Never Forget You (51).

Charles Novi

Crime School (38); King of the Underworld (39); Singapore Woman (41); Underground (41); The Mysterious Doctor (43); The Blackmailer (43); Crime by Night (44); Shine On, Harvest Moon (44); The Desert Song (43); To Have and Have Not (44).

Albert Nozaki

Sorrowful Jones (49, with Hans Dreier); Bride of Vengeance (49, with Roland Anderson, Hans Dreier); Appointment with Danger (51, with Hans Dreier); When Worlds Collide (51, with Hal Pereira); The Ten Commandments (56, with Hal Pereira, Walter Tyler).

Martin Obzina

First Love (39); The Invisible Man Returns (40); The Flame of New Orleans (41); Son of Dracula (43); The Amazing Mrs. Holliday (43); Fired Wife (43); Frankenstein Meets the Wolf Man (43); His Butler's Sister (43); Honeymoon Lodge (43); How's About It (43); The Mad Ghoul (43); Never a Dull Moment (43); Rhythm in the Islands (43); Sherlock Holmes Faces Death (43); Bowery to Broadway (44); Gypsy Wildcat (44); Moonlight and Cactus (44); The Merry Monahans (44); Dead Man's Eyes (44); Sherlock Holmes and the Spider Woman (44); House of Frankenstein (44); The Suspect (45); The Mummy's Curse (44); Night Club Girl (44); The Pearl of Death (44); Spider Woman (44); On Stage Everybody (45); Pursuit to Algiers (45); The Woman in Green (45); That Night with You (45); Dressed to Kill (45); Little Giant (45); Lover Come Back (45); Strange Conquest (45); House of Dracula (45); The Killers (46, with Jack Otterson); Black Angel (46); Heaven Only Knows (47); Jungle Goddess (48); Highway 13 (48); Arson, Inc. (49); The Green Promise (49); Sky Liner (49); Thunder in the Pines (49); Deputy Marshal (49); Davy Crockett — Indian Scout (49); One Too Many (50); M (51); Joe Palooka in Triple Cross (51); The Highwayman (51); The Sword of Monte Cristo (51); Lady in the Iron Mask (52).

Charles Odds

The Bridge of San Luis Rey (44); Dark Waters (44); Sensations of 1945 (44); Captain Kidd (45).

Cary Odell

My Sister Eileen (42); City Without Men (43); Two-Man Submarine (43); Destroyer (43); Ever Since Venus (44); The Impatient Years (44); Sing While You Dance (44); Cover Girl (44); Johnny O'Clock (47); Blind Spot (47); To the Ends of the Earth (48); The Dark Past (48); The Loves of Carmen (48); We Were Strangers (49); The Reckless Moment (49); The Secret of St. Ives (49); Cargo to Capetown (50); No Sad Songs for Me (50); Boots Malone (51); The Brave Bulls (51); Death of a Salesman (51); Flame of Stamboul (51); The Harlem Globetrotters (51); The Member of the Wedding (52); From Here to Eternity (53); Storm Center (56); 20 Million Miles to Earth (57); Bell, Book, and Candle (58); They Came to Cordura (59); Homicidal (61); Mr. Sardonicus (61); The Notorious Landlady (62); Kid Galahad (62); Seven Days in May (64); The Patsy (64); Hawaii (66); Cool Hand Luke (67); The Gypsy Moths (69); Mr. Majestyk (74).

Robert A. Odell

Occasionally Yours (20); A Little Fraid Lady (20); Dangerous Pastime (21); A Certain Rich Man (21); The Mysterious Rider (27); Tom Sawyer (30); King of the Jungle (33); The Eagle and the Hawk (33); Torch Singer (33); 3-Cornered Moon (33); Alice in Wonderland (33, with William Cameron Menzies); Six of a Kind (34, with Hans Dreier); Ruggles of Red Gap (35, with Hans Dreier); Border Flight (36, with Hans Dreier); Hold 'Em Navy (37, with Hans Dreier); King of the Gamblers (37, with Hans Dreier); Partners in Crime (37, with Hans Dreier); Beau Geste (39, with Hans Dreier); The Light that Failed (39, with Hans Dreier);

Unmarried (39, with Hans Dreier); Mystery Sea Rider (40, with Hans Dreier); A Night at Earl Carroll's (40, with Hans Dreier); Road to Singapore (40, with Hans Dreier).

Jack Okey

Torment (24); The White Moth (24); Old Loves and New (26); Sally (29); Showgirl in Hollywood (30); The Dawn Patrol (30); 5 Star Final (31); The Last Flight (31); I Am a Fugitive from a Chain Gang (32); Tiger Shark (32); The Crowd Roars (32, with Anton Grot); Private Detective 62 (33); Female (33); The Kennel Murder Case (33); 42nd Street (33); Footlight Parade (33, with Anton Grot); Central Airport (33); Lilly Turner (33); The Merry Frinks (34); Fashions of 1934 (34, with Willy A. Pogany); Flirtation Walk (34); Wonder Bar (34, with Willy Pogany); Bordertown (35); Lydia (41, with Vincent Korda); The Jungle Book (42, with Vincent Korda); Johnny Come Lately (43); Higher and Higher (43); The Master Race (44); Passport to Adventure (44); Show Business (44); None but the Lonely Heart (44, with Albert D'Agostino); Experiment Perilous (44); Johnny Angel (45); It's a Wonderful Life (46); Till the End of Time (46); The Spiral Staircase (46, with Albert D'Agostino); Deadline at Dawn (46); Crackup (46); Out of the Past (47); Night Song (47); Rachel and the Stranger (48); Adventure in Baltimore (49); The Set-Up (49); Double Deal (50); Born to Be Bad (50); The Racket (51); Hard, Fast, and Beautiful (51); Black Beard the Pirate (52); Devil's Canyon (53); A Bullet for Joey (55); Bengazi (55); Screaming Eagles (56); Run of the Arrow (57); The Missouri Traveler (58); The Young Land (59).

Harold G. (Harry) Oliver

Grim Game (19); Behind the Door (19); Below the Surface (20, with Hobart Bosworth); Down Home (20); Partners of the Tide (20); Face of the World (21); The Hill Billy (24); Don Q, Son of Zorro (25, with Anton Grot, Edward M. Langley, Harold Miles); Little Annie Rooney (25, with Jack Schulze); Sparrows (26); 7th Heaven (27); Street Angel (28); The Gaucho (28); The River (28); Lucky Star (29); Sunny Side Up (29); They Had to See Paris (29); City Girl (30, with Ben Carré, William S. Darling); Lightnin' (30); Liliom (30); Song o' My Heart (30); Scarface (32); Tillie and Gus (33); White Woman (33, with Hans Dreier); The Cat's Paw (34); Viva, Villa! (34); Mark of the Vampire (35); Vanessa, Her Love Story (35); The Good Earth (37, with Cedric Gibbons, Arnold Gillespie, Edwin B. Willis); Of Human Hearts (38).

Eric Orbom

Tess of the Storm Country (22, with Anton Grot); Abbott and Costello in the Foreign Legion (50); The Strange Door (51); Bedtime for Bonzo (51); Spartacus (60, with Alexander Golitzen).

Frank D. Ormston

Hypocrites (14); Samson (14); Dumb Girl of Portici (16); For Husbands Only (17); Japanese Nightingale (18); Kismet (20); Beloved Cheater (??).

Jack Otterson

Carolina (34); One More Spring (35); The Magnificent Brute (36); Three Smart Girls (36); This Way Please (37, with Hans Dreier); You're a Sweet Heart (37); The Rage of Paris (38); Sinners in Paradise (38); Son of Frankenstein (39, with Richard Riedel); You Can't Cheat an Honest Man (39); Tower of London (39); 7 Sinners (40); The Bank Dick (40, with Richard Reidel); My Little Chickadee (40); The Wolf Man (41); So Ends Our Night (41, with William Cameron Menzies); It Started with Eve (41); Hellzapoppin (42); The Spoilers (42); Arabian Nights (42); The Mad Doctor of Market Street (42); Arizona Cyclone (43); Cheyenne Roundup (43); Mug Town (43); Boss of Hangtown Mesa (43); The Amazing Mrs. Holliday (43); Hi'Ya Chum (43); It Comes Up Love (43); Raiders of the San Joaquin (43); Sherlock Holmes Faces Death (43); The Killers (46, with Martin Obzina); Song of Scheherezade (47, with Eugene Lourie); Michigan Kid (47); The Vigilantes Return (47); Pirates of Monterey (47).

Paul Palmentola

The Girl and the Gorilla (43); The Devil Bat (43); Tiger Fangs (43); Shake Hands with Murder (44); Sweethearts of the USA (44); Waterfront (44); Bluebeard (44); The Contender (44); Delinquent Daughters (44); Dixie Jamboree (44); I Accuse My Parents (44); Men on Her Mind (44); Minstrel Man (44); The Monster Maker (44); Swing Hostess (44); Thundering Gun-Slingers (44); When the Lights Go on Again (44); Johnny Doesn't Live Here Any More (44); The Kid Sister (45); The Phantom of 42nd Street (45); Rogues Gallery (45); Strange Illusion (45); Crime, Inc. (45); Fog Island (45); The Lady Confesses (45); The Man Who Walked Alone (45); Nabonga (45); Freddie Steps Out (46); Betty Co-Ed (47); Last of the Redmen (47); Little Miss Broadway (47); Glamour Girl (47); Sweet Genevieve (47); Two Blondes and a Redhead (47); Marylou (48); The Prince of Thieves (48); Racing Luck (48); Manhattan Angel (48); Jungle Jim (48); Triple Threat (48); I Surrender Dear (48); Boston Blackie's Chinese Venture (49); Kazan (49); Make Believe Ballroom (49); Chinatown at Midnight (49); The Lost Tribe (49); The Mutineers (49); Barbary Pirate (49); Mark of the Gorilla (50); State Penitentiary (50); Tryant of the Sea (50); Chain Gang (50); Last of the Buccaneers (50); Captive Girl (50); Jungle Jim in Pygmy Island (50); Revenue Agent (50); Fury in the Congo (51); Hurricane Island (51); Jungle Manhunt (51); The Magic Carpet (51); Purple Heart Diary (51); When the Redskins Rode (51); A Yank in Korea (51).

Max Parker

The Road to Yesterday (25, with Anton Grot, Paul Iribe, Mitchell Leisen); Eve's Leaves (26); The Volga Boatman (26, with Anton Grot, Mitchell Leisen); Turkish Delight (27); The Hawk's Nest (28); The Yellow Lily (28, with Anton Grot); Gold Diggers of Broadway (29); Public Enemy (31); The Warrior's Husband (33); The Power and the Glory (33); The Worst Woman in Paris (33); Grand Canary (34); I Am Suzanne (34); Satan Met a Lady (36); Marked Woman (37); Sh! the Octopus (37); Green Light (37); A Slight Case of Murder (38); Men Are Such Fools (38); Each Dawn I Die (39); The Roaring 20's (39); Devil's Island (40); Invisible Stripes (40); It All Came True (40); Brother Orchid (40, with Carl Jules Weyl); Manpower (41); The Hard Way (43); Princess O'Rourke (43); Arsenic and Old Lace (44); Cloak and Dagger (46); Deep Valley (47); Secret Beyond the Door (48).

Hal Pereira

Double Indemnity (44, with Hans Dreier); Ministry of Fear (44, with Hans Dreier); And Now Tomorrow (44, with Hans Dreier); And the Angels Sing (44, with Hans Dreier); Jane Eyre (44); Mystery of Fear (44); A Medal for Benny (45, with Hans Dreier); You Came Along (45, with Hans Dreier); Blue Skies (46); The Goldbergs (50); The Redhead and the Cowboy (50, with Henry Bumstead); My Favorite Spy (51, with Roland Anderson); The Mating Season (51, with Roland Anderson); Darling, How Could You (51, with Roland Anderson); That's My Boy (51); Peking Express (51); Red Mountain (51); Silver City (51); Dear Brat (51, with Henry Bumstead); Submarine Command (51, with Henry Bumstead); Sailor Beware (51, with Henry Bumstead); Rhubarb (51, with Henry Bumstead); Here Comes the Groom (51); When Worlds Collide (51, with Albert Nozaki); Ace in the Hole/The Big Carnival (51); Detective Story (51, with Earl Hedrick); Carrie (52, with Roland Anderson); Come Back, Little Sheba (52, with Henry Bumstead); The Greatest Show on Earth (52, with Walter Tyler); Shane (53, with Walter Tyler); Flight to Tangier (53, with John Goodman); The Country Girl (54, with Roland Anderson); The Naked Jungle (54, with Franz Bachelin); Rear Window (54, with Joseph McMillan Johnson); The Rose Tattoo (55, with Tambi Larsen); To Catch a Thief (55, with Joseph McMillan Johnson); That Certain Feeling (56, with Henry Bumstead); The Ten Commandments (56, with Walter Tyler, Albert Nozaki); The Man Who Knew Too Much (56, with Henry Bumstead); Funny Face (57, with George W. Davis); Vertigo (58, with Henry Bumstead); Ladies' Man (61); Breakfast at Tiffany's (61, with Roland Anderson); Love with the Proper Stranger (63, with Roland Anderson); The Nutty Professor (63, with Walter Tyler); Hud (63, with Tambi Larsen); The Odd Couple (68).

William Pereira

Aloma of the South Seas (41, with Hans Dreier); New York Town (41, with Hans Dreier); Since You Went Away (44, p.d. with Mark-Lee Kirk, a.d.).

Hans Peters

Dressed to Thrill (35); The Road to Glory (36); Heidi (37); Rebecca of Sunnybrook Farm (38); Submarine Patrol (38); The Little Princess (39, with Richard Day, Bernard Herzbrun); The Hound of the Baskervilles (39, with Thomas Little, Richard Day); Adventures of Sherlock Holmes (39, with Richard Day); Tarzan's Desert Mystery (43); Stage Door Canteen (43); Tarzan Triumphs (43); Music for Millions (44); The Picture of Dorian Gray (45); Twice Blessed (45); Thrill of a Romance (45); The Green Years (46, with Cedric Gibbons); Easy to Wed (46, with Cedric Gibbons); Song of Love (47); If Winter Comes (47); The Beginning or the End (47); Act of Violence (48); The Great Sinner (49); Battleground (49, with Cedric Gibbons); Border Incident (49); The Red Danube (49); Key to the City (50); Kim (50, with Cedric Gibbons); The Red Badge of Courage (51, with Cedric Gibbons); Scaramouche (52); The Prisoner of Zenda (52); Small Town Girl (53); Diane (55); Moonfleet (55); High Society (56, with Cedric Gibbons); Lust for Life (56, with Preston Ames, Cedric Gibbons); Tip on a Dead Jockey (57); Man on Fire (57); High School Confidential (58); The Miracle (59); Girl's Town (59); Bachelor in Paradise (61); Boy's Night Out (62); The Hook (63).

Robert Peterson

Arizona (40, with Lionel Banks); One Dangerous Night (43); The Boogie Man Will Get You (43); Stand by All Networks (43); Dangerous Business (46); Dangerous Millions (46); Night Editor (46); The Phantom Thief (46); Strange Journey (46); The Devil's Mask (46); Backlash (47); Jewels of Brandenburg (47); Bulldog Drummond Strikes Back (47); The Lone Wolf in London (47); The Wreck of the Hesperus (48); Leather Gloves (48); Ladies of the Chorus (49); Holiday in Havana (49); And Baby Makes Three (49); Knock on Any Door (49); Tokyo Joe (49); The Walking Hills (49); A Woman of Distinction (50); The Fuller Brush Girl (50); In a Lonely Place (50); Saturday's Hero (51); Sirocco (51); Scandal Sheet (52); The Big Heat (53); Human Desire (54); Five Against the House (55); The Long Gray Line (55); The Last Frontier (55); Hot Blood (56); The Garment Jungle (57); Decision at Sundown (57); The Last Hurrah (58); Edge of Eternity (59); Ride Lonesome (59); Two Rode Together (61); Underworld USA (61); Zotz! (62); Experiment in Terror (62); The Outlaws Is Coming! (65).

William Andrew (Willy) Pogany

The Devil Dancer (27); Palmy Days (31); Tonight or Never (31); Unholy Garden (31); The Mummy (32); Dames (34); Wonder Bar (34, with Jack Okey); Fashions of 1934 (34, with Jack Okey); Dante's Inferno (35, with Ben Carré).

Van Nest Polglase

A Kiss in the Dark (25); Lovers in Quarantine (25); Stage Struck (25); The Magnificent Flirt (28); Untamed (29, with Cedric Gibbons, Richard Day); Bed of Roses (33, with Charles Kirk); Chance at Heaven (33, with Perry Ferguson); Little Women (33, with Hobart Erwin); Morning Glory (33, with Charles Kirk); Anne Vickers (33, with Charles Kirk); Flying Down to Rio (33, with Carroll Clark); The Past of Mary Holmes (33); Melody Cruise (33); Emergency Call (33); No Marriage Ties (33); One Man's Journey (33); Midshipman Jack (33); Ace of Tonight (33); Professional Sweetheart (33, with Carroll Clark); Christopher Strong (33, with Charles Kirk); Romance in Manhattan (34, with Charles Kirk); Finishing School (34, with Albert D'Agostino); Rafter Romance (34, with John H. Hughes); This Man Is Mine (34, with Carroll Clark); Of Human Bondage (34, with Carroll Clark); The Lost Patrol (34, with Sidney Ullman); Spitfire (34, with Carroll Clark); The Gay Divorcee (34, with Carroll Clark); The Fountain (34, with Carroll Clark); Bachelor Bait (34, with Carroll Clark); Long Lost Father (34, with Al Herman); Roberta (35, with Carroll Clark); Village Tale (35, with Carroll Clark); Jalna (35, with Charles Kirk); The Last Days of Pompeii (35); I Dream Too Much (35, with Charles Kirk); In Person (35, with Carroll Clark); Star of Midnight (35, with Charles Kirk); Break of Hearts (35, with Carroll Clark); The Informer (35, with Charles Kirk); The Return of Peter Grimm (35); Sylvia Scarlet (35); Laddies (35, with Perry Ferguson); The Nitwits (35, with Perry Ferguson); Top Hat (35, with Carroll Clark); Alice Adams (35, with Perry Ferguson); Annie Oakley (35, with Perry Ferguson); Mary of Scotland (36, with Carroll Clark); Swing Time (36, with Carroll Clark); The Plough and the Stars (36); Follow the Fleet (36, with Carrol Clark); Mummy's Boys (36); Muss 'em Up (36); The Ex–Mrs. Bradford (36); The Lady Consents (36); A Woman Rebels (36, with Perry Ferguson); The Big Game (36); The Big Shot (37); Fight For Your Lady (37); Forty Naughty Girls (37); Living on Love (37); Meet the Missus (37); Music for Madame (37); New Faces of 1937 (37); On Again, Off Again (37); Sea Devils (37); Shall We Dance (37, with Carroll Clark); Stage Door (37); Super Sleuth (37); The Toast of New York (37); Too Many Wives (37); The Woman I Love (37); Hitting a New High (37); A Damsel in Distress (37, with Carroll Clark); Winterset (37, with Perry Ferguson); Affairs of Annabel (38); Carefree (38, with Carroll Clark); I'm from the City (38); The Law West of Tombstone (38); A Man to Remember (38); Room Service (38, with Al Herman); The Saint in New York (38); Tarnished Angel (38); Vivacious Lady (38, with Carroll Clark); Condemned Woman (38); Having a Wonderful Time (38, with Perry Ferguson); Bringing Up Baby (38, with Perry Ferguson); In Name Only (39, with Perry Ferguson); Love Affair (39); The Story of Vernon and Irene Castle (39, with Perry Ferguson); Bachelor Mother (39, with Carroll Clark); Fifth Avenue Girl (39, with Perry Ferguson); Alleghany Uprising (39); Five Came Back (39); The Girl from Mexico (39); The Great Man Votes (39); Gunga Din (39, with Perry Ferguson); The Hunchback of Notre Dame (39); Mexican Spitfire (39); Panama Lady (39); Reno (39); That's Right—You're Wrong (39); Abe Lincoln in Illinois (40); Primrose Path (40, with Carroll Clark); They Knew What They Wanted (40, with Mark-Lee Kirk); Vigil in the Night (40, with L.P. Williams); Curtain Call (40); Dance, Girl, Dance (40); I'm Still Alive (40, with Albert D'Agostino); Kitty Foyle (40, with Mark-Lee Kirk); Laddie (40); Let's Make Music (40); Lucky Partners (40, with Carroll Clark); Married and in Love (40); Mexican Spitfire Out West (40); My Favorite Wife (40, with Mark-Lee Kirk); Millionaire Playboy (40); Millionaires in Prison (40); One Crowded Night (40); Pop Always Pays (40); The Stranger on the Third Floor (40); Sued for Libel (40); Tom Brown's School Days (40); Too Many Girls (40); Wagon Train (40); You Can't Fool Your Wife (40); You'll Find Out (40); All That Money Can Buy (41); The

Bandit Trail (41); Citizen Kane (41, with Perry Ferguson, Hilyard Brown); Cyclone on Horseback (41); The Gay Falcon (41); Look Who's Laughing (41); Mr. and Mrs. Smith (41, with L.P. Williams); Suspicion (41, with Carroll Clark); Tom, Dick and Harry (41, with Mark-Lee Kirk); What a Woman! (43, with Lionel Banks); The Fallen Sparrow (43); Together Again (44, with Stephen Goosson); A Song to Remember (45, with Lionel Banks); Kiss and Tell (45, with Stephen Goosson); She Wouldn't Say Yes (45, with Stephen Goosson); Gilda (46, with Stephen Goosson); The Thrill of Brazil (46, with Stephen Goosson); The Crooked Way (49); The Admiral Was a Lady (50); The Fireball (50); The Man Who Cheated Himself (50); Johnny One-Eye (50); Never Fear/The Young Lovers (50); Silver Lode (54); Passion (54); Cattle Queen of Montana (54); Escape to Burma (55); Pearl of the South Pacific (55); Tennessee's Partner (55); Slightly Scarlet (56); The River's Edge (57).

Fred Preble

Hitler's Hangman (43); Isle of Forgotten Sins (43); My Son, the Hero (43); Shep Comes Home (48); Frontier Revenge (49); Ringside (49); Son of a Badman (49); Son of Billy the Kid (49); Zamba (49); Square Dance Jubilee (49); Red Desert (49); The Dalton Gang (49); Gunfire (50); I Shot Billy the Kid (50); Train to Tombstone (50); Border Rangers (50); West of the Brazos (50); Crooked River (50); Hostile Country (50); Radar Secret Service (50); The Girl from San Lorenzo (50); The Fighting Stallion (50); Federal Man (50); King of the Bullwhip (50); Korea Patrol (50); Blazing Bullets (51); Man from Sonora (51); The Hoodlum (51).

Jerome Pycha, Jr.

The Daring Young Man (43); Underground Agent (43); Escape in the Fog (45); My Name Is Julia Ross (45); Rhythm Roundup (45); Youth on Trial (45); The Gay Senorita (45); A Close Call for Boston Blackie (46); Deadline for Murder (46); The Gentleman Misbehaves (46); The Girl of Limberlost (46); Prison Ship (46); Rendezvous 24 (46); Out of the Depths (46); Curley (47); The Fabulous Joe (47); Let's Live Again (48); Here Comes Trouble (48); Who Killed Doc Robbin (48); Jungle Patrol (48); The Gay Intruders (48); Texas, Brooklyn & Heaven (48); The Girl from Manhattan (48); Unknown Island (48); Silent Conflict (48); Cover-Up (49); Strange Gamble (49); The Great Dan Patch (49); Prehistoric Women (51).

Merrill Pye

Mr. Wu (27, with Richard Day, Cedric Gibbons); Broadway Melody (29); Our Modern Maidens (29, with Cedric Gibbons); Our Blushing Brides (30, with Cedric Gibbons); Sins of the Children (30, with Richard Day); Freaks (32, with Cedric Gibbons); David Copperfield (34, with Cedric Gibbons); Reckless (35, with Cedric Gibbons); The Great Ziegfeld (36, with Cedric Gibbons, John Harkrider); Presenting Lily Mars (43); DuBarry Was a Lady (43); Bathing Beauty (44); Meet the People (44); Ziegfeld Follies (46, with Jack Martin Smith, Cedric Gibbons, William Ferrari); North by Northwest (59, with Robert Boyle, William A. Horning).

Charles F. Pyke

The Falcon in San Francisco (45); The Devil Thumbs a Ride (47); Thunder Mountain (47); Under the Toronto Rim (47); The Arizona Ranger (48); Variety Time (48); Make Mine Laughs (49); The Threat (49); Border Treasure (50).

Jack R. Rabin

Lost Honeymoon (47); Repeat Performance (47); Love from a Stranger (47); Adventures of Casanova (48); The Man from Texas (48); The Noose Hangs High (48); Raw Deal (48); Micky (48); Northwest Stampede (48); He Walked by Night (48); The Spiritualist (48); Red Stallion in the Rockies (49); Reign of Terror (49); Rocketship XM (50, special effects); Unknown World (51, co-a.d., co-prod.).

Hans Radon

Alias Mr. Twilight (46); Crime Doctor's Man Hunt (46); Just Before Dawn (46); Mysterious Intruder (46); The Return of Rusty (46); For the Love of Rusty (47); King of the Wild Horses (47); Secret of the Whistler (47); Shadowed (47); The Thirteenth Hour (47).

Natacha Rambova

Camille (21); Salome (22, also costumes); Monsieur Beaucaire (24).

Maurice Ransford

Little Tokyo, USA (42, with Richard Day); The Pied Piper (42, with Richard Day); Wintertime (43); Immortal Sargeant (43, with Richard Day); The Moon Is Down (43); He Hired the Boss (43, with Richard Day); Lifeboat (44); Sweet and Low Down (44); Captain Eddie (45); Hangover Square (45, with Lyle Wheeler); Leave Her to Heaven (45); Somewhere in the Night (46); The Foxes of Harrow (47, with Lyle Wheeler); 13 Rue Madeleine (47); The Walls of Jericho (48, with Lyle Wheeler); Road House (48); Mother Is a Freshman (49, with Lyle Wheeler); Twelve O'Clock High (49, with Lyle Wheeler); Oh, You Beautiful Doll (49, with Lyle Wheeler); Panic in the Streets (50, with Lyle Wheeler); Under My Skin (50); As Young as You Feel (51); I'd Climb the Highest Mountain (51, with Lyle Wheeler); The 13th Letter (51, with Lyle Wheeler); The Desert Fox (51, with Lyle Wheeler); Niagara (53, with Lyle Wheeler); Titanic (53, with Lyle Wheeler); King of the Khyber Rifles (53, with Lyle Wheeler); Black Widow (54, with Lyle Wheeler); The Bottom of the Bottle (56, with Lyle Wheeler); Love Me Tender (56, with Lyle Wheeler); Desk Set (57, with Lyle Wheeler); From the Terrace (60, with Lyle Wheeler); Snow White and the Three Stooges (61, with Jack Martin Smith).

Max Ree

Rio Rita (29); Seven Keys to Baldpate (29); Tanned Legs (29); The Case of Sergeant Grischa (30); Dixiana (30); Hit the Deck (30); Leathernecking (30); Beau Ideal (31); Cimarron (31); Girl Crazy (32); Carnegie Hall (47).

Elias Harry Reif

Gun Talk (47); Death Valley (47); Money Madness (48).

Nicolai Remisoff

Captain Caution (40, with Charles D. Hall); The Heat's On (43); Something to Shout About (43); Guest in the House (44); Young Widow (46); The Strange Woman (46); Lured (47); Dishonored Lady (47); No Minor Vices (48, p.d.); The Red Pony (49, p.d.); The Big Night (51); When I Grow Up (51).

Hugh Reticker

Red Hot Tires (35, with Anton Grot); Stranded (35); The Walking Dead (36); Dangerously They Live (41); Across the Pacific (42); Background to Danger (43); Truck Busters (43); The Doughgirls (44); Between Two Worlds (44); In Our Time (44); The Horn Blows at Midnight (45); Nobody Lives Forever (46); Of Human Bondage (46); Shadow of Woman (46); Humoresque (46); The Time, the Place, and the Girl (46); April Showers (48); Wallflower (48); The House Across the Street (49); Homicide (49); Night Unto Night (49); This Side of the Law (50).

Richard Riedel

Son of Frankenstein (39, with Jack Otterson); The Bank Dick (40, with Jack Otterson); The House of Seven Gables (40); Never Give a Sucker an Even Break (41); Night Monster (42); Flesh and Fantasy (43); Ghost Catchers (43); Hers to Hold (43); Hat Check Honey (44); Her Primitive Man (44); Weird Woman (44); Ali Baba and the Forty Thieves (44); Destiny (44); Sudan (45); Here Come the Co-eds (45); Men in Her Diary (45); Shady Lady (45); Frontier Gal (45); See My Lawyer (45); That's the Spirit (45); She Wrote the Book (46); Canyon Passage (46); Idea Girl (46); The Time of Their Lives (46); The Ghost Steps Out (46); Pirates of Monterey (47); Ivy (45, with William Cameron Menzies); Larceny (48); Family Honeymoon (48); Illegal Entry (49); Abbott and Costello Meet the Killer, Boris Karloff (49); Calamity Jane and Sam Bass (49); Francis (50); South Sea Sinner (50); Comanche Territory (50); Saddle Tramp (50); Outside the Wall (50); Comin' Round the Mountain (51); Meet the Invisible Man (51); Tomahawk (51); Finders Keepers (51); Hollywood Story (51); The Fat Man (51); No Room for the Groom (52); Red Ball Express (52); The Lawless Breed (52); Drums Across the River (54); Saskatchewan (54); This Island Earth (55, with Alexander Golitzen); I've Lived Before (56); The Land Unknown (57); Imitation of Life (59); Pillow Talk (59, with Alexander Golitzen); Portrait in Black (60); Hell Bent for Leather (60).

Frank A. Richards

Gunman's Code (46); Lawless Breed (46); Something in the Wind (47); Buck Privates Come Home (47); Rustler's Roundup (47); The Vigilantes Return (47); Feudin', Fussin', and a-Fightin' (48); Tap Roots (48); Red Canyon (49).

Fred Ritter

California Joe (43); Canyon City (43); Hands Across the Border (43); Overland Mail Robbery (43); Pistol Packin' Mama (43); The Cowboy and the Senorita (44); Good Night, Sweetheart (44); The Laramie Trail (44); The Mojave Firebrand (44); Pride of the Plains (44); Cheyenne Wildcat (44); Code of the Prairie (44); Hidden Valley Outlaws (44); End of the Road (44); Sheriff of Las Vegas (44); Sheriff of Sundown (44); Silver City Kid (44); The Cherokee Flash (45); The Great Stagecoach Robbery (45); Man from Oklahoma (45); Sheriff of Cimarron (45); Trail of Kit Carson (45); Corpus Christi Bandits (45); Hitchhike to Happiness (45); Thoroughbreds (45); Alias Billy the Kid (46); Conquest of Cheyenne (46); Days of Buffalo Bill (46); The Inner Circle (46); Night Train to Memphis (46); Red River Renegades (46); Sheriff of Redwood Valley (46); The El Paso Kid (46); Saddle Pals (47); Along the Oregon Trail (47); Homesteaders of Paradise Valley (47); Last Frontier Uprising (47); Northwest Outpost (47); Santa Fe Uprising (47); Vigilantes of Boomtown (47); Wild Frontier (47); Carson City Raiders (48); Train to Alcatraz (48); Macbeth (48); Prince of the Plains (49); Daughter of the Jungle (49); Omoo Omoo, the Shark God (49); Rimfire (49); Navajo Trail Raiders (49); The Arizona Cowboy (50); Rodeo King & the Senorita (51); The Arizona Cowboy (50); Rodeo King & the Senorita (51); Secrets of Monte Carlo (51).

Stan Rogers

Salute to the Marines (43); Dark Delusion (47); Alias a Gentleman (48).

Herman Rosse

King of Jazz (30); Frankenstein (31, uncredited with Charles D. Hall); Murders in the Rue Morgue (32); The Emperor Jones (33).

Arthur Royce

The Fighting Buckaroo (43); Law of the Northwest (43); A Tornado in the Saddle (43); Junior Army (43).

Wade Rubottom

Abbott & Costello in Hollywood (45); Two Smart People (46); The Arnelo Affair (47); Tenth Avenue Angel (48).

Jack Schulze

The Invisible Fear (21); Mighty Lak' a Rose (23); Madonna of the Streets (24); A Son of the Sahara (24); Joanna (25); The Lady Who Lied (25); Little Annie Rooney (25, with Harry Oliver); My Son (25); Irene (26); My Best Girl (27); Happy Days (29); Born Reckless (30); On Your Back (30); So This Is London (30); The Brat (31); The Count of Monte Cristo (34); The Last of the Mohicans (36); The Man in the Iron Mask (39); My Son, My Son! (40); The Son of Monte Cristo (41); Cheers for Miss Bishop (41).

Gabriel Scognamillo

The Merry Widow (34, with Cedric Gibbons, Frederic Hope); Andy Hardy Meets Debutante (40); For Me and My Gal (42); Thousands Cheer (43); High Barbaree (47); Singapore (47); Undercover Maisie (47); The Wistful Widow of Wagon Gap (47); Rogue's Regiment (48); Love Happy (49); Black Hand (50); Mystery Street (50); Right Cross (50); It's a Big Country (51); The Light Touch (51); The Great Caruso (51); The Story of Three Loves (53, with Preston Ames); Twist All Night (62); The Balcony (63); The 7 Faces of Dr. Lao (64); Angel, Angel Down We Go (69).

E.E. Sheeley

Foolish Wives (22, with Richard Day); Merry Go Round (23, wtih Richard Day, Erich von Stroheim); The Hunchback of Notre Dame (23, with Stephen Goosson); Phantom of the Opera (25, with Ben Carré, Charles D. Hall, Sidney Ullman).

Everett Shinn

Polly of the Circus (17); The Bright Shawl (20, with Wiard Ihnen); Janice Meredith (23).

Jack Martin Smith

Wizard of Oz (39, uncredited with Cedric Gibbons, William A. Horning, Arnold Gillespie); I Dood It (43); Whistling in Brooklyn (43); Broadway Rhythm (44); Meet Me in St.

Loius (44, with Cedric Gibbons, Lemuel Ayers); Yolanda and the Thief (45); Ziegfeld Follies (46, with Cedric Gibbons, Merrill Pye, William Ferrari); Holiday in Mexico (46); The Pirate (48); Words and Music (48); Easter Parade (48); Summer Holiday (48); On the Town (49); Madame Bovary (49); Nancy Goes to Rio (50); Summer Stock (50); Royal Wedding (51); Show Boat (51); An American in Paris (51, with Preston Ames, Irene Sharaff, Cedric Gibbons); The Belle of New York (52); Million Dollar Mermaid (52); I Love Melvin (53); Dangerous When Wet (53); Valley of the Kings (54); Teenage Rebel (56, with Lyle Wheeler); Bandido (56); Carousel (56, with Lyle Wheeler); Bigger than Life (56, with Lyle Wheeler); Peyton Place (57); The Best of Everything (59, with Lyle Wheeler, Mark-Lee Kirk); Can Can (60); Snow White and the Three Stooges (61, with Maurice Ransford); Cleopatra (63, with John de Cuir, Hilyard Brown, Herman Blumenthal, Elven Webb, Maurice Pelling, Boris Juraga); Goobye Charlie (64, with Richard Day); Von Ryan's Express (65, with Hilyard Brown); The Agony & the Ecstasy (65, with John de Cuir); Fantastic Voyage (66, with Dale Hennesy); Valley of the Dolls (67, with Richard Day); The Sweet Ride (67, with Richard Day); The Boston Strangler (68, with Richard Day); Planet of the Apes (68, with William Creber); Justine (69, with William Creber); Butch Cassidy and the Sundance Kid (69, with Philip Jeffries); Tribes (70, TV with Richard Day); Emperor of the North Pole (73); Bug (75); The Reincarnation of Peter Proud (75); Snow White and the Three Stooges (61, with Maurice Ransford); Tora, Tora, Tora! (70, with Richard Day).

Oliver Smith

The Band Wagon (53, with Preston Ames, Cedric Gibbons); Oklahoma! (55, with Joseph Wright); Guys and Dolls (55, with Joseph Wright); Porgy and Bess (59).

Perry Smith

Cowboy in the Clouds (43); Frontier Fury (43); Hail to the Rangers (43); Redhead from Manhattan (43); Robin Hood of the Range (43); Saddles and Sagebrush (43); The Desperados (43); Two Senoritas from Chicago (43); Cyclone Prairie Rangers (44); Saddle Leather Law (44); U-Boat Prisoner (44); The Unwritten Code (44); The Vigilantes Ride (44); Wyoming Hurricane (44); None Shall Escape (44); Boston Blackie Booked on Suspicion (45); Boston Blackie's Rendezvous (45); Leave It to Blondie (45); Sagebrush Heroes (45); Life with Blondie (45); Blondie Knows Best (46); Blondie's Lucky Day (46); Hit the Hay (46); The Notorious Lone Wolf (46); Renegades (46); The Red Stallion (47); Stepchild (47); The Big Fix (47); The Devil on Wheels (47); Philo Vance's Secret Mission (47); Love from a Stranger (47); Philo Vance's Gamble (47); Railroaded (47); The Prairie (48); Blondie Hits the Jackpot (49); Blondie's Big Deal (49); Girl's School (49); Johnny Allegro (49); Kill the Umpire (50); The Palomino (50); Blondie's Hero (50); Beware of Blondie (50).

Ted Smith

Gold Is Where You Find It (38); Dodge City (39); Torrid Zone (40); High Sierra (41); Gentleman Jim (42); Captain of the Clouds (42); Action in the North Atlantic (43); The Mask of Dimitrios (44); Conflict (45); San Antonio (45); Objective Burma (45); Three Strangers (46); The Verdict (46); Her Kind of Man (46); Pursued (47); Cheyenne (47); Embraceable You (48); Silver River (48); Fighter Squadron (48); Colorado Territory (49); Flaxy Martin (49).

J. Russell Spencer

The Great Dictator (40); Tonight We Raid Calais (43, with Richard Day); Happy Land (43); Holy Matrimony (43); Bermuda Mystery (44); The Eve of St. Mark (44); Sunday Dinner for

a Soldier (44); Nob Hill (45); Cluny Brown (46); Wake Up and Dream (46); Margie (46);
Dragonwyck (46); Nightmare Alley (47); The Late George Apley (47); Give My Regards to
Broadway (48); The Luck of the Irish (48); That Lady in Ermine (48); A Letter to Three Wives
(49); The Big Lift (50); An American Guerilla in the Philippines (50); Where the Sidewalk
Ends (50, with Lyle Wheeler); You're in the Navy Now (51, with Lyle Wheeler); Les
Miserables (52); Lydia Bailey (52, with Lyle Wheeler).

Rudolph Sternad

In Old Chicago (38, with William Darling); Suez (38); Rose of Washington Square (39, with
Richard Day); Little Old New York (40, with Richard Day); Young People (40, with Richard
Day); You'll Never Get Rich (41, with Lionel Banks); The Talk of the Town (42); You Were
Never Lovelier (42); The More the Merrier (43); First Comes Courage (43); There's
Something About a Soldier (43); Abroad with Two Yanks (44); Mr. Winkle Goes to War
(44); Over 21 (45); Tonight and Every Night (45); 1,001 Nights (45); The Bandit of Sher-
wood Forest (46); Perilous Holiday (46); It Had to Be You (47); Down to Earth (47); Dead
Reckoning (47); Port Said (48); The Return of October (48); Walk a Crooked Mile (48); A
Kiss for Corliss (49); Home of the Brave (49); Champion (49); The Men (50); Three
Husbands (50); Cyrano de Bergerac (50); Davy Crockett—Indian Scout (50); The Scarf (51);
High Noon (52); The 5,000 Fingers of Dr. T (53); Not As a Stranger (55); The Defiant Ones
(58); On the Beach (59); Inherit the Wind (60); Judgment at Nuremberg (61); Pressure Point
(62); It's a Mad, Mad, Mad, Mad World (63); Lady in a Cage (64).

Erich von Stroheim

Merry Go Round (23, with Richard Day, E.E. Sheeley); Greed (24, with Richard Day, Cedric
Gibbons); The Wedding March (28, with Richard Day).

James Sullivan

Klondike Kate (43); The Hairy Ape (44); Tomorrow, the World (44); Bandits of the
Badlands (45); The Cheaters (45); Mexicana (45); Story of G.I. Joe (45); In Old Sacramento
(46); The Invisible Informer (46); That Brennan Girl (46); The Pilgrim Lady (47); That's
My Man (47); The Web (47); The Fabulous Texan (47); The Gallant Legion (48); Old Los
Angeles (48); Slippy McGee (48); Sons of Adventure (48); Angel on the Amazon (48); Wake
of the Red Witch (48); Out of the Storm (48); I Jane Doe (48); Hellfire (49); Sands of Iwo
Jima (49); The Fighting Kentuckian (49); Too Late for Tears (49); Surrender (50); Hills of
Oklahoma (50); Salt Lake City Raiders (50); Singing Guns (50); Women from Headquarters
(50); Flying Leathernecks (51); Belle Le Grand (51); The Wild Blue Yonder (51); Around
the World in 80 days (56, with William Cameron Menzies, Ken Adam).

Frank Paul Sylos

Bank Alarm (37); The Moon and Sixpence (42); Corregidor (43); Career Girl (43); Alaska
Highway (43); Danger! Women at Work (43); The Girl from Monterey (43); Harvest Melody
(43); High Explosive (43); I'm from Arkansas (43); Jive Junction (43); Minesweeper (43);
Submarine Alert (43); Submarine Base (43); Three Russian Girls (43); Tornado (43); Lady
in the Death House (44); One Body too Many (44); Take It Big (44); Dangerous Passage
(44); Dixie Jamboree (44); Double Exposure (44); Gambler's Choice (44); Dark Mountain
(44); The Navy Way (44); Timber Queen (44); Aerial Gunner (44); When Strangers Marry
(44); Machine Gun Mama (44); Dillinger (45); The Great Flamarion (45); The Enchanted
Forest (45); Jealousy (45); One Exciting Night (45); Follow that Woman (45); High

Powdered (45); Scared Stiff (45); Suspense (46); A Scandal in Paris (46); The Fabulous Suzanne (46); Gas House Kids (46); Hot Cargo (46); People Are Funny (46); Swamp Fire (46); They Made Me a Killer (46); Tokyo Rose (46); Adventure Island (47); Return of Rin Tin Tin (47); Private Affairs of Bel Ami (47); The Burning Cross (47); Dragnet (47); Big Town (47); Danger Street (47); Fear in the Night (47); Hollywood Barn Dance (47); I Cover Big Town (47); Jungle Flight (47); Killer Dill (47); Seven Were Saved (47); Gas House Kids Go West (47); Big Town After Dark (47); The Gangster (47); Gas House Kids in Hollywood (47); Heading for Heaven (47); The Pretender (47); Smart Woman (48); So This Is New York (48); Ruthless (48); Blonde Savage (48); Albuquerque (48); Big Town Scandal (48); Shaggy (48); The Babe Ruth Story (48); The Hunted (48); Bungalow 13 (48); The Checkered Coat (48); Grand Canyon (49); Caught (49); I Cheated the Law (49); Tough Assignment (49); Red Light (49); Satan's Cradle (49); Holiday Rhythm (50); Hi-jacked (50); Motor Patrol (50); Baron of Arizona (50); The Return of Jesse James (50); Again . . . Pioneers (50); Second Chance (50); The Great Plane Robbery (50); Drums in the Deep South (51); Danger Zone (51); Bride of the Gorilla (51); F.B.I. Girl (51); G.I. Jane (51); Kentucky Jubilee (51); Little Big Horn (51); Pier 23 (51); Savage Drums (51); Yes Sir, Mr. Bones (51); The Bushwhackers (51); Leave It to the Marines (51); Varieties on Parade (51); Roaring City (51); 99 River Street (53); The Steel Lady (53); The Mad Magician (54); Men in War (57).

Dean Tavoularis

Ship of Fools (65); Inside Daisy Clover (65, with Robert Clatworthy); Bonnie and Clyde (67); Candy (68); Zabriske Point (70); Little Big Man (70); The Godfather (72); The Conversation (74); The Godfather, Part II (74); Farewell, My Lovely (75); Apocalypse Now (77); One from the Heart (82); Hammett (83).

Vincent Taylor

Mark of the Lash (48); Triggerman (48); Dead Man's Gold (49); Sheriff of Medicine Bow (49); The Fighting Ranger (49); Gunning for Justice (49); Bandit Queen (50); Roll, Thunder, Roll (50).

A. Leslie Thomas

The Thrill of Brazil (46); The Walls Came Tumbling Down (46); The Swordsman (47); The Black Arrow (48); The Man from Colorado (48).

Alexander Toluboff

Love (27, with Cedric Gibbons); Mockery (27); Anna Karenina (27, with Cedric Gibbons); The Cossacks (28); Diamond Handcuffs (28); Grand Hotel (32, with Cedric Gibbons); Rasputin and the Express (32); Queen Christina (33, with Cedric Gibbons, Alexander Golitzen, Edwin B. Willis); The Painted Veil (34); The Cat and the Fiddle (34); Shanghai (35); Mary Burns, Fugitive (35); Every Night at Eight (35); Trail of the Lonesome Pine (36); Big Brown Eyes (36); Spendthrift (36); History Is Made at Night (37); You Only Live Once (37); Vogues of 1938 (37); Stand-In (37); Algiers (38); Blockade (38); Trade Winds (38); Stagecoach (39, with Wiard Ihnen).

Alexander Trauner

Love in the Afternoon (57); Witness for the Prosecution (58); One, Two, Three (61); Irma la Douce (63).

William H. Tuntke

Son of Flubber (63, with Carroll Clark); The Misadventures of Merlin Jones (64, with Carroll Clark); Mary Poppins (64, with Carroll Clark); The Monkey's Uncle (65, with Carroll Clark); That Darn Cat (65, with Carroll Clark); The Gnome-mobile (67, with Carroll Clark).

Walter Tyler

The Man in Half Moon Street (44, with Hans Dreier); The National Barn Dance (44, with Hans Dreier); Henry Aldrich, Boy Scout (44, with Hans Dreier); You Can't Ration Love (44, with Hans Dreier); Hold That Blonde (45, with Hans Dreier); Kitty (45, with Hans Dreier); The Blue Dahlia (46, with Hans Dreier); Ladies' Man (47, with Hans Dreier); Unconquered (47, with Hans Dreier); A Foreign Affair (48, with Hans Dreier); Whispering Smith (48, with Hans Dreier); Samson and Delilah (49, with Hans Dreier); Riding High (50, with Hans Dreier); A Place in the Sun (51, with Hans Dreier); The Greatest Show on Earth (52, with Hal Pereira); Shane (53, with Hal Pereira); The Ten Commandments (56, with Hal Pereira, Albert Nozaki); The Nutty Professor (63, with Hal Pereira).

Sidney Ullman

Phantom of the Opera (25, with Ben Carré, Charles D. Hall, E.E. Sheeley); The Lost Patrol (34, with Van Nest Polglase).

Joseph Urban

Humoresque (20); The World and His Wife (20); Whiff of Heliotrope (20); Inside of the Cup (20); Passionate Pilgrim (21); Straight Is the Way (34); Proxies (??); The Restless Sex (20); The Bride's Play (21); Wild Goose (27); The Woman God Changed (??); Buried Treasure (21); Enchantment (21); Get-Rich-Quick Wollingford (21); Just Around the Corner (38); Back Pay (22); Beauty's Worth (22); Boomerang (25); Find that Woman (18); When Knighthood Was in Flower (22); The Young Diana (22); Sisters (22); Little Old New York (23); Adam and Eve (23); The Enemies of Women (23); The Valley of Silent Men (22); The Go Getter (37); Face in the Fog (22); Snow Blind (21); Under the Red Robe (23); The Great White Way (24); Janice Meredith (24); Yolanda (24); Never the Twain Shall Meet (25); Zander the Great (25); The Man Who Came Back (31); Doctors' Wives (31); East Lynne (31).

Robert Usher

She Done Him Wrong (33); Now and Forever (34, with Hans Dreier); Rumba (35, with Hans Dreier); Peter Ibbetson (35, with Hans Dreier); Goin' to Town (35, with Hans Dreier); Desire (36, with Hans Dreier); The Big Broadcast of 1937 (36, with Hans Dreier); Angel (37, with Hans Dreier); Artists and Models (37, with Hans Dreier); True Confessions (37, with Hans Dreier); Zaza (38, with Hans Dreier); Bluebeard's Eighth Wife (38, with Hans Dreier); Midnight (39, with Hans Dreier); The Cat and the Canary (39, with Hans Dreier); Man About Town (39, with Hans Dreier); The Ghost Breakers (40); Arise, My Love (40, with Hans Dreier); Victory (40, with Hans Dreier); Rangers of Fortune (40, with Hans Dreier); Those Were the Days (40, with Hans Dreier); Hold Back the Dawn (41, with Hans Dreier); I Wanted Wings (41, with Hans Dreier); Louisiana Purchase (41, with Hans Dreier); Nothing but the Truth (41, with Hans Dreier); My Favorite Blonde (42, with Hans Dreier); Morocco (42, with Hans Dreier); China (43, with Hans Dreier); No Time for Love (43, with Hans Dreier); Practically Yours (44, with Hans Dreier); Till We Meet Again (44, with Hans Dreier); The Chase (46); The Sin of Harold Diddlebock (47); Mad Wednesday (47); Vendetta (50).

George Van Marter

The Crime Doctor's Strangest Case (44); The Whistler (44); The Town Went Wild (44); A Wave, a Wac, and a Marine (44); Hollywood and Vine (45); Little Iodine (46); Susie Steps Out (46); Whistle Stop (46); Adventures of Don Coyote (47); Gunfighters (47); The Spirit of West Point (47); Open Secret (48); Blonde Ice (48); Arthur Takes Over (48); Half Past Midnight (48); Coroner Creek (48); Fighting Back (48); Night Wind (48); Daughter of the West (49); Fighting Man of the Plains (49); Champagne for Caesar (50); Joe Palooka in the Squared Circle (50); Slaughter Trail (51); New Mexico (51); Storm Over Tibet (51).

Leonard (Leonid) Vasian

Song of Russia (43); Cabin in the Sky (43); Young Ideas (43); Gentle Annie (44); The Seventh Cross (44); Keep Your Powder Dry (45); What Next, Corporal Hargrove? (45); It Happened in Brooklyn (47); My Brother Talks to Horses (47); High Wall (47); Scene of the Crime (49); Tension (49); Father of the Bride (50); Devil's Doorway (50); Father's Little Dividend (51); The Painted Hills (51); The Strip (51).

Carl Jules Weyl

The Florentine Dagger (35); The Case of the Curious Bride (35, with Anton Grot); Personal Maid's Secret (35); The Payoff (35); We're in the Money (35); The Singing Kid (36); Bullets or Ballots (36); Kid Galahad (37); The Adventures of Robin Hood (38); The Amazing Dr. Clitterhouse (38); Confessions of a Nazi Spy (39); Dr. Ehrlich's Magic Bullet (40); All This and Heaven Too (40); Brother Orchid (40, with Max Parker); The Letter (40); Out of the Fog (41); Desperate Journey (42); Yankee Doodle Dandy (42); King's Row (42, with William Cameron Menzies); Mission to Moscow (43); The Constant Nymph (43); Watch on the Rhine (43); Passage to Marseilles (44); The Corn Is Green (45); Saratoga Trunk (45); The Big Sleep (46); Escape Me Never (47); Cry Wolf (47).

Lyle Wheeler

Little Lord Fauntleroy (36, uncredited with Sturges Carne); The Garden of Allah (36, with Sturges Carne); A Tale of Two Cities (36); A Star Is Born (37); Nothing Sacred (37); Prisoner of Zenda (37); The Adventures of Tom Sawyer (38, with William Cameron Menzies, Casey Roberts); Made for Each Other (38, with William Cameron Menzies); Young in Heart (38, with William Cameron Menzies); Gone with the Wind (39, with p.d. William Cameron Menzies); Intermezzo (39, with William Cameron Menzies); Rebecca (40); That Hamilton Woman (41, with Alexander Korda); Smilin' Through (41); Babes on Broadway (41); Cairo (41); The Jungle Book (42); Keeper of the Flame (42); Woman of the Year (42); Bataan (43); A Guy Named Joe (43); Sweet Rosie O'Grady (43, with James Basevi, Joseph C. Wright); Harrigan's Kid (43); Dragon Seed (44); 30 Seconds Over Tokyo (44); Laura (44, with Leland Fuller); Bermuda Mystery (44); Ladies of Washington (44); Take It or Leave It (44); Wing and a Prayer (44); Sweet and Low Down (44); The Big Noise (44); In the Meantime, Darling (44); Irish Eyes Are Smiling (44); Something for the Boys (44); Winged Victory (44); Sunday Dinner for a Soldier (44); The Keys of the Kingdom (44, with William Darling); Hangover Square (45, with Maurice Ransford); A Tree Grows in Brooklyn (45); Leave Her to Heaven (45); Thunderhead—Son of Flicka (45, with Chester Gore); The Spider (45); Circumstantial Evidence (45); Captain Eddie (45); A Royal Scandal (45); The Bullfighters (45); Caribbean Mystery (45); State Fair (45, with Louis Creber); The House on 92nd Street (45); The Dolly Sisters (45); Fallen Angel (45); Billy Rose's Diamond Horseshoe (45); Molly and Me (45); Don Juan Quilligan (45); A Bell for Adano (45, with Mark-Lee Kirk); Junior Miss (45); Nob Hill (45); Where Do We Go from Here (45); Anna and the King of Siam (46, with William

Darling, Richard Day); 13 Rue Madeleine (46); Doll Face (45); Behind Green Lights (46); Colonel Effingham's Raid (46); Do You Love Me (46); Shock (46, with Boris Leven); Dragonwyck (46); A Walk in the Sun (46); Sentimental Journey (46); Strange Triangle (46); Cluny Brown (46); Centennial Summer (46); Three Little Girls in Blue (46); My Darling Clementine (46, with James Basevi); Smokey (46); Wake Up and Dream (46); The Foxes of Harrow (47, with Maurice Ransford); Boomerang (47); Captain from Castile (47); Kiss of Death (47); Nightmare Alley (47); The Ghost and Mrs. Muir (47, with George W. Davis, Richard Day); Daisy Kenyon (47); Forever Amber (47); Mother Wore Tights (47); The Shocking Miss Pilgrim (47); Carnival in Costa Rica (47); The Late George Apley (47); Gentleman's Agreement (47, with Mark-Lee Kirk); Call Northside 777 (48, with Mark-Lee Kirk); The Art Director (48, documentary); Sitting Pretty (48); When My Baby Smiles at Me (48); Scudda Hoo, Scudda Hay (48); Deep Waters (48); Fury at Furnace Creek (48); Green Grass of Wyoming (48); The Iron Curtain (48, with Mark-Lee Kirk); The Street with No Name (48); The Walls of Jericho (48); Give My Regards to Broadway (48); That Lady in Ermine (48); The Luck of the Irish (48); Cry of the City (48); Apartment for Peggy Wright (48); Roadhouse (48); Unfaithfully Yours (48, with Joseph C. Wright); Yellow Sky (48); The Snake Pit (48, with Joseph C. Wright); That Wonderful Urge (48); You Were Meant for Me (48); Escape (48); Chicken Every Sunday (48); Come to the Stable (49, with Joseph C. Wright); Letter to Three Wives (49); Mother Is a Freshman (49, with Maurice Ransford); Down to the Sea in Ships (49); Mister Belvedere Goes to College (49); The Fan (49); The Beautiful Blonde from Bashful Bend (49, with George C. Davis); It Happens Every Spring (49); House of Strangers (49); You're My Everything (49); Slattery's Hurricane (49); I Was a Male War Bride (49); Thieves Highway (49); Father Was a Full Back (49); Everybody Does It (49); Oh You Beautiful Doll (49, with Maurice Ransford); Pinky (49); Prince of Foxes (49, with Mark-Lee Kirk); Dancing in the Dark (49, with George C. Davis); Sand (49); The Big Lift (49); Whirlpool (49); Twelve O'Clock High (49, with Maurice Ransford); All About Eve (50, with George W. Davis); Under My Skin (50); When Willy Comes Marching Home (50, with Chester Gore); Mother Didn't Tell Me (50); Cheaper by the Dozen (50); Three Came Home (50, with Leland Fuller); Ticket to Tomahawk (50, with George C. Davis); Love that Brute (50); The Gunfighter (50); Where the Sidewalk Ends (50, with J. Russell Spencer); Broken Arrow (50); Stella (50, with Mark-Lee Kirk); My Blue Heaven (50); Panic in the Streets (50, with Maurice Ransford); I'll Get By (50); Mister 880 (50, with George C. Davis); No Way Out (50); The Jackpot (50, with Joseph C. Wright); An American Guerilla in the Philippines (50); Wabash Avenue (50, with Joseph C. Wright); For Heaven's Sake (50); Halls of Montezuma (50); Two Flags West (50); David and Bathsheba (51, with George Davis); On the Riviera (51, with Leland Fuller); The House on Telegraph Hill (51, with John DeCuir); Fourteen Hours (51, with Leland Fuller); Bird of Paradise (51, with Albert Hogsett); Follow the Sun (51); The Model and the Marriage Broker (51, with John DeCuir); I'd Climb the Highest Mountain (51, with Maurice Ransford); Call Me Mister (51, with Joseph C. Wright); The 13th Letter (51, with Maurice Ransford); I Can Get It for You Wholesale (51, with John DeCuir); You're in the Navy Now (51, with J. Russell Spencer); Half Angel (51, with John DeCuir); Rawhide (51, with George C. Davis); As Young As You Feel (51); The Frogmen (51); The Guy Who Came Back (51); Take Care of My Little Girl (51, with Joseph C. Wright); Meet Me After the Show (51, with Joseph C. Wright); Mr. Belvedere Rings the Bell (51, with John DeCuir); The Secret of Convict Lake (51); The Day the Earth Stood Still (51); People Will Talk (51); The Desert Fox (51, with Maurice Ransford); Love Nest (51); Anne of the Indies (51); Let's Make It Legal (51); Golden Girl (51); Elopement (51); Fixed Bayonets (51); My Cousin Rachel (52, with John DeCuir); The Snows of Kilamanjaro (52, with John DeCuir); Viva Zapata (52, with Leland Fuller); Phone Call from a Stranger (52); Red Skies of Montana (52); Monkey Business (52); What Price Glory? (52); O. Henry's Full House (52); Lure of the Wilderness (52); Something for the Birds (52); Bloodhounds of Broadway (52); Night Without Sleep (52); My Wife's Best Friend (52); My Pal Gus (52); Stars and Stripes Forever (52); Five Fingers (52); Return of the Texan (52); The Pride of St. Louis (52); With a Song in My Heart (52); Belles on Their

Toes (52); Deadline USA (52); The Outcasts of Poker Flat (52); Kangaroo (52); Lydia Bailey (52, with J. Russell Spencer); Diplomatic Courier (52, with John DeCuir); Wait Till the Sun Shines, Nellie (52); We're Not Married (52); Don't Bother to Knock (52); Dreamboat (52); Les Miserables (52); The Way of a Gaucho (52); Ruby Gentry (52, wtih James Basevi); The Robe (53, with George W. Davis); Titanic (53, with Maurice Ransford); The President's Lady (53, with Leland Fuller); The I Don't Care Girl (53); Niagara (53, with Maurice Ransford); Treasure of the Golden Condor (53); The Silver Whip (53); Taxi (53); Destination Gobi (53); Down Among the Sheltering Palms (53); Call Me Madam (53, with John DeCuir); Tonight We Sing (53); The Desert Rats (53); The Girl Next Door (53); Powder River (53); Pickup on South Street (53); Dangerous Crossing (53); The Farmer Takes a Wife (53); White Witch Doctor (53); Gentlemen Prefer Blondes (53); Inferno (53); City of Bad Men (53); Mr. Scoutmaster (53); A Blueprint for Murder (53); How to Marry a Millionaire (53); King of the Khyber Rifles (53, with Maurice Ransford); Beneath the Twelve Mile Reef (53); Desiree (54, with Leland Fuller); Hell and High Water (54); Prince Valiant (54); River of No Return (54, with Addison Hehr); Three Coins in the Fountain (54, with John DeCuir); Demetrius and the Gladiators (54); Princess of the Nile (54); Garden of Evil (54); Broken Lance (54); The Egyptian (54, with George W. Davis); Woman's World (54); Black Widow (54, with Maurice Ransford); There's No Business Like Show Business (54, with John DeCuir); Love Is a Many Splendored Thing (55, with George W. Davis); Daddy Long Legs (55, with John DeCuir); Prince of Players (55, with Mark-Lee Kirk); The Racers (55); Untamed (55); A Man Called Peter (55); Violent Saturday (55); The Magnificent Matador (55); Seven Year Itch (55, with George W. Davis); Soldier of Fortune (55); House of Bamboo (55); How to Be Very, Very Popular (55, with John DeCuir); The Virgin Queen (55); Seven Cities of Gold (55); The Left Hand of God (55); The Girl in the Red Velvet Swing (55); The View from Pompey's Head (55); Good Morning Miss Dove (55); The Rains of Ranchipur (55); The King and I (56, with John DeCuir); Teenage Rebel (56, with Jack Martin Smith); The Bottom of the Bottle (56, with Maurice Ransford); The Lieutenant Wore Skirts (56); Carousel (56, with Jack Martin Smith); The Man in the Grey Flannel Suit (56); On the Threshold of Space (56); Hilda Crane (56); The Revolt of Mamie Stover (56, with Mark-Lee Kirk); The Proud Ones (56); D-Day the Sixth of June (56); Bigger than Life (56, with Jack Martin Smith); Bus Stop (56, with Mark-Lee Kirk); The Best Things in Life Are Free (56); The Last Wagon (56); Between Heaven and Hell (56); Love Me Tender (56, with Maurice Ransford); The Girl Can't Help It (56); The True Story of Jesse James (57); Three Brave Men (57); Oh Men! Oh Women! (57); Heaven Knows, Mr. Allison (57); Boy on a Dolphin (57); The Desk Set (57, with Maurice Ransford); The Wayward Bus (57); An Affair to Remember (57); A Hatful of Rain (57); Bernadine (57); Will Success Spoil Rock Hunter (57); The Sun Also Rises (57, with Mark-Lee Kirk); Stopover Tokyo (57); The Three Faces of Eve (57); No Down Payment (57); April Love (57); The Enemy Below (57); Peyton Place (57); Kiss Them for Me (57); A Farewell to Arms (57, uncredited, p.d. Alfred Junge, a.d. Mario Garbuglia); A Certain Smile (58); Sing, Boy, Sing (58); The Gift of Love (58); These Thousand Hills (58); The Long, Hot Summer (58); South Pacific (58); The Young Lions (58); Ten North Frederick (58); Fraulein (58); The Fly (58); From Hell to Texas (58); The Bravados (58, with Mark-Lee Kirk); The Fiend Who Walked the West (58); The Hunters (58); The Barbarian and the Geisha (58); In Love and War (58); Mardi Gras (58); Inn of the Sixth Happiness (58); A Nice Little Bank that Should Be Robbed (58); The Diary of Anne Frank (59, with George Davis); Journey to the Center of the Earth (59, with Franz Bachelin, Herman A. Blumenthal); Rally Round the Flag Boys! (59); The Remarkable Mr. Pennypacker (59); The Sound and the Fury (59); Woman Obsessed (59); Warlock (59); Compulsion (59, with Mark-Lee Kirk); Holiday for Lovers (59); A Private's Affair (59); Blue Denim (59); Say One for Me (59); The Blue Angel (59); The Man Who Understood Women (59); The Best of Everything (59, with Mark-Lee Kirk, Jack Martin Smith); Beloved Infidel (59); The Hound Dog Man (59); Even Thieves (60); The Story on Page One (60); Can-Can (60); Wake Me When It's Over (60); Wild River (60); The Story of Ruth (60); From the Terrace (60, with Maurice Ransford); Let's Make Love (60); Advise and Consent (62); The Cardinal (63); The Best Man (64); In Harm's Way (65);

The Big Mouth (67); Where Angels Go, Trouble Follows (68); The Swimmer (68); Marooned (69); Tell Me that You Love Me, Junie Moon (69); Doctors' Wives (70); The Love Machine (71); Bless the Beasts and Children (73); Posse (75); Flight to Holocaust (77, TV movie).

Harrison Wiley

Driftwood (28); Nothing to Wear (28); The Power of the Press (28); Say It with Sables (28); The Scarlet Lady (28); The Sideshow (28); Submarine (28); Behind Closed Dors (29); The Donovan Affair (29); Flight (29); Wall Street (29); The Younger Generation (29); Ladies of Leisure (30); Prince of Diamonds (30); Rain or Shine (30).

Lawrence P. Williams

Vigil in the Night (40, with Van Nest Polglase); Mr. & Mrs. Smith (41, with Van Nest Polglase); Forever and a Day (43).

Edwin B. Willis

Queen Christina (33, with Cedric Gibbons, Alexander Golitzen, Alexander Toluboff); Anna Karenina (34, with Frederic Hope, Cedric Gibbons); Maytime (37, with Cedric Gibbons, Frederic Hope); Captains Courageous (37, with Cedric Gibbons, Arnold Gillespie); The Good Earth (37, with Harry Oliver, Cedric Gibbons, Arnold Gillespie).

Joseph C. Wright

The Woman of Bronze (23); Daring Youth (24); The Unholy Three (25); The Exquisite Sinner (26); The Man Who Laughs (28, with Charles D. Hall); Golf Widows (28); The Sea Wolf (30); Delicious (31); Manhattan Melodrama (34); Born to Be Bad (34, with Richard Day); Rose Marie (36); Day Time Wife (39, with Richard Day); Swanee River (39, with Richard Day); He Married His Wife (40, with Richard Day); Down Argentine Way (40, with Richard Day); The Great Profile (40, with Richard Day); Tin Pan Alley (40, with Richard Day); The Mark of Zorro (40, with Richard Day); Lillian Russell (40, with Richard Day); That Night in Rio (41, with Richard Day); A Very Young Lady (41, with Richard Day); Weekend in Havana (41, with Richard Day); Blood and Sand (41, with Richard Day); Swamp Water (41, with Richard Day, Thomas Little); Orchestra Wives (42, with Richard Day); Springtime in the Rockies (42, with Richard Day); Quiet Please, Murder (42, with Richard Day); My Gal Sal (42, with Richard Day); This Above All (42, with Richard Day, Thomas Little); The Gang's All Here (43, with James Basevi); Coney Island (43, with Richard Day); Sweet Rosie O'Grady (43, with James Basevi, Lyle Wheeler); Stormy Weather (43); Greenwich Village (44); Pin-Up Girl (44, with James Basevi); Irish Eyes Are Smiling (44); Billy Rose's Diamond Horseshoe (45); Three Little Girls in Blue (46); Do You Love Me (46); I Wonder Who's Kissing Her Now (47, with Richard Day, Boris Leven); Mother Wore Tights (47, with Richard Day); The Snake Pit (48, with Lyle Wheeler); Unfaithfully Yours (48, with Lyle Wheeler); Come to the Stable (49, with Lyle Wheeler); Wabash Avenue (50, with Lyle Wheeler); My Blue Heaven (50, with Lyle Wheeler); The Jackpot (50, with Lyle Wheeler); Call Me Mister (51, with Lyle Wheeler); Meet Me After the Show (51, with Lyle Wheeler); Take Care of My Little Girl (51, with Lyle Wheeler); On the Riviera (51); Golden Girl (51); Gentlemen Prefer Blondes (53); Man with the Golden Arm (55); Guys and Dolls (55, with Oliver Smith); Oklahoma (55, with Oliver Smith); The Strange One (57); Flower Drum Song (61, with Alexander Golitzen); Days of Wine and Roses (62); The Wrecking Crew (68).

Alfred Ybarra

This Is a Family (44); Goin' to Town (44); The Fugitive (47); Adventures of Casanova (48); Sofia (48); Borderline (50); One-Way Street (50); The Bullfighter and the Lady (51); Big Jim McClain (52); Blowing Wild (53); Hondo (53); The High and the Mighty (54); Track of the Cat (54); Run for the Sun (56); Legend of the Lost (57); Marines, Let's Go (61); The Comancheros (61); Major Dundee (65); Duel at Diablo (66); Hour of the Gun (67).

Paul Youngblood

Roll on Texas Moon (46); Under Nevada Skies (46); Bad Bascomb (46); Courage of Lassie (46); Robin Hood of Texas (47); Oregon Trail Scouts (47); Spoilers of the North (47); Stagecoach to Denver (47).

Bibliography

Albrecht, Donald. *Designing Dreams*. New York: Harper & Row, 1986.
Ames, Preston. "An American in Paris: The Ballet." *Production Design* vol. 1, no. 11 (Nov. 1952), 6ff.
Armitage, Merle. *Warren Newcombe*. New York: E. Weyhe, 1932.
Balio, Tino. *United Artists*. Madison: University of Wisconsin Press, 1976.
Barsacq, Léon. *Caligari's Cabinet and Other Grand Illusions*. Boston: New York Graphic Society, 1976. Rev. and ed. by Elliott Stein.
_____. *Le Décor de Film*. Paris: Seghers, 1970.
Basten, Fred E. *Glorious Technicolor*. New York: Barnes & Co., 1980.
Bawden, Liz-anne. *The Oxford Companion to Film*, London: Oxford University Press, 1976.
Baxter, John. *Hollywood in the Thirties*. San Diego: A.S. Barnes, 1968.
Baxter, Peter. *The Cinema of Josef Von Sternberg*. New York: A.S. Barnes, 1971.
_____, ed. *Sternberg*. London: The British Film Institute, 1980.
Beaumont, Harry. Scrapbooks. Lincoln Center Library Collections, New York.
Beaver, Frank E. *On Film*. New York: McGraw-Hill, 1983.
Behlmer, Rudy. *America's Favorite Movies*. New York: Frederick Ungar, 1982.
Blumenthal, Herman. "Models." *Production Design*, no. 11 (1951), 16ff.
Bordwell, David, and Janet Staiger, Kristin Thompson. *The Classical Hollywood Cinema*. New York: Columbia University Press, 1985.
Brown, Karl. *Adventures with D.W. Griffith*. New York: Farrar, Straus & Giroux, 1973.
_____. "SPFX 101: An Introductory Course," *American Film*, vol. 10, no. 10 (Sept. 1985), 54–59.
Brownlow, Kevin. *The Parade's Gone By*. New York: Alfred A. Knopf, 1968.
Carey, Gary. *All the Stars in Heaven: Louis B. Mayer's MGM*. New York: E.P. Dutton, 1981.
Carrick, Edward, comp. *Art and Design in the British Film*. London: Dennis Dobson, n.d.
Carringer, Robert L. "Who Really Wrote *Citizen Kane?*" *American Film*, vol. 10, no. 10 (Sept. 1985), 43ff.
"Central Park Casino, Joseph Urban, Architect." *Architectural Record*, vol. 66 (1929), 97–108.
Chaplin, Charles. *My Autobiography*. London: Penquin, 1964.
Chierichetti, David. *Hollywood Director: The Career of Mitchell Leisen*. New York: Curtis, 1973.
Clarke, Frederick, and Steve Rubin. "Forbidden Planet." *Cinefantastique*. vol. 8, nos. 2–3 (1979), 6–67.
Corliss, Mary, and Carlo Clarens. "Art Direction," *Film Comment*. May/June, 1978, 25ff.
Croce, Arlene. *The Fred Astaire & Ginger Rogers Book*. New York: Vintage Books, 1972.
Crowther, Bosley. *The Lion's Share: The Story of an Entertainment Empire*. New York: E.P. Dutton, 1957.

Culhane, John. *Special Effects in the Movies.* New York: Ballantine, 1981.
Curtiss, Thomas Q. *Von Stroheim.* New York: Farrar, Straus and Giroux, 1971.
Deschner, Donald. "Anton Grot: Warners Art Director, 1927–1948." *Velvet Light Trap.* vol. 15 (fall 1975), 18–22.
Deshazo, Edith. *Everett Shinn.* New York: Clarkson N. Potter, Inc., 1974.
Deutelbaum, Marshall, ed. *"Image" on the Evolution of the Film.* New York: Dover, 1979.
Durgnat, Raymond. "Art for Film's Sake." *American Film.* vol. 7, no. 7 (May 1983), 41–45.
Eames, John D. *The MGM Story.* New York: Crown, 1982.
Edmonds, I.G., and Reiko Mimura. *Paramount Pictures and the People Who Made Them.* New York: A.S. Barnes, 1980.
Eisner, Lotte H. *The Haunted Screen.* Berkeley: University of California Press, 1969.
Elly, Derek. *The Epic Film.* London: Routledge & Kegan Paul, 1984.
Everson, William K. *American Silent Film.* New York: Oxford University Press, 1978.
Feuer, Jane. *The Hollywood Musical.* Bloomington: Indiana University Press, 1982.
Filmarchitektur: Robert Herlth, Deutsches Institut für Film und Fernsehen. Munich: Uni-Druck, 1965.
Fitzgerald, Michael G. *Universal Pictures.* New Rochelle, N.Y.: Arlington House Publishers, 1977.
Franklin, Joe. *Classics of the Silent Screen.* New York: The Citadel Press, 1959.
Gambill. "Harry Horner's Design Program for 'The Heiress.'" *Art Journal,* fall, 1983, 223–230.
Genné, Beth. "Vincente Minnelli's Style in Microcosm: The Establishing Sequence of 'Meet Me in St. Louis.'" *Art Journal,* fall, 1983, 247–254.
Giannetti, Louis. *Understanding Movies.* Englewood Cliffs, N.J.: Prentice-Hall, 1972.
Gibbons, Cedric. "Interview." *Theatre Arts Monthly.* Oct. 1937, 783–798.
————. "Motion-Picture Sets." *Encyclopaedia Britannica.* vol. 15 (1946), 858ff.
Gill, Brendan. "Movies as Architecture." *Film Comment.* vol. 10, no. 4 (July-Aug. 1974), 28–29.
Goldberger, Paul. "Home Worthy of Oscar—In Hollywood," *New York Times.* Nov. 6, 1980, 23–24.
Goldner, Orville, and George E. Turner. *The Making of King Kong.* New York: Barnes & Co., 1975.
Goosson, Stephen. "Little Lord Fauntleroy." *Production Design.* vol. 1, no. 4 (April 1952), 16–19.
Gottfried, Martin. *Broadway Musicals.* New York: Abrams, 1979.
Grace, Henry. Scrapbooks of Set Stills. Archives, Academy of Motion Picture Arts and Sciences, Hollywood.
Guinness, Alec. "The Guinness Book of Records." *Film Comment.* March 1986, 37ff.
Gussow, Mel. *Don't Say Yes Until I Finish Talking: A Biography of Darryl F. Zanuck.* New York: Doubleday & Co., 1971.
Hambley, John, and Patrick Downing. *The Art of Hollywood. A Thames Television Exhibition at the Victoria and Albert Museum.* London: Thames Television, 1979.
Hammond, Paul. *Marvellous Méliès.* London: Gordon Fraser, 1974.
Harmetz, Aljean. *The Making of the Wizard of Oz.* New York: Knopf, 1977.
Haver, Ronald. *David O. Selznick's Hollywood.* New York: Alfred A. Knopf, 1980.
Haworth, Ted. "Production Designer vs Art Director." *Film Comment.* May/June, 1978, 36.
Hayne, Donald. *The Autobiography of Cecil B. DeMille.* Englewood Cliffs, N.J.: Prentice-Hall, 1959.
Heisner, Beverly. "Morris Lapidus and the Architecture of the Movies. *Postscript: A Journal of Film Culture and the Humanities.* Fall 1981, 8–17.
Henderson, Robert M. *D.W. Griffith: His Life and Work.* New York: Oxford University Press, 1972.
n.a. "Here's the Chaldean Who Built Babylon." *Photoplay.* vol. 11 (Feb. 1917), 83.
Hirsch, Foster. *The Dark Side of the Screen: Film Noir.* New York: A.S. Barnes, 1981.

_____. *The Hollywood Epic.* London: Tantivy Press, 1978.

Hirschhorn, Clive. *The Universal Story.* New York: Crown, 1983.

_____. *The Warner Brothers Story.* New York: Crown, 1979.

Honeycutt, Kirk. "Research that Makes Movies 'Real'." *New York Times.* March 1, 1981, 18D.

Hopkins, George James. "From 'Then to Now'," *Production Design,* vol. 2, no. 5 (1980), 8ff.

Horner, Harry. Seminar Transcript. American Film Institute, Feb. 1970.

Hossent, Harry. *Gangster Movies.* London: Octopus Books, 1974.

Jewell, Richard B., and Vernon Harbin. *The RKO Story.* New York: Arlington House, 1982.

Jones, Ken D., and Arthur F. McClure. *Hollywood at War, the American Motion Picture and World War II.* New York: A.S. Barnes, 1973.

"Joseph Urban, Architectural League." *The Art News.* vol. 30 (1932), 9.

Kael, Pauline. *The Citizen Kane Book.* London: Secker and Warburg, 1971.

Katz, Ephraim. *The Film Encyclopedia.* New York: Putnam's Sons, 1979.

Koenig, John. *Scenery for Cinema.* Exhibition Baltimore Museum of Art. Baltimore: New Process Press, 1942.

Koszarski, Richard. *Hollywood Directors, 1914–1940.* London: Oxford University Press, 1976.

_____. *Universal Pictures/65 Years.* New York: Museum of Modern Art, 1977.

Krautz, A., ed. *International Directory of Cinematographers, Set- and Costume Designers in Film.* Munich: Saur, vol. 1, German Democratic Republic (1946–1978), Poland, 1981; vol. 2, France, 1983; vol. 3, Albania, Bulgaria, Greece, Rumania, Yugoslavia (to 1980), 1983; vol. 4, Germany (to 1945), 1984; vol. 5, Denmark, Finland, Norway, Sweden (to 1945), 1986; vol. 6, Supplemental, new entries, additions, corrections 1978–1984, 1986; vol. 7, Italy (to 1986), 1987; vol. 8, Portugal and Spain (to 1986), 1988; vol. 9, CSSR and Hungary, 1989; vol. 10, Soviet Union, 1989.

Krinsky, Carol Herselle. "Joseph Urban." *Macmillan Encyclopedia of Architects.* 1983; vol. 4, 245.

Kreuger, Miles, ed. *The Movie Musical from Vitaphone to 42nd St.* New York: Dover, 1975.

Kuter, Leo. "Production Designer." *Production Design.* vol. 1, no. 3, March 1951, 11ff.

Larkin, Rochelle. *Hail, Columbia.* New Rochelle, N.Y.: Arlington House Publishers, 1975.

Laurent, Hugues. *Memento d'Architecture Appliquée à la Decoration de la Film,* vols. I & II, Paris, Institut des Hautes Etudes Cinematographiques, 1966.

_____. *Rudiments d'Art Décoratif et d'Ameublement en Général,* Paris, Institut des Hautes Etudes Cinematographiques, 1965.

Leven, Boris. "What Is a Production Designer?" *Film Comment.* May/June 1978, 36.

Lourie, Eugene. *My Work in Films.* New York: Harcourt Brace Jovanovich, 1985.

_____. "The River." *Production Design.* Feb. 1951, 5ff.

McClay, Howard. "Pre-Production Planning." *Production Design.* Jan. 1952, 6ff.

MacGowan, Kenneth. "The New Studio Art." *Motion Picture Classic.* March 1919, 16ff.

Mandelbaum, Howard, and Eric Myers. *Screen Deco: A Celebration of High Style in Hollywood.* New York: St. Martin's Press, 1985.

Marill, Alvin H. *Samuel Goldwyn Presents.* South Brunswick, N.J.: A.S. Barnes, 1976.

Marner, Terence S., and Michael Stringer, comps. *Film Design.* New York: Barnes and Co., 1974.

Marner, Terence St. John. *Film Design.* London: Tantivy Press, 1974.

Marchi, Virgilio; Guido Cincotti and Fausto Montesanti. *La scenografia cinematografica in Italia.* Rome: Bianco e Nero Editore, 1955.

Martin, Floyd W. "D.W. Griffith's 'Intolerance': A Note on Additional Visual Sources." *Art Journal.* fall 1983, 231–233.

Meehan, John. "Death . . . Goes to a Party." *Production Design.* vol. 1, no. 5 (May/June 1951).

MGM Matte Collection, University of Southern California, Special Collections.

Minnelli, Vincente. *I Remember It Well.* New York: Doubleday, 1974.

Naumberg, Nancy. *We Make the Movies.* New York: Norton, 1937.

"Obituary, Cedric Gibbons." *New York Times,* July 27, 1960, 29.

Osborne, Robert. *50 Golden Years of Oscar.* La Habra, Calif.: ESE California, 1979.

Palmer, James W. "An Extension of Reality: Setting as Theme in *The Servant,*" *Mise-en-Scène.* (Spring 1980), 44–48.

Parkinson, Michael, and Clyde Jeavons. *A Pictorial History of Westerns.* London: Hamlyn, 1972.

Paul, William. *Ernst Lubitsch's American Comedy.* New York: Columbia University Press, 1983.

Perry, Ted. "Sergei Eisenstein: A Career in Pictures." *American Film.* Jan.-Feb., 1983, 46–51.

Pickard, Roy. *The Hollywood Studios.* London: Frederick Muller, 1978.

Pitkin, Walter, and William M. Marston. *The Art of Sound Pictures.* New York: Appleton, 1930.

Riley, Michael M., and James W. Palmer. "An Extension of Reality: Setting as Theme in *The Servant,*" *Mise-en-Scène.* vol. 2 (spring 1980) 44–48.

Rockett, Will H. "Landscape and Manscape: Reflection and Distortion in Horror Films." *Postscript: Essays in Film and the Humanities.* vol. 3, no. 1 (fall 1983), 19–34.

Salt, Barry. "Film Style and Technology in the Thirties." *Film Quarterly.* vol. 30, no. 1 (1976), 19–32.

Sarris, Andrew. *The Films of Josef Von Sternberg.* New York: Museum of Modern Art, 1966.
————. *Interviews with Film Directors.* Indianapolis: Bobbs-Merrill, 1967.

Scherle, Victor, and William T. Levy. *The Films of Frank Capra.* Secaucus, N.J.: Citadel Press, 1977.

Schulberg, Budd. *Moving Pictures.* New York: Stein and Day, 1981.

Sennett, Ted. *Hollywood Musicals.* New York: Abrams, 1981.
————. *Warner Brothers Presents.* N.p.: A Castele Books, Inc., Edition, 1971.

Stradling, Harry. "Richard Day Rides to an Academy Award." *Production Design.* Feb.-March, vol 2, nos. 2-3 (1952), 7.

Sylbert, Richard. "Dialogue on Film." *American Film.* Dec. 1985, 12ff.

Taylor, Deems. "The Scenic Art of Joseph Urban: His Protean Work in the Theatre." *Architecture.* vol. 69 (1934), 275–290.

Teegan, Otto. "Joseph Urban." *Architecture.* vol. 69 (1934), 250–256.

Theatre Crafts, the Magazine for Professionals in Theatre, Film, Video, and the other Performing Arts, is currently one of the few periodicals that regularly carries articles on art direction in films.

Thomas, Tony, and Jim Terry, with Busby Berkeley. *The Busby Berkeley Book.* New York: New York Graphic Society, 1973.

Thomas, Tony, and Aubrey Solomon. *The Films of 20th Century-Fox.* Secaucus, N.Y.: Citadel Press, 1979.

Urban, Joseph. *Theaters.* New York: Theatre Arts, 1929.

Vardac, A. Nicholas. *Stage to Screen: Theatrical Method from Garrick to Griffith.* Cambridge, Mass.: Harvard University Press, 1949.

Vogelgesang, Shepard. "The New School for Social Research, New York City, Joseph Urban, Architect." *The Architectural Record.* vol. 67, no. 4 (1930), 305–309.

Watts, Stephen, ed. *Behind the Screen: How Films Are Made.* New York: Dodge, 1938.

Weinberg, Herman G., comp. *The Complete Greed.* New York: Arno Press, 1972.
————. *Josef von Sternberg: A Critical Study of the Great Film Director.* New York: E.P. Dutton, 1967.
————. *Stroheim. A Pictorial Record of His Nine Films.* New York: Dover, 1975.

Wing, Ruth, ed. *The Blue Book of the Screen.* Hollywood, Blue Book of the Screen, Inc., 1923.

Willis, Carol. "Zoning and *Zeitgeist:* The Skyscraper City in the 1920's." *Journal of the Society of Architectural Historians.* vol. 45 (March 1986), 47–59.

Index